D1500381

The Village that Died for England

by the same author

On Living in an Old Country
A Journey Through Ruins

The Village that Died for England

The Strange Story of Tyneham

PATRICK WRIGHT

Jonathan Cape
London

For Claire, Edward, Nicholas and Richard – who preferred Chapman's Pool to the Tank Museum

First published 1995

1 3 5 7 9 10 8 6 4 2

First published in the United Kingdom in 1995 by Jonathan Cape
Random House, 20 Vauxhall Bridge Road, London SW1V 2SA

Random House Australia (Pty) Limited
20 Alfred Street, Milsons Point, Sydney
New South Wales 2061, Australia

Random House New Zealand Limited
18 Poland Road, Glenfield
Auckland 10, New Zealand

Random House South Africa (Pty) Limited
PO Box 337, Bergvlei 2012, South Africa

Random House UK Limited Reg. No. 954009

A CIP catalogue record for this book
is available from the British Library

ISBN 0–224–03886–9

Papers used by Random House UK Limited are
natural, recyclable products made from wood
grown in sustainable forests. The manufacturing
processes conform to the environmental regulations
of the country of origin.

Phototypeset by Intype, London
Printed and bound in Great Britain by
Clays Ltd, St Ives PLC

CONTENTS

Part Four The Scouring of Tyneham Valley (1943–61)

Part Five Slugging it Out with the Tyneham Action Group (1968–75)

Part Six After the Great Disillusionment

LIST OF ILLUSTRATIONS

PREFACE AND ACKNOWLEDGMENTS

It was early in 1984 that I visited the Isle of Purbeck, curious to see the coastal landscape that had inspired the perfect but fatally contaminated English world imagined in Mary Butts's pre-war novel, *Death of Felicity Taverner*. As I wandered the militarised zone around Tyneham, I was surprised less by tankfire than by long suppressed memories of the years I had spent at boarding schools in Dorset — a period that came to an inglorious but welcome end in 1968. I remembered an institutional atmosphere in which idealism — and this book is all about the splendours and woeful inadequacies of English idealism — did not always triumph over eccentricity and prejudice, and a pastoral landscape in which the residues of war were deeply embedded.

The first school I attended, Port Regis in the Blackmore Vale, is now a most opulent-looking establishment, but in the early Sixties it had an austerity to match the disused prisoner-of-war camps in an adjacent field: wire, prefabricated huts, and the word 'Ablutions' stencilled on a gaping door. Violin lessons were compulsory — as were bowel-movements, to be ticked off on a wall chart every morning. Biggles was in the library and his young admirers spent their spare hours constructing slow tank-like vehicles out of old wooden cotton reels, candle-wax and rubber bands.

In those years the beaches still bore signs warning of unexploded mines, and it was quite possible for schoolboys to return from seaside excursions with pockets full of live shells washed up by the post-war tide. I spent months researching Rolf Gardiner, an organic farmer and youth leader who plays a considerable part in this book, before it dawned on me that I had actually heard him speak in the mid-Sixties, when he visited Bryanston School to declaim against mechanisation and the motor-car, and to rally his adolescent audience against the coming idea that the future of the countryside lay in tourism and leisure.

I would not have lingered so long had this strangely tank-rolled landscape only possessed such disconcerting personal resonance, but it proved to have far wider reach than that. Remade by generations of writers and artists, its heaths and cliffs have achieved totemic status in the national imagination. The thought of its green hills has been carried around the globe, and into the most terrible military engagements, by generations of armoured soldiers. In *On Living in an Old Country* (1985) I adapted a phrase from one of François Mitterand's election posters to describe this idealised southern geography as 'deep England'. It was Dorset that I had in mind then, and I have been investigating the Royal Armoured Corps' stretch of its coast ever since. I started out knowing very little, but I was convinced that one of England's more telling twentieth-century stories must be coiled up behind its wire.

To begin with, I thought I was only indebted to a little-known novelist of the Thirties but my obligations were actually many from the start, and they have since grown more extensive than I can adequately acknowledge. Many people have spared time to talk with me, and I am grateful to everyone whose conversation is cited in the book.

In the Lulworth area I have benefited more than may immediately be evident from discussions with Mrs Josephine Taylor, Colonel Sir Joseph Weld, Mr Wilfrid Weld, Jack Scutt, Harry Westmacott, Denise Wright, Joan Townend, Alan Brown, Valerie Mitchell, Rena Gould, Peter Gould and Keith Lewis. It is proper also to acknowledge that, thanks to heroic local fundraising (and, eventually even a grant from English Heritage), St Andrew's Church, East Lulworth, is no longer in the near-derelict condition here described.

The architectural interlude (Chapter 19) could not have been written without the assistance of Andrew Holmes, Jeanne Sillett, Peter Wilson, Nigel Coates, David Greene, Paul Shepheard, Martin Lazenby and Fred Scott. My understanding of Rolf Gardiner and his circle has been greatly increased by Rosalind Richards, John Eliot Gardiner, Margaret Gardiner, Andrew Best, Peter Hood, Liz Waller, Michael Pitt Rivers, Teddy Bourke, Michael Dower, Norman Oddy, Sir Harrison Birtwistle, Peter Farquharson, G. D. H. Harthan, Betty Galton, Angus Fowler, Dame Sylvia Crowe and Malcolm Chase. Others who have helped include Claire Lawton, David Alan Mellor, Ian Patterson, Sue Clifford, Frances Partridge, Jamie Muir, Sarah Benton, Colin Ward, Richard Mabey, Peter Jewell, James Lefanu, David Greenhalf, Francis Kelly, Joanna Bailey, Michael Pickwoad, Simon Relph, Neal Ascherson, Peter Mitchell, Stuart Hall, Claire Harman, Emanuel Litvinoff, Roy Cobb, Arthur Grant, Roger Peers, Ruth Colyer, Gillian Barlow, Judith Stinton, Alan Swindall, Trevelen Haysom, Norman Moore,

Adam Curtis, John and Caroline Montagu. Andrew Watson has photographed various parts of the area for me. Kola Krauze has kindly drawn a map, and Andrzej Krauze has contributed a small collection of tanks.

Besides being a leading participant in this story, Rodney Legg is a one-man cultural institution in Dorset, and an unusually generous one at that. I have followed up many leads from his books, articles and conversation. Anyone seeking further information about the landscape of the Lulworth gunnery ranges should consult his *Lulworth Encyclopaedic Guide*, to be published by his Dorset Publishing Company in 1995. I am also grateful to him for granting me permission to quote from his letters.

I cannot name the secondhand book dealers to whose shelves I owe many fortuitous discoveries, but I would like to acknowledge the assistance of the following libraries and archives: the Tank Museum at Bovington; the National Army Museum; the British Library; the House of Lords Record Office; the library of the Dorset Natural History and Archaeological Society at the County Museum, Dorchester; Cambridge University Library; the Public Record Office; the Dorset Record Office; Dorset County Library; Weymouth Borough Library; the Fellows' Library at Eton College; Karl Marx Memorial Library; the Tate Gallery; the Imperial War Museum; the National Film Archive at The British Film Institute.

My earlier articles on this contested landscape appeared in *New Society* (31 January 1986), *The London Review of Books* (24 November 1988) and the *Independent* magazine (19 October 1991): my thanks respectively to Tony Gould and Paul Barker, Karl Miller and Mary Kay Wilmer, and Ian Parker. More recently, I have been writing for the *Guardian*, and am sincerely grateful for the charitable view its editors have taken of my protracted absence. I have been fortunate in having the assistance of a grant from the K. Blundell Trust, and I was also helped in the early stages by an award from the Nuffield Foundation's Small Grants Programme.

I would like to thank General Mark Bond for permitting me to quote from family documents; Mrs Rosalind Richards, who has granted me permission to quote from Rolf Gardiner's papers; Mrs Penelope Massingham, who has allowed me to make extensive use of H. J. Massingham's writings; and Lord Portsmouth, who has generously allowed me to quote from Lord Lymington's letters to Rolf Gardiner. Jeanne Sillett and Peter Wilson have kindly allowed me to reproduce their work and Mrs Camilla Bagg has granted me permission to quote from the unpublished writings of Mary Butts.

My agent, John Parker, has eased difficulties of the corporate kind, and done much more besides. Neil Belton has been an invaluable accomplice as my editor for ten years now; and I am enormously grateful both to Veronica Horwell, who found ways of pruning my overgrown draft without ever resorting to Lord Hinchinbrooke's slasher, and also to Marion Steel who made further suggestions and prepared the final version for print.

This book is the sequel to — and also, in an unanticipated sense, the forerunner of — my previous volume, *A Journey Through Ruins*. Both are focused on small but revealing stretches of minor road and they are intertwined in material and method alike. Much of what I discovered in the Tyneham valley demanded an urban perspective, so I broke off to go 'botanising on asphalt', in Walter Benjamin's phrase, and soon found that Dorset had a considerable presence on Dalston Lane, north-east London. The books form a pair — *Walking on Crichel Down*, Volumes Two and One.

Fulbourn,
January 1995

The corner of a corner of England is infinite
and can never be exhausted

Hilaire Belloc

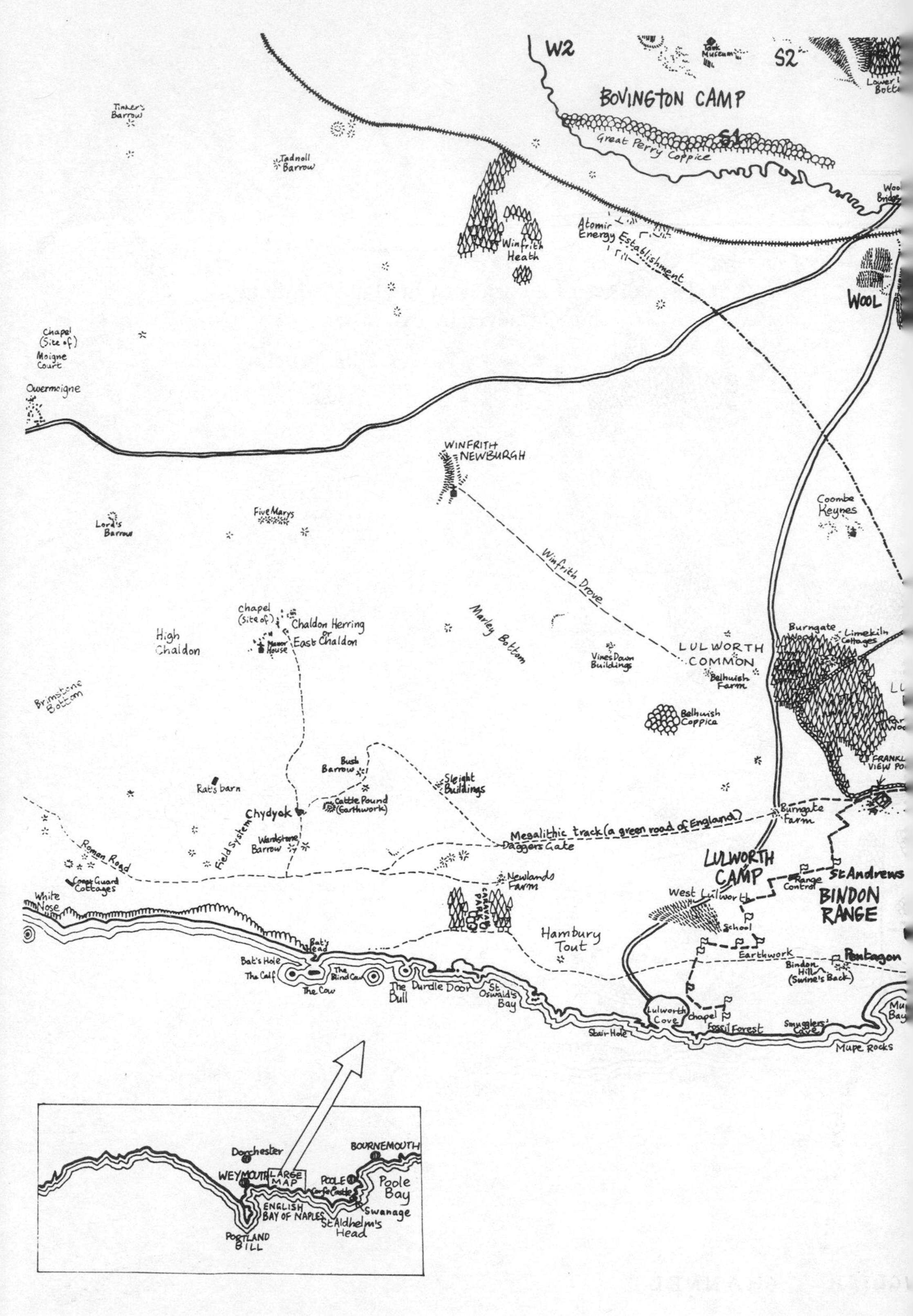

W2
Tank Museum
S2
Lower
Bovington Camp
S1
Great Perry Coppice
Tinker's Barrow
Tadnoll Barrow
Winfrith Heath
Atomic Energy Establishment
Wool Bridge
Wool
Chapel (Site of)
Moigne Court
Owermoigne
Winfrith Newburgh
Coombe Keynes
Lord's Barrow
Five Marys
Winfrith Drove
Marley Bottom
Chapel (site of)
Chaldon Herring or East Chaldon
Manor House
High Chaldon
Brimstone Bottom
Vines Down Buildings
Lulworth Common
Belhuish Farm
Burngate Wood
Limekiln Cottages
Belhuish Coppice
Bush Barrow
Sleight Buildings
Rat's barn
Chydyok
Cattle Pound (Earthwork)
Field System
Wardstone Barrow
Megalithic track (a green road of England)
Daggers Gate
Burngate Farm
Roman Road
Coast Guard Cottages
Newlands Farm
Caravan Park
Lulworth Camp
Range Control
St Andrews
Bindon Range
West Lulworth
School
White Nose
Bat's Head
Bat's Hole
The Calf
The Cow
The Blind Cow
Hambury Tout
Earthwork
Pentagon
Bindon Hill (Swine's Back)
The Bull
Durdle Door
St Oswald's Bay
Lulworth Cove
Chapel
Stair Hole
Fossil Forest
Smugglers' Cave
Mupe Rocks
Dorchester
Bournemouth
Weymouth
Large Map
Poole
Poole Bay
Corfe Castle
English Bay of Naples
Swanage
St Aldhelm's Head
Portland Bill

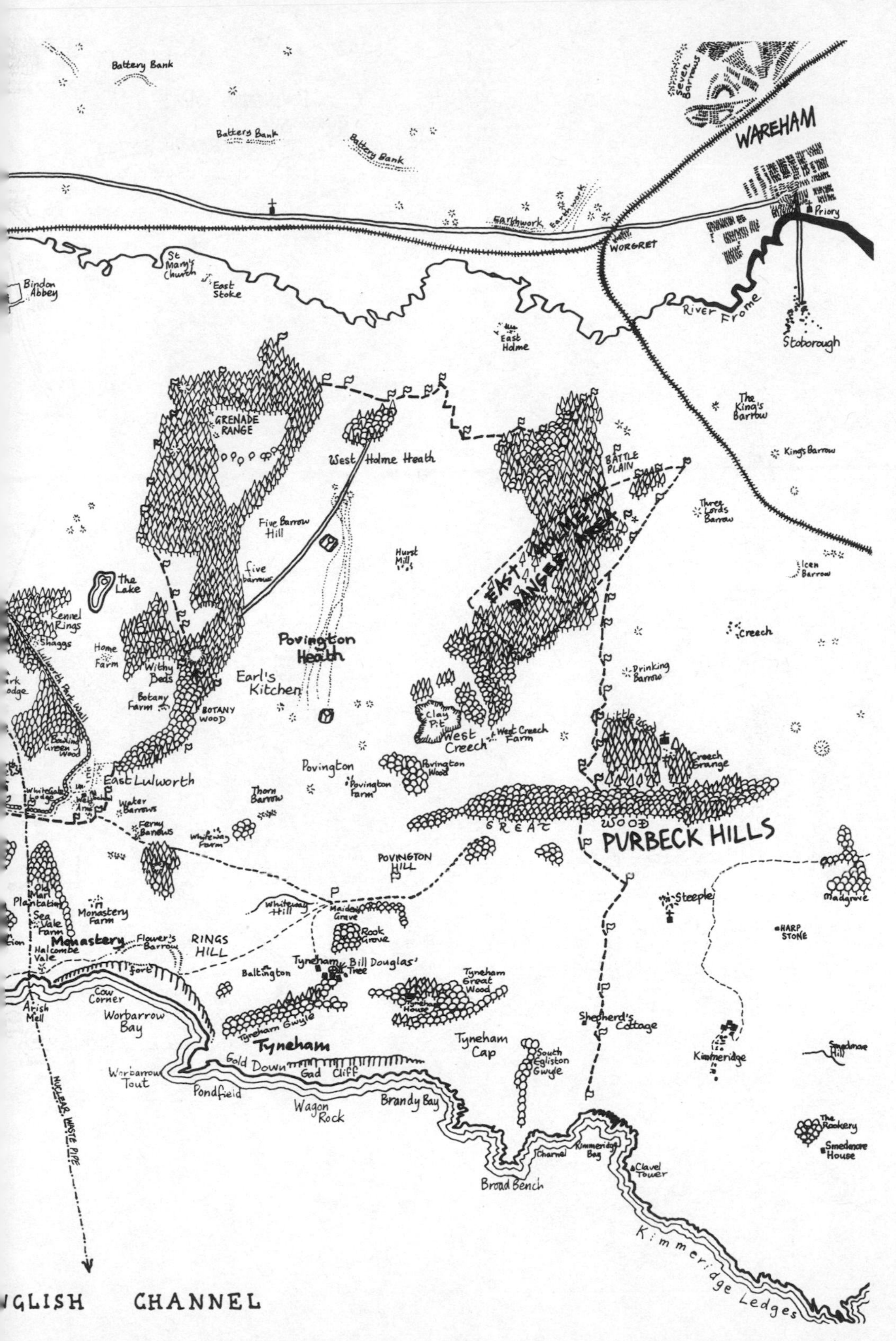

Battery Bank
Battery Bank
Battery Bank
Seven Barrows
WAREHAM
Priory
Earthwork
Earthwork
WORGRET
St Mary's Church
East Stoke
Bindon Abbey
River Frome
Stoborough
East Holme
The King's Barrow
Kings Barrow
GRENADE RANGE
West Holme Heath
BATTLE PLAIN
Three Lords Barrow
Five Barrow Hill
five barrows
Hurst Mill
Icen Barrow
The Lake
Kennel Rings
Shaggs
Lulworth Park Wall
Home Farm
Withy Beds
Povington Heath
Earl's Kitchen
Creech
Drinking Barrow
Botany Farm
BOTANY WOOD
Clay Pit
West Creech
West Creech Farm
Creech Grange
Povington
Povington Wood
Povington Farm
East Lulworth
Thorn Barrow
Water Barrows
Ferny Barrows
Whiteway Farm
GREAT WOOD
PURBECK HILLS
POVINGTON HILL
Steeple
Madgrove
Old Marl Plantation
Monastery Farm
Whiteway Hill
Maiden Grove
Sea Vale Farm
Rook Grove
HARP STONE
Monastery
Flower's Barrow
RINGS HILL
Halcombe Vale
Tyneham
Bill Douglas' Tree
Baltington
Fort
Tyneham Great Wood
Cow Corner
Arish Mell
Worbarrow Bay
Tyneham Gwyle
Tyneham House
Tyneham
Shepherd's Cottage
Tyneham Cap
Kimmeridge
Smedmore Hill
South Egliston Gwyle
Gold Down
Gad Cliff
Worbarrow Tout
Pondfield
Wagon Rock
Brandy Bay
NUCLEAR WASTE PIPE
The Rookery
Smedmore House
Charnel
Kimmeridge Bay
Clavel Tower
Broad Bench
Kimmeridge Ledges
NGLISH CHANNEL

PART ONE

New Bends in the Rolling English Road

Snowdrops have been a picture this year, as have violets. The lighter mornings have heralded increased birdsong. Spring cannot be far away.

Dorset Natural History and
Archaeological Society Bulletin, March 1994

ONE

TWO VIEWS OF A DAMAGED HILL

I HAD LEFT London just as the pulsing of the last night clubs was giving way to the greasy chirrupping of the inner city dawn chorus, but I came unstuck at Waterloo. A bleary-eyed ticket inspector directed me on to the wrong train, and it was past midday by the time I set out up the western edge of Bindon Hill, stepping out on the springy downland grass that Mr Philip Brannon, artist and author of the Victorian guidebook with which I had equipped myself, called 'richly verdant turf of exquisite softness'.[1] There were oxe-eye daisies among the scattered flints, snail shells and rabbit droppings — along with wild thyme and the curious hairy-flowered plant known as kidney vetch.

Walking east along the old track that follows the long spine of Bindon Hill, I passed a brick radar station with which the controllers of the firing range monitor vessels at sea. Large fragments of shrapnel lay rusting on the turf, and the steep northern flank of Bindon Hill was gouged by tank fire. The plain below was marked by numerous tracks, bunkers, dumps and shattered target tanks, one of which clanked sporadically in the wind.

There were other walkers on that ancient green road: a couple with two overfed dogs, which had made it up the hill only to collapse panting in the ditch beneath an old Iron Age embankment; a sinewy old man who strode by in khaki shorts, stabbing at the earth with a tall staff of cork-screwed hazel; and another solitary fellow who had a little teddy-bear strapped to his rucksack and a serious line in understatement. 'A bit drafty,' he shouted as an immense gust of wind swept in from the sea and flicked us both clean off the path.

I found the amateur botanists, whose field trip I had intended to join several hours earlier, perched high above chalk cliffs at Bindon's western edge. A mixed party with considerably more females than males, the members of the Dorset Natural History and Archaeological Society were settled in clusters on that never ploughed turf slope, their backs arched against the militarised zone. Most concentrated on the coastal view to the west, a prospect that still seemed to epitomise everything that is most precious about the southern English landscape.

Some used binoculars to survey the cliffs and promontories that stretch away towards the distant profile of St Adhelm's Head. Others studied the foreground, following the tightly wired path as it sank down through the sudden breach in the chalk at their feet, crossing the little stone beach of Arish Mell Gap, and then rising up steeply through the folded turf of Halcombe Vale to the crest of Rings Hill, where the embanked Iron Age camp of Flowers Barrow is outlined against the sky. The ruins of Monastery Farm could be seen just inland from Arish Mell Gap, named after the Trappist monks who lived here nearly two centuries ago when 'the most perfect silence and tranquillity reigned throughout this little vale'.[2]

Despite the ripped turf and red flags, this forbidden scene still seemed to aspire to an Arcadian condition. Brown bullocks tried casually to mount one another in the fields below; a stonechat perched momentarily on a spear of Devil's Bugloss; and an obliging army warden called Kiwi climbed up to discourse on the incidence of orchids on the firing range: Pyramid, Marsh and Early Spotted were to be found here, he thought, but the Bee was not so common as it had once been. The impossibly rare Military Orchid wasn't mentioned at all. Nor was the large discharge pipe that has run so prominently through Arish Mell Gap since 1959, carrying radioactive waste out to sea from the Atomic Energy Establishment a few miles inland on Winfrith Heath.

I passed the members of that field trip again after they had wound their way down the southern flank of Bindon Hill. One group was observing a townsman who had allowed one of his inappropriately shod young sons to clamber halfway up a cliff near Mupe Rocks and was now trying to retrieve him in a rising tide. Others were examining carefully selected blades of grass with the help of a magnifying glass, and bandying Latin terms.

I left the firing range through a gate close to the low-lying stone house called Little Bindon. Pressed up against the military fence, this would look unexceptional but for the large buttresses and bricked up Gothic window arches that indicate an ancient and ecclesiastical origin. The Cistercian Abbey of Blessed Mary is said to have been founded here in 1149 — shortly before it was removed a few miles inland to Great Bindon, where it would command the area until its demolition shortly after the Dissolution of 1539.

For a time in the late Eighties, Little Bindon was tenanted by a well-spoken and welcoming young man, a convalescent of the modern world who had gone native in the religious history of his landscape. This latter-day hermit lived here by candlelight, hewing wood and drawing water from the well. On summer weekends, he opened the little chapel at the eastern end of his retreat and invited walkers to admire the coved ceiling and a rigged galleon scratched into the wall hundreds of years ago.

Sometimes this bright-eyed fellow could be met walking back towards his retreat around Lulworth Cove, carrying his provisions in plastic. He hardly seemed out of place, for although the eighteenth-century vicar who wrote the first county history of Dorset, was content to describe the cove as 'a basin or creek, environed by high cliffs',[3] others have recognised it as a freakish place. Thomas Hardy had his way with the cove, throwing drowned bodies on to the beach, wrapping it in fear of Napoleonic invasion, and making his own poem of the unsubstantiated rumour that John Keats stopped here on his last consumptive journey to Rome, to compose the undying sonnet 'Bright Star, would I were stedfast as thou art'.[4] But a disillusioning strangeness was in the rocks too; indeed, a language of astonished geological observation trickles out of the late eighteenth century, when advocates of the Sublime cultivated an appetite for the 'agreeable horror' of such picturesque places,[5] and then filters down through the guidebooks of the nineteenth century.

To begin with, Bindon Hill rises up formulaically enough at the head of the cove: a 'lofty and irregular precipice' towering behind the 'elegant curve' of a beach and opposite the 'rocky horns' that stand at the narrow breached entrance. But then comes a series of 'prodigious convulsions', which break through the 'richly verdant turf' of this idyllic prospect to thrust the rude underside of things into view.[6] The industrious sea cuts away at the less resistant strata to produce channels 'of the most frantic shapes' through which it pours with an 'awful roar'.[7] The rock strata rise up from the depths — buckling, colliding, and squeezing each other into strangely contorted shapes. They defy the Book of Genesis by throwing out the fossilised debris of successive worlds that existed before ever Adam delved and Eve span.

This contest between idealised appearance and obtrusive material reality took a different form in the early twentieth century, for the place became a film-set. This was the work of Cecil M. Hepworth, a pioneer of the early British cinema, who thought nothing of making certain improvements on his favourite location. In 1911, finding no suitably picturesque cottage with the sea at its door, he had shingle carried up from the cove and planted a fake beach in the garden of an appropriate dwelling in the village. In 1913 he came back to film Sir Johnston Forbes-Robertson's production of *Hamlet*. A mock Castle of Elsinore was built on the cliffs, and visitors to London's Museum of the Moving Image can still see the eccentric rocks of Lulworth holding their own against the melodramatic gestures of those windswept Edwardian actors.[8] Things had quietened down considerably by 1951, when the picture of Lulworth Cove was used in the Festival of Britain, to show the productive geology on which an innovative and mechanised chapter of our flagging island story was now to be founded.[9]

For my Victorian guide, Lulworth Cove was a place of material strangeness, but this famous natural amphitheatre is now also devoted to seasonal exhibitions of the great British class structure, which can be every bit as arched as the rocks. Visitors tend to pause at the narrow entrance to the beach, only spreading out into their differences after they have surveyed the suddenly revealed cove. A man with a metal detector is circumnavigated first by an elderly lady, who walks to a considerable distance before unfolding her sketching stool, and then by a party of hard-hatted geology students intent on inspecting the blue clay at a significant point in the cliff. Affluent continental yachtsmen stand at anchor in the centre of the cove, sipping drinks as they watch an English volunteer force splash their way through an implausible outward-bound exercise involving portable radios and a raft made of oil drums and planks. An indigenous Lulworth fisherman sits reading an old thriller among the defiantly scattered tools of his trade: sodden old boats, coiled rope and blue plastic sheeting, rusted links from a vast chain. His demeanour confirms the county historian's version of what happened on 4 October 1754, when a whale passed near the cove: 'the country people endeavoured to take him; but he broke from them, and was found dead a few days after, near the Isle of Wight, having been much wounded'.[10]

Like all the best coastal resorts, Lulworth Cove has the jumbled ambience of a place that exists in several different dimensions at once. Walking up from the sea the visitor can enjoy the sight of these competing Lulworths. A discreet family from the upper reaches of the middle class sits in a cottage garden, studiously ignoring the vulgar trippers. Hikers stride through purposefully, pressing back with affronted eyes against the commercialised squalor that stands between them and the superior pleasures of the cliff path. Local fishermen drive through in battered, country and westernised vehicles. Their finest redoubt is a decidedly unthatched terrace of former coastguard houses that lies athwart the village and makes no concessions to the rambling and lilified look of the cottage across the road. This is the domain of the Millers, a family of many branches whose members have worked this coast for generations. Mrs Miller herself is sometimes to be seen sitting in the gateway, offering boiled crabs as a primeval alternative to the more conventional tourist offerings.

In the Eighteen Sixties, Lulworth could be described as 'the sweetest of England's southern nooks': a 'retired' place by comparison with nearby railway resorts like Weymouth and Swanage. If the Dorset naturalists are anything to go by, the 'scientific wanderers' to whom Brannon dedicated the place are still putting up a fight. I was sitting in the outdoor café by the car park when they arrived for tea. Those in the van wasted no time clearing the tables around them with conventional weapons drawn from the arsenal of rural class war: glacial smiles; over-confident 'borrowing' of untaken chairs from nearby tables. In a moment, the south-west corner of the café had been taken.

Having seen this party at work, it was easier to understand why some of the natives of Lulworth Cove appear to have had second thoughts about saving the environment. The cause is amply advocated in the leaflets sold from the conservationist shack down by the sea, but you only have to linger late in one of the restaurants here, and the cook will eventually emerge to offer free advice on the best way to deal with spare oak trees. Undeterred by a council preservation order, he had put paid to one in his garden near Wool by injecting it with a hefty dose of Agent Orange, the defoliant with which the American military denuded large tracts of Vietnam and which this native son of Dorset claimed to have procured with the help of a military friend.

Jumping at the Woodside

A few hundred yards north of that large car park above the cove, the road veers right past the village hall and a thatched bus shelter. West Lulworth soon trails off into a string of modest private houses, and then gives way to the recently much fortified perimeter fence of the Royal Armoured Corps gunnery school — an exceedingly permanent-looking establishment that still goes by the name of 'Lulworth Camp'.

There is a guardhouse and barrier at the entrance, together with an old Comet tank parked behind a little chain. The monster looks photogenic enough, silhouetted against the ridge of Bindon Hill with the name 'Cotswold' painted on it in large white letters. But any such impression is quickly compromised by the heavily armed soldiers who step out nervously every time a car slows, to ensure that the photographer isn't actually reconnoitring for the IRA.

The B3070 follows the route of the ancient ridgeway into Purbeck. Long since metalled, this once dimpled track remains a resolutely minor road, winding along between embanked hedges of foaming may. Soon enough, a gap in the wire opens into one of England's most incongruent roadside attractions. A sign announces this to be the 'Franklin Viewpoint', explaining that it was constructed by the Royal Armoured Corps gunnery school through the generosity of Mr J. Franklin of West Lulworth, who provided 'plant and materials'. A motorist pulling in could be forgiven for wondering exactly what materials can have been contributed. A few tons of gravel have been dumped on the ground and spread about a bit, and a rudimentary picnic bench has been contrived from concrete and recycled timber. A row of bullet-shaped bollards of white concrete marks the point beyond which cars must not venture; and a coil of rusted barbed wire rises up just beyond.

It seems that this generous sponsor may not have been granted even the limited immortality of the average commemoratively endowed park bench. In recent years, the whole place has been tidied up, planted with a forest of signs and enlarged as a more official regime overtakes the improvisational age of mutual back-scratching between local traders and the gunnery school. The name is in question too. Indeed, an altogether more prominent sign suggests that this is no longer the Franklin Viewpoint at all, but the 'Bindon Firing Range Spectator's Car Park', adding that 'it is advisable to cover your ears while firing is in progress'. Another illustrated notice tells tank spotters how to differentiate a Chieftain from a Scorpion or a Scimitar. A small armoured-car turret is mounted like a sculpture on a plinth of Purbeck stone. Its sign promises that money rolled down the upthrust barrel will be sent to the Army Benevolent Fund.

Visitors park and gaze out over this makeshift entanglement of wire and surreal instruction. A control tower commands the large tarmac area from which the tanks fire. There are odd-looking ramps, and steps that rise up into buildings that no longer exist. There are observation posts, hangers, sheds of wood and corrugated iron, camouflaged marquees and an assortment of poles and curiously arranged planks, which lie about between clumps of gorse and new plantations of military fir. There are the countless miles of wire that characterise every military landscape; and though there are many hues of green, the colour scheme shifts in a sequence that follows no overall design. Even the most permanent of military bases retain something of this provisional look, their equipment looking as if merely scattered or dropped.

Beyond this area the land falls away for half a mile or so and then rises up into the even ridge of Bindon Hill, once known as a resting-place for migratory birds. The landscape has since been resurveyed according to military perspective. Large black signs bearing single red numbers appear at regular intervals along the length of Bindon Hill: starting with a '4' on the west side of Arish Mell Gap and rising as they go west towards Lulworth Cove. Patches of white show where the firing of live shells is particularly concentrated, and a long groove is cut along the base of the hill behind a moving target rail. The facing slope is sufficiently crumped and pitted to recall the shattered landscape of the Western Front, but Bindon Hill still dips down poetically into Arish Mell Gap, an inverted triangle of suddenly revealed sea that opens, as the Victorian Philip Brannon described, between 'two lofty chalk heads as a verdant picture in a bold frame'. The Napoleonic wars were a distant memory by the 1860s, but Brannon still expected his reader would be 'disposed to descant with politico-military wisdom on the defenceless state of this easy landing place to an enemy.' After standing at the Franklin Viewpoint, however, it is impossible to see Arish Mell Gap in that way ever again.

This alluring and defenceless opening of the mother country has been roughly treated since the tanks arrived. The Army may have spared some of the orchids, but it has brought the Victorian appreciation of this place, which emphasised its seclusion and its vulnerability, to an obscenely literal-minded conclusion. A later commentator, F. J. Harvey Darton, records that Bindon's flank was still 'dark with pines' at the end of the Great War, but there is no sign of these now except for a scraggy clump of Scots pines just inland from Arish Mell. Maiden Plantation may originally have been set to embellish a pastoral view, but for the Royal Armoured Corps's artist, whose picture adorns a notice in the Franklin Viewpoint, this tuft lends a vulgar suggestiveness to the Gap that has been so sorely abused in the twentieth century: first taken from behind by its own defenders and then penetrated with a large pipe full of radioactive waste. F. J. Harvey Darton had something other than this ghastly sub-Freudian reduction in mind when he promised the unique delights of a place that 'satisfies always and fully'.[11] He never walked into the nearby Weld Arms, as I once did, to find a group of young officers from the Queen's Own Hussars chortling about 'barrel droop', said to beset Challenger tanks when their gun tubes get heated up.

Some visitors will be dismayed to find such brutal use made of this exquisite landscape, but they only have to glance at their fellow Franklinites to recognise that the sense of violation is very much part of the attraction. The tanks line up on the tarmac a couple of hundred yards away and the onlookers share the perspective of the trainee gunners as they blast away, splitting sight from sound and leaving them to recombine chaotically in the car park: the flash and recoil register first, and then a vast thunderbolt crashes in just behind them, jolting the cars and shocking young infants into tears or gleeful shrieks. As the noise fades, the tiny sounds of the pastorale reassert themselves — the metallic tinkling of twine rapping against flag poles, and the trilling of blithe and habituated larks that haven't missed a note. The tanks have truly entered the idyll and seized hold of its heart.

I've sat here and watched as an armoured car fired a red flare down towards Arish Mell Gap, cheered on by a cluster of enthusiastic children. I've seen elderly men sunk in wartime reminiscence, while their wives maintain a respectful silence beside them. The Franklin Viewpoint can be especially dramatic at night. I drove into it at about 11.30 one warm July evening, parking in a line of silent and unlit cars. Stars glimmered beyond the distant ridge of Bindon Hill. I could hear the steady throbbing of diesel engines, and some fragmented snatches of conversation. Then came a sudden white flash — bright, but too brief to illuminate the overall scene — and the car was rocked by an explosion that then started rolling about like a stereophonic special effect on an early heavy metal album. After bouncing back and forth between Rings Hill and Bindon, it rolled itself up into another resounding thump and then died away into those idling engines. A bright light suddenly went on at the foot of the ridge and a tank started blasting streams of tracer at it with a machine gun. I could see exhilarated faces in the cars, and a little further away a group of young men sitting on the roof of their van and toasting the show with cans of lager.

Such is the Ministry of Defence's commitment to public education that larger demonstrations have been mounted on the Bindon range. I joined the Press for one such excursion in May 1993. It was the usual disjointed collection of scribblers that gathered on the tarmac that morning: a sloppy bunch by comparison with the soldiers, many of whom sported virile moustaches and jutting close-shaven jaws. Everyone was intrigued to see a silver grey coach pull in with 'Good News Travel' written on its side, and even more so when nine Russian soldiers stepped down. Dressed in camouflaged fatigues, with Arish Mell-shaped triangles of blue and white striped vest at their open collars, they ambled over to the VIP lounge beneath the control tower.

Soon enough the 'press corps' were marshalled into open army trucks and driven off to the theatre in Lulworth Camp, to be briefed by officers who stood up in front of tawny velveteen curtains that infused the whole event with an atmosphere of amateur dramatics. Colonel Bryan Gordon-Smith explained that his men were in the business of 'dismantling the capabilities of the Cold War'. More specifically, the object of today's exercise was to blow up tanks, as agreed under the Conventional Armed Forces in Europe treaty. The UK had agreed to destroy 183 tanks in all, and of the various methods allowed — severing, crushing, conversion to civil use — the British had chosen explosives. Some fifty Chieftains were to be blown that week at Lulworth, and the 'resultant hulks' would be left there to be used for target practice. The Russians had yet to begin on their far greater 'reduction liability' of 10,000 tanks, but their inspection team was here to ensure that no cheating took place. The Commander of 5 Field Squadron of the Royal Engineers then went through the anatomy of the tank, identifying the places where his men were placing their charges. It was, he said, 'excellent training for my soldiers, who rarely get the opportunity to put explosive theory into practice'.

At the foot of Bindon Hill we were shown an assortment of tanks that had already been blown in a picturesque manner. The photographers took their pick of the gun tubes — bent, split or twisted. Then we were driven back to the tarmac beneath the control tower. The photographers lined up, training their biggest lenses on the three tanks that had been selected for the final explosion. Some regretted that the Army had lacked the aesthetic sense to place these exhibits where they would have been silhouetted against the shining cleft of Arish Mell Gap, but a junior officer was already handing out latex ear plugs. Right on cue, the three Chieftains blew simultaneously with a high vertical flash and a vast plume of smoke, which had shot up past the ridge of Bindon Hill before the bang hit the tarmac beside us.

It only remained for the Russian Colonel Sergei Slepnev — his long bony face waiting patiently for the interpreter to catch up — to inform the gathered journalists that he would never have believed it had he been told, even two years previously, that he would be here in Lulworth, observing such a thing as a guest of the British Army. The young British officer who accompanied me — he had, as he explained, only 'come along for the jolly' — was not convinced that the threat was really over. But the show had gone well, and the nation found a more encouraging message in its papers the next morning: exit the Cold War as a few thin threads of smoke drifting away through Arish Mell Gap.

TWO

REFORMATION IN THE PARK

A WALL CAN BE a cruel thing even in rural Dorset, like a brand or a bloody knife in the ground. Hurdles of coppiced hazel may traditionally have sufficed to enfold the sheep, but it takes stone and brick to keep people in their places and to set the mark of property on the earth. Thomas Hardy broke his poor stonemason, Jude the Obscure, against this hard fact; and it applies on the B3070 too, even though the passerby may fail immediately to see it.

For in contrast to the military wire on the coastal side of this lane, pious Thomas Weld's wall opposite looks as soft as enduring brick and stone possibly could. Built in the last decades of the eighteenth century, much of it along the ridge and ditch of a thirteenth-century deer park, it joins the road just west of the Franklin Viewpoint: a much-creepered thing that runs behind a row of oaks for a few hundred yards, and then emerges to form an agreeably liquid blur of red and grey outside the car window. It rises as high as ten foot in places but is usually lower and generous with glimpses of the green world within. Still effective as a sign of aristocratic enclosure, the wall has aged to become a dappled, eye-pleasing thing. Variegated by lichens, lifted by tree roots and undermined by badgers and rabbits, it has long since been converted into a habitat.

The main gate opens into a landscaped tranquillity that could hardly stand in greater contrast to the gross exhilarations of the Franklin Viewpoint. The drive winds up through a grove of well-placed trees, curving round to disappear behind an eighteenth-century stable court. The sound of gunfire frequently resounds, but the bits of apparatus that lie on the grass here are quite unlike those on the other side of the wall. They pertain to horses rather than tanks and reveal this to be a place where, at the appointed season, young ladies guide their mounts over sponsored fences with names like 'Green Bump' and 'Pallisade and Pheasant Feeder'.

Lulworth Castle stands in the middle, an imposing square building with four towers at its corners. Constructed as a romantic hunting lodge in the seventeenth century and turned into an opulent residence in the eighteenth,

Lulworth is a sham castle, built for envious show; and its ruin lies close to the high tower of St Andrew's Church. Turner treated the church tower as a lighter but equal counterpart to the castle, setting the pair — a well-harmonised and wooden architectural couplet — into the Arcadian background behind cows and a fishing swain. In earlier eighteenth-century prints the church often seems more reduced, a mere landscape feature placed behind the castle to lend a little Gothic romance to the ladies and gentlemen who promenade on the castle lawns while contented rustics roll the grass and distant ships sail by through Arish Mell Gap.

The oldest building in Lulworth Park, St Andrew's stands isolated among trees north of a small wicket gate in the surrounding wall. Its fifteenth-century tower rises up through four diminishing stages with pinnacled buttresses at each corner. Curious stone corbels protrude from beneath its embattled parapet, and a rank harvest of weeds, shrubs and saplings sprouts from its rusty carstone sides. The visitors' book contains appreciative comments contributed over many years. One who had apparently felt like a trespasser remarked that 'So many "Private's" make one shy of entering'; but others seemed to appreciate the seclusion: 'One of the few places the Yanks haven't tried to buy'; 'Old England at its best. Keep it as it is.' And yet, as is so often the way in Old England, time seems to be running out. The plaster is falling; green mould creeps up the damp walls; and a notice announces that 'This church is under threat of closure.'

The churchyard has tumbled down the years too. I once unearthed the end of an ornate cast iron bench here, and foraging creatures have brought bones to the surface. Some of the monuments reveal this to be the last resting-place of faithful servants to the Welds, buried here with due tribute. But there are older stones too, now as cracked and tilted as the upended rocks of Lulworth Cove, which still stammer out urgent moral instructions. The Garlands were well-established tenant farmers, but I had to peel back ivy and moss and wait for the shadows to lengthen before I could decipher their communication:

Rejoice oh young man in thy youth;
But let thy pleasure be,
Forever go armed with truth,
And strict sincerity.
For though thy life extended may,
Beyond the age of Man;
In pain and grief t'will pass away

And fuddenly be gone;
Therefore, all God's Commandments mind,
As long as thou haft breath;
Then sweet contentment here you'll find,
And peace at laft in Death.

One Sunday in August 1992 I raised the congregation of St Andrew's to a grand total of nine. The organist struggled to raise a tune, and the elderly parson turned out to be an equally determined fisher of men. After welcoming us to this decrepit place, he urged us all to find 'a new world in Jesus'.

When it was time for the sermon, he climbed into the pulpit to recall how, years ago, he had once been in the habit of reading *Which*, the magazine of the Consumers' Association. Perplexed by the detailed information provided about washing-machines, fridges and radios, he had resolved to read only the summaries. This turned out to be strangely unsatisfactory and he soon gave up the magazine.

At this point the vicar paused, letting his words wander out into the modest and unaisled nave where they scuttled about between rows of empty pews, occasionally bumping into lonely congregationists, who sat there anticipating an attack on the materialistic values of the consumer society that mistook a twin tub washing-machine for the key to Heaven. But the vicar drew a different conclusion. So it was, he said sternly, with the Church of England's new services and prayer book. The modern church was in danger of becoming altogether too sheepish about its mission, and of settling for a 'summary of the faith' rather than the whole gospel. We were falling short of the perfection of God daily, weekly, monthly: 'Why are standards so high? Because they represent conditions before the fall.'

Standing by the churchyard gate, I mused upon the vicar's difficulty. There was a soul-stirring view to the south, with Flowers Barrow looming up over the trees and one of the Royal Armoured Corps's red boundary flags fluttering before the sea in Arish Mell Gap. But, closer up, St Andrew's seemed to drift in a green void. A lone ash stands in the pasture beyond the gate, accentuating the sense of emptiness. The vicar may have looked at all those empty pews and worried about the faithlessness of modern times; but I had a different absence in mind: not just where is the congregation, but what has happened to the village from which its members might have come?

English Heritage at Work

Tropical sailors of old were susceptible to a disease called calenture, in which they mistook the sea for green fields and tried to step out into it, but nobody has named the disorder that has left successive vicars of East Lulworth to imagine a busy village in the lightly ridged ocean of grass surrounding their church. This settlement does not appear on any hiker's map, but there can be no doubt that it once existed. A pictorial map drawn by Margaret Weld in 1721, shows cottages by the church, with cultivated fields, hedges and garden plots planted with fruits and vegetables. The houses may not be as numerous as those that cluster around the church in a later portrayal, but one of them has a plume of smoke curling up from its chimney pot; and there are people too, loading hay or riding down towards the sea at Arish Mell.

Things have changed in Lulworth Park, and it is not just the sound of gunfire that carries news of this fact into the dank recesses of St Andrew's churchyard. 'After a long day the fun is set, but it shall rise again at the resurrection of the just and fhine for ever.' So says one weathered old tombstone, but I had hardly sorted out the f's and the s's when a modern Dorset vernacular drifted in from the north, a gruff voice complaining of 'so much fucking rain and so much fucking wind'. On another occasion, I was just leaving the churchyard, when a small executive coach with 'Victory Tours' emblazoned on its side rattled over the cattlegrid and pulled up by the castle immediately to the north of St Andrew's. A company of well-dressed men in suits descended, and then stood about balancing hard hats on their heads: no Russian officers, these were the Commissioners of English Heritage and they had come to inspect one of their largest restorations.

At the estate office in the old stable block, Mr Wilfrid Weld, the present owner, explained that the castle was the commanding centre of the Weld estate, which owns some 12,500 acres here, the bulk of it being land that was first aggregated by the Cistercian abbots of Bindon Abbey and then redistributed by Henry VIII. The first Weld bought the estate in 1641, but it was Thomas Weld, who owned Lulworth in the late eighteenth century, who gave it its present form. It was he who had the wall built, and it was also he who shifted that considerable proportion of East Lulworth to make way for his park. Drawing on a detailed archaeological and ecological survey recently commissioned by the estate, Weld explained that the houses near the church are recorded on a map dated 1770/1, but that they were levelled shortly after that. It is not known whether their removal was sudden or spread over a number of years, and neither was it clear whether the evicted tenants were rehoused elsewhere on the estate.

I once bumped into Mark Girouard at the castle. But although the scholars and architectural historians have certainly been down to scrutinise the ruins and to wonder just how much Thomas Weld did to complete the transformation of this former hunting lodge into a palatial residence, the site is normally left to the stoneworkers who tell a ruder story. 'We're the whipping boys,' they say with a snort at the unlikely thought of their manager. Gazing up into the vaulted spaces of English Heritage's organisation, these stoneworkers identified large redundant areas: 'I've got two and a half people looking after me,' said one, brandishing an internal staff newsletter that brims over with the wasteful pieties of good corporate communications.

'We are the closest thing to Joe Public that English Heritage has got,' explained another, adding that he wouldn't dream of visiting his own organisation's sites. Perhaps the Weld estate would be able to make something of Lulworth Castle, but it would never rival a really good attraction like the Yeovilton Air Museum or, for that matter, the Franklin Viewpoint just over the wall.

These stoneworkers had a point when they suggested that, tanks apart, the park has hardly ever resounded with the real din of history. For centuries the guidebooks have been getting by on a few bare facts: counting up the Royal visits and telling how the castle suffered when garrisoned by parliamentary forces during the English Civil War.

Yet history entered Lulworth Park in another way too. Thomas Weld moved a village and built a wall when he extended his park in accordance with the Whig fashion for 'improvement', but he was also responsible for the lovely Palladian building that stands beside a ha-ha at the end of the old castle lawn. This is the Great Chapel of St Mary's — built to a design by John Tasker in 1786 and reputed to be the first free-standing Roman Catholic church erected in England after the Reformation. I came to mass here the Sunday after attending the service in St Andrew's. There were forty or so people in the mixed congregation, and battered old heaps parked alongside brand new BMWs under the old chestnut tree outside. The chapel had recently been restored, with further assistance from English Heritage, to its original eighteenth-century opulence. Freshly painted celestial scenes adorned the domed ceiling, and the altar, made in Rome with no expense spared, looked as rich as ever with its alabastar and marble and its tabernacle of lapis lazuli and amethyst.

Mr Wilfrid Weld was there to serve Father Michael Murphy, who delivered his homily in a gentle Irish voice. After welcoming visitors, Father Murphy measured out the long threads of history that bind the Roman Catholic Church to the landscape around Lulworth. He honoured the memory of St Adhelm, whose staff is said to have taken root in the ground, and he quoted from Llewelyn Powys, a writer who had lived on the high downs of the Weld estate sixty years previously, and written of ' "the eternal hills of Dorset" — a lovely expression that'.

In the words of their own family historian, the Welds were 'the wealthiest of the old Catholic families of the Squirearchy'.[1] Both priests now make ecumenical gestures, but the short distance between these two churches also measures a long history of religious antagonism, which is built into the fabric of Thomas Weld's wall. The Welds had to be vigilant throughout the eighteenth century. In 1714, a mob from Poole came out to the castle, shouting curses on 'their Jesuit priest'. The house had already been searched and only left with such weapons as were deemed necessary for repulsing any pirates who might land at Arish Mell, and Margaret Weld wrote a letter describing their exposed position: 'We are daily threatened with the populace to which we now lie exposed, and on Monday the ninth instant between eight and nine o'clock in even actually insulted at our doors by some of them, though no harm was done.'[2]

Thomas Weld was also familiar with these tensions. During the Gordon Riots of 1780, he wrote to his nearby friend James Frampton to secure safe refuge for his family in case the disorder spread to south Dorset;[3] and even though George III had permitted him to build his chapel on condition that it looked like a mausoleum rather than a church, he was still subject to double-taxes levied on Catholics and barred from joining the Dorset Yeomanry. Considerable difficulties followed from his decision to establish a monastery for a small group of Cistercian Trappists displaced by the French Revolution, which had converted their silent Normandy retreat into a cannon foundry.[4] Thomas Weld brought them to Lulworth in 1794, and built the Monastery of St Susan down at the old 'Sea-farm' a few hundred yards from Arish Mell Gap. This institution, into which the monks moved under cover of night in March 1796, survived through the Napoleonic

Wars, but drew such scandalous accusations that it was eventually closed under government pressure in 1817 and the monks repatriated to France.

The scandal, which was to reverberate for more than a hundred years, began before the monastery was opened.[5] In 1795, Thomas Weld was attacked in a poem called 'On the Building of a Monastery in Dorsetshire'.[6] The anonymous poet, who was in no doubt that monks and friars are 'more formidable than hostile ships', turns Weld into 'Numa', a 'zealous papist' who befriends the grey-hooded monks who are first seen creeping like monstrous spies into a cave by the shore. Numa and his monks bring their own kind of extinction to East Lulworth: 'Behold us! not indeed yet numerous,/ but daily so becoming to our faith/ Half Lulo's people have already turned.' Even the parish clerk has succumbed to the alien rites and pageantry which are 'wont to fascinate the people'. By 1801, when a second anonymous poem appeared, the 'contagion' had spread to 'two parts in three' of the village.[7] Two years later Thomas Weld was offering a reward of £100 for the apprehension of whosoever was responsible for the 'industriously circulated' rumour that Napoleon himself was hidden in the castle or in the monastery at Arish Mell, along with arms and ammunition.[8]

So the tanks of religious hatred break through the picturesque aspect of Lulworth Park, turning Thomas Weld's removal of the village into an act of religious war and establishing a hostile tension between the castle and the tower of St Andrew's. The first of those anti-papist poems treats the newly isolated tower as a yet unbroken hostage to the diabolical Numa, who explains to the monks that 'All that you see is mine, that Church alone excepted.' The same idea seems to have occurred to Denis Bond, who was rector of nearby Steeple and Tyneham until his death in 1795; for it is recorded that when he came to preach at St Andrew's, he would 'inveigh so loudly against the Pope that the Welds (R.C.) could hear his harangue in the Castle'.[9]

These animosities have long since cooled, but the notice of closure served on St Andrew's in 1990 remains the delayed-action consequence of Thomas Weld's decisions. Having had the bones of his ancestors removed from the family vault at St Andrew's to the mausoleum under the Great Chapel of St Mary's in 1787, Weld took down the medieval body of the church and replaced it with a smaller nave and chancel that quite lacked the quality of his new edifice. Victorian antiquarians would condemn these humiliating 'improvements' outright, claiming that 'the architecture is of a very mean character'.[10] The Great Chapel would have its historical moments (in 1790

Bishop Carroll was consecrated there, the first Bishop of Baltimore and 'foundation stone of the American hierarchy',[11]) but St Andrew's only sank into local obscurity, as the difficulties of sustaining it on a dwindling base of Protestant parishioners steadily grew. Numa's 'contagion' was apparently still advancing in the 1860s, when Dorchester architect John Hicks surveyed the church prior to a second rebuilding in which his employee Thomas Hardy was involved. As Hicks wrote in support of a wider public appeal: 'The population of East Lulworth at the last census was 450, nearly three-fourths of whom are Roman Catholics and those who still remain in communion with the Church of England are almost without exception poor. The Great Tithes of the Parish, and the whole of the land (with the exception of the Glebe) are the property of a Roman Catholic Landlord, who has refused on religious grounds to contribute.'[12]

By 1961 the church was once again 'in a most pitiable condition', and another appeal was launched in 1967. The population of East Lulworth had fallen to under three hundred, and there were 'only about a dozen Anglican families in the village'. As Revd John Stone concluded for the benefit of those visitors who might trickle through, 'Our need is desperate, and local resources are so very limited. Please come to our aid.'

Low Road to Tolpuddle

East Lulworth, or the surviving part of it that still lies along the outside of Thomas Weld's wall, was described as a 'dependent' village back in the Eighteen Sixties, and it remains so to this day.[13] Wilfrid Weld's father, the late Colonel Sir Joseph Weld, lived in the manor house here until his death in 1992. Having inherited the estate in 1935, he became well known as 'the last of the old squires'. When I met this former Lord Lieutenant of Dorset in March 1989, he unfolded a picture of East Lulworth that was still wrapped in unembarrassed Tory paternalism. There had never been any 'development' in East Lulworth, he explained. The estate had indeed sold cottages, barns and building land elsewhere, but not in East Lulworth: 'You've got to resist people,' he said, adding that to sell cottages would be to introduce 'weekenders', who tend to kill a place.

There are still some in the village who wonder whether this long tradition of Catholic paternalism is entirely beneficial. They point to the fact that the shop has recently closed, and observe that the couple who recently made such a go of The Weld Arms, East Lulworth's only pub, have moved on too. 'Feudalism,' they say, 'is bad for the soul'; it saps people's initiative, and encourages moaning.

And it is true that this charmingly undeveloped village has its own way of nursing grievances. People will point to the rotting windows of their rented homes and observe that when cottages fall empty now, the Weld estate is renovating them for holiday letting. Even those who have no arguments with the present can be full of sharpened reminiscence about how severe things used to be. Perhaps they remember the fate of the family who once farmed in a bucolic little hollow called Wood Street — said to have been evicted after three generations from buildings later allowed to crumble, and still made to pay for every fruit tree that had disappeared during their long tenancy. Or they may remember how the children in the village of Coombe Keynes, just north of East Lulworth, used to be called in every time a Weld drove by because it was better to skulk indoors than to stand curtseying at the roadside.

Others approach the point obliquely, suggesting it might be worth taking a look at *Rough Shoot*, a film shot in East Lulworth in 1953, which turns the gates of Lulworth Park into the entrance to the County Mental Hospital, and takes even more offensive liberties with the squire. In this Cold War thriller the upright and patriotic Colonel Sir Joseph disappears to make way for a man called Hassingham, a weak-minded drunkard who has developed dangerous foreign affiliations through his Austrian and perhaps even slightly Jewish wife. Communism has replaced Catholicism as the alien creed, and Hassingham is in the pocket of evil plotters who, were it not for the intervention of an American hero, would successfully have landed a Soviet agent to steal the plans for Britain's atom bomb.

The village in the grass around St Andrew's has attracted a modest amount of archaeological attention. The first information emerged in 1959, when the Atomic Energy Authority dug the trench for its nuclear effluent pipe. The eighteenth-century remains included hand-made brick and fragments of ashlar, architrave from a door, clay tobacco pipes, glass bottles, bits of bone and oyster shell, and a refuse pit that was duly sectioned. As the investigating archaeologist concluded: 'Together, all these finds give an impression of the "material culture" of the people in East Lulworth before the eviction sometime between c. 1785–95.'[14] At least thirty-five dwellings are said to have been removed, approximately half the existing village of

East Lulworth. They were probably made of traditional Dorset cob, plastered with earth and lime.[15]

Yet in the remaining segment of East Lulworth, people have a different way of holding on to that lost organic community. I discovered this by accident, a couple of years after coming down to Lulworth Park with Stuart Hall to make a television programme for the Open University. We had stood together by St Andrew's, and surveyed the empty field. 'Where's the village?' asked Stuart, and I answered, just as we had rehearsed, that the Welds had moved it to put this pleasing green view in its place. The remark seemed uncontroversial, especially since I was only repeating what Mr Wilfrid Weld himself had told me. However, the year after our programme was first transmitted, I was recognised in the road in East Lulworth, and swept into a house to meet an elderly lady who wanted to thank me for having stated so clearly what had happened to the village in the park. The late Mrs Rena Gould had much to say in praise of the Welds, and she was certainly no anti-papist. Yet, as a resolute member of the Church of England, she declared it one of the more abject facts of Lulworth life that, in the early decades of the century, villagers were still converting to Rome in the hope of ingratiating themselves to the Squire. 'I was glad you said that,' she repeated.

In reality, however, the tribute for keeping alive the memory of that extinguished village in the grass belongs to someone quite different. John Fitzgerald Pennie grew up in East Lulworth during the time of Thomas Weld's improvements to the park, the son of a Protestant family. Born in 1782 to parents who lived as servants in St Andrew's vicarage, Pennie was a prodigious phenomenon. His literary endeavours were not encouraged; indeed, such was his father's hostility that he was obliged to write under hedges or in barns and stables. An old maiden aunt, on hearing that her young nephew was determined to write a play, 'absolutely screamed with horror, overset three or four flower-pots filled with her choicest plants, and nearly fainted on a bed of young sprouting asparagus'.[16] But Pennie, having written a tragedy by the age of fifteen, went on to compose the prolix and barely readable verse epics and plays about ancient Britain that would gain him some temporary reputation as 'the Bard of the West' and a self-taught 'genius' who made the most of his 'ill-fated' life, vigorously exploiting its 'deep night of darkness, want, and misery' in his perpetual search for patrons.[17]

Described by his obituarist as 'the poet of antiquarian lore', Pennie paced about among the ancient earthworks of Flowers Barrow and Bindon Hill, conjuring them into great camps of the Durotriges. He was partial to Druids, but it wasn't just on their behalf that he fashioned a magic lantern capable of letting 'a bygone world, the relics of which are dust, live again in the glowing colours of imagination'. Indeed, in his autobiographical *Tale of a Modern Genius*, which he published under the pseudonym 'Sylvaticus', he repopulated the emptied acres around the reduced and isolated parish church of St Andrew's, and it is thanks to him that the village lives on — a romantic memory pulled from the minds of the elders who had lived through Thomas Weld's transformations.

After gathering up 'the simple legends' that were 'yet remembered by the few that love to be garrulous of by-gone days', East Lulworth's oral historian took up his chosen position somewhere near the wicket gate, peered over Thomas Weld's wall into 'the verdant park' with its 'luxuriance of waving woodlands', and used the powerful apparatus of his mind's eye to project his own Tory idea of a lost 'English Heritage' back into that recently cleared scene.[18]

He begins by restoring the medieval church and rebuilding the old manor house that was said once to have stood so close to the west door of the church that 'From the great hall of this stately mansion, its possessors could behold through the western window of the church tower, the wax tapers shedding their consecrated light on the high altar.' Then he reintroduces the village. First on to that enclosed ground are 'the cottages of the neighbouring peasants', each one hung with festive garlands. 'Yonder village-green' comes next, and it too seems to land close by the church, pinned down by a maypole. The sprightly sound of viol and pipe starts up, and the whole organic scene begins to move as 'vigour, youth and beauty' step up to mingle in 'the joyous dance'.

So the local heroes walk out once more on to the green. John Stubbs was 'the stoutest wrestler within nine miles of the village' and his chosen partner is Betty Adams, the parish-clerk's daughter, who steps up to dance in 'a short gown of the largest and most gaudy-coloured flowers, with here and there the figure of a man in the mixed costume of a Turk and a Chinese introduced between'. George Ford was 'the undaunted chief of the smuggling sea-gangs along the southern coast'. He could jump a turnpike gate from the ground, and had often carried twenty-four-gallon casks of brandy up from the seashore at one time. Then comes Ben Roberts, a smuggler who was never happier than when dancing with Mary Wilmot. He would shower her with contraband luxuries — 'shewy gewgaws, ribbons of many colours, beads, dollars of tea' — but Mary Wilmot was 'a thoughtless, vain, idle, laughing coquet — a very jilt'. She preferred the excise officer and only laughed as 'poor Ben Roberts' retreated heartbroken to the stable where he shot himself.

Sentimental tragedy of the sort that would only just be redeemed by Thomas Hardy also engulfed fair Jane Gilbert, 'one of the merriest in the May-pole dances'. She doted on Henry Standley, 'the wild, but handsome game keeper and sporting companion of a half-witted squire in the neighbourhood'. But, having 'triumphed over her virtue', this worthless fellow disappeared to London where he sank into 'voluptuous dissipation' and never came back to marry her as pledged. Jane eventually hanged herself from the rafters of a barn, where she was found with a lock of Henry's hair on her bosom. As a suicide, she was buried at midnight near a crossroads on an adjacent hill. The mountain winds solemnised her 'dismal obsequies', and the cliffs themselves seemed to shriek as 'the horrid stake' was driven through her body. Earth was heaped up around the stake like a tumulus, and the site was still known as 'The Maiden's Grave'.

Hearing the pealing bells that once heralded the evicted community's festivals, Pennie takes the side of the old church tower against the usurping castle beyond — recalling how it 'lifted its pinnacles above the straw-roofed cottages that clustered around it, and confronted with a noble and venerable dignity the proud battlements of that lofty pile'. May-day opens with the 'peasant-maidens' gathering flowers in dewy fields and woods. They pick 'magical fox-gloves' from around the elm trees that, beyond the clearance, had so long served as 'the rendez-vous of the young, the sportive, and the idle, and the meeting-place of the aged and garrulous'. Those maidens would be out again at 'Harvest-home', dancing behind the last waggon as it came in from 'the moonlit fields, covered in boughs and garlands of flowers'. They were there too for the 'ancient and rural feast of sheep-shearing', when 'the flocks of a thousand valleys and mountains were gathered together to be washed in the flowing stream, and then stripped of their burthensome fleeces', by shearers who would later go on to 'a great banquet served up in smoky hall on maple dishes'.

As for 5th November, no one could mistake the enthusiasm with which Pennie fills his reimagined village with the din of guns and bells, and thickens its air with the smoke of bonfire and tobacco in his evocation of that riotously anti-papist celebration. He shows women chattering 'with an unbounded volubility of plots and popish treasons', while a tremendous bonfire blazes on the reinstated village green 'like an Indian suttee', and delighted children dance around the flames. Then 'the horrible effigies of his Holiness the Pope, and the frightful bugbear of Guy Faux' are brought out to be burnt. The Clerk's daughter, Betty Adams, brought out 'the straw-stuffed Pontiff of Rome' swinging it round by the arms and hurling it 'exultingly into the bonfire, amidst an universal yell'. She then took the first draught from the double-handed brown jug, and chanted 'the following exquisite stave':

Destruction to the French and Pope,
I do long to see the hour:
Confusion to them that do set them up,
Or aid their hellish power!
Huzza! my boys, huzza!

These defiant words were immediately 'chorused by all the rustics, who then joined hands, and sang and danced round the fire, till the Pope and the arch-traitor Faux were both consumed to ashes'.

For Pennie, Thomas Weld's wall was at once an emblem of Catholic pride and the symbol of a system of enclosure and 'improvement' that had driven the rural virtues from the land. The village elders remembered a time when there had been twenty-five barns in the parish. These 'rustic halls' may have been full of cobwebs, but that had not deterred the 'laughing villagers' who would hang a cord of lanterns over the beams and then gather to dance their jigs and reels, and toast the crazy fiddler with 'brown jugs of lamb's wool' — a native brew of ale and roasted apples. In the modern era of the wall, there were not four of these 'good old store-houses of plenty' remaining.

Turning off his lantern, Pennie glanced back at that stolen ground by the captive church, and faced the bitter truth of his own times: 'Alas! Those good old times of hilarity, plenty, and their constant concomitant — Content are banished from us; while poverty, oppression and an overwhelming principle of absurd pride have joined to sweep away every vestige of those manners and hospitable customs of our forefathers . . .' Tracing the descent of that expropriated peasantry through 'the parish annals of vice, fraud and crime' and into 'the wretched abodes of pauperism', he foreshadowed another geological convulsion that would soon threaten the 'wavy woods' and 'flowery lawns' of Lulworth Park. Thomas Weld had removed a village and caused a wall to be built, but as the surrounding poverty grew and the parish relief system started to break, he also gave the land on which a workhouse was erected at Wool in 1796, collaborating in this endeavour with his landowning friend, James Frampton of Moreton.

If that name is familiar to this day, it is because 'Improvement' raised the spectre of insurrection. James Frampton, who was also a magistrate, came into his own in 1830, three years after the publication of Pennie's forgotten book, when the impoverished countryside was convulsed by machine-breaking, rick-burning and other rural protest. Unusual notices were posted in Dorset, like one that sought information about two incendiarists who had been seen riding through the county, with 'something different from a common riding stick', which was suspected to be 'an Air Gun, from which a small Shell is thrown, which ignites after a certain time'.[19] Frampton went to Bere to recruit special constables to keep the peace, and, finding the populace provoked by this measure, came back to Moreton to fortify his house against the anticipated mob: arming it, sealing up the lower windows and, in the words of a visitor, ensuring it was 'barricaded like an Irish mansion'.

East Lulworth had its own unusual experiences that year, not least because Lulworth Castle served as an asylum for Charles X, the Bourbon King of France who had fled his country in frightened apprehension of the mob. Charles's cringing fear of the crowd on the quayside at Poole was deplored by some, including the Duke of Wellington, who feared it would set a bad example for English malcontents.[20]

Fortunately, James Frampton was there to protect the Weld estate too. When notice was received on 30th November of an 'intended rising' at the adjacent villages of Winfrith, Wool and Lulworth, this ruthless magistrate rode out to meet them with 'a large body of farmers' equipped with short staffs and the new name of a 'constabulary force'. They headed for Winfrith, where the premises of an unpopular clergyman were said to be in danger, but found the mob to be less fierce than expected. 'Urged on from behind hedges, &c., by a number of women and children', the men only advanced 'respectfully, and with their hats in their hands, to demand increases of wages'. Frampton read the Riot Act when they would not disperse, but they still pushed forward. One of the offenders was promptly 'collared', but 'he slipped from his captors by leaving his smock frock in their hands'. Hearing that another mob was advancing from Lulworth, Frampton rode off to threaten them with similar promises of deportation to Van Diemen's Land. They appear to have been easily quelled, for when this dispenser of 'aristocratic justice' got back to Moreton,[21] he told his sister that the Lulworth mob had consisted of 'fine-looking men, and particularly well-dressed, as if they had put on their best clo' for the occasion'. Having quelled Lulworth's only recorded act of political rebellion, Frampton went on to secure lasting fame for himself a few years later as the corrupt and overzealous persecutor of the Tolpuddle Martyrs.[22]

As for J. F. Pennie, I was disappointed not to find his grave in the churchyard of St Andrew's. The funeral of Pennie and his wife Cordelia is entered in the East Lulworth register of burials, but their obituarist suggests they had resolved not to lay their bones in that captive place. After dying within two days of one another in 1848, they were interred in 'a secluded and picturesque spot' of Pennie's own choice — somewhere, as may be imagined, within sight of Flowers Barrow, which East Lulworth's modern genius once judged to be a Roman camp but later decided was 'wholly of British construction' and a fit burial place for the 'Aboriginal inhabitants' of his region.

THREE

STILL LIFE IN THE DESERTED VILLAGE

Began learning a new song. Heard a great many discords
Teacher's Log, Tyneham School, 30 April 1873

THE ROAD TO Tyneham breaks off the B3070 just before East Lulworth. Long since metalled but still known as the Whiteway, it winds up on to a high chalk ridge that wheels round from the cliff-top heights of Flowers Barrow to form the outer rim of the Isle of Purbeck. Thomas Hardy may have imagined King Lear raging on the great expanse of heath to the north, but it is now blasted in a different sense — carved with tank battle runs, target tracks and, further east, a vast clay quarry. Blue butterflies flutter over the whale-backed down of Povington Hill, competing with red flags and the complicated bye-laws governing the administration of the range — spelt out clause by bureaucratic clause on a noticeboard.

After running north along the ridge for a few hundred yards, the road turns sharply at the all but forgotten site of the 'Maiden's Grave' described by Pennie, and starts to sink down past the concrete plinth of a recently removed military checkpoint, and through a little stilly wood of oak, ash and hazel. The first prohibitions are spelt out in black and white: NO VENDORS NO HAWKERS NO CAMPERS and NO OVERNIGHT STAYS. Further on there are older signs of chipped red enamel, still ablaze with the warnings of an earlier age: DANGER. THERE ARE BOMBS AND UNEXPLODED SHELLS INSIDE. THEY CAN KILL YOU . . .

To drive down into the Tyneham valley is to sink into a zone where even the sharpest of actualities seems overtaken by myth. This was a well-loved place before history broke in to destroy it during the Second World War. Its small Elizabethan mansion lacked the aristocratic opulence of Lulworth Castle, but for nearly five hundred years it had belonged to the Bond family, well-established members of the Dorset gentry. *The Times* photographed the harvest here in August 1929, spreading the result — a horse-drawn harvester set off against valley and sea — over half a page. There could scarcely have been a more heart-stopping picture of England

— a perfect fold in the downs, touched with eternity despite the distant outline of Mrs Wheeler's modern bungalow on the cliff above Worbarrow Bay.

The summer prospect remains compelling even without the golden oats. The land swoops down from Flowers Barrow, exposing a sheet of ocean before circling the odd conical headland known as Worbarrow Tout, and then rising up again into the limestone of the inner Purbeck ridge, where a turf horizon marks the top of Gad Cliff, still soaked in the smuggling romance of James Meade Falkner's novel *Moonfleet*. There are sheep and cattle in the valley, and abandoned farms, their yards piled high with great black plastic bags of silage. Thistles, gorse, bracken and ragwort grow in the neglected fields, and there is scattered evidence of military use too: a scarlet concrete bollard in the middle of a field, more rusting target tanks and, down on the beach, concrete dragon's teeth placed during the Second World War to deter enemy landings. Painted numbers creep incongrously below Gad Cliff, and a large '3' sits on Worbarrow Tout too.

The most prominent feature nowadays is a recently much expanded car park called the 'Tyneham Village Viewpoint'. As for the village, to begin with it is hard to see anything beyond the welter of signs. Few of the visitors who drop the requested parking fee of thirty pence into the collection post sense any irony in the sign declaring that 'All proceeds help with the upkeep of Tyneham village.' Metal detectors are banned, dogs must be kept away from sheep and cows, and visitors are ordered to 'Enjoy the Wonderful Views'. Thc numbered posts of a 'Tyneham Trail' are scattered more discreetly through the village, each one explained in the accompanying leaflet — published with a grant from the Teachers' Fund of the School Curriculum Development Committee — that provides little drawings of the houses as they were before 1943, and names their evicted inhabitants.

Vigorously kept up by the Army, Tyneham village has the hectic flush of a place that has been restored way beyond the point of no return. The overgrown churchyard has been cleared and put to lawn that wouldn't look bad outside a government computer centre. The gravestones have been scrubbed so clean that even the most crooked ones seem filled with the desire to stand to attention. The pond has been bulldozed into new life as an eco-system with bullrushes, irises and the inevitable little island too. The ruined cottages of Post Office Row have also been robustly treated, their fallen roofs removed and their walls reduced to an officially recognised safe level and capped with cement.

Tyneham has been reinstated as an evocative visual aid. Television crews are sometimes to be found here, especially on weekends close to Remembrance Sunday when visitors may be asked to muster a sentence about their impressions of the place. I once came across a school visit. A representatively urban and multicultural class were standing knee-deep in the first cottage of Post Office Row, looking over the ruins of this extinguished Dorset village as if they were exploring some recently excavated ancient Babylonian site. 'Do you think there was a kitchen here?' asked the teacher, as his charges peered around the cramped space that had once been home to Shepherd Lucas and his family. 'What evidence have you got that they had a bathroom?' he asked an Asian girl. 'You're making assumptions all along the line.'

Outside the old post office next door, some elderly folk were bending over to read the signs inside a telephone box — an unusual model of magnolia concrete with red glazing bars and an ornamental metal finial, which rises up through four enamelled TELEPHONE signs to celebrate new powers in the air with the help of a spear blade thrust aloft. This over-restored freak gleams as if it were new, but connoisseurs will recognise it immediately as a rare example of the K1 kiosk, introduced by the post office in the early Twenties. Now locked against the threat of vandalism, it has a 'closed' sign cutely placed inside the door. The old wartime notices on the backboard — 'I am on war work. If you must use me be brief' — turn out to be colour photocopies.

Further up Post Office Row there is a symbolic oak tree, planted next to the church gate to mark the coronation of George V, and beside it the village tap with words from the Gospel according to St John inscribed in its stone: 'Whosoever drinketh of this water shall thirst again. But whosoever drinketh of the water that I shall give shall never thirst; but the water that I shall give him shall be in him a well of water springing up into everlasting life.' The Tyneham Trail leaflet commends the tap as 'a typical example of the Victorians' desire to promote the scriptures'.

The small church of St Mary the Virgin contains tablets commemorating the Bonds and their faithful servants, and, by the altar, a large stained glass east window made by Martin Travers in 1924, and commissioned by Warwick Draper, who lived at Worbarrow Bay, to commemorate his deceased wife Grace. It shows a Madonna and Child, set against a weeping willow and is rounded off with biblical words in which the whole of

Creation — Mountains and Hills, Seas and Floods — praises and magnifies the Lord forever.

Of the two unmodernised Bibles on display in this partly thirteenth-century building, the one said to be the last used in the church has been restored by the Royal Armoured Corps, and is now dedicated to 'the parishioners of Tyneham and Worbarrow'. The other, which was presented by two former villagers, stands across the chancel, open at the Book of Daniel where Persia was divided and the clash of great armies resounded overall. Looking down at that story of distant warfare and expropriation, I found phrases drifting up through the glass and, in the absence of any supervising vicar, coupling wildly with the story of Tyneham and its military evacuation: 'The robbers of thy people shall exalt themselves to establish the vision . . . ', 'He shall enter peaceably even upon the fattest places of the province; and he shall do *that* which his fathers have not done . . . ', 'And they shall pollute the sanctuary of strength, and shall take away the daily *sacrifice*, and they shall place the abomination that maketh desolate . . . '

The rest of the church is devoted to a secular exhibition that hails Tyneham's evicted villagers in the same naturalistic spirit as it greets the fulmars and shags of Gad Cliff. The old fields and hedges are delineated on a map, each granted its traditional name — Longmead, Lower Limekiln, Old Cowleaze. Limpid colour drawings show yoked oxen, an ancient 'Iron Age' plough with a single wooden share, and medieval field systems which can still be seen as 'low ridges' when the sun is low in the sky. One drawing suggests how Flowers Barrow might have looked when its green rings were filled with wooden shacks and commanded by a clan chieftain with a slingshot in his hand.

The story of Tyneham's evacuation is easily reconciled with this prehistoric world. To begin with, as a sign explains, the RAF and Army were billeted in the village, but as the military build-up increased before D-Day, the valley was cleared on the order of Churchill's War Cabinet. Villagers received a month's notice, and an official pledge that they would be able to return to their homes once the emergency was over, but they had to be gone by 19 December 1943. So they filed, patriotically, out of their valley, but only after pinning a note to the church door: 'Please treat the church and houses with care. We have given up our homes, where many of us have lived for generations, to help win the war to keep men free. We shall return one day and thank you for treating the village kindly.'

Outside by the Coronation Oak a father barks orders at his young daughters. 'Stay on the path,' he shrieks. 'Do I make myself very, very clear. You'll get blown up otherwise.' The girls run on regardless, only pausing when they reach the old stone-tiled schoolhouse. Built by the Bonds in 1856, Tyneham National School was closed by the Board of Education as the roll dwindled in 1932. The log-book tells of school mistresses and their struggle to maintain standards in a valley where nature itself seems to have conspired against them. The children are generally well versed in religious subjects, but arithmetic, grammar and general discipline remain a constant battle. Attendance fails for many reasons besides illness — smallpox, diphtheria — and the weather ('not quite so good an attendance today owing to the inclement tendency of the weather this morning' — 27 June 1871). Perhaps the mackerel were in the bay, the harvest was being brought in or, as was reported on Ascension Day 1876, the militia were at West Lulworth and the children had gone over to stare. In 1874, the schoolmistress recorded that even the grass was against her: it was high and very wet, and it kept the little ones from coming to school. There were upsetting occurrences, like the funeral of a third standard girl who died of 'brain fever' in 1872: the children were 'much distressed at the sight of the funeral but sufficiently composed to go to the grave each with a bunch of flowers'.

On Empire Day the school would be visited by the Bonds and addressed, perhaps by its appointed correspondent, who in 1905 'tried to impress on the minds of the children the responsibility that rested on each true Englishman to uphold the honour of England in whatever country they were, and that as they grew older and had to go out into the world, and some of them, perhaps to foreign lands, to strive never to do anything to disgrace the name of Englishmen'. The children would sing God Save the King as the Union Jack was hoisted, and then go on to recite poems by Rudyard Kipling and to sing 'suitable songs' like 'Brittania's sons on every shore'. Mrs Bond might then present each child with an orange — there was a famously productive orange tree in the conservatory at Tyneham House — and a holiday would be declared for the afternoon.

Like the rest of the village, Tyneham School was tightly managed by the Bonds and their rector. Visiting inspectors from the Education Department were worried about sanitation arrangements. They recommended printed copybooks, and regretted the harshness disfiguring the children's note-singing. Some commended Tyneham's as 'a good village school', while others threatened to impose a fine 'unless improvement is made in arithmetic'. The various standards studied set poems: in 1890 these are listed as including Wordsworth's 'Foresight', Miss Yonge's 'The Mother's Book' and Longfellow's 'Discovery of the North Cape'. Oliver Goldsmith's 'The Deserted Village' was set for the higher standards in 1892. 'Watching for Pa' was among the songs, and Object Lessons included plum pudding, St George and the Dragon, posting a letter and the Union Jack.

The state's presence in this valley has hardened since the days of the school inspectors, or the post office engineers who came to install the telephone box in the severe winter of 1929. The GPO had already made some concessions to Mr William Bond, whose conditions extended far beyond his refusal to have such a disturbing device as a telephone in Tyneham House. They had agreed to install an already outdated K1 model, rather than the current K2, which, being red all over and equipped with nocturnal illumination, was considered far too obtrusive. Yet they were still cursed by a rector who wanted none of their modern improvements. As for their original misplacing of the kiosk by the pond, rather than outside the post office, this is said to have enraged William Bond so much that he went home and suffered a stroke.[1]

The ruined schoolhouse was repaired in the Eighties and opened as a gallery and museum. Its educational message is still full of poetry — albeit only that of military public relations. Offering its own surreal tribute to the tank, it repeats the myth of Tyneham, stripping it of social content and turning it into an ecological and archaeological saga. The visitor is informed that the Royal Armoured Corps has saved Tyneham and its valley from the fate of so much of Dorset's traditional landscape. There has been no commercial development, no deep ploughing to destroy the medieval field systems, no pesticides or herbicides to silence the valley's naturally polyphonic spring. The most arresting image, which showed the Army blasting away in the gorse, was labelled 'Co-operation — the Army creating small pools for dragonflies in the wet heathland area . . . '

That exhibition struggled valiantly to bring the story to a happy conclusion, but some visitors remain unconvinced by the new ecological settlement. I once heard an elderly lady, returned to England for a holiday after many decades in Canada, worrying about the fate of the poor villagers. She was promptly engaged by a burly range warden, who wasn't going to listen to any of this sentimental nonsense. 'The villagers don't even want to come back,' he said, adding that some of them were probably pleased to leave too: 'You imagine the life,' he continued, gesturing at the ruined cottages, 'no electricity, no water, everything owned by the same man.' The

Army had done the villagers a big favour — booting them out into a world of statutory rights and hot and cold running water in the bathroom. But the lady wasn't having it. 'It's still wrong,' she muttered, striding off disconsolately.

The best testimony to this unresolved argument was to be found in the visitors' book, confidently placed with the assurance that 'your comments and suggestions will be appreciated'. An inscription signed 'Richard Attenborough and family', protested at the mess left by a passing film company, and another regretted that 'the telephone box is an eyesore'. Some lamented the fate of the village in terms that would certainly not have been appreciated by the Ministry of Defence: 'Such devastation to a once beautiful area!' wrote 'One who was stationed here in 1943'. Another described Tyneham as 'a small pocket of humaneness in a sterile desert of uncanny beauty, like a viper or a scorpion. Deathly. I cry for thee Tyneham.' Somebody wondered 'Does Tyneham point the way to resolving the Inner City Problem?' and an indignant child had scrawled: 'How would you like it if someone came along and blew your house up! Traitors!' One freeborn Englishman grunted 'Fuck off Army and Don't Come back.' Others observed that without the Army to 'preserve and freeze' it, Tyneham would only have suffered a different destruction by the 'developers' and 'yuppies'.

By the end of 1990, that strange book of condolences had been removed from the old schoolhouse, never to be seen again. I last leafed through it during the Easter weekend that year, when the argument was still resounding. One of the final entries declared 'I think it was a jolly good idea (the army taking over and kicking all the riff-raff out). It is a pity they don't take over the whole of Dorset and irradiate the lot. Bloody peasants!' That one was signed 'General Sir John Hackett'.

Should Villages be Allowed to Crouch?

> The ruined spendthrift, now no longer proud,
> Claimed kindred there, and had his claims allowed.
>
> Oliver Goldsmith (The Deserted Village)

Alain Robbe-Grillet, the French experimental novelist, once took his stand against the kind of literary writing that was prepared to describe a village as 'crouching' in the hollow of a valley. From the moment this sort of metaphor was used, he objected, the village became a dependent place that could hold no surprises. It wasn't just that the village would lose nothing if it were merely 'situated' in its valley. For Robbe-Grillet, the word 'crouching' also functioned like a tank in the service of sentimentality, blasting the village out of independent existence and then opening its shattered ruins to occupation: 'If I accept the word "crouching" I am no longer merely a spectator; I become the village for the duration of the phrase, and the hollow of the valley functions as a cavity into which I would like to disappear.'[2]

Tyneham is surely the village that proves his point. It has suffered a double annihilation — evacuated by the Army, and then further obliterated by the mythologies that have moved in to ghost its every detail. For if Tyneham 'crouches', it does so at the centre of a remarkable posthumous cult: extinction has granted this remote English village a strange numinosity, alluring and repulsive at once.

To begin with Tyneham was merely one obscure village among others. Once evacuated and sealed up behind the wire, however, it was raised into a new perspective which endowed its smallest detail with special significance. It was reborn as a perfect English village of the mind, one that belongs on the same map as Stanley Spencer's Cookham, Edward Ardizzone's Little Snoreing, and, for that matter, the unlucky Fifeshire village of Auchtermuchty adopted by Margaret Thatcher's favourite journalist, Sir John Junor: 'And why did I write about Auchtermuchty? Because I wanted a sort of Brigadoon place which had been bypassed by the modern world and in which old-fashioned virtues still persisted.'[3]

I remember the late Miss Margaret Bond remarking on the great uprising of interest in all things to do with the extinguished village in which she had grown up and wondering what could possibly motivate it. Among the evidence she showed me was an article somebody had copied for her from the Winter 1980 issue of a quarterly magazine called *This England*.[4] The article was a wan and unexceptional thing. Elegiac and set to the usual diminishing sequence of minor chords, it followed the same formula as countless other pieces that have projected Tyneham's story over the fifty years since its evacuation. The authors followed those patriotic villagers as they left their homes with 'sad but brave hearts knowing by their sacrifice that they could help Britain win the war'; and they noted that 'officialdom' not only failed to let them enjoy their last Christmas in the village, but then reneged on the promise that they would one day be allowed to return.

And yet the context provided by *This England* for Tyneham's story was also revealing. Now claimed as Britain's largest heritage quarterly, with an estimated print run of 160,000 copies and a legion of expatriate readers, *This England* was launched as 'a quarterly reflection of English life' from Grimsby in Spring 1968. As the publisher of six county magazines, the founder and editor Roy Faiers reckoned that the time was right to project the same values at a national level. Convinced that parochialism was a virtue, he hoisted the flag of St George in his first issue: 'Instead of politics, we shall bring you the poetry of the English countryside ... Instead of bigotry, we shall portray the beauty of our towns and villages.'

This England built its world almost entirely out of dwindling residues. Its country was full of branch lines, threshing machines and traditional English customs like the Cornish Furry Dance. There were nostalgic steam engines too: Roy Faiers rode the Flying Scotsman, and yearned for a time 'when machines needed man'. *This England* favoured heroic soldiers, Baden Powell and poets of the landscape like Thomas Hardy and Patience Strong. Dismissive of his critics, Faiers stressed the importance of 'looking back with pride'.[5] The letters pages burgeoned as expatriate readers remembered an England of threepenny bits, hedgerows and simple family pleasures. In the words of one correspondent, writing in the spring of a strike-bound year, *This England* was 'a breath of fresh air' in an 'atmosphere of pollution'.[6]

Sadly, however, *This England* was really lost England all along. Roy Faiers asked his readers to take a look at the English pound note: 'Once you could spend it anywhere in the world and proudly. Now all you get for it is a handful of pesetas and a smile of sympathy.' One modernising reform after another was met with the same riposte: 'It may be clever and modern and progressive. But it's certainly not English.'[7] Faiers was appalled by the state of England's schools and wondered 'How can you feel proud in a pair of jeans?' He worried about the creeping 'Sovietisation' of England, and encouraged his readers to join the late Ross McWhirter's National Association for Freedom. One reader wrote from Cape Town: 'Rest assured that you have armies and armies behind you, not the least of which are in those corners of foreign lands which are forever England'.[8]

By the time *This England* got around to featuring Tyneham's story, something unusual was happening to the photographs too. Their evocative quality seemed strangely intensified by what they refused to show. There were no motorways, no industrial cities, no suburbs to interfere with the thatched idyll. The same selectivity was applied to people. There was a certain ethnic appeal to the old Dorset shepherd who adorned *This England's* cover in Spring 1979, wearing a smock just like the one that magistrate James Frampton had seen pulled from an escaping protestor in the Winfrith 'riots' of 1830. But the problem, as Faiers wrote about immigration in Autumn 1976, is that 'the knowalls have opened the flood gates until our cities throb with trouble'. 'England,' he said 'is *our* home. Heathrow is our front door.'

By Winter 1980, when Tyneham made its first appearance, every item was ghosted by this implicit interpretation of England. The cover of that very issue showed schoolboy choristers in 'a northern church'. The accompanying text remarked that these reluctant angels probably had conkers and catapults in their pockets — it was quite unnecessary to spell out that these emphatically lit English lads were all white.

So it has been more generally with Tyneham. The story of that village has its local integrity, but it found much of its broader significance among those who were disposed to share Roy Faiers's conviction that 'we need a revival of the spirit to wrest us from social and moral disintegration'.[9] Requisitioned at a time of undoubted national emergency, this loyal village went on to become the mythologised symbol of an England that was to be betrayed in its own name through every day of the peace that followed: it became a symbolic plague village of the welfare state — even the Lidice of the post-war settlement.

Tyneham may have died for the war, but at least it had been spared the many degradations of the post-war period. The schoolroom offers an ecological version of this fable but the Tyneham valley escaped more than the pesticides of modern agriculture or the Godless food industry that would have industrialised the cottage pigs and, if government explanations are correct, given the cattle BSE. Nobody ever came here to put metal over its dimpled tracks; to fluoridate the drinking water or fill the lanes with Subtopian lamp-standards. There had been no consumerism or television to foster aberrant desires, no immigration to pollute the village's native stock, no metrification to confound the valley's innate sense of measure; no welfare state to homogenise its community, weaken the robust character of its villagers, or carp about the fatty diet. No liberal progressives had ever come to tamper with the school curriculum, modernise the liturgy or put a woman in the pulpit. Tyneham's natives had been spared the humiliation of waking up to find themselves suddenly in Europe and obliged to augment the ancient dialect of their valley with words like Maastricht. The over-restored phone box in Post Office Row holds the key to the meaning of this vividly reimagined valley. In Tyneham, history is still fitted with a Button B: press it and you get your money back in pounds, shillings and heavy pence.

Once obliterated, Tyneham was reborn as the symbolic valley where traditional English virtues held out in sharply polarised opposition to the destructive trends of modern life. It became a vale of true soulfulness whose people still lived in the time of good neighbours: decent folk who wouldn't know what to make of John Major's poor cry of 'Back to Basics' because they had never left their instinctive values behind. Tyneham was surely the homeland that burned so bright in the mind of Captain Hilary Hook, when he came home from his hill in Kenya, saying 'I'd always planned to lay my bones in England', only to find himself in a barely recognisable country full of supermarkets and tin-openers, which he could hardly operate: 'I've lived with natives bringing in firewood all my life . . . '[10]

As time went by, this crouching village would come to be marked off not just with red flags, but with conspiracy theories of a simplified and sometimes vicious kind. Thanks to its posthumous cult, Tyneham became emblematic of the wider cultural syndrome, endemic in post-war Britain, that leaves its victims unable to grasp the modern world except through allegorical fables of malign encroachment. To follow the coast path through this still forbidden valley is to cross the thin stretch of no-man's land that separates England from it lunatic fringe. It is to tread patriotic turf with the retired army officers who thought of raising private armies against Harold Wilson, and to risk encounter with those paranoid natives in the Conservative Party who whispered that the City of London was only riven by scandals during the late Eighties, because it was controlled by a 'tightly-knit Jewish network'.

By the mid-Eighties, when I first noticed the phenomenon, nearly every national newspaper seemed to have had at least one correspondent camping out in the Tyneham valley. The fellow may not even have known he was there, but his job was to review current developments from the perspective of the vale of extinguished virtues at the back of so many disappointed English minds. At that time, the best clues as to the precise shape of this expropriated landscape were provided by the *Sunday Telegraph*, and particularly by a column called 'My Country Right or Wrong?', which offered weekly glimpses of the world as seen through the eye of one Tyneham man after another. Enoch Powell lamented the loss of the Britain that gave itself away in 1972, surrendering sovereignty to the Common Market. Chris Patten praised 'our generous and instinctive pragmatism', now so sadly threatened by 'credit card spivvery', 'municipal totalitarianism' and the rising tide of 'yobbery' that destroyed direct grant schools and put housing estates into our villages. He dared to hope for a resurgence of the 'civilised Blimp'.

Chapman Pincher talked about his sense of umbilical attachment to the soil of England, and then listed its supposed enemies: foreign agents, subversives, traitors, Asian and Afro-Caribbean immigrants. According to Michael Wharton, who for years wrote the *Daily Telegraph*'s Peter Simple column, our descent had been so speedy that 'to fear for England now is not just to look back to some distant or imaginary "golden age" '. The decline of recent years was plain to see, whether it be the responsibility of 'factory farming, industrial forestry and gigantic road schemes' or of the leisure and tourism industries, which would inevitably turn England into a theme-park and 'universal suburbia', or the rise of 'the Arts' at the very time when religious belief, morality and culture were collapsing. To gaze down over the Tyneham valley through Wharton's eyes was to see not 'the environment', which Wharton dismisses as 'that most specious of modern themes', but an earthly, God-given paradise that was still recognisable as 'the Creation'. But then a fog of racial anxiety swept in to darken this lovely view: 'England, until lately a homogenous nation, had been part-colonised by large numbers of alien and unassimilable people'.[11]

Creeping erosion worried Terry Waite, whose 'My Country Right or Wrong?' was published on 11 January 1987, shortly before this footloose emissary to the Archbishop of Canterbury was taken hostage in Beirut. He celebrated the forsaken language of the Book of Common Prayer, and regretted the secular spirit that 'devours everything within its path'. Politicians could say what they liked, but 'our nation will not be invigorated until we recover a pride in our heritage': a heritage that includes donating to charity and showing a proper respect for art and the ancient buildings that 'tell us a great deal about the souls of our forefathers'.

Peregrine Worsthorne, the McCarthyite dandy and editor who was eventually both knighted and sacked for his attempt to relaunch the *Sunday Telegraph* as the *Tyneham Echo*, made his own burlesque contribution to this column in 1986, remarking that 'In the olden days I found it easy to take pride in pretty well everything about Britain.' Such, however, had been the degeneration that he now found that his patriotism owed more to the past than the present 'and smacks heavily of nostalgia'. Returning to his old haunts, he found things 'changed almost out of recognition ... The character of many beloved towns has been ruined; familiar landscapes desecrated. On the Underground I feel surrounded by aliens.' Tyneham man finds himself driven to desperate thoughts: 'To be frank it would not be difficult for me to become disloyal to this country. If a far-left government came to power, abolished the monarchy, nationalised private property, set up people's courts — did all the things, for example, advocated by Tony Benn — treason would become an option very much worth considering ... '

The capacity of Tyneham's fable to accommodate the whole post-war history of the nation was first brought home to me by Margaret Thatcher's Secretary of State for Education, Kenneth Baker, and more particularly by the bestselling anthology of *English History in Verse* he published in 1987. Asked to review this already much-praised work, I hastened down to Tyneham for inspiration. Opening it as I sat by the bullet-scarred rectory, I found myself confronted with another collection of vigorously managed ruins: clipped fragments, poems reduced to snippets, so much so that even Sir Kingsley Amis had suspected a kind of 'literary philistinism' was at work. Baker had assembled his whole anthology on the Tyneham principle, reducing the entire tradition of English poetry to the folkloric rhymes of a lost English valley. Eager to see how Baker had ended his version of England's story, I turned to the last page and found a fragment — as carefully scrubbed as the tombstones in Tyneham churchyard — of T. S. Eliot's 'Little Gidding', serving as Baker's version of Churchill's pledge.

What, I wondered, did Mr Baker make of the years since 1940, when T. S. Eliot stood in the failing winter light of his 'secluded chapel' and knew so surely, in the palpable danger of that moment, that 'History is now and England'? Margaret Thatcher's Secretary of State for Education had chosen the Coronation of Queen Elizabeth II as his formal end-point, but he actually had trouble getting through 1945, the year of Labour victory. A. P. Herbert's 'Mr Churchill' was there, but after that the story died away in minor ditties by Noel Coward and William Scammell. Regretting the 'remarkable shortage' of 'good, straight' verse written about 'public events in England over the past thirty years', Baker had adopted a policy of charitable evacuation. Those few post-war poets who did manage to stay true to England were offered assisted places in more lustrous parts of our island story. Geoffrey Hill came to stand next to Shakespeare in the England of Plantagenet Kings; C. H. Sisson found himself in the bracing reign of Henry VIII; and Philip Larkin joined Wilfred Owen for the Great War.

So Tyneham was to outlive itself — a local anecdote that found epic reverberations in the post-war culture of national decline, its valley becoming the subjective correlative to the grim ditch we were all stuck in. This wider interpretation is grossly unfair to the people who lived here, and yet the challenge was never just to disentangle the historical truth of what had happened here from the usurping myths. For the cult of Tyneham is like history itself — full of different potentialities.

There may be a Tyneham valley in every truly Tory heart, but it is not just for commentators on the right that England is a forbidden valley full of apparently lost causes. Turn from the *Sunday Telegraph* to the *Guardian*, and there will still be writers who arrive at their sense of English nationality by diminishment, fencing off the obtrusive modern world. Twenty or so years ago Edward Pearce was an abrasive polemicist in *Free Nation*, the paper of the National Association for Freedom, but he is now the *Guardian*'s master of the Tyneham idiom. We hear it in his hymn of praise for the Three Choirs festival in Worcester — a 'disgracefully English affair' that he celebrates in opposition to the Edinburgh festival with its 'socially impactive experimental theatre'. 'Much of England has receded. But the choral tradition, like swans and cricket, survives. And what it does here — a sort of Evensong with lift-off — is simple, open-ended pleasure.'[12] Tyneham had no pub to be polluted by barrels of lager, with its 'unintelligent dullness', but there was a beer seller, who may well have sold the regionally distinctive real ale Pearce prefers — 'the almost, but not quite sweetness of Eldridge Pope's Royal Oak from Dorset'.[13] Pearce gives us Tyneham as a sprinkling of obscure and perhaps even Latin words hurled into the superficial stream of journalistic prose, but it also comes through as a kind of unresearched instinctiveness, one minute elegiac, and the next snarling defiance which prefers insult to reason as it lashes out against the 'smarties', the cliques, the people with more money or airtime. When Pearce champions the unrestrained virility of Mr Alan Clark, he reveals that Tyneham has escaped 'political correctness' too.

Yet a serious cultural syndrome can't be judged by its froth alone. So, we turn to the *Guardian*'s pages in search of deeper resonances — perhaps to John Gray, the former Thatcherite political theorist, who now worries about the destructive triumph of monetarism and urges the Labour Party to adopt the discarded political and ethical priorities that belonged to the old Tory party.[14] Or to the dying but still splendidly defiant television dramatist Dennis Potter, who knew all about the deformations that imperialism worked on the English character but pressed through that easy observation to commend the patriotism it deformed: we were, as he said of the non-conformist mining villages of the Forest of Dean where he grew up during the war, 'a brave and steadfast people' whose best values had been reflected in the works of the 1945 Labour government — now being 'so brutally and wantonly and callously dismantled'.[15]

When I visited Tyneham in the Autumn of 1985, I drove straight into a film set. The ruins of Post Office Row had been covered with old-style thatched frontages, and a square tower had been added to the church. A young black carpenter in the construction crew explained that Tyneham was being turned into Tolpuddle, for the filming of *Comrades* by the Scottish director Bill Douglas. As I later found out, Tyneham had been selected from over 130 Dorset villages, which Douglas had examined and found too modernised. He had been captivated by the 'totally unspoilt' quality of the Tyneham Valley, remembered by his set designer as a place without chainsaws or pylons where it was 'as if time had stopped'.[16] So the metallic grip of the Army would briefly be replaced by what the leading Tolpuddle Martyr, George Loveless, once called 'the iron hand of your land and money-mongering taskmasters'.[17] There, once more, were the shire horses, archaic seed-drills and stooks of the idyll. Douglas brought a gipsy fiddler, a chained escape artist and a dancing sailor to the village green, mounting a full Harvest festival of the bountiful kind that J. F. Pennie's village elders had remembered from pre-enclosure days.

Like Pennie again, Douglas restaged the 'good times', taking the side of the rick-burners and machine-breakers of the 1830s and filling the laborious valley with portents of just insurrection — the scraping of scythes being sharpened, or the sight of fat scurrying cockroaches being put to the torch. His film shows noble but sorely exploited landless labourers, 'the most beautiful people in the whole world' as his James Loveless remarks, setting them in heroic counterpart to the opulent landowner, Mr James Frampton — for Douglas 'a black figure in his soul and history',[18] who rides by in a carriage, his family laughing under the parasols of idle luxury as half-starved labourers sweat in his fields. By recasting it as Tolpuddle, Bill Douglas briefly won Tyneham back from the reactionary mythologies of *This England* and the columnists of 'My Country Right or Wrong?', turning it in a contrary direction that still made the most of its nostalgic appeal.

As Douglas wrote of the moment when his chained martyrs followed the villagers who had filed out of the valley in 1943, 'it is as if they will never come back to this place; or to the tree on the village green, drifting away; or to the landscape so familiar to them, this landscape that even now stretches forth in an explosion of light, rich but oblivious'.[19]

Douglas saw *Comrades* as a political film — sufficiently to hope (vainly) that it would be released before the election in which Margaret Thatcher won her third term. It was not widely shown in Dorset (there were brief screenings in Bridport and Wareham), but the set became a major local attraction. Initially, the Army had been warned that it would hardly go down well with conservation-minded visitors, but the designer now suggests that it might actually have 'helped to popularise Tyneham in a different way'.[20] Built with the co-operation of the gunnery school ('When they weren't shooting, we could') it was left standing for months so that a final sequence could be filmed in February 1986. The winter gales blew the tower off the church and the old phone box was smashed to pieces as scaffolding supporting parts of the reconstructed street came crashing down. A local vicar was upset to find this village landmark negligently 'tossed aside', but an Army spokesman quickly promised to restore it, with the financial assistance of Skreba Productions. He hoped that the kiosk would be complete with buttons A and B again, although he regretted that it would have to be kept locked, 'because of vandalism'.[21]

I discussed this incident with Miss Margaret Bond, whose father William Bond had succeeded to Tyneham in 1898, and she thought it was a pity too: a replacement is 'never the same thing as having the original, is it?' And yet the film set had impressed her: 'wonderfully done, that ... I mean you couldn't believe the things weren't ... I had to go and tap them to see that they weren't real.' Not having seen *Comrades*, Miss Bond had no views on what Bill Douglas had done to her valley; matching its beautifully filmed autumnal and, later, snow-covered landscape with his own meditation on illusionism and class power; turning the vicar into a bent instrument of aristocratic oppression; and introducing a Methodist chapel in which George Loveless would pray 'Give us the vision Lord to see beyond the narrow confines of the field.' She couldn't see why any Tyneham villager could possibly have wanted to join the Labour Party in the days of her family's stewardship.

Miss Margaret Bond went on to explain that her father had died in 1935, and that it was a 'mercy' he didn't live to see what was coming to the village. Opposed even to a telephone in Tyneham House, he would surely have 'had a fit' if he had seen what the Army would do with tanks.[22] Ralph Bond, who succeeded William and saw the whole takeover through, would surely also have had things to say about the present ecological definition of the valley. His other sister Lilian remembered him as a keen natural historian. On coming home from Eton for the holidays, he would form his sisters into a Natural History Society, to which he gave lectures. He made a drinking place for animals in Tyneham Great Wood and devoted much energy to the Dorset Natural History and Archaeological Society. But Ralph Bond's interests as a natural historian were hardly those of the abstracted green spirit that governs the valley now. He would surely have been taken aback by the notice, planted at the beginning of the Tyneham Gwyle by the Dorset Heritage Coast authorities, which announces that: 'the woodland of Tyneham, if left untouched by man, would be mainly of oak and ash, and particularly rich in birds, animals and flowers'. He would have wondered where these latterday conservationists got the idea that the carefully tended 'woodland of Tyneham' might ever have been left 'untouched by man'.

He would also have been surprised to discover that the destructive invader had changed again — not the telephone; not the trippers who, as Margaret Bond could remember, were already peering through the windows of Tyneham House in the early years of the century; not even the Army. Under the new settlement, the threat to this sylvan scene is now seen to lie in the fact that 'the fast-growing "alien" sycamore has been introduced'. The sycamore becomes a kind of illegal immigrant — appallingly fertile, and inclined 'to force out native species of tree to produce a wood much poorer in flora and fauna'. So severe is the situation, that an arboreal ethnic cleansing might soon have to be carried out in the Tyneham valley. The notice predicts that 'man may have to intervene through "woodland management" ' to remove the sycamore so that 'native trees' can survive and the 'abundant wildlife they support' may flourish. It seems that the Bonds were deluded when, after the Great Gale of 1929, they were saddened by the loss of the old sycamores in Tyneham Great Wood, which had provided a nesting place for owls.[23]

Too bad also that the late Bill Douglas was not content to uproot a sizeable sycamore tree when he turned Tyneham into Tolpuddle. Instead he had the thing moved a hundred yards or so and then replanted (once the range wardens had disposed of an unearthed incendiary shell) just north of the church so that Tyneham would have its version of the great sycamore — known as the Martyrs' Tree and for years preserved by the National Trust with funds from the Trade Union Congress — under which Loveless and his comrades used to gather to talk and from which they are said to have picked leaves to use as bookmarks for their Bibles before being transported to Australia.

PART TWO

The Rolling English Tank: The Battle of Bindon Hill (1916–29)

A man coming through a hedge first selects a weak spot (point of attack), he then forces his arms through the branches (penetration), and pushing them outwards (envelopment), forms a sufficiently large gap (base of operations) to permit of his body (army) passing easily through the hedge (enemy's defences). The operation of penetration with tanks is just the same.

Brevet-Colonel J. F. C. Fuller, D.S.O., 1920[1]

FOUR

FIRST SIGHTINGS

So simply had event followed event at Mockery Gap, as generation followed generation, that nothing had ever occurred that caused so great an excitement as this new appearance.

T. F. Powys (1925)

EARLY ONE OCTOBER morning in the mid-1930s, a young woman named Joan Begbie visited the Lulworth area with the intention of walking over Bindon Hill with her two dogs: 'Mr Bundy, a tough little brindled griffon, and Bill, a sentimental bull terrier'. She considered Dorset to be 'the grandest place for walking in I know'. Invariably, 'it was good to be on the springy turf again'.

A few years previously Miss Begbie had published *Walking in the New Forest*, and she was now hard at work on the sequel, *Walking in Dorset.*[2] It was not her ambition to 'please the historian, archaeologist or geologist' — indeed, she professed cheekily to enjoy 'a hedger's gossip more than the wisest scientific treatise' — but Miss Begbie nevertheless wound her way down towards East Lulworth in a mood of historical reverie. She thought respectfully of the Welds with their 'unswerving devotion' to the Roman Catholic faith and their long association with the surrounding landscape. She remembered Thomas Weld, both fleetingly and inaccurately, as the man who, 'wanting to enlarge his park, pulled down the whole of the original village of East Lulworth and rebuilt it outside his new wall', but she was more exercised by the romantic associations of a site that is actually not quite visible from the road. Miss Begbie was thinking of Julia Woodforde, the girl from West Lulworth who had disguised herself as a soldier in order to enter the Monastery of St Susan where she had first met her 'Trappist lover', the Irishman James Power whose 'hair-raising' stories of the French Abbot's brutality had eventually precipitated the closure of that controversial retreat by Arish Mell Gap.

Arriving at the Weld Arms in East Lulworth, Miss Begbie found the landlord's son to be 'all courtesy'; he moved a waggon so that she could leave her car in the barn and he told her a way to reach Arish Mell Gap through fields and woods, thereby avoiding altogether the B 3070, a minor road that she, a true walker, disdained as 'the Lulworth Cove highway'. Before her unleashed dogs were through the first field, Miss Begbie had fallen into a rhapsodic mood. The glistening fields stretched out around her and Flowers Barrow 'brooded' over the whole delightful scene. A solitary magpie flew across her path but Miss Begbie put this ill omen from her mind.

Soon she had crossed a single strand of wire and followed Monastery Farm Lane into a wood that rang with birdsong. Entering this 'place of verdurous lights', Miss Begbie felt as if she were inside Nature's freshest watercolour. As she advanced the transparent green and gold screen ahead of her seemed to become 'suffused with a misty blue' which thickened almost imperceptibly and then suddenly revealed itself as the sea. Eagerly, she pressed forward through a swing gate to emerge 'at the head of a wooded green valley going down to blue water and ending in fair white cliffs and the lofty hills, Bindon and Rings'. 'Here,' as Miss Begbie wrote, 'was Arish Mell Gap.' The dogs 'darted joyously down to the furze coverts', but Miss Begbie drew back on her heels and 'dratted the magpie' with all her heart. Great Bindon had been enclosed; and rising from the wire 'on his first steeps, and surmounting his summit, were crimson flags'. Miss Begbie stopped at Sea Vale Farm to ask a woman in the gateway what the flags might mean: 'Oh, it's the Tanks,' she said gazing rapturously up at the hill, 'their ranges is on Bindon Hill, and they're just going to start firing. But they'll be done by twelve o'clock, and you can go up there then.' So Begbie had no choice but to leash her dogs and return reluctantly to the metalled 'Lulworth Cove highway'. The firing commenced as she passed Lulworth Camp, causing her to 'raise her dander' to such a pace that she nearly missed the 'green way' which facilitated her escape to the west — up on to the downs from which she would turn to see Bindon Hill, 'savage with gunfire and bristling with crimson banners'.

If one thing is certain about Miss Joan Begbie, it is that she knew exactly what she would find when she set out for her walk that morning. By the mid-Thirties the tank was well established in Dorset and, thanks to a great clamour of opposition, its presence on the slopes of Bindon Hill was known throughout the land. Miss Begbie dramatised her walk, contriving to recapture the initial sense of shock that so many had felt when the tanks laid permanent claim to this unrivalled stretch of their country.

From the very first experimental trials of this uniquely British invention, the tank was a noisy machine in an English garden. Invented in an attempt to break the unexpected stasis of trench warfare in France and Belgium, it was first tested in pastoral and sometimes classically aristocratic settings. Late in September 1915, a wooden prototype called *HMS Centipede* was taken to the experimental ground of the 'Trench Warfare Department' at Wembley Park. 'Guarded by sentries and screened off in an enclosure such as might have sheltered a coker-nut [sic] shy or the fat lady at a fair', the wooden model was shown to gathered officers: some from the Admiralty Landships Committee, which was responsible for developing the tank with resources procured by Winston Churchill, then First Lord of the Admiralty; and others from the Ministry of Munitions and General Headquarters in France.[3]

By December, when a working prototype called 'Mother' was put on display, Wembley Park was considered insufficiently secret, and a 'lonely field within a mile of Lincoln Cathedral' had been chosen instead.[4] Late in January, both 'Little Willie' and 'Mother' were taken by night to Hatfield Park for demonstrations over a specially designed 'steeple chase course' built on the edge of Lord Salisbury's private golf course.[5] There were simulated trenches, and a swamp had been made by damming a stream. Asquith was unable to attend the demonstrations on 2nd February, but the spectators did include Lord Kitchener, Lloyd George, Chancellor Reginald McKenna, and A. J. Balfour who, having replaced Churchill at the Admiralty, was duly taken for a ride in the tank. On 8th February, a special trial was arranged for King George V, and he too went for a ride.

Further trials, and also training for the first tank crews, were held on a five acre patch of Lord Iveagh's estate at Elveden near Thetford. Evacuated at a week's notice, the 'Elveden Explosives Area' was soon 'more ringed about than was the palace of the Sleeping Beauty, more zealously guarded than the Paradise of a Shah'.[6] Here in Suffolk's big shoot country, tanks disported over a reconstructed section of the Western Front while cherry blossom followed hoar frost in melting from the trees, and Lord Iveagh's partridges fled for cover. In July, Lloyd George came along to inspect the tanks' progress. Wearing the flowing cloak that also distinguished his visits to the Western Front, he watched as twenty-five of those famously geometrical, lozenge-shaped tanks slid forward to shatter the peace. During a later demonstration a tank knocked down a tree twenty-six inches thick. Meanwhile, local people speculated that the Army was tunnelling right through to Berlin.

The Elveden Explosives Area had been abandoned as too small by the end of 1916. From October the Tank Corps was based at Bovington Camp near Wool: a shanty of huts had been taken over, along with some 1,000 acres of heathland, which the War Office had first acquired for use as a rifle range in 1899.[7] The tanks first went into action in the Battle of the Somme on 15 September 1916, but their arrival in Dorset a month later was still shrouded in official secrecy. Roads were closed to civilian traffic and local residents were told to pull down their blinds and stay in back rooms as the tanks, or 'Hush Hushes' as they were still known at the time, were brought down the zealously guarded road from Wool station.

The Headmistress of the Catholic school in Wool, Miss J. I. Bohs, wrote a poem telling how the tanks 'descended on the lowly vale of Wool' at eight o'clock one morning, obliging the village folk to creep about 'in fear with bated breath'. Armed sentries greet 'the little milk girl' with cries of 'Halt! show your pass'. The dairyman was angry because he couldn't send off his milk, and the postman had to go well out his way to cross the river. Only a small boy called Leo Burden 'chances the fate of being shot' and dares to peep. He later rushes into the class room demanding to be allowed to write the following essay: 'I've seen a tank and its about thirty feet long and is has big has an house and has got four funnels and a lader out side and lots of smoak and six men go in thro' a hold and its covered with a rick cloath and then the policeman cum so I cum on too.'[8]

There was resistance from the outset. Local lore still makes much of a stubborn Dorsetshire peasant who refused to leave his field, only to find soldiers building a screen around him where he stood. There was also talk of a farmer who, when asked to keep to his back rooms while the machines went by, replied that he had 'no objection to helping the authorities to keep the "Secret of the Tank", only unfortunately one had broken down, and had been towed into his farmyard, and there left for 48 hours'.[9] The farmer eventually identified himself as James Spicer of Bovington Farm, pointing out that he had actually used his own horses to tow the broken Behemoth into his yard. As for the intransigent countryman who had been barricaded in his field, Spicer could commend his devotion to duty: 'My shepherd was pitching out a fold for sheep in a field adjoining the road

1 The Franklin Viewpoint, 1989

2 Arish Mell Gap and Bindon Hill from Flowers Barrow, 1992

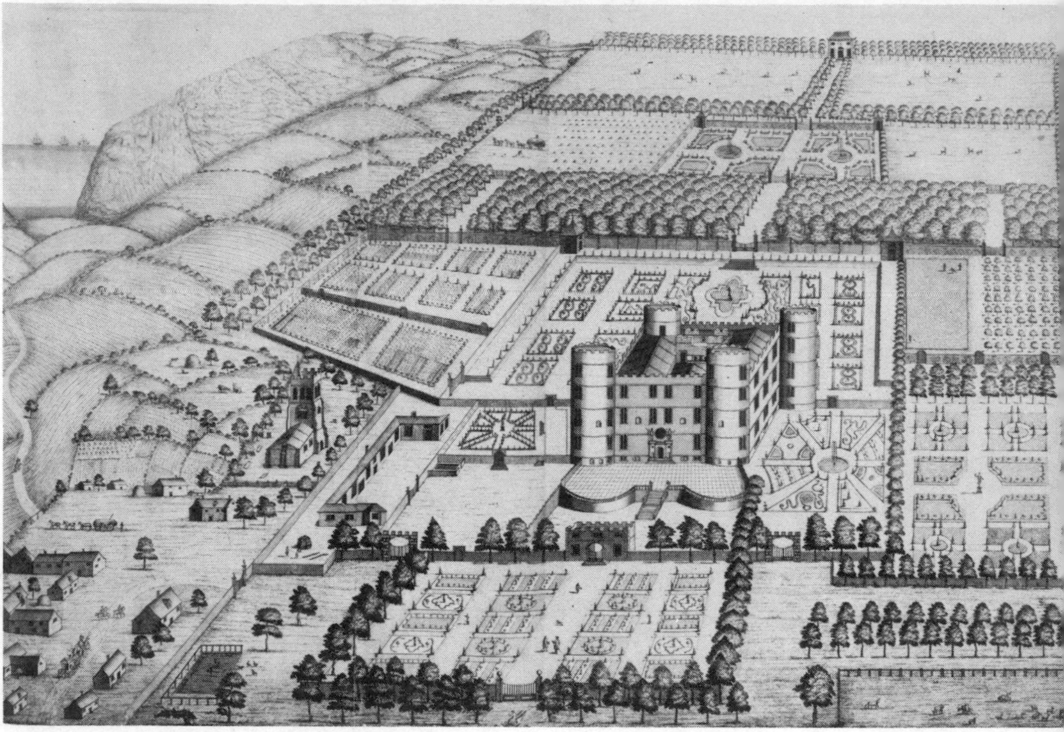

3 Lulworth Castle delineated by Margaret Weld, 1721

4 East Lulworth picturesque, *c.* 1890

5 Tyneham under conversion for Bill Douglas's *Comrades*, 1985

6 Tyneham as Tolpuddle, with relocated Martyrs' Tree to the right, 1985

7 East Lulworth drama, *c.* 1926. Theodora Weld, centre, with unknown partner and village cast on steps of the castle; Herbert Weld in peaked cap behind right

8 Medium tanks firing at moving target range on Bindon Hill, late 1920s

where the Tanks had to pass; a soldier went to him and told him he was to go home and shut himself in ... The shepherd told him he could not as the sheep would run over the fields of roots and injure themselves, but the soldier insisted on his going. The outcome as they pitched some hurdles end ways round the shepherd, made him turn his back to the road and the soldiers mounted guard over him, to see he did not turn his head to look at the Tanks as they passed.'[10]

Bovington Camp went through a great surge of expansion over the next two years. Extra camps were set up at Swanage and another for the Depot Reserve Unit at Worgret, near Wareham. In July 1918 it was decided that the Tank Corps should be doubled in size over the next twelve months, and, in the words of J. F. C. Fuller, the tank tactician who for a time was the officer in command of Bovington, 'nearly half a million pounds worth of buildings were sanctioned without estimates being called for, so important was it now considered that not a day should be lost in the Tank Corps preparations for 1919'.[11]

Bindon Hill fell to that onslaught. As one veteran put it: 'Near Lulworth Cove, where trippers used to make pilgrimage before the war, a battle-practice range came into being.'[12] The transformation, which began in 1916, was less simple for the people on the ground. St Andrew's Farm, on the site, was immediately evacuated: 'We had very short notice to get out of there,' remarked Nelson Thompson, who, more than half a century later, would remember moving out in the dead of night.[13] A few astonished sentences are all that remain of another displaced native, who watched his cottage birthplace disappear under a storm of canvas that soon gave way to more permanent huts built by prisoners of war: 'It went from grass and they built it and built it and built it — they haphazard everything. They took all the hill away nearly into West Lulworth — right from East Lulworth, right from Arish Mell, right through.'[14] So the tanks crawled their way up Quarr Hill and across the downland to Lulworth. These slow-moving machines were already celebrated for the mobility they would restore to modern warfare, but the road from Wool to Lulworth was a narrow lane, and terrible delays occurred whenever the tanks were abroad. For the people of the Weld estate, sudden immobility became the order of the day: as elders still remember, rustic time was thrown clean out of joint.

The secrecy that enshrouded the initial gunnery training makes it hard to verify the rumour that West Lulworth post office suffered a direct hit during the early months. But it also ensured that the new establishment was adopted as a favourite location by Lieutenant C. Patrick Thompson, a Biggles-like character who wrote romantic spy stories for the magazine *Flying*. 'The Stunter' concerns a suspicious-looking stunt plane which keeps travelling between South Dorset and France, prompting the worried remark ' "My good man . . . he passes clear over your bally Tank parks. There's not a county in England so chock-full of 'Prohibited Area' placards." '[15] Another tale called 'Dope' exploits Lulworth's secret new powers. A fleet of German submarines is said to be operating off the Dorset coast: indeed, 'I have heard that one of the submarines floated Lulworth way, and being spotted by a class at artillery practice, was assaulted by a mighty shell storm and vanished for ever from the ken of man.'

After the war, public and parliamentary pressure for retrenchment of the armed forces combined with the boneheaded attitudes of the top brass to call the future of the tank into question. Trench warfare was said to have been an unrepeatable aberration, and the tank could be written off as an obsolete freak. According to Liddell Hart, the post-war military catch-phrase, especially among the cavalry school, was 'Back to 1914'. J. F. C. Fuller's contrary assertion that the day of the horse had passed for ever drew massive counterfire from a military hierarchy that preferred to talk of abolishing the tank battalions altogether.[16]

Between 1918 and 1920, however, the tank continued to make its case, compelling not just by conventional firepower but by the 'moral effect' of its deterring appearance. The Commander-in-Chief of the British Army on the Rhine attributed the continued 'prestige' of the British troops in Germany to the 'enormous effect of tanks on the civil population';[17] and there was rising interest in what they might do in Mesopotamia, India, Egypt, Iraq and the Soviet Union, where three detachments had been sent to assist the failing White Russian forces in the struggle against Bolshevism. Fuller noted that tanks were also proving useful 'in those areas where law and order was threatened'. In January 1919 there had been 'a call for tanks to overawe rioters in Glasgow', and there was daily demand for armoured cars in Ireland, where nationalist resistance to British rule threatened to turn violent. Such was the situation that year that one impeccably right-wing veteran of the threatened Tank Corps was prepared to hope for the best: 'Since the authorities have discovered the value of tanks during industrial disturbances, and in Ireland, they may harden their hearts against the Treasury, and the Tank Corps may tide over this bad hour with the help of Trade Unions and Sinn Fein. It will be the first time that either institution has served a useful purpose.'[18]

The Tank Corps survived this period of indecision. A proper uniform and badges were established; and in 1923 the Corps, which had secured the King as its Colonel-in-Chief, received a royal title and was made part of the regular Army. The permanent status of the Royal Tank Corps had immediate consequences in Dorset. Bovington Camp needed extending yet again and plans were also drawn up for the gunnery school at Lulworth, leased as it had been from the Weld estate under the Defence of the Realm Act of 1916.

The War Office had not previously had to worry about the legality of such land acquisitions, but emergency procedures would only last for as long as officials managed to extend the Great War. For ordinary people, this catastrophe came to an end in 1918, but the bureaucratic termination was not announced until August 1921, and from then, the future of lands taken over during the war was very much in question.

Conditions of 'financial stringency' combined with political sensitivity to make it impractical for the War Office to initiate compulsory purchase orders all round the country; but for a time, its officials worked on the assumption that rights of way closed up during the war could be kept that way for two years after the cessation of hostilities, that is until 31 August 1923, and that three further years might then be obtained with the consent of the Railway and Canal Commission.[19] By May 1922, however, their lawyers had decided not only that the War Office was quite wrong in thinking that there was 'no question of owners having representation' at the Commission's hearings, but also that unless more than fifty 'controversial sites' were processed by the end of the following August, all the closed highways on them would 'automatically reopen' the following morning — in less than four months. This schedule was quite impossible to meet, so War Office officials hastily drafted a bill that would allow them to stay put if they had filed application with the Commission.

The War Office appears not to have counted the Lulworth gunnery school among its most 'controversial' sites. It was more concerned about closing roads running through an ammunition dump in Bramley, Hampshire; and also with Porton in Wiltshire, where its officials saw a 'very remote' chance of the local quarter Sessions approving the permanent closure of cart tracks. They knew, however, that in pressing for an extension they were courting unpopularity. Even during the war, requisitioning had brought sharp condemnation, with eminent business men writing to *The Times* to protest against 'the arbitrary methods of Jacks in Office'[20]; and opposition would be greater now that civil society was no longer wholly dominated by the warring State. After being scaled down by the Cabinet, the War Office's bill was enacted by the Commons on 26 July 1922, but it was widely felt, even by members who supported Bonar Law's government, that 'the tentacles of the War Office should not be extended any longer'.[21]

The decision to purchase Bindon Hill had been made by 22 January 1923, when the Commanding Royal Engineer at Weymouth sent a letter to Mr Archdall Ffookes, Clerk to the Dorset Lieutenancy, making what he presumed to be a merely procedural request. The land in question was required by the War Department and 'I should be much obliged therefore if you would be so good as to obtain the signature of two Deputy Lieutenants of the County of Dorset to each of the two Certificates, cause the full names and addresses of the Deputy Lieutenants to be inserted at the beginning of the Certificates to be attested in the usual manner, and return the Certificates to me as soon as possible.'[22]

Over the next few months some of the War Office's claims would be settled. The Weld estate was prepared to surrender the odd stretch of heath to the expanding tank range over at Bovington, but it took an entirely different view of the 973 acres bordering on the ancestral seat of Lulworth Castle, which the War Office now wanted to turn into a permanent gunnery school.[23] Like his deputy Lieutenants, Lord Ilchester and Mr Bond, Lord Lieutenant Shaftesbury was a prominent member of the landed aristocracy; and there could be no question of his county giving passive consent to such an outrageous act of expropriation.

FIVE

BIG GAME HUNTING IN WESSEX

ENGLAND'S NEWSPAPERS WERE not short of stories in the month of August 1923. George V may have sailed on uneventfully at Cowes, but President Harding of the United States had died suddenly in San Francisco, and a juicy murder trial was underway at the Old Bailey: the accused being a certain Madame Fahma, a French woman who, at the height of a terrible thunderstorm, had killed her wealthy Egyptian husband in the Savoy Hotel — an act for which she was acquitted, to the satisfaction of a public hardly needing a jury to convince it that the victim had been a vicious dog who deserved nothing less. The newly independent Irish free state was undergoing its first election; and Germany was seething with hyperinflation and revolutionary unrest, much inflamed by France's recent occupation of the Ruhr in pursuit of unpaid reparations.

And yet the southern shire county being what it was, a little breeze of pastoral resistance only had to spring up in Dorset and a firm wind would soon be gusting along Fleet Street. By the beginning of August, when Lord Shaftesbury brought out the Dorset County Council against the War Office's plan for Lulworth, the battle for this threatened 'beauty spot' had been joined by *The Times*, which noted that the firing had already made Lulworth Castle 'uninhabitable', and also that the War Office's proposal was 'likely to meet with firm opposition'.[1]

By 4 August, the *Manchester Guardian* also regretted the threat to this 'lovely stretch of the Dorset coast': although the tank was 'a native of Dorset' and, unhappily, an 'indispensable national possession', there could be no excuse for indulging it 'to this remarkable extent'.[2] But it was *The Times's* unnamed 'Special Correspondent' who had the inside story from Dorchester. Describing local feeling as 'very bitter against the proposal' and praising Lulworth Cove as 'one of the best-known beauty spots in the South of England', he observed that the council, of which he may well have been a member, was 'particularly bitter against the curt way in which the official intimation was received by the authorities concerned'.[3]

Local opinion certainly seemed resolute in its opposition. Revd John

Lawrence, the vicar of St Andrew's, that ancient Protestant church in Lulworth Park, sent *The Times* (and the Prime Minister) a resolution in which East Lulworth Parish Council protested 'very strongly' against the proposal, which would destroy a rare and much valued part of 'remaining' England.[4] The County Council was joined in its stand by the Dorset Natural History and Archaeological Society, whose membership included Mr Archdall Ffookes as well as Lords Shaftesbury and Ilchester.[5]

The *Observer* supported this emerging front by eliciting protests from 'eminent men intimately associated with the area'. The aged Thomas Hardy came out in defence of this part of 'Hardy Country', which, for him at least, was of older provenance: 'I join the protest against such a foolish proceeding as establishing a gunnery school that will ruin a beautiful holiday spot enjoyed by millions since the reign of George III, that monarch included.'[6] A longer statement was provided by Sir Alfred Fripp of West Lulworth. This eminent surgeon, who numbered the King among his patients, had been in the habit of 'renewing himself in the scenes of his youth', returning to Lulworth for his holidays and drawing succour from the memory of its 'Dorset lanes, the lines of its cliffs and horizon, its pageant of seasons, its peace'.[7] Fripp would shortly be commissioning Sir Edwin Lutyens to build Weston House near the top of the private road known to less fortunately placed residents as 'Millionaire's Row', and he was contemptuous of the hirelings who planned to disturb his retirement: 'The long suffering and inarticulate tax-payer, during the war, became accustomed to decisions of this kind being taken by comparatively minor officials. But the public is now tired of Dora [the Defence of the Realm Act] and all her works, and expects the amenities of civilisation shall once more be observed by those who, after all, are the paid servants of the public.'

The War Office informed the *Observer* that it was weighing up the protests and still withholding final judgement. So the gentlemen of Dorset kept up the pressure. On 12 August, the MP for South Dorset, Major R. D. T. Yerburgh, communicated his objection.[8] His statement was corroborated by Warwick Draper of 'Sheepleaze' in Worbarrow Bay, the man who, that same year, commissioned Martin Travers to make the stained glass window in Tyneham Church: 'Permit me, on behalf of the residents and, more particularly, the fishermen of this bay ... to urge the public and national need for preventing this monstrous local nuisance.'[9]

On 6 August, the *Daily Graphic* joined the protest with an article by its regular columnist S. P. B. Mais. Writing under the heading 'Tanks in Dorset Paradise', Mais opened with a flourish:

> I have just returned from collecting shells on a Dorset beach. It is not a game that I recommend to the many boy scouts or girl guides who are in camp near by. In fact, a kindly government has erred on the side of generosity in the number of notices which it has placed in prominent positions all over the hillside warning the public to leave all shells or pieces of shell alone. There have been fatal accidents.

Mais alleged that Lulworth Cove had originally been included in the War Office's scheme: 'So little do the authorities know ... that when it was pointed out to them that their western boundary extended to a point 900 feet west of a beauty spot at least as famous and often visited as Clovelly they said that "west" was a misprint for "east".' He talked to the worried fishermen, and was glad to relay the protest of one: 'I fought for this bit o'land, and when I come oam they try to starve me out of it.'

Accompanied by Sir Alfred Fripp, Mais walked from the Cove to Arish Mell Gap, strolling over a pastoral landscape made tense by the explosive contributions of the tank. Sweeping his arm over the contested acres, Fripp described the area as a unique distillation of all that was most essential about the English landscape. Here, he said, 'you have every variety of scenery imaginable: 'Cornish cliffs, Devon sands, Sussex Downs, Yorkshire wolds, Northumbrian moors'. 'And always shells,' added Mais, 'treading warily' and shying at the mistaken sight of a discarded beer bottle.

Coming down from Bindon Hill, this columnist set out for Lulworth Castle where he looked forward to meeting a patriotic Lord of the Manor who had 'generously allowed the War Office to use his property, imagining, naturally, that due reparation would be made when the time came to remove the tanks'. In reality, Mr Herbert Weld Blundell was not Lord of any of the Weld estate's many manors, and he had been nowhere near Lulworth when the tanks first laid claim to Bindon Hill in 1916. Indeed, such were Mais's misconceptions, that he must wait at the entrance to Lulworth Park, while some truer facts are mustered about the elderly gentleman waiting to receive him at the end of the drive.

In the late Eighties the memory of Herbert Weld Blundell still revolved over East Lulworth, catching light like a mirrored sphere suspended from a lost ballroom ceiling, and casting sharply differentiated impressions into the various corners of the rural class structure. Miss Margaret Bond, formerly of Tyneham, remembered Herbert as an ancient and somewhat skulking fellow — she could still see him reading *The Times* in an armchair in the hall — who was, nevertheless, a considerable improvement on the 'very queer' Lancashire Weld Blundells who had lived at Lulworth Castle before him. Colonel Sir Joseph Weld, who inherited the Weld estate on Herbert's death in 1935, spoke of him as a highly intelligent but cranky fellow who was full of gimmicks. A chain-smoking enthusiast for herbal cigarettes, he ate date jam with a spoon and came up with an unusual scheme for housing his villagers in flat-roofed cottages of moulded concrete.

Modestly placed villagers offer a very different picture of the seigneur, glimpsing him across vast social distances that were anything but diminished by physical proximity. An elderly man who, as a boy, had been employed to take money at the summer car park on the road down to Arish Mell Gap, remembers a sudden and furious reprimand breaking over him like a thunderbolt. A former housemaid, who once looked up to see him from a stairwell, still quakes a little as she describes catching the master's glance as if it were a bullet. Someone else recalls that Herbert Weld Blundell wouldn't allow people to walk across the park within view of the castle: when he was in residence, Anglican parishioners had to follow the park wall all the way round and approach St Andrew's church through the wicket gate to the south.

Herbert Weld Blundell was a God-like figure of inscrutable mood and arbitrary decision, and his park was altogether more enchanting than the grassy place that can be visited now. Witnesses remember a walled Paradise with exotic trees and shrubs, peacocks on the great flowered walkways, lawns tended by four or five gardeners, and a row of cannons, said to have been retrieved from the wreck of a French warship. They tell a Puck-like story about the chipped statue of a Roman centurion that stands in Bowling Green Wood: so powerful was the spell of Lulworth Park that the village children half-believed that this stone centurion came to life each day, stepping down from his plinth and walking over to the castle for lunch. 'People were servile then,' as one happily relocated daughter of East Lulworth says.

The elders remember the squire's peaked yachting cap, and also his car: a convertible Rolls Royce with a shining metal W specially mounted on it so that Herbert could easily pick it out in a row of identical vehicles. And they remember his wife too. For in 1923, this septuagenarian bachelor had surprised everyone by marrying 23-year-old Theodora Morrison, the daughter of a Protestant family, thought to have been an actress on the London stage. The shock of this unexpected event still raises a few wrinkled eyebrows in the village, but even if Theodora had once, as rumour suggested, been Herbert's god-daughter, she turned out to be more than just a 'delicate' and 'ethereal' presence on the arm of her elderly squire — 'pretty if not beautiful' as the late Rena Gould remembered. Theodora was keen on crossword puzzles, a newspaper innovation of that time, but she also did much to brighten East Lulworth life, taking steps to overcome the denominational schism in the village. She brought together children from both Catholic and Protestant schools for pageants and a joint Christmas party, and she produced them in a memorable production of *A Midsummer Night's Dream*.

Mais and the other reporters who wrote about Lulworth in August 1923 were inclined to describe Herbert Weld Blundell as the deeply rooted Squire of Lulworth, but he had actually only just moved in. At that time, the Weld estate was the property of Herbert's cousin, Reginald Joseph Weld Blundell, and Herbert, whose own address was given as Ovington Square, London SW3, appears only to have arrived on the scene in 1923, by which time the estate was being administered 'in lunacy' by court-appointed receivers on behalf of the absent Reginald, who would not survive the year. Herbert leased the castle and associated sporting rights from the end of March, at an agreed rent of £425 per annum.[10]

Herbert dropped the Blundell from his name by deed poll in 1924, but he wouldn't actually inherit the Weld estate until the late Reginald's equally absent brother Humphrey died in 1928. Once installed in the Castle, however, he was soon established as a pillar of the establishment. He became Rear Commodore of the Royal Dorset Yacht Club, having long been a familiar presence at Cowes with his celebrated 120 foot yacht 'Lulworth', a sloop-rigged vessel with a distinguished record in competition with George V's 'Britannia'. He joined the South Dorset Conservative and Unionist Association, which would eventually appoint him President in February 1927.

Colonel Sir Joseph Weld remembered Herbert as an enthusiast for the Trans Siberian railway, who once took a train to Peking 'just for the fun of it', having provisioned himself for the three week journey with two roast chickens. Yet this excursion was modest by comparison with the adventures of his younger days. In 1900, Weld Blundell had joined the Boer War as a special correspondent for the *Morning Post*, which printed his dispatches alongside those of the young Winston Churchill. He wrote as a participant-observer, entering skirmishes on which he reports, and applying the language of hunting to the Lovat's Scouts he saw leading a company of the Highland Light Infantry up on to terrain where the wily Boer would at last be within firing range. These guides were like 'stalkers in a deer forest', and 'the day was a vindication of, if not a triumph for, what a sportsman would call "spying" and "reconnoitring", as against the too often perfunctory operation known as military scouting'.[11] While British forces herded their enemies into the twentieth century's first concentration camps, Weld Blundell was urging fastidious readers to understand that the Boer had long since departed from the code of honour: 'we are forced to face the ugly fact that we are now fighting with mere savages'.[12]

As a man who had been able to take his pick of the Victorian world, Weld Blundell had travelled widely as an explorer, archaeologist and big game hunter. He had journeyed through Persia in 1891, staying as a guest of the Bahtiari Ikhania at Mal-i-mir, and led an expedition to Persepolis, bringing back moulds of some of the reliefs for the British Museum and the Louvre. In 1895, he had gone to Libya to inspect the relics of the ancient Grecian settlement in Cyrenaica — his journey only made possible by the intervention of Lord Rosebery, the Foreign Minister.[13] Taking his bearings from ancient sources like Callimachus's 'Hymn to Apollo', he led his camel train across 'an undulating tract of generally fertile, but almost totally deserted country abandoned like an ill-kempt garden to the hand of nature'; and then, as they descended on to 'the great red-soiled plain of Merj', imagined himself 'coming out of the Malvern Hills and on to the plains of Hereford in primeval days'.

Weld Blundell had also been much interested in Abyssinia, the last of the independent kingdoms of Africa. The British Legation to the court of King Menelek had been set up in 1897, and Herbert visited in spring the following year, accompanying the British diplomatic representative as he went to take up his appointment in Addis Ababa. He was there when the representative was received in state at Menelek's palace, and later entertained the Royal Geographical Society with a colourful account of the event.[14] They were led to the reception by 'a variegated mob of men armed with samples of all the guns ancient and modern, dressed in flowing shammas ornamented by a broad red stripe'. Herbert saw lion-killers who wore a fringe of the animal's mane around their heads, reminding him of the blonde wig of a bald-headed comedian, and elephant-killers with chains hanging from their ears. As for the emperor himself, 'His Majesty, though very dark in complexion, with not very regular features, has charming manners and a particularly pleasant voice, while his face is quite redeemed from the effect of the type, by a most intelligent mobile expression and an amiable smile that makes his features almost handsome.'

He had returned the following year to journey through southern Abyssinia with his hunting friend, Lord Lovat and Dr Reginald Koettlitz, a geologist who would later join Scott's Antarctic expedition. After leading his scientific caravan into an area where 'the gun has not yet penetrated in large numbers', he came across a huge rogue elephant 'sauntering along with an easy roll through the bamboo not 250 yards off' and got 'a good shot behind the shoulder'. He took his final blast when the stricken creature charged but swerved away at about thirty yards. Weld Blundell's trophy turned out to be 11 feet 11 inches to the top of the shoulder, which seemed, with one duly mentioned exception, to be the biggest recorded. Lord Lovat's turn came the next day, when he took on 'a fine active female with a good shot between the eye and ear'. Lovat stood firm when the wounded animal charged — until, at a distance of some five yards, he 'gave her a good one almost exactly on her forehead over the juncture of the trunk. This swung her round as quick as a teetotum and I, standing close by, got a shot into her as she turned. This considerably diminished her ardour, and after getting away about 200 yards, we found her very sick, standing motionless, and Lord Lovat gave her the *coup de grâce*.'[15]

Had it been invented a few decades earlier, the machine that was to cause so much outrage at Lulworth could have served in Weld Blundell's arsenal of elephant metaphors: after rushing 'like an engine, into the bamboo', and then bursting out again 'like a torpedo, charging right home', that stricken female might have slowed to come rolling forward like a tank too.

Neither the attraction of modern machines nor the thrill of testing them in wholly inappropriate places had passed Herbert by. Before the Great War he had contributed an introduction to a book about the adventures of Captain Bede Bentley. In 1907, Bentley, an adventurer who would later claim, falsely, to be the originator of the tank,[16] had set out to drive a Wolseley motor-car to Addis Ababa in order to present it to Emperor Menelek. Sponsored by the *Daily Mail*, Bentley travelled with his butler, a brindled bulldog named 'Bully' and large supplies of bully beef, Oxo cubes and Bath Oliver biscuits. There were leopards to shoot, but these Burberry-clad heroes also had to deal with the tribal 'Niggers' who lurked dangerously in the terrain, albeit with some 'splendid young animals' among their naked and 'glistening black' women.[17]

Mr Weld Blundell also knew about the spellbinding power of large guns. In 1906, he published his own translation of an Amharic 'History of King Theodore' he had obtained in Addis Ababa.[18] Written by an Abyssinian chronicler, this told the terrible story of King Theodore, an unusually brutal predecessor of Menelek's, who, feeling betrayed by Queen Victoria's emissaries, imprisoned a number of Europeans and then demanded that they prove their western superiority by making a vast gun big enough to carry a thousand pound projectile. The terrified Europeans, many of whom were missionaries, set to work, taking ancient bronze urns and casting a mortar or 'bomba' of such a size that 'a man could get into it and come out again, the other end'. Said to have weighed between fifteen and sixteen thousand pounds, this totemic object was named Sebastopol by King Theodore, who ordered it to be dragged from the foundry at Debra Tabor to his stronghold at Magdala, high up on the Abyssinian plateau — a terrible journey that lasted over six months. The bomba was drawn with five ropes, each with scores of natives and slaves pulling it — as many as eight hundred were necessary in some places. The British soldiers, who had come to liberate the captive Europeans, are said only to have laughed when they saw the great weapon, which ended up abandoned in a village square. The allegory was crueller still, for Magdala only fell because the British Expeditionary force was able to use the road that Theodore had built so that he could move this vast and utterly useless bomba up to his fortress.[19]

Herbert Weld Blundell could appreciate the mythology of the incongruent war machine in Abyssinia, but he was not inclined to extend a similarly imaginative welcome to the tanks shattering the peace of his newly leased Lulworth home. On reaching the castle, S. P. B. Mais found himself sitting in the gun-room 'of that square, much-betowered historic castle, which so many English Kings have decided to honour', while the Lord of the Manor 'inveighed against the high-handed action of his overlords'. Asserting, quite inaccurately, that a Weld had built this house in the late sixteenth century, Mais admired the spirit in which Herbert fired out his best line: 'Even the Huns never did a thing like this.'

SIX

LULWORTH'S UNPOPULAR FRONT

THE PHILISTINISM OF THE Royal Tank Corps seemed to be confirmed when an 'authoritative source' at Bovington Camp described Bindon Hill as 'admirable natural butts for the firing practice'.[1] Gunnery ranges have to be somewhere, he said, and surely 'national defence counts for something' — even in a post-war society obsessed with the 'privileges of the holiday tripper'.

This was provocation enough to bring Herbert Weld Blundell charging out of his wooded park. He conceded that there had been no protestation when the War Office 'came in to the outer park of Lulworth Castle' and 'put their guns up against the road past the garden walls': 'in the great world-struggle everybody willingly did what they could to assist their country' — assuming, all the while, that the gunnery school would be closed when the War was over. As the acting head of an estate that had lost its younger heirs in that disastrous engagement, Mr Weld Blundell spoke out in uncompromising terms:

> They gave up their lives and their property; they waived their rights, and, without murmuring, were prepared to submit to annoyance and loss at the hands of the military authorities. All this was done from motives of patriotism, and now the War Office seems to be extremely indignant because, with the war won and peace reigning again, the public object to living under war-time conditions and refuse to submit to a military dictatorship.[2]

Lulworth Castle was already rendered 'uninhabitable and unlettable', and the new plans threatened to close up the road to Arish Mell Gap and also the walk from East Lulworth village. Compensation was doubtless an issue, but Herbert Weld Blundell thrust his standard into higher ground: 'It may suit some people to say that owners of property, who have been there for three hundred years and who have built all the houses, farm buildings and roads that make the difference in food and wage-producing values between an agricultural property and barren heath or downs, have no rights and ought to submit to have their property taken away and their home ruined, but such confiscation by military authorities involves a principle that concerns everyone from the highest to the lowest.'

The newspaper correspondence pages testify to the ardour with which the southern middle class stepped out to join the resistance movement that Herbert Weld Blundell and his lordly colleagues on the County Council were mustering on the green slopes between that 'much betowered historic' castle and the chalk cliffs of Bindon, where England rose up and culminated against the sky. These incandescent letter-writers urged fellow readers to 'do what you can to save the soul of England from the damnation of utilitarianism'[3] and demanded that the 'names and positions of all those head officials who are responsible for the present lapses should be published so that the public may know where the blame lies'[4]. They shuddered at the thought of tanks, 'with the hideous memories of murderous war which they evoke',[5] and, as they signed off — whether from Oxford, Ely, or Wandsworth Common — they proved that the true lover of Dorset was not necessarily a resident of the county at all.

A cultivated weekly like the *Nation and Athenaeum* was pleased to see 'many signs of revolt against the contempt displayed by public departments for aesthetic and historical values'.[6] But how far down the British class structure would Weld Blundell's rallying cry actually be heard? *The Times's* Special Correspondent was hopeful, noting that, while Lulworth may always have been 'appreciated by the few', it had 'never been appreciated by so many people as at present' thanks to the advent of the motor-coach: 'on most days this summer as many as thirty of these conveyances can be seen drawn up in the neighbourhood in the middle of the day'. A local reporter shared this vision of broad national solidarity, offering thanks to the charabancs through which 'the beauty spots are becoming enshrined in the hearts of the inhabitants to an extent that has not been possible before'.[7]

Yet the frailty of Weld Blundell's cause is suggested by its hesitant treatment in the paper of the advancing Labour Party. Dedicated to the noble purpose of 'restoring the soul of the British people', George Lansbury's *Daily Herald* had plenty to be going on with in 1923. Its typical letter-writer was not a clergyman or artist worried about threatened 'beauty spots' but someone like Mr David Koffman, who wrote from Dalston Lane, London E.8, urging support for the *Herald's* current financial appeal on the grounds that its pacifism alone made it a vital antidote to 'the dope dished up by the millionaire press'.[8]

The *Herald* was no more pleased than the *Daily Mail* to see 'Historic Relics Threatened', but it would not join in the Battle of Bindon Hill anything like so promptly. Indeed, this skirmish between the rural aristocracy and the military state was left to 'Rovator', the rambling correspondent whose preference was for northern landscapes, and who only got round to Mr Weld Blundell's troubles late and with considerable scepticism. 'Judging by the daily press,' began this friend of the open road, 'a great number of people are getting concerned about the fate of the Lulworth Cove area.'[9] He wondered what could possibly justify this 'burst of anxiety' considering that Lulworth had 'long been saddled with a military camp, and the villagers have had time to learn to accept it as part of the place'.

But suddenly Rovator awoke to the special charms of Lulworth: 'Yes, there is something in these old hills, something subtle that grows and grows with the years and that breathes peace and contentment.' Without exactly coming out against the tank range, he allowed that 'there are beauty spots at which we wish to linger' and that 'the Hills of Purbeck — when they have captivated us — make us long to live with them for all time'. That is as close as anyone could reasonably have expected a socialist newspaper to get to siding with the Tory Squire of Lulworth, who, if village memory is correct, didn't hesitate to take the conventional steps to ensure an appropriate result in General Elections — letting it be known that 'If the Tory Party don't get in I'll sack half my staff.'

Many people took up their pens to defend the England that was threatened at Lulworth but the moralised opposition between Tank and their threatened Beauty Spot would not command the field as they expected. The intrusion of other themes is clearly visible in an article published by *The Times* on 3 September 1923. A classic of its type, 'The Defence of Arish Mell' was written by an unnamed correspondent who reflected on his own attachment to this threatened part of Dorset:

> We have, most of us, a little spot somewhere in the world that we look upon almost as our property; we resent meeting strangers there, and we only mention it, if it is within a radius of a thousand miles, to our very closest friends. We console ourselves, when the daily round becomes too oppressive, by building castles, or even cottages in its air — little white-walled cottages with green doors and shutters and with roses climbing up towards the roof. Some day we will retire there to find rest and contentment.
>
> Until the War Office proposed to take possession of part of the Dorset coast and to turn it into a Tank gunnery school, I had fondly imagined Arish Mell and Worbarrow Bay were mine. Everyone knew

Lulworth Cove — indeed, it has become the daily meeting place of scores of motor-charabancs from Bournemouth and Weymouth — but few people stopped at East Lulworth to walk down the lane, past rambling old Monastery Farm, to Arish Mell Gap, and still fewer climbed over that formidable ridge of the Purbeck Hills to visit Worbarrow, a wonderful little bay protected by a wonderful little headland.

To my surprise, the newspapers were full of protests against the iniquity of the War Office for proposing to use Arish Mell Gap for its nefarious purposes. I should no longer have to fight alone against the great Government Department for wishing to deprive me of that which it had given me — for it had led to my discovery of Arish Mell at the beginning of the war, by sending me there to look after a coast patrol whose duties were to arrest imaginary spies and to discover imaginary submarines. Most of my sentries were London boys, who were unused to the stillness of the Dorset nights, so that I used to crawl on hands and knees to visit my posts, lest I should be shot by one of my own sentries. But I forgave the War Office for inflicting this indignity on me, since it was only owing to its mysterious workings that I was ever out on the Purbeck Hills when the moon turned them into a wonderland of black and silver.

And now there spring up hundreds of other defenders of Arish Mell Gap. Have so many others then poached rabbits and pheasants on their way home from visiting their sentry posts? Have so many spent idle hours under the trees of Lulworth Park? Have so many others forgotten present-day soldiering as they pottered about in the Roman camp that looks down on Worbarrow Bay?

The Englishman has a sentimental affection for chalk cliffs. The ramparts of Dover have taught him to prefer white cliffs even to the red sandstone of Devon and the granite of Cornwall. He loves the close-bitten turf that crowns them, the milky blue sea at their feet. Perhaps it is this fact which gives the Lulworth opponents of the War Office so many unexpected allies, for there are few finer chalk cliffs in England than those which the Tank gunners would snatch from us. In my selfishness, I like to think that it is this inherent love of chalk cliffs generally, rather than an intimate affection for the Lulworth cliffs in particular, which has impelled so many people to write to the papers about it.

Would that the originators of the War Office scheme had stood by me on Worbarrow beach one day not so very long ago when the mackerel were being landed. The symphony of silver fish and blue sea, of afternoon mist and white cliffs, would surely have convinced them of the iniquity of disturbing this blue and silver peace by the noise of a gunnery school, with all the miseries from the years of war that it would recall.

For this correspondent, Arish Mell Gap was the place of discovery where an Englishman found himself at his most attuned and patriotic: an ideal realm where wishes could be kept against the harsh drift of time beyond the ridge, and where nature sprang eternal in a symphonic movement that would surely have interested Sir Edward Elgar.

And yet this moving testimonial to Arish Mell adds up to a strangely reluctant rallying cry. It is not just that the refined pleasures of Arish Mell are actually defined against the vulgar enthusiasms of Lulworth's charabancs, or that a cultured officer can appreciate what leaves his Cockney troopers merely bored and jumpy at the trigger. Even within his own class the writer faces the additional problem of being unable to defend Arish Mell without breaking its secret. So he resorts to an ingenious patriotic abstraction, concluding that the people who have risen up for Arish Mell are actually champions of a deeply felt image. The 'close-bitten turf', 'milky blue sea' and chalk cliffs are part of an 'inherent' English geography that others would know from elsewhere, and it is this more abstract landscape that is to be defended against the War Office. The true people of Deep England don't have to beat their way over every down and dale to know where they belong; and inversely, as this writer is relieved to discover, every time one of them does take to the hills the experience remains unique.

'The Defence of Arish Mell' was governed by a blunter inconsistency too. If the author owed his own knowledge of Arish Mell to the Army that had stationed him there during the early years of the Great War, then how could he sustain the idea that he was also defending civilisation against barbarism?

There is abundant evidence that the tank men who served at Bovington and its outlying camps were appreciative of the landscape too. Alec Dixon came to Worgret Camp in 1919, and was soon a member of 'the small community of bookmen' who were accustomed to meeting in 'the smelly coffee shops of Tintown'.[10] Dixon may have shared Bovington's dream of desertion, which was apparently to 'hire a dinghy at Lulworth Cove' and then to be picked up by a passing packet steamer, but his years as a 'tinned soldier' were not without their consolations: he relished 'the air of mystery' in the landscape, read Thomas Hardy and walked out into the Purbeck Hills: 'a wild, free country of legends and heroes'. He shared this enthusiasm with many of his fellows — including T.E. Lawrence, that 'true Viking of the Machine Age' who was then serving at Bovington as 'Private Shaw', and suspected of being 'a newspaper bloke on the lookout for some dope about tanks'.

The *Tank Corps Journal* reveals the officers at Lulworth to have been fully aware of their sudden notoriety. As one contributor wrote in September 1923: 'A certain liveliness has been imparted to the peacefulness of Lulworth life by the printer's ink storm that has been raging around our devoted heads. We feel quite proud of the fame that has so suddenly descended on us . . . but we are rather hurt at being considered as blots on the landscape.'[11]

The gunners of Lulworth were inclined to lampoon their critics as oversensitive souls, but they had their own romantic way of gazing up the length of their contested firing range. In January 1924, for example, the writer of 'Lulworth Notes' revealed that the practising gunners were caught up in their own fantasy of the place: 'In imagination we see the fair slopes of Bindon disfigured by the countless dead; one bright youth ceased his slaughter only on the hoisting of the red flag, a token of surrender, by the butt party.'[12] Similarly in April, when the old 'Tank Park' at Lulworth was abandoned for 'a detached residence consisting of one large room and quite a number of modern conveniences' – the *Tank Corps Journal* remarked appreciatively that the new park was 'beautifully situated near a lovely little wood with a charming outlook upon Bindon Hill and Arish Mell Gap'.[13] Bindon Hill and Flowers Barrow had been taken into the recent war, a patriotic image at the back of many a tank soldier's mind.

As it advanced on Lulworth, the tank found more such cracks in the defenders' fortifications, widening them as it approached. The first explosive challenge was tossed by a spokesman from Bovington Camp, who observed, 'it's all very well for people to write to the papers and say there are plenty of other sites . . . but they do not say where these sites are, and wherever we go, it seems to me we shall have to occupy some bit of countryside'.

Salisbury Plain seemed a fine alternative to some of Lulworth's defenders,[14] but when the suggestion was mooted in the *Daily Graphic* it only elicited a wounded response from a correspondent in Salisbury, who objected that people in Wiltshire 'read with horror the suggestion of a Dorset – a Wessex – man, that what he is protesting against should be dumped on to Salisbury Plain. It is a blow in the back from a friend.' After describing the military depredations that Salisbury Plain was already facing, he tried to guide Lulworth's tanks into somebody else's backyard: 'Are there no Sussex Downs, no Yorkshire moors, no dreary wastes anywhere that can be used?'[15] The tank folk at Lulworth Camp offered their own mocking contribution to this farcical debate: 'No bright spirit, for instance, has yet thought of the Sahara; Siberia has not been mentioned; neither have the rocky fastnesses of Tibet, where surely an ideal locale for our noisy demonstrations could be found.'[16]

The objectors had trouble with the civilian population too. As Weld Blundell's lieutenant in Lulworth Park, Revd John R. Lawrence, Vicar of St Andrew's and Chairman of East Lulworth Parish Council, was happy to enumerate the thoughts of all 'lovers of Lulworth' in a letter to *The Times*:

> 1. Surely it is immoral, surely it is not right, that such a spot should be commandeered, apart from necessity.
> 2. Another of 'The Stately Homes of England' (so fast disappearing), with all their meaning is destroyed.
> 3. Dorset, the country, England, claims it: for its beauty, scientifically, for its history and remains.[17]

But some Dorset people were scarcely impressed by this line of argument. The Wareham and Purbeck Rural District Council had early observed that, while the resident of Lulworth Castle might well protest, the people of West Lulworth hadn't complained – presumably because they recognised a rare source of income when they saw one.[18]

Rayner Goddard, KC, a barrister to various London banks who also served as Recorder of Poole and owned a fine house in West Lulworth, replied that no complaints had been received by the local Council for the very good reason that objectors had been instructed to address their complaints to the Marine Department of the Board of Trade.[19] He had submitted objections as early as August 1922 'at the request of the fishermen', and a petition signed in the village had also been sent. Some of the most 'monstrous' provisions had then been dropped, including those that would have made it a criminal offence for a child to paddle on the beach or for a boat to be rowed across the cove between 7 am and 3.30 pm.

Goddard was a formidable recruit. Known as 'Doggie' on account of his bulldog-like countenance, he was only at the early stages of a career that would later bring him notoriety as a judge who is said to have been quite unsparing in his application of the rope, birch and cat-o'-nine tails.[20] Goddard must have been an intimidating figure even before he was appointed to the High Court bench in 1932, but a growing section of Dorset opinion remained incurably delinquent.

Herbert Weld Blundell also rushed in to dispute the emerging economic arguments in defence of the Lulworth gunnery school. He conceded that 'there may be many people at West Lulworth who are glad to have a camp to trade with, but that is because they do not know that the firing practice has effectively stopped the chance of Lulworth Cove developing into an important and flourishing watering place'. The tanks had already made Lulworth Castle 'uninhabitable', threatening the Weld estate's future as a residential estate worth some £7,000 a year to labour and employees. So the War Office's plan might not, so the squire threatened, turn out 'as cheap as it looks'.

By the end of August, however, those 'strong expressions of opinion in favour' of the tanks had been amplified by the Mayor of Wareham, who ventured that the closure of Lulworth gunnery school would probably bring about the removal of 'the vast majority' of troops from Bovington camp too, thus depriving the regional economy of between £2,000 and £3,000 per week and ending the 'considerable amount of civil employment directly connected with the camp'. The plain truth, as the traders of Wareham knew after the closure of the Depot Reserve Unit's camp at Worgret, was that 'beauty spots do not feed hungry men'.[21] This defence of local trade was coloured by class resentment. One rural district councillor wanted to know 'what is at the back of the opposition to the camp? Is it the land-owners?' Doubting the patriotism of the objectors, he remarked that 'Some of them seem to object to Tommy Atkins.'

Of the three main resisters in Lulworth Park, the barrister held his counsel at this point. The Catholic Squire pressed on with his own economic arguments, eventually even commissioning a scheme to convert Lulworth Cove into a fully commercialised 'plage'.[22] Pushed on to the defensive, the Protestant Vicar of St Andrew's also felt obliged to emphasise the development potential of the area. Citing the spectacular growth of Bournemouth and Swanage he offered up Arish Mell and Bindon Hill to the same lucrative prospect: 'Let this part of Dorset develop (and be retained for such) in some possible future. "Floreat!" but not as a camp.'[23] This desperate vision might conceivably have mollified a few shopkeepers, but it would do nothing for those cultivated 'men of Dorset' who had rallied to the defence of Arish Mell — but not in order to see it built up like Bournemouth. Complicated by the emergence of renegade local interests, the opposition between Tank and Beauty Spot had lost its moral clarity.

False Victory

The War Office's lease was resolved temporarily with the help of the Commons, Open Spaces and Footpaths Preservation Society. In July 1924 a spokesman had called for 'vigorous public protest' against the Lulworth proposal,[24] but the Under-Secretary for the War Office, Colonel Ashley MP, informed the society's secretary, Mr Lawrence Chubb, that it was 'of prime importance that the camp should be retained, and appealed to the society not to influence public opinion to impede the scheme'.[25] So Chubb made a deal. If the War Office would give the public 'reasonable access to the cliffs and to the ancient paths, the society would be happy to use its good offices with the landowners'.[26] Chubb drew up the headings of an agreement that would extend the lease for a maximum of three years while the War Office found another site, but this arrangement failed when the War Office pressed for five years, and 'declared itself unable to bind itself definitively to evacuate the site even at the end of five years'. Eventually, it was agreed that the gunnery range should remain in place on a temporary basis until August 1924.

Towards the end of this term, the War Office attempted to secure a further extension, but Mr Justice Sankey, who presided over the hearing, dismissed the application on the grounds that Lulworth Cove was one of 'the beauty spots of England', and also that the first agreement brokered by Chubb had been based on the explicit understanding that the land would revert to the Weld estate by the end of August 1924.

Victory was celebrated immediately, but while 'all lovers of Dorset scenery' were said to be 'emphatic in their expressions of satisfaction', the War Office only picked up the blunter cudgel of compulsory purchase.[27] Asked in the House of Commons what the War Office's intentions now were, Mr Walsh, Secretary of State for War, announced that the War Office had decided 'to exercise their powers of purchase under the Acquisition of Land Acts' but would 'stay proceedings as soon as the owners of the land granted a short lease on suitable terms'.[28]

So bureaucracy triumphed over justice, beauty and truth. Rayner Goddard KC wrote to inform readers of *The Times* that, despite the expiry of its lease, the Royal Tank Corps was still firing across footpaths and sealing off the road joining West and East Lulworth.[29] Since no attempt had been made 'to stop those of us who since August 31 have disregarded the notices by walking and driving along the road through the camp', Goddard concluded that the signs were 'no more than bluff and humbug'.[30] He closed on a haughty flourish:

> six weeks ago about 15 shells fell into the sea one after another in a line with the east point of the Cove, hundreds of yards outside the limit of the danger zone, and just where the Weymouth steamer turns to port to enter the Cove. Fortunately the steamer was not due, and such boats as were out were to the westward. No sort of warning had been given. This occurrence can be proved by several credible eye-witnesses. The next time it happens I suppose a War Office official will attend the inquest to express polite sympathy with the relatives,

> and to emphasize, with perfect accuracy, that the law imposes no liability on the Crown to make compensation for such regrettable incidents.[31]

Herbert Weld Blundell also wrote to *The Times*, affirming that he had it 'from the highest authority' that 'it is a question of money', and then blaming the situation on officials of the kind that 'the rest of the Army, in graceful recognition of that portion of their persons that shows most brilliance, designate as "Brass hats" '.[32] He closed his letter with a memorable paragraph in which the conventions of the stiff upper lip were to be seen at their most commanding:

> If a mere owner might state his case, it might perhaps be mentioned that the 'devastated area' is the most vital portion of the whole estate, lying from the gardens to the sea, the Tanks' sheds being placed, in order to get as long a range as the confined space admits of, up against the garden and park walls, giving the effect of a battle raging for five days a week when in full practice and thereby making the residence uninhabitable — a disappointing result of all the members of the family who could serve being killed down to a second cousin, a boy of 12. The hostile army of Cromwell only stripped the lead, which could be replaced; the conquest by the British Army of the most important parts of the estate would be the equivalent of confiscation.

From this moment of outraged clarity, Weld Blundell fell back into reluctant negotiation. By September 1925, notice of compulsory purchase had been withdrawn and a five year lease had been agreed, back-dated to run from 1 September 1924. There would be no firing on Saturdays, Sundays or Bank Holidays. Walkers would be allowed access to the various cliff paths on the summit of Bindon Hill when the range was not in use. Moreover, while the War Office would be entitled to use the land until September 1929, 'there is an understanding that Lulworth will be evacuated at an earlier date if suitable alternative accommodation can be elsewhere secured'.[33]

So victory was celebrated again. *The Times* welcomed the success of what had certainly been a 'hard-fought campaign'. Calling obliquely for an end to hostilities ('the country will probably not wish to grudge the military authorities the extra four years of possession'), it pronounced 'the moral' of Bindon Hill: 'No one will deny that the War Office and other Departments of State must have land; but it must not be land which, for one reason or another, has so endeared itself to the public that its forfeiture becomes a national loss.'

SEVEN

TANKS AGAINST ASPIC

IN 1925 LULWORTH COVE was chosen as the subject for a poster in Shell's 'See Britain First' series, but the defenders of Bindon Hill were already disappointed in their hope that the motorised fame of their threatened beauty spot would further empower their resistance to the tank. The War Office had displayed little sense of strategy beyond a mulish refusal to budge backed by threats of compulsory purchase, but the fatal flaw in Lulworth's defences was much older than the tanks. So deeply was class antagonism buried in the landscape that the smallest blade of downland grass seemed to exist in two polarised dimensions at once. The defenders of Bindon Hill may have had poetry, scientific interest and refined aesthetic appreciation on their side of this division, but the more pragmatic perception of the Wareham traders could also lay claim to history.

F. J. Harvey Darton had the example of interwar Dorset in mind when he wrote that England was 'in danger of becoming two nations', divided between those who came to the countryside to look and those who remained there to be seen. On one side were the 'foreigners' who drove in from the suburbs and cities; and on the other were the residual folk of a dying countryside whose final humiliation was apparently to be adopted as picturesque 'exhibits for inspection' by 'motorists, hikers, weekenders'.[1]

Contrary to some opinion, the rise of this onlooking perspective was not the fault of Thomas Hardy. Lulworth certainly had a prominent place in the 'Wessex of Romance' — that evocative country of background locations to which the early twentieth century tried to reduce Hardy's altogether more demanding writings.[2] But, as Hardy himself implied when he spoke against the tanks on Bindon Hill, the modern touristic view of the Dorset coast actually derived from the late eighteenth century when George III favoured Weymouth as a place of summer resort, coming down to practise some restorative sea-bathing after recovering from his first bout of madness in the summer of 1789. Weymouth was an obscure backwater then, doomed by its ancient loss of the wool trade to Poole. It was chosen partly because the Prince of Wales had adopted Brighton and, only a year before, plunged it into such debauchery that the town was now said to be deserted by decent people whenever the Prince and his retinue were due.[3] So the Royal party took a house from the Duke of Gloucester, and transformed Weymouth's fortunes in a few seasons.[4]

Weymouth greeted George III with successive convulsions of loyalty, offered, as Fanny Burney remembered, in 'a truly primitive style'.[5] In this atmosphere, which was said by the anonymous author of a novel called *A Trip to Weymouth* to reverberate 'with the plaudits of loyalty and joy', the convalescent monarch could go some way towards relaunching his troubled reign.[6] It had to be conceded that 'the lustre of royalty has ever been shunned by the philosophic mind', yet in Weymouth at least the Royal presence could still serve as an 'incitement to the moral and social virtues'; indeed, as a female character in *A Trip to Weymouth* remarks, Royalty 'does you more good than all the drugs in the world'. George was feted not as an expansionist 'enlarging the boundaries of his dominions' — he could hardly be that after his troubles in America and Europe — but as a 'patriot king': 'the wise governor, the man of justice' who honours agriculture and 'keeps a truly paternal eye' on the 'liberties, morals and well-being of his people'.[7]

The native populace may have been content to mount 'excessive' displays of patriotic loyalty, but the polite society that flocked to join George at his summer resort could hardly spend all its time gazing at the portly monarch as he chatted in the fields, or sniggering at the unsophisticated sincerity of the country people who followed their monarch on his visits to Lulworth Castle and other nearby county seats. The theatre provided 'entertainment quite in the barn style',[8] but Mrs Siddons was not at her best in the comic roles chosen to cheer the convalescent King. As Fanny Burney remarked, 'nothing but the sea at Weymouth affords any life or spirit'.[9] The just discovered bay may have been 'very beautiful, after its kind', but enhancements were plainly necessary if this new resort was to be distinguished from a rustic backwater. So the visitors used imagery derived from the Grand Tour to convert this rude native scene into a refined Italianate wonder. The Bay of Weymouth was redesignated 'The English Bay of Naples' — a transformation that would only gain in poignancy a few years later when the Napoleonic Wars put an end to continental travel.

There was plenty of formulaic pastoral stuff involved in this conversion: every movement of the air became a prophylactic zephyr blown by the Goddess of Health; every bump in the surrounding landscape was hymned as 'Pindus' flowery top'.[10] It was not until long after the Royal heyday had passed that the native rocks of Dorset woke up to their new vocation and started to mimic Vesuvius in the appropriate manner (the cliff at Holworth began to omit steam in 1824, and then actually burst into flames in 1826–7), but the conceit was well established by then. Countless polite beachcombers had picked up stones and shells on the sands at Weymouth, and compared them with those that might be found near Naples; and the geological comparison had long since entered the scientific world too. Visitors to Sir Ashton Lever's museum near Blackfriars Bridge in London would find an exhibition of 'inflammables' in which 'Coal very much resembling wood from the cliffs near Weymouth' was placed alongside 'Native yellow sulphur from Vesuvius'.[11]

The native people could apply for their own places in this improved and newly picturesque scene, but only on certain terms. There was always room for rude but healthy 'Dorsetshire yokels' with patriotic bunting in their hatbands. There was ample accommodation for pastoral shepherd boys and also for elderly swains, like the retired couple in *A Trip to Weymouth*, who sat at the door of a bucolic cottage in Purbeck, o'ershaded by spreading ivy and gazing out to sea as 'the fleets of commerce' pass by on 'the swelling tide'.[12]

The English Bay of Naples was adopted by Thomas Hardy — who incorporated its landmarks into his early novel *The Trumpet Major*, and then went on to introduce more profound themes. But the sentimental gloss that had been smeared over this coastal scene persisted through the nineteenth century, long after the railways had turned Weymouth into a bustling middle class resort, and the Welds had felt obliged to introduce admission charges at Lulworth Park to discourage visitors of the less desirable type.[13] The Italianising tradition was renewed by the Victorian watercolourist Alfred Downing Fripp, father of the surgeon Sir Alfred Fripp, who spent many years painting in Italy, and then brought his 'delicate and tender touch' home to West Lulworth, where he wasted no time setting his more indigenous neighbours in tinted amber.[14] He perched darling fisherboys on the rocky shoreline, decorating them with the oddly shaped cork floats of their trade. His piping shepherd boy stands on a sheep-dotted chalk cliff with a loyal old English sheepdog at his feet. He is blessed with golden curls, rosebud lips and flaunting blue eyes that appear to have been ringed with mascara.

This Georgian sentimentality persisted into the guidebooks of the early twentieth century. Among the best known of these was *Highways and Byeways of Dorset* by Sir Frederick Treves, an eminent Victorian surgeon who lived, or at least kept a house, in West Lulworth. Treves's book, which first appeared in 1906 but was still popular during the early years of the tank, remembered West Lulworth to have been: 'as picturesque a hamlet of thatched cottages as could be imagined, with its spring of clear water issuing from the hill, its mill-pond where a great sheep washing was held once a year, and its mumbling old mill'. Though 'numerous red brick villas and lodging-houses' had since done much to rob the place of its 'ancient charm', the village still had its 'queer old church'. As for East Lulworth, Treves managed to turn this wholly owned and, indeed, abruptly relocated settlement into a monument to English freedom and individuality: a 'delectable' hamlet of 'engaging thatched cottages and old-fashioned gardens, facing all ways, for each has been placed as some man's heart desired it'.

This picturesque view was not always appreciated by the people it portrayed in such banal terms. It remained impervious to history, its tinted glass quite unclouded by the riots of the 1830s, or the numerous surveys demonstrating that Dorset's agricultural workers were among the very poorest in the land. For Alfred Downing Fripp, even the signs of this notorious poverty could apparently be incorporated into the idyll — he liked the painterly challenge of a garment that had given out at the knee, and appears to have found virtuous qualities in the patches on his shepherd boy's smock.

Against this background, it is not surprising that the impending departure of the tank, celebrated by *The Times* on 21 September 1925, should have occasioned second thoughts in the locality by the end of October, when a public inquiry was held by the Board of Trade to consider the bylaws which would establish the range under the new and apparently final lease. Objections were maintained by Mr William Bond of Tyneham and Mr Rayner Goddard KC among others, but the officers in charge of the Lulworth Gunnery School had an easier time than expected.

The gunnery school was then under the command of Lieutenant-Colonel C.N.F. Broad and his senior gunnery instructor, Major T. Darwell. These innovative pioneers had yet to receive the first really fast heavy tank (a model called 'The Independent', not introduced until 1926), but they were already 'filled with the spirit of mobility' and working to prove that a tank could fire accurately on the move.[15] Darwell promised that the current annual allowance of fifty shells per man was soon to be reduced to forty-five rounds per five men, and that in future firing would only be from three- rather than six-pounder guns.[16] But the wider case was put by Lieutenant-Colonel Broad, who claimed that relationships between village and camp had improved considerably since 1919, when soldiers had become restless and disorderly while awaiting demobilisation.[17] Broad reminded the local population that they 'could not have an omelette without breaking eggs': it could not be denied that the firing range brought certain disadvantages, but having counted up the advantages he reckoned that 'in the village there would be more grief than pleasure' when the School finally went.

Arguing this towards the end of 1925, Broad was considerably less isolated than the 'authoritative source' who had made the same heretical claims from Bovington two years earlier. The new Mayor of Wareham told the inquiry that his Town Council had recently passed a unanimous resolution 'supporting on national, economical, county, and local reasons the retention of the gunnery school'. The West Lulworth Parish Council had, by this time, also stopped dithering and come out in favour of retaining the camp. In their revised estimate, the 'financial value' of the tank gunnery school to the village was considerably greater than that of 'the tripper', who would doubtless keep coming anyway.

Broad could also claim the support of a body which, at the time when the first protestations were reported in the national press, had only made local news by marching behind band and banner in commemoration of the Tolpuddle Martyrs.[18] It was announced that, in Dorchester, a resolution had been passed unanimously at a recent district meeting of the National Union of Agricultural Workers, representing over 1,000 men. This had urged that the school should be retained at West Lulworth, as they considered it would be 'a waste of public money to remove it after spending a large sum on the present training centre'. Showing a collectivist disregard for the inconvenience suffered by Weld Blundell, their resolution had also insisted that 'the nation's interest came before those of individuals, and that the presence of the camp relieved unemployment in the district'.

The victory so decisively announced by *The Times* would be confounded as these local dissenters made common cause with the Royal Tank Corps. Here were Dorset people defending their own practical interests against the empty vistas of a lofty and aristocratic pastorale. Cravenly opportunistic as it certainly appeared to the defenders of Bindon Hill, this local perspective was not merely pragmatic. In lining up the tank against the 'individual' rights of the squire, the Union indicated that, far from being just a provider of jobs in a depressed area, this military machine also had considerable potential in the rural class struggle: an affronter of the squirearchy, and a kind of anti-deference machine.

Some indication of the tank's positive attraction as an anti-pastoral device is to be found in a book by Eric Benfield, a stoneworker and self-educated writer from the Purbeck village of Worth Matravers. In *Southern English* Benfield distinguishes his own 'personal' style of autobiography from the abject variety of the man who once wrote 'that when he was cycling along some country road he was run down by a car and he was delighted to find that he had been run down by the charming, if careless, Lady So-and-So. He apologised and that seemed all that there was to write about it.' Had he been Lady So-and-So, Benfield would have been delighted to run this cringing fellow down again. Indeed, 'I should use a tank for the second attempt.'[19] Rather the tank than the dumb, forelock-tugging charm of the deferential villager. Rather the tank than the kind of lady whose 'sole sum of work was perhaps arranging the flowers in some church' but who still explained that a man was 'bound to slip downhill unless all his days were occupied with useful labour'.[20] Rather the tank than rotten Georgian aspic.

EIGHT

EMPTYING OUT THE HOLLOW LAND

How was it that no-one of us ever found it till that day for it is near our country.

William Morris

THE PHOTOGRAPHER S.W. Colyer has left proof that Lulworth continued to attract its own unique kind of visitor in the interwar period, even if the fellow did seem like an eccentric throwback. Beside a photograph of the cove included in a book called *Unspoiled Dorset*, Colyer quotes from an elderly gentleman encountered there: ' "These coves are prophylactic. They are so isolated, wards in Nature's hospital. I go to them to be purged by sun, wind and water. Then I feel as Naaman did when he stepped out of Jordan." '[1]

In reality, however, that wishful Victorian distinction between Lulworth and nearby railway resorts like Weymouth and Swanage had already collapsed, opening a new front of antagonism: not just between visiting lovers of the picturesque and the indigenous folk who knew very well that a kettle cannot be boiled on beauty, but between refined visitors and the mass of vulgar trippers. In 1906, Edric Holmes could still hope for Lulworth: 'the great majority of seaside visitors seem to fight shy of any place that has not a station on the beach'.[2] Some twenty years later, Donald Maxwell found the place beyond polite description: 'On a Sunday afternoon in the summer it is possible to find Lulworth Cove a vast annex of the motor show at Olympia with a bank-holiday thrown in. The amenities of the place would be entirely spoilt if every single visitor was a paragon of good breeding and decorous behaviour. As great numbers of these visitors are not conspicuous for either of these things, the effect is better imagined than described.'[3]

Things were less bad on the other side of the Purbeck Hills. Over at Tyneham Great House, William Bond held out as best he could. When the coastguard station at Worbarrow Bay was closed down, he had even gone so far as to buy and level the redundant cottages so they could not be turned into holiday homes. But his daughter Margot could still remember looking up to find people wandering across the garden or peering in through the windows. There were camps in the Tyneham valley too: albeit wholly temporary ones on land owned by Mr Bond's less fastidious cousins who lived north of Tyneham at Creech Grange.

It was in the Twenties that the scoutmasters of Eton Collage lit upon this emblematic valley, and chose to hold their annual scout summer camps here. They rented a field between Tyneham village and Worbarrow Bay from Longman, the tenant of Baltington Farm, hiring tents, marquees and other equipment for the week-long occasion. The scouts went on rambles and engaged in 'night schemes', which involved taking prisoners and carrying significant mallets from one side of the valley to the other. They spent a lot of time erecting and servicing 'gadgets' constructed, according to the precepts of true woodcraft, out of logs, sticks, string and wire. 'The throne' was a large bench-like seat which granted Eton's 'beaks' symbolic elevation over the ordinary scouts at the camp fire. 'Dr Malden' seems to have been a privy.

The scouting 'beaks' would subject each camp to a detailed retrospective appraisal written in an exercise book and called, for obscure Etonian reasons, an 'Egg'.[4] The author of each of these curious documents would claim to have 'laid' his 'egg' for the critical attention of the other scouting 'beaks', who were invited to add their comments as the thing circulated between them. The surviving 'eggs' reveal the beaks to have been tireless searchers after perfection in the Tyneham valley. The author of one even included a little map showing just where every gadget, marquee and ring of bell tents would stand if Mr Longman's field could be made to conform to his idea of 'Utopia'. This ideal blueprint drew lukewarm response from a more pragmatic beak, who wrote 'I approve of Utopia in theory, but I am not sure that it will fit our present site.'

There was earnest deliberation about the placing of the flagpole, and about improving the singing. Perhaps it would be sensible to invest in a 'Hackney' song book, although there was caution on this front too: as one beak scribbled, 'Do not let us Prussianise our camp fires at all costs.' No one disputed the need for a 'definite signal' to herald the dawn of camp activities, but 'God defend us from a whistle — let it be a horn.' This measure was adopted in later camps, but still under review a few years later: 'I don't much like the Horn — as blown by most people it sounds like a Cow coughing. I think a little instruction is wanted.' The beaks were unanimous in deploring the villagers and summer visitors who insisted on joining their campfires. Appalled to find women sitting in their evening circle, they resolved that in future it would be as well to have 'a circle made by staves, or perhaps merely by persuasion' to keep these imposters at bay: 'We don't want to be unfriendly, but we do want to be alone.' So the search for perfection continued, until 1931 when the Eton scouts moved to an even more secluded site in a valley known as the Golden Bowl, at Encombe nearby.

The rising popularity of the Lulworth area left a number of its more sensitive admirers no choice but to fall back into the Tyneham valley, where they tried to reintroduce exclusivity to the landscape. So serious was the perceived threat that this entrancing fold in the downs was soon subject to literary manoeuvres that, in their determination to empty its landscape of imposters, seem to prefigure the military evacuation of 1943.

In 1925 Mills and Boon published *Bindon Parva*, a book of 'experimental stories' by George A. Birmingham, a pseudonymous vicar with south Dorset connections.[5] Bindon Parva was an imaginary Purbeck village in 'a hollow among the downs' somewhere near Tyneham or neighbouring Steeple. It is visited by an architect who, in a break from hacking out tasteless suburban villas, comes to this depopulated village in order to expose ancient murals recently discovered in the walls of its Norman church. This fellow finds himself lodging with the vicar, a mysterious and ascetic man named Maturin, who turns out to be 'on terms of familiarity with a number of dead men'. Unusually sensitive to the 'long abiding memories in the very stones' of his church, Maturin has a 'theory of the consecration of churches', according to which 'Human emotion, especially emotion of a very strong and sincere kind has the power of soaking into the walls of a building, charging the very stones with a certain energy which then gives out again years afterwards.'

Some people are far more attuned to the 'stored emotions' in ancient buildings than others. This special sensitivity was possessed by a visionary spirit, but it was certainly not available to the average gawping tripper. Scotland Yard might well be interested in using Maturin's architectural clairvoyance to solve crimes but practical application of these powers would 'vulgarise them at once'. 'You might as well advertise them', as the architect is told by his more sensitive senior partner, and that would be 'the last possible degradation of human nature . . . '

Birmingham's theory of architectural 'consecration' articulates the tension that animated many anti-touristic guidebook definitions of the Lulworth area as they tried to save its special charms from the oblivious masses. But the novelist Mary Butts expected considerably more from these southern Dorset acres. Born in 1891, she had grown up in Salterns, a large house near Poole which looked out over the Purbeck Hills, and moved into artistic circles in London shortly before the Great War — spending a large part of the Nineteen Twenties in expatriate Bohemia in France. In her post-war writing — especially the novels *Armed With Madness* (1928) and *Death of Felicity Taverner* (1932) — she drew on her memories of Purbeck to create a 'green transparent world' called, after William Morris, 'The Hollow Land'.

The 'Hollow Land' is a translucent country closely derived from the Purbeck Butts had known as a child in the first decade of the century. In *The Crystal Cabinet*, she recalled how she would take the ferry from Poole and then walk past Corfe Castle to reach her favourite sites on the coast:

> More and more I went further afield, often alone on foot from Salterns, across the great heath. Into the Goathorn woods, to the grey apple-orchard set in the open moor . . . Over to Worbarrow under Flower's Barrow and Arish Mell Gap. From Worbarrow Tout, past Gadcliff, up to the stone seat some Bond of Tyneham had placed, high above the sea, before the haunted, broken upland of Tyneham Cap. A 'pass no further' mark that bench, a boundary-stone between man and no man's land.[6]

Butts describes how she was seized by this remote land, and the geography of those walks returns in her writing, seen through a prism of retrospective mythologisation. The heath is a 'purple land' with bees, 'magenta risings, yellow sand holes' and 'black bunches of trees';[7] but once the Grail legend is activated it is also an 'infernal prairie' of bewilderment and confusion.[8] Corfe Castle is 'the hub of the down-wheel, set in its cup of smoke and stone'. The 'Hollow Land' lies on the little visited coast beyond that: a revelatory country 'made of turf hills, patched with small trees and stones and hammered by the sea'.[9]

The constituents of this irridescent landscape are organised within the remembered view down over Kimmeridge Bay from Gad Cliff or Tyneham

Cap. It features high downland with an 'enamel carpet' of flowers in its turf, sudden cup-like valleys, tumuli and unmetalled roads, both green and white. There is 'a chess-board of fields' and a 'village of extraordinary beauty'. An eighteenth-century house stands at the far end and, near at hand, there is a wood shaped like a clasped fan, which runs down from the heights of a turf ridge to 'a little secret cliff where England rose out of the harvested sea'.[10] From 1923, when it featured in her first book, this was Butts's 'Sacred Wood'.[11] Its trees converse with one another and there is profound meaning in the 'rearrangements of light on a leaf'.[12] The wood encloses the humble dwellings of a shepherd and a fisherman, but it also shelters a large and 'very old' stone house which stands surrounded by huge ilex, beech and oak trees. The two significant houses in this valley belong to the Taverner family. Shared between cousins, just as the Bonds shared the Tyneham valley, they are the ancestral homes of the more native members of the war-ravaged circle — young survivors of the Western Front, the Russian Revolution and the chaotic artistic scenes of post-war Paris and Villefranche — who have now returned in search of healing and reintegration.[13]

The 'Hollow Land' is 'enchanted and disenchanted with the rapidity of a cinema': its stream 'a running trap for light' and its landscape anchoring 'events, only part of which are happening on the earth we see'.[14] On this reverberant ground Butts staged the drama of Europe's post-war 'dis-ease' — a story of broken continuity and of a destructive 'revaluation of values' marking the end of culture. The 'Hollow Land' still has its indigenous population, but these natives are like gnarled and time-expired relics. The fisherman is a noble savage, but the shepherd is a troglodyte who 'comes home drunk in the moonlight, yelling obscene words to the tune of old hymns'.[15] Despite Butts's inclusion of these rusticated types, and her declared preference for peasants over vulgar tourists, the 'Hollow Land' is no longer a working landscape: the old stone quarry has a sculptor's studio built into it, and features only as the setting in which the mania of this war-damaged fellow can be displayed to dramatic effect.

The central characters in Butts's valley may pass as connoisseurs of futility in the wider post-war world, but in the 'Hollow Land' these assorted artists, writers, ruined aristocrats and dispossessed White Russians prove uniquely sensitive to the charms of a place that exists 'in one mode of the perfected'. They listen to the conversation of trees, whistle, and write poems. They relish the scents and wild flowers, and hear music in the rain.

Possessed of an 'exquisite turn for observation',[16] they have no regard for the spectacular 'amusements' favoured by town-dwelling tourists, but know 'fifteen ways of looking at a finch'.[17] Their refined minimalism is a mark of cultural superiority as John Cowper Powys once defined it:

> the less cultured you are the more you require from Nature before you can be roused for reciprocity. Uncultured people require blazing sunsets, awe-inspiring mountains, astonishing waterfalls, masses of gorgeous flowers, portentous signs in the heavens, exceptional weather on earth, before their sensibility is stirred to a response. Cultured people are thrilled through and through by the shadow of a few waving grass-blades upon a little flat stone . . .[18]

For Butts, 'the scenery seemed to be the play',[19] but the special attractions of the 'Hollow Land' were never to be confused with 'the posters and pretence that represent the Londoner's poor escape to the land' or with the enthusiasm of the 'gaping tourists' in vulgar clothes who kept pouring in on motor-cycles or in Ford cars. Butts tried hard to protect her Hollow Land from picturesque cliché, defining it as a place of ritual rather than the conventional kind of literary symbolism that had descended, so she saw it, in an unbroken line from the Romantic poets to the banal imagery that animated the tourist trade. As she once wrote in an appreciation of the Dorset-born artist Christopher Wood, their country was not just a place of 'short turf and chalk hills which are like nothing else on earth'; it also had a 'secret history' written across it 'in letters too large' for all but the most 'conscious' among the people bred there to read.[20]

William Morris' legendary 'Hollow Land' was remembered through a seething confusion of war and steel, and Butts also acknowledged the presence of the Army — unlike many of the guidebooks of that time, which continued to sing the praises of Arish Mell as if the tanks had never existed. A character in *Armed With Madness* looks back over the heath and sees 'a blazing plain from which an army might pop out';[21] and the Shepherd's wife knows all about the improvements that the military could bring to the rural economy: a toothless and diseased 'old trollop', she has spent many years selling herself to the soldiers at a nearby camp. In a poem called 'Corfe', Butts has a man crossing the rough grass: with his 'strong graceless khaki legs . . . treading the hill down'.[22] These references serve to anchor the ruinous memory of the Great War, which keeps breaking into Butts's Hollow Land: machine guns rattle away and poppies no sooner appear than they form a 'blood-mist'. A 'no man's land' is declared up by Tyneham Cap and clouds of mustard gas seem to drift across the 'Hollow Land': 'pockets of poisoned air' which are emblematic of all the destructive forces gathering beyond the chalk ridge.[23]

Butts's valley was threatened by forces considerably worse than the odd tank. The Hollow Land may have been 'exquisitely civilised . . . a nucleus, capable now of perfect expansion in terms of itself'; and Butts may have felt passionately that it was 'for us to apply the terms, not destroy the formula'. But history was set on the opposite course, and its juggernaut, unleashed by the Great War, was already pressing in to obliterate the gifted valley that should have served as the model for the reconstruction of all Europe. Butts defines the 'Hollow Land' against the materialist outlook that would reduce all passion and imagination to 'little tricks of the machine' and render any one life as meaningless as any other. She opposes the organic intelligence of her valley to the specialised and deformed knowledge of the mechanistic expert whose inventions are either machines designed to serve false needs or, like poison gas, the monstrous products of 'perfectible technique'. She values its unique aesthetic and spiritual quality against the crude financial interest of those who can think of nothing but 'Prupperty, prupperty, prupperty'.[24]

Butts planted her Sacred Wood with carefully laid 'Traps for Unbelievers' and posted her own offputting 'Warning to Hikers' on the ridge above.[25] In the poem named 'Corfe', she called on God to carry out deterrent adjustments on that Purbeck scene:

> God keep the Hollow Land from all wrong!
> God keep the Hollow Land going strong!
> Curl horns and fleeces, straighten trees,
> Multiply lobsters, assemble bees.
>
> Give it to us for ever, take our hints
> Knot up its roads for us, sharpen its flints,
> Pour the wind into it, the thick sea rain,
> Blot out the landscape and destroy the train.
>
> Turn back our folk from it, we hate the lot
> Turn the American and turn the Scot;
> Make unpropitious the turf, the dust
> If the sea doesn't get 'em then the cattle must.

Make many slugs where the stranger goes
Better than barbed wire the briar rose;
Swarm on the down-tops the flint men's hosts
Taboo the barrows, encourage ghosts.

Arm the rabbits with tigers' teeth
Serpents shoot from the soil beneath
By pain in belly and foot and mouth
Keep them out of our sacred south.

But the presence of the sacred in the Hollow Land was far too subtle to bring off this defensive engineering, and Butts was driven to desperate measures.

In *Death of Felicity Taverner* all the forces of destruction are concentrated in the figure of Kralin, a metropolitan Jewish blackmailer who was able, thanks to the 'dis-ease' of that broken post-war era, to marry the daughter of the house and drive her to suicide. This contaminating alien now intends to complete his achievement by taking over the ancestral landscape and killing it with the kind of commerce that mass tourism made possible. He plans a hotel, a row of bungalows along the low cliff, golf-links, a car park and a garage with petrol pumps which would destroy the view from the old house. The rolling English road down to the sea would be brutally straightened and tarred; and one of the old barns would be converted into a cinema. The Hollow Land would be reinterpreted according to a 'faked story' of its history. Having prepared 'one of the least-known places in England' in this way, Kralin would then complete its humiliation by advertising its attractions. The village, which was 'perfect as a single unit of antique building, would do half of the publicity for him',[26] and the blind, uprooted urban masses would dutifully pour in: 'All summer the greasy papers of their meals will blow about, the torn newspapers and the tins. They will blow to the boundaries of the Sacred Wood and clog in its thorns . . . '

Touristic development is symbolic of the whole cluster of destructive trends that threaten to overwhelm the Hollow Land — the degeneration that Butts sometimes described as 'The Tide'. As the embodiment of all these apparently triumphant evils, the Jew must go; indeed, the preservation of rural England depends upon his murder. Butts was no conventional reactionary or anti-Semite (she would describe her own political allegiances as similar to those of the Independent Labour Party), but she goes to the end that this fiction demands: giving the job to a deracinated White Russian, who sees in the 'grey thing' that is Kralin an embodiment of the same 'materialist' forces that had destroyed his world in the Revolution of 1917. He performs this unusual preservationist measure with grim satisfaction.[27]

So Lulworth's tanks achieved the additional virtue of being better than anti-Semitic murder. God may no longer have been there to heed Butts's call, but the War Office at least would prove capable of planting deterrent explosives in her endangered turf, and of reinforcing with wire the briar roses that already guarded the Sacred Wood. The only slug that would keep the marauders at bay was the famously 'Cubist' one that H. G. Wells had once dubbed a 'slug with spirit'.[28]

Butts would not have been impressed by this outcome. She died young in 1937, but it is highly unlikely that she would have seen anything positive in the tanks' advance. Not for her, surely, the fallen spirit of compromise in which one extoller of 'Unknown Dorset' settled with the tank. The former war artist and topographical writer, Donald Maxwell was sent down to Lulworth by the editor of the *Graphic* at the height of the agitation in the early Twenties. It soon became clear to him that 'the ease with which vast numbers of people can reach a given spot at the same time is going to be one of the scenic problems of the future'.[29] Disgusted by the surging vulgarity of Lulworth, he couldn't share the affronted sensibility of those who thought the presence of the tank in this area 'too horrible to contemplate'. By the time he reported back to his editor, he was in no doubt that the War Office, far from being 'the villain of the piece', was actually 'a noble protector of the natural scenery'.[30] Having weighed up the opposition between the Tank and the threatened Beauty Spot, he concluded that 'if people want to agitate about preserving the rural charm of England against aggression' they should 'do something to stop toast-racks of people rushing hither and thither through the secluded ways and leafy lanes of our lost Arcadia'.

NINE

THE SQUIRE'S LAST STAND

SHORTLY AFTER THE Armistice, there was amused speculation in the *Tank Corps Journal* about possible 'uses for tanks in peace time': farmers might put them into service as tractors or threshing machines; they might be redeployed as trouser presses, or used by the post office to deliver its notoriously slow telegrams. Some post-war showman should suspend a tank in the air, attach seats to its rotating tracks, and charge sixpence a ride on the 'Tank Roundabout'.[1]

The Tank Corps had been known from the start for its 'Esprit de Tank', but its demobilised veterans really did make ingenious attempts to cash in on their redundant but still charismatic machines.[2] The *Tank Corps Journal* published a verse tribute to Major Moffat of Thames Ditton, a veteran who had placed an advertisement in *The Times*, announcing his plans to set up 'joy-ride tanks' at a seaside resort and inviting 'several Ex Tank Corps Officers or others with capital' to join him in this experimental enterprise.[3] So the tank, which in some versions is said to have been first inspired by the sight of the big wheel in Battersea Park, finally proved its affinity to the vulgar exhilarations of Weymouth Sands.

Meanwhile Army manoeuvres constituted one of the big public attractions of those post-war years, proving that tanks could be compelling even in their absence. In September 1923, when the Battle of Bindon Hill was at full heat, the Press was following manoeuvres on the chalk of the South Downs and paying particular attention to the way in which the military overcame a new 'problem in mimic warfare'.[4] It had been judged impracticable to 'introduce a real tank into the lanes and hedgerows of Sussex', so their place was taken 'by a screen almost like a piece of theatrical scenery, in the creation of which the military has displayed an unsuspected talent for decorative painting'.

These simulated tanks were silent, so the crews were 'required to create a din approximating to that of a tank in action, and for this purpose the Army supplies them with rattles and motor horns and various other noise-creating devices . . . There is thus to be seen and heard advancing over the

Downs the plain spectacle of a painted screen, borne by a party of men creating many varieties of din supplied by nature and artifice.' *The Sunday Times* admitted that the result was not at all 'like a herd of elephants', in the simile said to have been used by one tank officer as he sailed into battle during the war, but the show was energetically presented nonetheless: 'While apologetically grinning at the painted pretence, Tommy conscientiously and vociferously fulfils his instructions to sound like a tank.'

However sound he may have been on elephants, Herbert Weld had never really grasped the imaginative force of the tank. He had seen these ironclad engines only as mechanical despoilers — the very opposite of anything that might be counted patriotic or cultured. But although it was partly thanks to base economic pragmatism that the tanks held their ground at Lulworth, they also demonstrated a far more positive power of attraction. This was already evident by August 1923, when an officer at Bovington — the one who described Bindon Hill as a natural firing butt — informed the *Bournemouth Daily Echo* that holidaymakers had found the tanks at Lulworth 'an additional attraction to the natural holiday charms of the district', and that the firing range was already drawing quite a crowd: 'Recently, while a demonstration was in progress the crowd of trippers watching it became so large that two lorry loads of troops had to be sent to Lulworth from Bovington to help in forming a cordon to keep them out of danger.'[5] Herbert Weld replied bluntly that while 'a few trippers might be attracted by an occasional tank demonstration . . . the vast majority of holiday visitors would prefer that these displays should take place elsewhere'.[6] But he was to be defeated as the tank went on to establish itself as a genuinely popular tourist attraction.

By the mid-Twenties the main camp at Bovington had acquired some of the features of a true historical site. No longer just an eyesore of mud, Nissen huts and rusting hulks, 'Tintown' was starting to claim a cultural significance of its own. Most of the tanks that had been brought back from the Western Front to litter the heath at Bovington were broken up for scrap metal, but a number were identified as interesting examples for early design and set aside for preservation. By November 1919, the *Tanks Corps Journal* was describing what it called a 'Tank Museum': 'In a small railed off enclosure near the Tank Schools there is a very interesting collection of Tanks, every type being represented from the Mk.1 to the latest infantry carrier. "Little Willie", the original experimental tank, made in the early days, is also present.'[7]

Visiting Bovington in 1923, Rudyard Kipling is said to have remarked on these rusting hulks, suggesting that they should at least be housed under a roof. Soon afterwards, they were moved to an open-sided shed in the Driving and Maintenance School, which made occasional use of them as educational curiosities. By 1926, the redesignation of this collection of rescued scrap-iron was complete:

> Those who knew Bovington in 1919 and 1920 will remember the mass of derelict tanks which at that time strewed the heath around the Camp. These have mostly been converted into scrap and removed, and the heath has, in parts at least, resumed its native bleakness. There is, however, still a small patch immediately north of the Driving and Maintenance School which is reminiscent of those days. It is an area of about an acre surrounded by a broken fence, and contains the remains of some twenty-six tanks. Blackberries grow among them in profusion, and often a rabbit may be found. In wet weather it is partly a lake. This is the Tank Museum.[8]

As support grew in the villages, the tank park over at Lulworth emerged as a place of surreal dynamism where onlookers could cheer as the habituated orders of the ancient regime were affronted. Long before the Franklin Viewpoint, the tank park had become a popular roadside attraction, a fairground full of bangs and smoke set off against the static tranquillity of the deer park on the other side of Herbert Weld's wall. Here was avant-garde action and excitement rather than landscaped privacy, church and poetic contemplation of trees.

The tank park placed a rival bid for all the qualities that had previously belonged on the other side of Herbert Weld's wall. Lulworth Park could appeal to the nation's sense of heritage, but the tank would upstage it as the futuristic spirit of progress — a vanguard force blasting its way through the idylls of class power. It could be embraced as a great inconveniencer of squires, a breaker of deference, and an excellent machine for affronting self-appointed spokesmen of 'local opinion' like Mr Rayner Goddard KC.

The park might still be presented as the organic centre of the agricultural round, but the tanks added their own explosive displays to the dwindled calendar of rustic festivity. The picturesque appreciation of the Dorset coast had been set on its modern course by George III, the 'patriot king'; but, as the proudest British invention of the Great War, the new war machine had more recently also been hailed as a 'patriot tank'.[9] This had been part of Lieutenant-Colonel Broad's case for the Lulworth gunnery school at the Inquiry of 1925, when he described the tank not as a bloodthirsty monster but as 'a great saver of life', which made it possible for twenty well-trained and protected soldiers to do a job that had previously demanded two hundred far more dangerously exposed ones.[10]

The tank even commandeered the paraphernalia of the Royal Visit. King George V was Colonel-in-Chief of the Royal Tank Corps, and when he visited Bovington in April 1928 he went over to the gunnery range at Lulworth, where he watched various displays before himself donning 'the distinctive headdress of the Tank Corps', entered a tank and started blasting away at Bindon Hill.[11] Lulworth Castle once provided refuge for a frightened French monarch, but the gunnery school had its exotic foreign visitors too. In March 1928, King Amanullah and Queen Surayya of Afghanistan were welcomed to England on a state visit. Surviving film shows these remote and long-suffering monarchs proceeding through a grimly metallic England full of war machines and armament factories, with the Grand National and Greenwich Observatory thrown in for light relief.[12] King Amanullah tries out a semi-automatic rifle at the BSA factory in Birmingham. He drives a new Rolls Royce at the factory in Derby and inspects warships at Portsmouth. On 20 March, the party came to the gunnery school at Lulworth, where they watched an old Mark V Star tank crash through a bush in a primitive demonstration of cross-country versatility. The King of Afghanistan then climbed into a modern Vickers tank for a ride.

As it trailed trails of populistic glory over the slopes and heaths of Dorset, the tank founded a new fellowship of the underdog and proved that patriotism need not be tied to a patrician imagery of hedgerows, chalk and turf. Brow-beaten trippers and anti-picturesque locals alike were welcome to embrace the modernist imagery of the new Behemoth. The tank park offered a way of winning the rural class struggle by means other than those sanctioned by the progressive theorists of political emancipation. As for Mr Weld's sadly disturbed eighteenth-century park, the literatteurs of Tintown knew how to wring a joke from the conflict between the tank park and that place over the wall. One ditty in the *Tank Corps Journal*, printed a few weeks before a 'futurist' ode beginning 'Crash . . . Rattle', was called 'We'll All Go A-Tanking today'. It imagined tanks male and female coquetting like promenading paramours as they trundled around in their 'tank park', eventually falling upon each other with clanking intimacy to beget that characteristic vehicle of modern tourism, 'a Ford'.[13] A photograph from a few years later, perhaps 1928, goes even further; it shows a tank demonstrating its superior powers against the towers of a mock, but decidedly Lulworth-like, castle.

The Curse of Tutankhamun

Mr Herbert Weld could ignore much of this gathering trend as he sat in his lofty castle, studying interim reports of the evacuation he was funding at the Babylonian site of ancient Kish, or writing articles about the waters of the Blue Nile and their potential for irrigation purposes. After weighing up the likely Egyptian response to the Sudanese exploitation of the waters on which both countries depended, he suggested, with a sweep of his explorer's hand, that the best outcome would probably be to take a sizeable area of Uganda and create a 'separate administrative unit', to be governed with due Egyptian involvement.[14]

By the end of that year, however, this man, who thought nothing of rearranging Africa with a few confident strokes of the imperialist pen, had been overtaken by such a catastrophic sequence of events that, sixty years later, some of East Lulworth's village elders were still reaching into the supernatural for explanations. It was said that the castle ghost, known as 'the Grey Lady', had been much seen in those years, an omen that boded ill for the Welds, and that Herbert was the victim of the 'Curse of Tutankhamun'. This mystic phenomenon, which became something of a popular cult in the Twenties, had already placed an occult charge in the mosquito bite that finished off Lord Carnarvon, and sent a python into Howard Carter's Egyptian residence to devour his pet canary; and it now came for the archaeological squire of Lulworth on the mistaken assumption that he also had been present when Carter's expedition opened Tutankhamun's tomb in 1923.[15]

At the end of 1928 Weld's young wife Theodora suddenly fell ill and died on Christmas Eve. Stricken by this unexpected blow, the squire had other difficulties too. He had spent large amounts of money modernising the castle, restoring its furniture and fitting it with the latest in central heating, but tax and death duties were pressing. As a staunch Tory, Herbert Weld knew that Lloyd George and his Liberal government 'had the honour of being the pioneer' of the 'extortionate taxation' that had 'denuded the country of its most cherished treasures and bled agriculture white by cutting off at its source its necessary capital'.[16] And now that Stanley Baldwin's Tory government had given way to the second Labour administration of Ramsay MacDonald, he could only regret that there was 'no prospect in the future of any government action that will not be for the worse'. In April 1929, arrangements were made for Sotheby's to dispose of both the early fourteenth-century Luttrell Psalter, which the Weld trustees had deposited with the British Museum some thirty years before, and the fifteenth-century Bedford Book of Hours which was also among the most valuable heirlooms of Lulworth Castle.

This must have seemed trouble enough, but the Great War had also planted the wholly unexpected 'booby trap' into which Lulworth's retired big game hunter was to fall only three days before those famous illuminated manuscripts were due to go under the hammer on 29 July 1929. As a result of an unexpected 'legal pitfall' discovered by the British Museum's lawyers, Herbert was informed that all the heirlooms and 'chattels' in Lulworth Castle were apparently the property of Mrs Mary Angela Noyes, wife of the poet Alfred Noyes.

As Mr Weld pointed out, this outcome was the very opposite of that intended by the ancestors. In 1869, the furniture, pictures, manuscripts and books had been settled 'for the use and enjoyment of the person entitled to the hereditaments in such a way that they should always go as heirlooms with the Castle', but, as was now discovered, an old law upset this precautionary measure, demanding that the heirlooms go to the heir mentioned in the entail who first reached the age of twenty-one. The heir in question had been killed in action during the War, dying, as Herbert explained, 'with three lives between him and the enjoyment of the property'[17] and his widow, now remarried, was Mrs Alfred Noyes. Weld took his case through the courts, but his Appeal was rejected only a few hours before the sale. So he lost his heirlooms and his right to dispose of the 'chattels' in the castle — including many pieces of furniture that he claimed to have 'rescued out of old lumber rooms' and restored at a cost of thousands, only to find that they too formed part of 'the "inheritance" of Mrs Noyes'.

Colonel Sir Joseph Weld remembered an uncle telling him that Herbert could probably have come to terms with Mrs Noyes, but that this possibility was snuffed out by his 'terribly rude' sisters, who wrote 'the most disgusting letters' cursing this accidental heiress.[18] Herbert returned to Lulworth in dismay and, with the taxman pressing, instructed Savills to sell approximately a third of the Weld estate at auction: East Lulworth would be retained, but offers were to be invited on numerous cottages and farms in outlying villages like Wool, Winfrith Newburgh and East Chaldon, and great tracts of farmland reaching right up on to the downs and cliffs west of Lulworth Cove.[19]

Further catastrophe struck on the morning of Thursday, 29 August 1929. As the story goes, Weld had just finished breakfasting in the castle with his secretary and his Scottish estate manager. They may have discussed the approaching sale, reported in that very morning's edition of *The Times*. But their conversation was suddenly interrupted by a servant girl, Fanny Simons, who had looked up to see flames pouring out from a top floor window in one of the castle's towers. The neighbourhood was alerted by a footman, who rang the medieval time-bell at the top of the castle, and Weld joined his hastily arrayed estate workers in trying to confine the blaze to its source in a linen room. When the fire extinguishers ran out they formed a line up the staircase and tried pass up water in buckets, but 'the smoke was too dense and Mr Weld and those with him had to retreat'.[20]

The fire brigades arrived from Dorchester, Weymouth, Swanage and Poole, but they too were thwarted. The water, drawn from a tank under the rose garden, ran out just as the blaze had been brought under control, and fire broke through again while nearby wells were found and quickly exhausted. As a fire chief would later explain, 'every pond and pool in the district' was tried without avail. A fire engine sent down to Lulworth Cove to get sea water got stuck in a ditch, and an attempt was made to get a continuous hose up from the sea by stationing three fire engines along the road to Arish Mell Gap — a 'policy of desperation'[21] that was thwarted by low pressure and also by the fact that the different fire brigades were equipped with non-standardised hoses that could not be connected together.

So the castle burned. Two firemen were rushed to hospital in Dorchester with terrible injuries: they had suffered such a shower of red-hot lead from the collapsing roof that 'their shoulders looked as if they were wearing an extra cape of metal over their uniforms'.[22] The famous 'King's Room', which was reported to have been 'one of the most complete apartments of period furniture in the world' was destroyed early on — a reporter claimed to have stood in the hall and watched the magnificent four poster bed in which George III had slept blazing like 'a bonfire'. By the end of the day the whole building had been gutted.

All sorts of people rallied round to join the estate workers in rescuing the contested heirlooms and chattels: Roman Catholic priests, holiday-makers, and the 'whole village of East Lulworth'[23] led by Mr Doddington, who would later provide Weld with a bed for the night. Valiant assistance was also provided by thirty-six Girl Guides from Bournemouth who happened to be camping in Lulworth Park. They were reported to have distinguished themselves by bravely 'dashing in' to carry out books and 'light articles of furniture and personal belongings'.[24] As the Captain of their troops reported, 'Our girls have been absolutely splendid ... They gave chocolate to the firemen and now they are doing picket duty by the salvaged goods.'[25]

The *Daily Mirror* took an aerial photograph of the smoking castle and spread it over the entire front page, and most papers featured a picture of Herbert Weld, the distraught 78-year-old squire. There he was, from the *Daily Herald* to the *Daily Telegraph*, with his peaked yachting cap and a monocle firmly gripped in one eye. But if some papers used a library picture, left over from their coverage of Cowes, others showed the 78-year-old squire of Lulworth on the fatal day itself. *The Times* caught him seated in plüs fours on a Regency chair with rescued furniture, paintings and tapestries heaped on the grass around him, staring ahead as the blaze brought exquisite eighteenth-century ceilings crashing down on three centuries of Weld history. According to the *Western Gazette*, he stood 'a little apart from the crowd that had gathered, watching the flames enveloping the upper parts of the building, and declining to listen to those who, solicitous of his welfare, urged him to come farther away from the spray of the hose, the smoke and falling stones'.[26] The *Bournemouth Daily Echo* went further, suggesting that 'Perhaps the most pathetic sight was the lonely figure of Mr Herbert Weld, the owner, looking on resignedly at the gradual destruction of his home ... When I saw him he was standing alone ... smoking a cigarette and looking up wistfully at the belching flames and smoke.' In later paragraphs, sub-titled 'Mr Weld's Emotion', it claimed that Weld had to be 'dragged by Girl Guides from the steps of the castle up which he kept running as the flames grew greater. "My castle", he cried despairingly — 'it is ruined!" '

Driven back on to their guidebooks, the reporters claimed, repeatedly, that the house had been built in the patriotic year of 1588, and many insisted, quite wrongly, that the Welds had been there ever since. They counted up the Royal visits, and mentioned the special interest of the chapel, from which furniture and even the altar had been removed when the fire threatened to spread.[27] As a Labour paper, the *Daily Herald* was inclined to stress 'the tremendous efforts' of the fire brigades, but there was no hint of resentment in its observation that Lulworth Castle had been 'in the same family for centuries', and it infiltrated no ironic inflection into the voice of the neighbour who explained that 'People in the village are very much upset by the calamity, as Mr Weld is a deeply-loved personality. He lost his wife only a while ago.'[28] *The Dorset County Chronicle* contrasted the 'thrilling scenes' of the conflagration with the happier memory of the last big event at Lulworth Park: a grand fête, which the South Dorset Conservative and Unionist Association had held here two summers previously. 'Then the chief figures in a wonderful scene in front of the Castle were Mr Weld, a most hospitable and kindly host, and his wife, a gracious and charming hostess.'[29]

A few people in East Lulworth still remember that ruinous day. Gazing off into the middle distance, they see bedding being hurled from the upper windows, and blue and gold curtains fluttering in the smoke-filled wind. They remember the obliterated ballroom, the famous King's bed, canopied, as one recalls, to look 'like St Pauls', and bloodsoaked bandages scattered on the lawn after the injured firemen had been taken away. Some remember the fire as the 'end of a dynasty', while others report a more personal sense of loss, like the former housemaid who remarked 'I felt it was my home being burned.' One man is still a little ashamed of the 'sheer relief' with which he realised he would 'not have to deliver coal to the castle any more'.

Letters testify to the pious spirit in which the Welds sought consolation in the unknowable nature of the Lord's ways, and also to the shock felt by local estate workers. One missive, addressed in large copperplate hand to 'Mrs Weld' by a retainer called Sargeant, seems to sum up the sense of fatal ruin:

> I feel this terrible tragedy most keenly, for my whole life has been devoted to the service of the family, and I love every bit of the Estate. It is all like parting with my very own! I had intended to write a week or two ago, to offer you and young Mr Weld my deep sympathy at the most unexpected tragedy of the Heirlooms, which, with the parting with so much more of the Estate by sale, was a great sorrow to me, and now comes this further crushing blow! I feel deeply for you and all the family — poor Mr Herbert Weld — it is too tragic for

> words . . . We have frequently said in the office that by the time young Mr Weld succeeded there would be nothing left but the Mansion and contents and now even these have gone![30]

There is no evidence to suggest that the fire had any cause other than the one Herbert Weld offered the *Daily Mail*: 'I think that an electric light wire fused. For many years the castle had had its own supply.'[31] But the elderly squire had suffered an extraordinary coincidence of disasters, and it is hardly surprising that the memory of the fire is still attended by rumour. One since-retired worker in the castle's restoration expressed the suspicion he shared with his colleagues: 'Weldy probably set fire to it,' he opined, adding that Tory squires were more or less above the law in those days, and he must have needed the insurance money. Colonel Sir Joseph Weld, who was to inherit the estate on Herbert's death, would give no quarter to this scurrilous idea, but he remembered being told that the insurance assessor who worked on the Lulworth claim (and who was said to have been on the scene surprisingly soon after the fire broke out) was in later years sentenced to the maximum term for fire-raising offences committed in league with the corrupt head of the London Fire Brigade. Colonel Sir Joseph added that the castle had been seriously underinsured, for £37,000, as he remembered, while the lowest estimate for its restoration came to £120,000. So the money was used to pay off other debts.

Tanks in the Park

It was on the day Herbert Weld's castle burned that the tanks made their triumphant entrance into Lulworth Park. Weld had wasted no time alerting the fire brigades of South Dorset by telephone, but the Royal Tank Corps also received a call for urgent assistance. The detachment of fourteen men, who hurried round from the gunnery school, included the man who was then chief gunnery instructor, Colonel Carter, and also Major Darwell. *The Universe*, a Catholic paper, was pleased to see these black-bereted men working in co-operation with the Girl Guides. 'With flames raging around them, the men threw books from the library shelves out of the window, and the girls carried them away to safety.'[32] The pictorial Press also gave prominence to these tank soldiers. Not content with printing a photo of two black-bereted soldiers standing guard over salvaged valuables on the lawn, the *Illustrated London News* also featured the armoured car in which they had arrived — a swart, large-wheeled metal machine parked on the grass in front of the smoking castle.[33] *The Graphic* miscaptioned its picture, describing the vehicle as 'a tank'.[34] Like the Girl Guides, the tank men were later commended by the head of the Dorchester fire brigade. It is reasonable to assume they were also included in the profuse thanks that Herbert Weld extended to all his helpers through the local papers.

As that emblematic picture demonstrated, the Royal Tank Corps had finally penetrated the deer park; and on Saturday, 31 August, Mr Weld had further reason to be grateful to its soldiers as they joined him in defending his gutted castle against a horde of invading trippers. It had been bad enough on the day of the fire, when crowds had turned up to watch the disaster. The *Bournemouth Daily Echo*'s reporter had declared 'the scene now is one that would impress a cinema audience': sightseers had come from all over the district, and hundreds of cars and motor-cycles were parked in the immediate vicinity of the castle. These uninvited spectators stood 'gazing in silent and sympathetic wonder', finding the heat so intense that many were reported to have discarded their outer garments. By the weekend the castle had been wired off behind 'Danger' signs, partly on account of the still unopened strong room exposed at its centre, but the sightseers came rushing back in even greater numbers.

Herbert Weld had retreated to London, leaving his abandoned castle in the hands of the Royal Tank Corps, which placed sentries at all the entrances to Lulworth Park, and also at the various houses, inns and village halls into which the salvaged valuables had been crammed. These guards refused entry to the gawping masses, and evicted the considerable number who scaled the park wall in order to catch a glimpse of the smouldering ruins. Mr Weld's miseries can scarcely have been mitigated by the reminder, provided by a correspondent to *The Times*, that Gainsborough had visited Lulworth Castle on one of his sketching tours and 'found inspiration in its neighbourhood for one of the best known of his landscapes', namely 'The Market Cart'.[35]

The disputed heirlooms and 'chattels' had been burned free of any obligation, legal or otherwise, that might tie them to Lulworth Castle, and more sales were to follow as Mrs Noyes exercised her claim — including one in which the Welds of Lulworth felt it wise to employ an anonymous agent to buy back certain ancestral portraits 'as the Noyes were certain to be there and would run us up if they saw a member of the family bidding'.[36]

Herbert Weld's aggrieved account of his fate, published in *Country Life*, drew counterfire from a distant relation who, as one of Mrs Alfred Noyes's trustees, was plainly incensed by his claim that Lulworth Castle had been 'stripped' of its treasures and furnitures: 'Discussion of personal affairs in the Press would, I am sure, be as distasteful to my cousin, Mr Herbert Weld, as to myself.'[37]

'It will be bad if it is left to bide,' so one old villager had remarked of the ruin; but Weld was not a man to give up easily. When full-scale restoration proved impractical, he scaled down his plans and tried to have an apartment built for himself in the relatively undamaged basement rooms beneath the castle terrace. He is said to have spent some £3,000 having a new floor laid and fitting the place out with fireplaces and doors, so there was never any question of his 'kennelling' in those dark rooms like the 'worthless Arabs' he had once seen squatting in forgotten ancient Greek tombs in the Cyrene. But this scheme came to nothing too. The builders had tried to stop the rain leaking into this opulent bunker but no amount of pitch would do the job: Herbert reputedly stepped into several inches of water on his first visit, and promptly went off to rent himself a house in West Lulworth. From there, he carried on with plans to increase the sorely taxed Weld estate's income from the holiday trade. He opened fee-charging public lavatories and, in 1930, installed the never less than hugely profitable car park above Lulworth Cove.[38] He ran a lucrative double trade down at Arish Mell Gap — opening it to visitors who probably didn't even notice that he was also selling off the scenic shingle to builders by the truckload.

Lulworth Park declined gently through the Thirties. Many estate workers lost their jobs at this time and moved on, sometimes with considerable bitterness; and the park lost much of its well-tended grandeur. Peacocks still wandered about, but many of the more opulent features — the great walks and wooded vistas, the richly flowered lawns — were in decline by July 1939, when the Dorset Federation of Women's Institutes mounted an ambitious historical pageant in Lulworth Park. 'The Spirit of Dorset', which reads like a dramatised Wessex variant of *Puck of Pooks Hill*, was enacted on the tree-lined lawns behind the ruined castle, and Thomas Weld's chapel was incorporated as a charming background feature.[39]

Set in a Celtic hilltop village the most revealing episode showed the subjection of Celtic Dorset by Vespasian's Roman forces. It opened with a pastoral view of Durotrigean women spinning, scraping hides and potting while their men stand about slinging stones. Two huntsmen then enter with a stag, which is placed on the village altar stone and dedicated by a Druid to the 'Great Ones'. The men dance round the altar stone, and a procession of girls carries branches of may through the scene; but this archaic idyll collapses as the Roman assault begins. As true Dorset men, the Durotriges would never have surrendered were it not for a low act of treachery, but their chief is slain, and the invaders enter the fort to offer the 'men of this Downland' the prosperity that only the Roman state can bring: 'Submit yourselves, and live, free men.' The Druid kneels to pick up a handful of native Dorset earth, which he hands to the Roman General in a gesture of submission. Speaking as one true Dorset man to another, the Roman General insists on honouring the British dead; indeed, in a magnanimous gesture, informed like the rest of this episode by Sir Mortimer Wheeler's recent discoveries at Maiden Castle, he urges the survivors to 'Take up your brave dead and bury them beside the gate they have so gallantly defended.'

The pageant was acted by locals organised through Dorset's various Women's Institutes – except, that is, for the victorious Roman soldiers, who were kindly provided by the Commanding Officer of the Lulworth gunnery school. The script leaves no doubt those Romans would eventually be seen to have conquered Old England for the better; and, with the Second World War only a few weeks away, who was to say anything else of the Royal Tank Corps soldiers who played them? By that time, the Lulworth gunnery school was on a new lease, dated from Christmas Day 1937 and extending for ninety-nine years.

PART THREE

Metal in the Turf: Three Improving Futures for a Lost Downland Valley (1930–42)

Gold is for the mistress — silver for the maid — Copper for the craftsman cunning at his trade. 'Good!' said the Baron, sitting in his hall, But Iron — Cold Iron — is master of them all.

Rudyard Kipling[1]

The grass will grow green with the returning Spring, the machines will rust and crumble into dust ...

Rolf Gardiner[2]

TEN

BACK TO THE STONE AGE

> To us the purity of the Downs, the 'chain of pearls', is everything; but others are already fashioned by the human mart into another way of seeing . . .
>
> Edmund Blunden (1931)

THE ARCHAEOLOGISTS WORKING on Herbert Weld's excavation of the Mesopotamian site of ancient Kish spent the amenable seasons of ten years 'digging through legend' to expose 'the very origins of human civilisation'.[3] They found a thick layer of alluvial silt, which they recognised as 'the Flood Stratum' even while remaining resolutely unconvinced by the archaic stories of the Deluge, said to have put an end to a mythical age in which God-like rulers lived for 900 or even 1,500 years. Their records have since been regretted as chaotic, but Fleet Street watched with keen interest as they dug into ancient temples and ziggurats, one of which turned out to have been refaced in the time of Nebuchadnezzar. As for the human burials, it was observed that, in accordance with ancient Sumerian custom, the body would normally be placed 'on its side with knees drawn up and one hand supporting the head'.

This discovery must have prepared Herbert Weld for the unusual request that came from of one of his tenants in the summer of 1933. Albert Reginald Powys, secretary of the Society for the Protection of Ancient Buildings, approached Weld on behalf of his brother Llewelyn, an epicurean writer and philosopher who rented the remote farm cottage he called Chydyok, high up on the downs west of Lulworth Cove. Llewelyn was apparently dying of tuberculosis and wanted his 82-year-old squire's permission to be buried on the downs, knees to chin in the prehistoric position.[4]

'Oh yes, Llewelyn,' say the elders of East Lulworth, taking evident pleasure in the now rarely visited memory of this unusual man. He was 'eccentric', and not always loquacious at a passing encounter, but a fine fellow nevertheless, who could be met walking out on the downs wrapped in a great cloak, and wearing an ancient Egyptian emblem around his neck.

They remember his wife, the American writer and early feminist Alyse Gregory whom Powys had met in Greenwich Village and brought to the Dorset downs from her job as managing editor of the influential literary magazine *The Dial*. There were his sisters too: Gertrude, who also lived at Chydyok, and Philippa, or 'Katie' as she was known, who was a bit of a 'boozer', but no real sin in that. Then there was Gamel Woolsey, an enigmatic young woman, also suffering from tuberculosis, from the American south. She was Llewelyn's downland lover, his muse and holy woman. The pair are said to have made vows to the moon,[5] and there were passionate meetings at ancient crossroads like Burngate or Daggers Gate on the prehistoric track between Powys's cottage at Chydyok and East Lulworth where Woolsey and her husband Gerald Brenan rented the little cottage adjoining the Weld Arms.[6] But it is not for cosmic sex or the imaginary 'Middle Earth' of her poetry that the elders remember Woolsey. Looking back across the yawning social distances, they associate her only with toasting forks — wire things with a Lulworth-like castle at the end, which one villager, Jack Scutt, remembers selling for her from his position as car-park attendant on the road down to Arish Mell Gap.

Herbert Weld had his trippers and his unwanted tanks. Yet there was another constituency on his depressed estate, renting buildings that were now surplus to the requirements of dwindling pastoral agriculture, or buying them at the none too successful sales in which he tried to dispose of holdings at the edges of his estate. These people — members or affiliates of what came to be known as the Powys circle[7] — were busily establishing not just a philosophy on his neglected downs, but also a literature, a politics, and even a foreign policy of sorts.

The most revealing path to Tyneham is by no means the quickest. It sets off in what any competent map-reader would swear was entirely the wrong direction and winds its way through this strangely colonised country. We can do without the camels, horses and native bearers that Herbert Weld took on his African forays, but we do need a guide: a man who walks the green roads with an old English sheepdog called Friday, respectfully introduced as 'a union by grace of the wild with the domestic'.[8]

H. J. Massingham was well known in the mid-Thirties as a prolific chronicler of England's dying countryside. He loved Wessex as 'a haunted land, magical, mysterious, indefinable' and counted Dorset the 'peremptory shire' within that marvellous kingdom.[9] So potent was its ancient landscape that he could sense 'the invisible presences' hovering 'even at Lulworth, whither trippers countless have tripped'. As a self-confessed 'purist in chalk', Massingham had long reckoned that 'in all England there are no hills more individual, more truly shaped according to each its own, powerful nature, and yet so comforting to the human spirit as the Dorset uplands'.[10] Like Kipling in Sussex, he marvelled to see those democratic hills 'sporting like primal whales, dolphins and behemoths in the flood of creation', describing Dorset's downland scene as 'a canvas that some medieval artist might have taken for his original in depicting the first world-thought of God'.

One 'ghostly evening' in the mid-Thirties, Massingham walked along 'the grassy and long silent road' that follows the spine of Bindon Hill, and then halted at its 'lofty edge' to gaze out over Arish Mell Gap. It was at this vantage point that I had come across the botanising members of the Dorset Natural History and Archaeological Society in 1989; and it pleased Massingham, nearly sixty years earlier, to sit there enjoying 'the positive emotion of repose' associated with 'these silent, ancient places'.[11] It is likely that the archaic earthworks set him thinking about the long duration of time against which the span of an individual life seems, as he had felt ten years earlier when reclining on the ramparts of Maiden Castle, as fleeting as 'the shadows of the rooks on the Downland turf'.

That 'scented turf' is tough and practical stuff, the delicacy of its flowers only matched by their ability to resist a tearing wind. Yet for many members of the generation that came through the Great War, to walk on it was to tread the ground of utopia itself. In 1923, W. H. Hudson had described this downland turf as 'the divine Mother's green garment',[12] but others went further, sowing it with poetic blossoms that today's scientific conservationists would hardly tolerate in their grassland management programmes. For F. J. Harvey Darton, the flowers were like stars and the snail shells like 'jewels from Aladdin's cave': walking along the chalk ridge above Tyneham, he had delighted in the 'eternal green' and felt it to be 'part of a world in which, to a Radical, Conservatism may well appear the creed of Utopia, rather than the abhorred dogma of the Primrose League'.[13]

Massingham also sensed special qualities in this 'high sweet turfen land'.[14] That springy, herb-rich turf was what generations of grazing and fertilising sheep had made of scrub, and it offered living testimony to a traditional husbandry faced with extinction in a fast mechanising world. Massingham could have held his own in the grass-telling company of the Dorset Natural History and Archaeological Society. Yet, for him, to count the flowers on a Dorset down was not 'a cataloguer's pride, but a sort of bead-telling in sun-worship';[15] shunning Latin pedantry, he preferred to press old vernacular names back into the forsaken English turf.

The signs of tank gunnery must have surrounded Massingham as he sat on the edge of Bindon Hill, but he too kept his back turned and his eye on the 'Titanic bluffs' of a coastline that was surely unmatched by 'any other littoral in England'.[16] The view out over Arish Mell and Worbarrow Bay became nationally famous in the Thirties. It served as a setting for A. E. W. Mason's romantic Armada novel *Fire Over England* (1936), and its photograph would adorn the endpapers of *Britain and the Beast*, a rousing defence of the threatened countryside in which Massingham joined ranks with the likes of the architect and former tank officer Clough Williams-Ellis, J. M. Keynes and E. M. Forster, who denounced the Army's red flags as so many lolling 'tongues of blood' and condemned the Tank Corps for 'the ruining of the land near Lulworth Cove'.[17] As the light faded, Massingham witnessed a startling 'scene of interpenetrated elements' in which the world seemed to revert to its own moment of creation. The great limestone headlands began to resemble 'a bank of storm-cloud' and the ocean stretched out 'ineffably calm' until 'its substance was gossamer, a carpet of evenly spread cloud-vapour'. Before long, land, sea and sky could hardly be told one from each other; everything had become ethereal.

Lifting up the Downs

One day in May, shortly after that revelatory moment of 'transparency', Massingham returned to visit his friend Llewelyn Powys in his remote cottage.[18] Parking their car at the old crossroads known as Dagger's Gate, he and his wife struck out along 'the old Bronze Age Way', a white road that 'undulated like a living thing' through downs of 'vivid green'. He remarked on the numberless daisies that starred the track, so that 'it flows white, a milky way among the green curves of a highland shaped like the cumulus clouds above it'; and he praised the gorse, which seemed 'lifted full into the heaven's eye', where it 'glittered and almost crackled with its sun-colour'. There were surely 'no downs in England more at home with infinite space than these'.

As he walked — his wife Penelope remembers counting the telegraph poles for orientation — Massingham was engaged in the romantic practice he once called 'Downland travelling'.[19] This distinctive period activity involved glorying in such relics and ancient potencies as remained on the chalk downs, but it also implied fierce opposition to the modern world. To walk away from Bindon Hill with Massingham is not to escape the local contest between tanks and the threatened beauty spot, but rather to find it amplified into a massive polarisation that threatens to engulf all humanity.

Massingham deplored the modern cult of the picturesque as 'a giant worm trailing its slime over the counties of England'.[20] People like William Gilpin, who promoted the picturesque at 'the fag-end of the eighteenth century', may have started the job, but for Massingham it was the Victorians who finally 'hacked apart' beauty and utility, leaving only the foul industrial cities and a broken countryside now used as 'an antidote to the squalor of practical urbanism'. In place of the populous and unenclosed countryside of traditional agriculture, where beauty had been an 'inevitable by-product of common use', came 'the country as scenery' and so much else that Massingham hated to see served up in the name of English heritage: 'the plush, the fancy embroidery, the sugared yarns, the Dorothy Perkins nooks and Birket Fosterish bowers'. Thanks to this poisonous cult, the working countryman had become a 'quaint' relic, his serviceable tools mere 'bygones'. Like J. F. Pennie, Massingham was dismayed to think that 'the festivities are over'.[21]

If dislike for the dead hand of the picturesque drove this 'downland traveller' up on to the unprettified chalk, where the signs of an 'antique dance between man and nature' were still written in the turf,[22] it also gave him a singular ability to find great heights where others would hardly see them. Stepping out along Herbert Weld's 'hedgeless no-man's-land',[23] Massingham saw the mid-Dorset chalk ridge running parallel to the north. To most eyes, this would appear low-lying and far off on the horizon, but Massingham described it as 'towering'[24] as if it were some vast Abyssinian plateau rising up to dominate the scene. So insistent was he on the loftiness of England's chalk downland, that he mounted a stout defence of Gilbert White, who had described the Sussex downs as a 'chain of majestic mountains', against doubters who kept insisting that, at their highest point, they didn't even reach 1000 feet above sea level.[25]

Perhaps the downs seemed larger before the tractor conquered all agricultural distance, but there is a pastoral convention at work here too. At his most formulaic, J. F. Pennie had described the rounded chalk ridge of the Purbeck Hills as 'that lofty range of mountains'; and Hardy's fine poem of the 1890s, 'Wessex Heights', also proclaims the downs as high places for 'thinking, dreaming, dying on', where a man could escape the 'mind-chains' of society's dreary vale. But Massingham gave this conventional loftiness a uniquely twentieth-century significance. He started by mustering topographical arguments in support of his claim that England's chalk downland should be granted 'the status of mountains': its 'repetition of like forms' created an 'illusion of infinite distance'; and its 'sweeps, bluffs and unencumbered folds' echoed the shape of cumulus clouds to such an extent that 'in summer the skies are a translated downs in white and blue'. Above the clutter of ordinary detail, the downland traveller was occupied only with essentials: 'Aloft, he breathes an air that tunes him to the grand, archaic, naked form of things'.[26]

Yet the decisive factor that made such a high country of England's chalk downland was different again. For twenty centuries this country had been 'the principal home of prehistorical man', and Massingham valued it as a 'palimpsest'. As he wandered the ancient green roads of England, he would read 'the turfscript of these abandoned downs',[27] convinced that the ancients could achieve a kind of 'vicarious life in us through the witchcraft of the Downland air and the pulse-stirring adventure of hunting them out'.[28] The old walks were 'to be translated as an inventory of homesteads, cattle-pens, open grazing grounds, cultivated fields and communication with the great highway between Wiltshire and Devon farther north'. As for the barrows, lynchets and tumuli, Massingham thought of them as 'the stepping-stones of the gods' or, ten years later, as 'a kind of Jacob's Ladder between Heaven and Earth'.[29]

So Massingham set about heightening Herbert Weld's 'sacred mountains', steepening their sides and raising them away not just from the local vulgarity of Lulworth Cove — for Massingham had more serious enemies than would allow for much trivial snobbery — but from the whole 'mechanised' civilisation governing the 'valley of lamentation' below. As he walked along the barely inclined track from Dagger's Gate, Massingham was actually scaling the allegorical alp he knew as Degeneration.[30] The Victorians may have argued, with Darwinian confidence, that the history of humankind followed an evolutionary progression from savagery to civilisation, but Massingham set his 'steep gradient' in the opposite direction, convinced that megalithic man, far from being a 'raging beast' who stood in dire need of civilisation, had actually been peaceable and far more in tune with the benign essence of human nature. Once he had made the ascent into 'skywedded' barrowland, he looked back through more recent civilisations — Celtic, Roman, Saxon, Norman or modern industrial — and knew that the road of 'progress' had run 'downhill all the way'.[31]

Massingham used diverse sources to reconstruct the good life once lived on Herbert Weld's chalk uplands. As a culturalist who believed in 'the psychic unity of mankind', he was contemptuous of racialist theorising and drew his picture of the archaic culture from 'primitive' peoples who survived in remote corners of the world: the 'hairy Anu' of Japan, or the apricot-growing Hunzas who still practised terrace agriculture in their high valleys near the North West Frontier. He dug deep into the archaeological records, even citing the findings of Herbert Weld's expedition to Kish to indicate the artistic superiority of the ancient megalithic culture.[32] 'The morning of the world' had left its gleaming shards in Dorset too. Massingham looked at the ancient chalk figure of the Cerne Giant, looming over the village of Cerne Abbas with vast phallus and mighty club, and knew him to be a sun-worshipping megalithic man. Staying at a remote farm near Bridport, he was enthralled to discover that some Dorset folk still followed 'the amazing custom of the couvade, or of putting the husband to bed when the wife bore a child': 'the goodman's wife (a very pretty and intelligent woman) told me that her husband always fell sick when she bore a child ... and, what is more always would'.[33]

Massingham would cite many learned tomes in support of his hunches, but he preferred the evidence of his own romantic eyes. Convinced that the archaic culture had given near perfect realisation to the unchanging 'matrix of humanity', he felt that there was no better way of penetrating its mysteries than to visit the ancient sites and attune yourself to their vibrations: 'Trust your eyes,' he wrote, 'take no books on your journey.'[34]

For this English shaman, the ancient Egyptian connection was plain to see: 'One has really only to run to over the artificial hill of Silbury, near Avebury to exclaim, "An Egyptian pyramid in earth".'[35] And that, really, was the nub of Massingham's early analysis: the megalithic sites on the chalk downland were the works of 'Ancient Mariners', who had come from Ancient Egypt via Minoan Crete. Massingham imagined the 'votaries' of this flint-hunting people entering Britain through the 'little bays and coves of this elysian coast' — places like Lulworth Cove and Arish Mell. He only had to wander those downs to know that the colonists had concentrated their settlements there for 'the sheer pleasure of dwelling on them ... I believe the ancients occupied the highlands of Dorset because they liked them.'

And yet Massingham also sensed disaster as he walked away from the tanks on Bindon Hill. 'Something happened,' as he remarked: 'a very sharp break indeed, the sharpest break, or, to use a biological term, "mutation" that has ever occurred in human affairs .. Nature and Man were living happily together, and then suddenly, without any forecast or portent of the great change, nature appears as the servant of man, and on her placid Downs were revealed the effects in earth and stone of this new commerce between them.'[36]

This catastrophe, which Massingham was inclined to treat as the basis for the myth of Lucifer's fall, cast people down from that angelic life in 'the starry gardens'. The 'instantaneous break' followed the ripening of seeds of destruction within the archaic culture. Increasing involvement in agriculture and mining led to the emergence of property and wealth, and, before long, a ruling class. Slavery and human sacrifice provided these pacific people with a bloodthirsty 'education in warfare'. The sun-god was transformed into a war-god according to the new precepts of metal and war; and 'the Earthly Paradise declined into El Dorado'.[37] The task of civilisation should have been to 'remove encumbrances from the living spirit of man'; but the shoddy twist of Degeneration was woven into its fabric: 'What civilisation has done for us is to open up a crowded paradise of possibilities for the perfect society and the "good life" of each member of it. What we have done with our heritage is crystallize those primary flaws of machinery and adjustment that accompanied its distribution.'[38]

The path up on to the chalk downs from Daggers Gate is now a well signposted stretch of the Dorset Heritage Coast on which the walker will encounter pleasantly whimsical sculptures, placed by the environmentalist organisation Common Ground, but for Massingham it was the high road to Avalon. He was satisfied that the Merlin of Arthurian legend was probably a wise man of the archaic culture, perhaps even the founder of Stonehenge;[39] and he sensed the memory of his sadly broken megalithic way of life in the persistent mythology of the Golden Age, where 'poetic imagination' was reconciled with 'historical fact'. It had been there in Hesiod, and it broke through again in the 'noble savage' of Jean Jacques Rousseau, who turned the Golden Age into 'an instrument of liberation', thereby preparing the ground for the French Revolution, with its goals of equality, liberty and fraternity.[40] It was kept alive by other visionary 'teachers of humanity' like Blake, Shelley and Robert Owen, the founder of Socialism. It takes considerable effort of imagination to see this now, when so many of the nation's prehistoric residues survive only as pathetic island relics in the midst of vast prairie-like fields; but in the Twenties and Thirties, they still had the strength to issue an uncompromising indictment of modern civilisation. People gazed out over the turf rings of Eggardon or Flowers Barrow; and they knew that life could be otherwise. As the leading philosopher of this downland tendency, H. J. Massingham wrote, 'the supreme value of the Golden Age as an idea is the historical justification it gives to a totally different conception of life from those already prevalent'.[41]

The Tank Enters Prehistory

Massingham's hymn of praise to Downland Man was founded on a 'diffusionist' idea of prehistoric culture that now stands discredited in archaeological circles. But his poetic invocation of the downs also had a contemporary meaning. This traveller, who wandered through one violently extinguished 'Camp of Peace' after another, was himself the survivor of a war that had, as he would later remember, 'virtually exterminated his generation'.[42] Such is the real measure of the symbolic height he granted to the Dorset downs. As he walked up from Daggers Gate, Massingham was climbing the precipice that divided the high aspirations of his generation from the mud of the infernal trenches in which so many of them had died.

F. J. Harvey Darton met the terrible 'marches' of the Great War, by writing *The Marches of Wessex* ('What is Peace? I have tried to imagine some of its chapters, as they may still be read in broken letters in a few places in one English county'),[43] but Massingham's response was more comprehensive than this. He believed that 'our social life and our human values are threatened with the same cataclysm that overwhelmed the ancient world', and he was quite explicit about the advance of war into the modern age: 'the spear has become the bomb, the bronze dagger the bayonet, while the savage feud has progressed onwards and upwards to the shock of lacerated millions'.[44]

Massingham hurled the example of his archaic 'society organised on the basis of peace'[45] against the warrior leaders of his own time. Written only a few years after the war, his article 'Maiden Castle; A Theory of Peace in

Ancient Britain' is prefaced with two epigrams quoted with undisguised contempt from contemporary politicians. In the first, the Tory Lord Birkenhead pooh-poohs those who hoped the League of Nations might secure peace, saying that 'human nature is combative' and 'rewards stout hearts and sharp swords'. In the second, the Labour MP, Dr Haden Guest, tells the House of Commons that 'there was no antithesis between war and peace because there never had been in the world as yet a real condition of peace'.[46] In a 'metallic age', so Massingham had written in 1918, 'thought must seem to be hard and flat'.[47] With its 'Camps of Peace' undefiled by war-profiteers or the dehumanising institutions of centralised power, his prehistoric Golden Age was a tribute cut out of chalk and flint and offered as an alternative to the official war memorials of the victorious State.

Before the Great War, Massingham was associated with the *New Age*, a journal known for its anti-Fabian 'guild socialism'; and he considered the violent mutation that brought his archaic megalithic culture tumbling down to have been of the same order as the catastrophe that had 'virtually exterminated' his generation.[48] The nomadic predators who sacked the hilltop settlements anticipated the marauding 'man of action' Massingham saw in the modern business man.[49] Their opportunistic eye for wealth placed these rapacious accumulators among the forerunners of 'usury', the Biblical offence that Massingham, writing in the last year of the Great War, defined as 'the sin of buying cheap to sell dear ... of self-interest as the ruling motive of the social life'. The metallic innovators of the Bronze and Iron Ages anticipated both 'the iron claw of industrialism' that had gripped the western world since then, and the subsequent triumph of militarism — equally dependent on 'the quantitative standard of accumulation, the distinction between the process and the fruits of wealth', which had 'plunged us all into this unspeakable misery'.[50] Theirs was the expropriating initiative that the founders of modern Britain had merely reiterated: 'Dutch William, who sold his purse to the Bank of England, the great lords of the Enclosures, the Victorian frock-coats headed by Adam Smith, Malthus, Cobden and Darwin'.[51]

Those early predators cleared the path for centralised power — the story of which was, for this Guild Socialist, never better than 'a tale told by a State idiot'.[52] After the sacking of Massingham's Arcadia, it was only a matter of time before an idea of 'Mechanical "evolution" ' would be 'misapplied to human life' to produce the theory of progress driving western civilisation relentlessly towards its own death.[53]

Since the cataclysm that destroyed the Golden Age was so closely connected to the Great War, it is not surprising that the peace-loving communitarians of Massingham's megalithic culture should display all the best qualities of Edwardian Guild Socialists. Their primitive communism had never degenerated into a 'mechanical officialism' that wanted only to 'rearrange and redistribute the mechanism of life upon its existing basis',[54] and neither had it taken the Fabian turn 'from the contemplation of human values at odds with existing institutions to the idealisation of the most powerful and the least human of institutions — the idolatry of the State'.[55] The hilltop settlements represented an archaic federation of independent producers: 'little townships and communities' of the sort that, during the last years of the Great War, Massingham was drawing from the vision of William Morris. Self-sufficient, producing and owning their own resources, threaded together by 'itinerant bands of players', their world proved that 'the intensity of local life, character and art need never harden into prejudice and exclusiveness', just as long as there was 'toing and froing' along those ancient green roads to keep them 'aerated with new ideas'.[56]

These sun-worshipping primitives enjoyed a personal freedom remarkably like that advocated by D. H. Lawrence, whom Massingham met and admired; and they probably wore sandals too. They lived in pleasurable harmony with nature and were untroubled by 'state coercion' or military conscription, which 'mechanically simplifies human variety'. They lived close to 'the concrete realities of life' and may even have watched birds as Massingham himself learned to do immediately after the war — seeing them as marvellous bundles of world and thought, and finding reintegration in their quiet observation.[57]

Their culture had not been divided by modern specialisation or the kind of aestheticism that Massingham associated not just with mannered art, but with military men who thought in terms of 'technical contrivance and design and who do not see flesh and blood in flanks and salients'. Little is known about the language of this happy megalithic folk, but it will have been an accented and common speech of the kind that Massingham yearned for now that dialect was dying and 'even children and farm labourers patter the verbal imperialisms' of commerce, centralised Press and State.[58] Their conception of art may not have included 'cutting out a frock' or 'hoeing a potato patch', as the young Massingham dreamed the reconnected art of his time might do, but it was certainly born of 'the practical uses and spiritual needs of the community' and expressive of 'men's and women's wonder, satisfaction in and apprehension of the miracle of daily life, life shared and life experienced'.[59]

Massingham preferred not to acknowledge the tanks on Bindon Hill, but his books are crawling with tanks even when he doesn't name them. Their phantom is evoked every time he denounces the 'metallic' form of civilisation that he saw advancing unstoppably to crush every human resistance;[60] and whenever he regrets that modern civilisation had substituted 'the belief in the perfectibility of machines' for a prior 'belief in the perfectibility of man'.[61] It is there when he deplores H. G. Wells, often hailed as the first Futurist dreamer of the tank, as an exemplary thinker of the 'Machine Age'; and again when he denounces the whole compact of industrialism, State centralisation and usury that had caused the Great War as 'the metal Juggernaut whose fuel is human blood'.[62]

As a downland traveller of the twentieth century, Massingham had learned to tell the difference between a stooping hawk and a mechanical killing machine:

> a battleship, a tank, are hideous, however ingeniously made, because their purpose is purely wasteful and destructive. They represent the energy of the community spilled over into a sombrely unproductive end. A hawk, who is also a killing machine, is fierce, but neither ugly nor cruel, because to kill is a necessity of his existence. And I think it is a safe axiom that necessity, provided it really be necessity (there's the rub), is neither ugly nor cruel.[63]

At Stonehenge, he had seen 'Tanks, rows of sheds roofed with corrugated iron, a snowstorm of tents, aerodromes and other warty growths, expressing what Mr Robert Graves calls "the military art" ';[64] and he regretted that the 'improvised encampment' of his age would leave no relics to future archaeologists except corrugated iron.[65] But then he surveyed the barbed wire that made Stonehenge look like a 'super-shell dump',[66] and found it grimly appropriate that this pre-eminent stretch of downland should be 'kidnapped into military bondage'.[67] Being later than Avebury, Stonehenge was the work of a megalithic culture already in decline. Recent excavations suggested it had been used as a site of human sacrifice and, since war was the child of that degenerate aberration, Massingham concluded that the great stone circle actually stood to the military hardware around it in the relationship of 'father to son'. Similar things might have been said about the tanks at Bindon Hill, fortified as a 'beach-head' by early Iron

Age settlers in the fifth century BC. But though he did once call Bovington Camp a disfiguring rash,[68] Massingham felt no need to mention the tanks at Lulworth Gunnery School. He had already built their metal into his theory of the broken English downs.

Dorset's Last Megalithic Man

We may reasonably imagine our downland traveller touched by despondency as he approached the flint cottage of Llewelyn Powys. Horrified by the thought of a mechanised civilisation in which the individual was 'drowned' in the centrally directed 'mass-mind',[69] he was only a little consoled to know that a few people still held out against the alienating tide.

Massingham's own list of surviving megalithic spirits included W. H. Hudson, the author of *Nature in Downland*, whom he found living in Bayswater, but still recognised as 'purely primitive ... he came into our midst out of what existed before civilisation was'.[70] He found the same archaic qualities in the doomed craftsmen and countrymen who lingered on from pre-industrial England: the husbandmen whose redundant tools he collected into his 'hermitage', and whose passing he never ceased to lament.[71] It is unlikely that the old land labourers with whom he used to play shove ha'penny in the local pub would have thanked him for comparing them with the 'primitives who roamed the earth for a hundred thousand years without taking a single step into the foreign country of civilisation',[72] but Massingham meant only tribute when he described them as 'the last of the primitive stock which owns nothing of England and yet is more English than all her sons'.

Llewelyn Powys, however, was surely the greatest of these survivors. No sooner had Massingham finally arrived at the isolated house called Chydyok, than he fell into animated conversation with this extraordinary man 'whom illness had struck down to be the hermit of this wilderness'.[73] He watched as, with 'emaciated arms', Powys removed 'flint implements he had picked up on the downs from their cabinet'; and expounded on them — scrapers, celts and arrow heads — with eyes burning in his bearded face 'like the gorse on the hillside'. Such had been this man's heroic struggle for life that his face was 'as worn as the sea-cliffs, but as brilliant as I had seen them in the sun'. His enveloping quietness seemed to share in the primal force of the waves tearing at the shingle below Bats Head and in the energy that streamed down in 'the gilded bolts of the sun'.

Never before had Massingham known a man whose nature was so attuned to the land where he lived. It was hard to put a name on this evident genius, but Massingham knew it was not what would ordinarily be expected in the son of a rector from Somerset. He sensed it as 'an element estranging, elf-like and a little feral and inhuman, a queer, wild, Pagan streak altogether vanished from the world'. Powys was 'the pard-like spirit of the elemental scenes', laid low by deathly sickness, but still equipped with 'primeval intensity of mind and sense'. Sitting in that little cottage with Powys, his wife Alyse Gregory and his sister Gertrude, Massingham felt that: 'The cosmos was their matrix, and as I had witnessed on Bindon, the material frame of the world dissolved into a dream, so I became aware of three human beings in whom dwelt its immortal essence.'

Llewelyn Powys was certainly given to megalithic gestures, and his repertoire extended far beyond the diet of fruit, nuts, milk and vegetables he derived from Reddie Mallet's book *Nature's Remedy or Nature's Cure*. In his Dorset, the moon hung like a sudden lantern over Flowers Barrow, and there were ancient sites which, especially if visited at midnight, had the power to 'break the bondage of cowardly thought'.[74] Until prevented by ill-health, Powys had walked out across a field of mangel-wurzels to sleep on the overgrown bank of a prehistoric 'boma' or cattle-pound near his house. Convinced that, with the exception of the odd shepherd, he was 'the first human being to lie here since neolithic days', he would gaze into the starry void, feel the sun and moon reasserting 'the ancient God-like influences' they had lost in the modern world, and 'experience intimations of the nature and scope of man's future'.[75]

For Llewelyn Powys the cliffs and downland of the Dorset coast sustained a poetic experience of the world in which 'to be alive is the prize above all prizes, to be out of the grave, the great exemption'. Up in this high and elemental fastness, he could escape being 'submerged by the common place', just as he had resolved always to do when, as a 25-year-old, he was first diagnosed as suffering from pulmonary tuberculosis.[76] In the seclusion of these abandoned downs, this countryman who regarded 'all social gatherings as devastating to intellectual thought',[77] could insist that 'the false values imposed on us are the products of mistakes caused by the high premium put upon personal property',[78] and get on with the job of explaining 'how poetic vision can serve us in our present age of steel and concrete'.

Known to his friends as Lulu, Powys strode about 'Luluizing' the downs in this potent way, stirring them up into a vivid explosion of cosmic revelation that owed nothing to the priests, whose doctrinal creed he judged to be 'a product of death'.[79] On one of his epic walks, he claimed to have seen the head of a fairy ascend from a faded and rust-coloured dock leaf and float into the sky — a vision, as he admitted in a candid letter, which 'invalidated my senses'.[80] Walking near East Lulworth, this sun-worshipping pagan drew up before a tall wood and bid his wife, Miss Alyse Gregory, 'Listen to the Godless wind blowing through the trees. It sounded the same when the Neanderthal men were coming up from the sea, when Christ was being crucified, when Epicurus was conversing in his garden.'[81] Following the word of a local fisherman, he discovered forgotten and all but impassable old smuggling paths, following one down to a remote cave where he wrapped a riband of seaweed around his brow and lay back to imagine the scent of mermaids as the waves boomed around him.[82]

He would step out through the downland turf ('stiff', 'flinty' and 'ewe-cropped'), and make his way along the narrow top of the perilous cliff called Bats Head to lie naked in a spot that remained perfectly calm even when a storm was blowing over the cliff. At the famous 'fossil forest' near Lulworth Cove, he clambered into a vast stone tree, which he called a 'sarcophagus-stone' or a 'coffin out of eternity', and, after sinking through the unfathomable depths of geological time, imagined the voracious Ichthyosaurus diving where shag and cormorant were now 'sharking for the flesh of fish on the lew side of Blind Cow Rock'. As for the prehistoric track or 'Roman road' which had brought Massingham up from Daggers Gate, for Powys it belonged not to modern walkers in their tweeds and windproofs, but to the unbowed tramps and gipsies with whom he shared it. He marvelled that 'sun-tanned Bedouins' of the heath were still crossing 'our shining macadam roads with desert dust upon their sandals'; like himself, they had 'never been duped into substituting the fake values of civilisation for the true values of life', and they offered a wonderful foil to 'our present industrial, mechanical, practical age'.[83]

Many people recoiled from this self-described 'Epicurean from the open fields' who believed that 'the secret of life' was to be found by gathering 'heightened realisations through the immediate subjective experiences of each of our mother-naked bodies'.[84] Some, including a number who looked in on this late megalithic scene from Bloomsbury, wondered at the pretentiousness of this prophet who seemed to 'produce his words' in the artificial manner of a film star;[85] while others deplored his brazenly 'amoral' outlook on sexual matters. 'Nothing is more villainous,' thundered Powys in reply to these critics, 'than the way people of conventional habits endeavour to tame, correct and inhibit the wild splendour of lust.'[86] A passage from Miss Alyse Gregory's diary, written at the time of Powys's passionate entanglement with Gamel Woolsey, leaves little doubt of the daunting complexities this 'passionate realisation of life' could bring to those Luluizing walks:

> Llewelyn: I have injured you and hurt you over and over. I know I have been cruel, but I do love you. My soul courts yours.
> A: The carline thistles are out, and the orchises are faded. Look, there is a scarlet pimpernel.
> Llewelyn: I do not know how I could have got through the last year if you had not been so sweet to me.
> A: Why do you think the butterflies, if their life is so brief, rest so quietly on the grass blades and flowerheads? Do you think they are satiated or half-drowsing their few moments away? I am so fond of the marble whites.
> Llewelyn: I think they are drinking, hourly from the flowers.
> A: Is that their food? But there is no nectar in a grass blade.
> Llewelyn: I will try to do better. Oh, I will, I will.
> A: I know it, my darling Llewelyn. You do try. I do understand. It's not your fault. It is the fault of life itself.
> Then he goes to meet Gamel.[87]

H. J. Massingham found much to approve in this revolutionary revivalist, who seemed to share his sense of the 'earth-life' with D. H. Lawrence.[88] Llewelyn might see fairies rising up from dock leaves, but he had spent five years, over the period of the Great War, as a convalescent sheep farmer in Kenya, and he had a more practical grasp of agriculture than many who dismissed him as a dotty pastoralist. Llewelyn Powys was a countryman through and through, who found his friends among the farmers, shepherds and fishermen. Locals would walk up to Chydyok to talk with him, and one Spring the Winfrith band even came up to play for him as he lay ill in his shelter.[89] A man of considerable local reputation, he undertook certain public commitments, trying to help the fishermen who came to him when their livelihood was threatened by a Navy surveying boat, and campaigning to have the Lodmoor marshes, east of Weymouth, acquired by the council as a nature reserve. He lost a lot of money in a famous libel case, after he and others, acting on the principle that 'a well descended spirit' should try to 'relieve suffering wherever it existed and at whatever cost', were sued for alleging cruelty in the conduct of a home for mentally handicapped children in nearby East Chaldon.[90]

Llewelyn Powys found nothing to respect in intellectuals like T. S. Eliot ('the tidy, well-disciplined Gabbitas-Thring tutor of our day ...'), or in fashionable young metropolitans who were so well adapted to 'the new mechanical inventions' that they had to be 'drunk with cocktails before they want to make love'.[91] He and his feminist wife preferred such aboriginal and 'primitive' peoples as remained on the earth. While staying in New York, Powys had welcomed Big Chief White Horse Eagle to tea, saying of this 'surviving king of all the Red Indians' that he has 'a noble exterior when seen with all his feathers, and a personal dignity, though I fear he has been sadly debauched by contact with vulgar people ...'[92] They visited the West Indies where, as Alyse Gregory recalled, the negresses were inclined to 'rock backwards and forwards, slapping their thighs with merriment' whenever their unconventionally clad megalithic visitor came into sight. Powys also saw much to admire, declaring 'these transplanted human beings' to be 'far more interesting than all the white people put together ... They revealed to me secrets of the sun, the life under the sun and moon that I could never have got from these chattering dressed up silly people who make their living out of these half-starved black men and then deride them.'[93] Powys paid his tribute to the countryfolk of Dorset by comparing them to the black people he had known in British East Africa, cherishing both for the unabstracted quality of their intelligence and their acute sense of political justice.[94]

Powys's country people did not have 'blind, intimidated brains' like the conventional 'good citizens' he once likened to 'silly sheep, woolproud, lambproud, but never soul proud', and he was pleased to take his place among them. He shared their accented speech,[95] and wrote articles for them in the local papers, explaining that 'It enchants me to have them read by these old-world labourers and cow herds and discussed in every tavern from Weymouth to Shaftesbury.'[96]

Plain-spoken and full of actuality, these admirable essays meditate on landmarks and other local phenomena, and reveal insights gleaned from beach-combers, fishermen, tramps and farm labourers. On Armistice Day,

Powys joined his readers in remembering 'These Jacks, and Bobs, and Harry's and Georges, and Walts, and Bills' who are 'utterly lost to Dorset', while commiserating with the women who had 'consoling exhortations about "glory" offered to them in exchange for the living bodies of their sons', and who surely deserved better than to be fobbed off by a popular Press spouting about 'the immortal dead'.[97]

Powys came up with carefully chosen heroes or 'worthies' for his Wessex readers: people like Joseph Arch, the 'hedgerow lecturer' who founded the National Agricultural Labourers' Union and whose visit to Dorset was still remembered by an old man in Winfrith. He wrote about William Barnes and Thomas Shoel, the eighteenth-century farm labourer of Montacute who became a poet and composer of sacred music, and a great witness to the hardship facing the farm-hand when 'the labouring classes of England, cheated of their independence by the arbitrary Enclosure Acts, were entering upon a long period of degradation'.[98]

He celebrated the Tolpuddle Martyrs, contributing a piece to the booklet published in 1934 to accompany the annual Trades Union Congress, held in Weymouth that year to mark the centenary of their deportation.[99] His article begins with the graffiti (or rather 'graphetai') carved by agricultural labourers in the chalk walls of an old farmstead, Rats Barn, in a wild valley near his cottage. Some of these initialled dates went back to 1825, and 1830 appeared frequently too. Powys imagined those Bible-loving and noble-headed men joining the 'rioting' labourers of Winfrith in 1830, advancing 'respectfully, with their hats in their hands' to demand an increased wage; and then being dispersed by James Frampton and his special constables. Powys was in no doubt of the justice of the Tolpuddle Martyrs' cause, or that their 'trial and conviction was what in America would be described as a "frame-up" engineered by class-interested magistrates under the connivance of the Whig government'. But his solution was not of a kind to worry Herbert Weld: 'As one reads accounts of the happenings of those days one longs for the powerful intervention of some honourable and magnanimous landed gentlemen of the kind that before now have not been unknown in Dorset. Where were the Lord Cranbornes, the Lord Shaftesburys, the Squire Sheridans, the Squires of Culver Dell, men diligent and strong to save their "humble and obedient labourers"?'

Powys once told Theodore Dreiser that his writings were concerned with 'matters deeper than Russian or German politics — indeed they are concerned with those low fields where Brother Billycock walks with Brother

Budding Belly under the sound sun of the heaven. I mean desire and hunger, and these mates don't give a damn about methods of government.'[100] And yet, as he followed his ancient downland track through the Thirties, this prophet of 'godless faith'[101] became increasingly committed to the 'middle of the road' in a political sense too. He had once declared that 'surely everybody who has thought honestly about the subject must be a socialist',[102] but having long ago seen a redcoated soldier chased down a Weymouth street and felled by a howling mob, he had always distrusted social programmes that 'imply a period of lawlessness' for 'the attainment of Utopian ends'.[103] It was from that position that he raised the English virtues of liberty, fair-play, tolerance and reason against leaders like Mussolini, Stalin, Hitler and anyone else who might consider 'jumping up for a paradise from buckets of blood'.[104]

Llewelyn was in favour of the old county order. He only had to visit Dorchester to be reminded of the virtues of old gentility, when compared with the mincing narrow-mindedness of those who owed their recent elevation to commerce and trade. Visiting a Dorchester shop, he came across a trio of those ' "new Dorset ladies" whose breath is withering to everything that is free and charming in life'.[105] Hearing these creatures talking about their troubles with domestic servants, Powys was distressed to think that 'simple Dorset maidens from happy villages perhaps under the protection of the Bond family, or of the Weld family, should be suddenly caught away, to find themselves in the power of these "roving Griffs or Harpies dread" '. He counted 'old Weld' alongside H. J. Massingham among the superior company of writers and philosophers who, unlike the censorious moralists, would grant him 'the kind of plenary indulgence' that was the classical attitude to such matters.[106]

The tanks could certainly be heard up at Chydyok, but Powys, who was attuned to downland sounds and once advised a correspondent to seek reassurance in the sound of 'a cowpat falling flat upon the grass', was not inclined to acknowledge their mechanical thunder. He knew about those metal machines, having heard about them during the Great War. In a letter to his brother Theodore, written during his African sojourn, he had cited their invention as proof of the anachronistic barbarism of war: 'The anomaly of war at this stage in our civilization is clearly seen by the importance which becomes necessarily attached to work, to action — to constructing a tank and carrying a bayonet effectively. Tanks should be constructed in the mind — such tanks would really avail the human race — religion, poetry, philosophy — these things only are of use.'[107] He would not grant the Lulworth gunnery school more than a footnote in one of his essays, taking it as the orientation point from which interested readers might trace the position of a stone head, perhaps late Roman, mounted low in the wall enclosing Lulworth Park to mark the spot where a young girl called Edith had been murdered over a century before. His instructions, which may be sufficiently explicit to account for the fact that the 'Edy Head' has since disappeared, explained that the stone was 'almost opposite the field gate that is to be observed some two or three hundred yards from the easterly entrance to the practising ground of the soldiers'.[108]

As for Herbert Weld's ruined castle and park, Massingham would surely have approved of the spirit in which Powys used to visit this sinking aristocratic enclosure in order to dwell upon the folly of vanity, pomp and worldly ambition. He liked to make his approach from Winfrith, walking along the old drove, then a 'marvellously wide green way', which suggested 'a track along which the Canterbury Pilgrims might have passed'. After remembering the common grazing rights that had been extinguished by the enclosures, he would enter Lulworth Park near Limekiln Farm, and follow the wooded lane past the 'ivy-mantled hollow tower' that still stands at the corner of Burngate Wood. He strolled beneath unforgettable beeches, and along woodland drives that, come springtime, would be bordered by short wild daffodils. He stood before the burned-out castle, declaring it 'a dolorous experience to view at close quarters this broken monument of family pride and to see the masses of seventeenth-century lead still clinging to the dizzy walls, suggesting to a capricious fancy lodged accumulations of grey unmelting blizzard ice . . . Once again the power of fire has been manifested and these ancient dormitories of privilege are now relegated to the chatter of saucy jackdaws and the screaming of the peacock tribe, preternatural and frightful.'[109]

One Good Friday he stopped to muse upon a derelict brougham carriage, languishing in a woodland glade on the edges of the park.[110] Once used to transport 'honourable Catholic dames' along the high roads, it had fallen into service as 'a vehicle for conveying faggots and brushwood', and now lay rotting under vast oaks, its wheels 'unrevolving in springy leaf-mould'. The blue-bells shooting up between its spokes showed the transient folly of civilised vanity when faced with the thrusting upward surge of vegetable sap, the 'agony and ecstacy of corporeal love'. Readers familiar with Powys's philosophy would have known, if only from the rising sap, that they were witnessing the 'wild rout' of Dionysius. Here was the 'vegetable god' — he of 'the vital leap' into 'exultant consciousness', whose presence might, according to Powys, suddenly be sensed in the rough smell of nettles in a ditch — rising up to bury the disintegrating luxuries of Lulworth Park in his interlacing 'riot of the visible'.[111]

As for his desire to be buried in the ancient manner, Herbert Weld granted Llewelyn the permission he requested, as can be gathered from a letter Llewelyn wrote to his brother John Cowper Powys in August 1933: 'It was a comfort to think that if I died I would be allowed to be buried in the garden a few feet from my shelter with knees and arms flexed and not crossed. This was through the old squire's intervention who knew my wishes.'[112] But although Powys was wasted to a guttering flicker of life when Massingham visited him in 1936, he had already outlasted the old squire. Herbert Weld died on 5 February 1935, obliging Llewelyn Powys to draw up another set of 'Instructions for the Despatch of my body in case of my death' in December that year:

> If I die abroad let my body be cremated and my ashes returned to Dorset. In the case of my dying at Chydyok let information be sent to Rivers Pollock and Gerald Brenan and let them come at once to Chaldon, and together or one or other of them with Mr Cobb go to Mr Joseph Weld (carrying Mr Herbert Weld's letter to show him) and ask him to confirm the old squire's permission for me to be buried on the south west corner of the Obelisk field — the place known to John Cowper Powys and to Mr Cobb. If he refuses to let them go to Barnaby Duke of Dorchester, with whom I was at school and ask him to allow me as much ground in his Holworth Farm as he would allow for the burying of a hog. I do not mind how obscure the ditch — any chalk pit would do, or nettle patch. Brimstone Copse would please me well. If he refuse, offer to *buy* the privilege. Should he still refuse then carry me to a crematorium at Southampton and bury my ashes at night in the south west corner of the Obelisk field and nothing said. In the case of leave being obtained to bury me openly then let the grave digger arrange that it would be easy to bury Alyse near me when the time comes. Let me be buried without a coffin and lying on my side and on no account let my arms be crossed.[113]

This unorthodox interment was not to take place — either in the garden at Chydyok, or in that nearby corner of the Obelisk field. Powys died while convalescing in Switzerland, on 2 December 1939 and, due to the intervention of the Second World War, his ashes could not be repatriated until 1947. The monument to Dorset's last Downland Man is a great rough slab of Portland stone up on the path near the Obelisk field. Carved in situ by Elizabeth Muntz, it confronts the passing walker with the God-defying but still scriptural words that Powys had chosen for his own epitaph: 'The Living The Living He shall praise thee.'

ELEVEN

RED DAWN

> It is so much easier to say that a man is a Bolshevik than to explain what he really thinks.
>
> H. J. Massingham (1919)

I HAD BARELY heard of the little village of East Chaldon before 1987 when I visited the estate office in Lulworth Park to interview Wilfrid Weld. After we had talked, Mr Weld kindly offered to show me something of his estate. We came to East Chaldon (or Chaldon Herring, in the name favoured by Llewelyn Powys), as we approached the western limits of the estate. I remember Weld slowing just outside the village to greet some people following a fox-hunt along a nearby ridge; but I only registered the village as a blur of well-placed prettiness: a few farm buildings and cottages, a triangular green, a pub called 'The Sailor's Return', and a marvellously rounded green hill called High Chaldon rising up just beyond the village: a visionary knoll which I did not then recognise as Dorset's answer to the various cosmological heights featured in Herbert Weld's travels: the Gebel Akhdar or 'Green Mountain' near the Mediterranean coast of Libya; or the twin ziggurats of Harsagkalamma in ancient Kish, a name that his archaeologists translated as 'Mountain of the World' and associated with the earth god Enlil and his consort Ninlil.[1]

A couple of years later, I returned to look at two listed cottages, which the Weld estate was then offering for sale. A thatched house with ivied walls of stone and brick, St Nicholas Cottage was thought to date from the seventeenth century and would, so the estate agent claimed, provide its purchaser with 'accommodation of great charm and character'. Offers were invited in the region of £175,000. Also thatched, the second property was less forthcoming. Identified only as 4/5 East Chaldon, it consisted of two adjoining stone cottages in a row of three on the corner of Chydyok Road, a lane that provides access to a few council houses before culminating in the gated track leading up to the remote farm building that was once home to Llewelyn Powys. Being in 'a very poor state of repair' these sunken-roofed hulks would require 'complete refurbishment', and were offered at only £80,000.

For any would-be cottager with a couple of hundred thousand pounds to spare, both these places would have had considerable potential. But by then I knew considerably more about East Chaldon, and I could feel the disillusioning ghost of Valentine Ackland at my side. A tall, Eton-cropped figure wearing trousers, jacket and tie, she had lived here in the Thirties and carried out her own highly critical survey of the villagers' cottages. I could hear the debunking upper class voice of this convent-educated and now assertively lesbian young woman, as she dismissed every claimed 'attraction' of these rustic dwellings with a contemptuous riposte. The little wooden windows may look alluring enough, peeping out under the brow of thatch, but they are actually so tiny that only the most miserly portion of light could ever reach through them. Savills' brochure talked about inglenook fireplaces and ancient bread ovens but Ackland matched this with woeful tales of chimneys that smoke unless the door is perpetually open and of damp, beetle-infested walls from which sodden plaster falls. She scattered rats everywhere too — including one that had recently bitten a baby in the throat as it slept in its cradle upstairs.[2] Even the post office that was here in the Thirties has gone, leaving only the dangerous consolations — and Ackland knew all about them as one who used to write 'DD' in her diary for every day when she managed to be 'Devoid of Drink'[3] — of the 'excellent public house'.

Could this, I wondered of 4/5 East Chaldon, have been the very row of thatched cottages that Ackland 'went over' in her relentless, anti-idyllic manner in 1935? These, as she told readers of *Left Review*, had been superficially 'renovated inside, with a lick of whitewash and some putty stuffed in the worst cracks of the window-sills'.[4] Inspecting the cramped cave-like interior of one of these two-bedroom cottages, where a Weld estate workman warned her that ' "Thik house be all buggy up the walls," ' she observed that it had recently housed a family of six children, along with mother, father and the mother's brother — said locally to have fathered most of the children ('You'd expect it then,' as her informant remarked her). After roundly condemning this hovel — the tiny fireless bedrooms; the damp stone-floored pantry hardly five and a half feet high, where a sixteen-year-old daughter had recently been put to die of TB — she remembered how a farm labourer, who had formerly lived in one of these cottages, had spoken out: ' "What those houses need is a red jacket." ' Ackland relished this incendiary phrase, quite unlike anything ever used by an estate agent, explaining that it came 'straight from the more glorious days of our county. The days of rick-burning'. Unfortunately, the houses were actually receiving 'a white jacket' as they were 're-dressed for the next comers' and made into the 'smartest possible whited sepulchres'.

That red jacket may only have been the threadbare residue of an ancient insurrectionary tradition, but Ackland, for whom the burning of Lulworth Castle had apparently not been enough, took it up as romantic proof that there was 'good blood' in the English countryside yet and that the hard-pressed rural workers only needed to 'have their memories jogged' to resume the struggle. This was the briar that she would plant at her own fiercely unpicturesque cottage door, and the following year she exhibited it again in *Country Conditions*, her book about the miseries of country life in a barely disguised East Chaldon. This time the fire-raising labourer is named Fred Dory, and described as a representative villager, albeit of unusually acute political intelligence: 'indeed, Dory is directly in the tradition of the local men, his ancestors, who in 1830 joined with the men of the neighbouring village in a demonstration that brought the local landowner tumbling out of his bed in a sweat of anxiety, to parley with them for long enough to allow the militia to come and settle the argument'. The sister of that hated magistrate and landowner, James Frampton, may have recorded that the crowd which mustered in Winfrith came out in their Sunday best and had to be urged on from behind hedges by their wives, but for Ackland this ancient moment of glory was not to be diminished by such depressing details. By this time, indeed, Dory was fitting his old red jacket not on to his own former abode, as he had been in *Left Review*, but on to 'the very row of cottages in which he is now living'.[5]

Half a century later it is abundantly clear that the ill-housed country workers did not decide to 'take steps', as Ackland had hoped they might. Yet for a while in the Thirties even Llewelyn Powys, of whom Valentine Ackland would later write 'What an earthquake of a miracle',[6] was ready to go some distance with Ackland and her more systematic sister in militancy, the novelist Sylvia Townsend Warner. In 1935, he wrote to thank 'my two darling children' for the presents they had sent up the track to lighten his convalescence.[7] He was grateful for the photograph of the deathmask of Akhenaton, the pacific, sun-worshipping ruler of ancient Egypt; but the grapes turned out to be sour, prompting this Dionysian to observe that all shopkeepers were inclined to cheat over grapes, which 'have a false value as symbols of conspicuous waste on the sideboard of the bourgeoisie'.

Perhaps he was teasing, but there can be no doubt that Ackland and Warner were working hard to convert this remote corner of the Weld estate into a hotbed of Communism. For them, the faded red jacket of East Chaldon memory glowed with the reflected light of a glorious Soviet future in which tanks would be left to rust while the light aircraft of the workers' state swooped down to spray pesticides over collectivised fields, and contented workers on scarlet tractors revitalised the soil with artificial fertilisers. Red flags — just like those at the gunnery school on Bindon Hill — would flutter over the whole productive scene.

Fables of a Sinking Down

If East Chaldon had become the cultural centre of the Weld estate by the Nineteen Thirties, this was largely due to the presence of Theodore F. Powys, who, in 1904, had moved to this remote settlement from Studland, where he had been increasingly bothered by tourists. He married a local girl and bought from the Weld estate a ninety-nine year lease on Beth Car, a red-brick villa at the western edge of the village, which, though sometimes said to have been designed by Thomas Hardy himself, had no picturesque charms at all. Powys was rather proud of the 'ugliness' of his house, telling readers of the *Countryman* that 'If you look for sweet williams beside our door, you will find only bindweed . . .'[8] Following his example, other Powyses came to live in the area, or visited repeatedly — Llewelyn, Philippa, Gertrude and John Cowper among others — and T. F. Powys's presence also drew a succession of unrelated writers and artists to the village.[9] Sylvia Townsend Warner, who was then a young musicologist and composer engaged in a Carnegie-funded project to publish a collection of fifteenth and sixteenth-century English church music, first visited the area at Easter 1921. She came down with friends, staying at the Weld Arms in East Lulworth and surprising her company when she stripped off and waded into the sea at Arish Mell Gap.[10] She visited East Chaldon a little later, drawn by T. F. Powys, about whom she proposed to write, and, settling there with Valentine Ackland — who had arrived as Mrs Molly Turpin, to recover from a short-lived marriage. David Garnett and Liam O'Flaherty were among the visitors in the early years of 'Powys mania'; and even Lady

Ottoline Morrell, the literary hostess of Bloomsbury, came down for a few uncomfortable days.

While the squire sat in his castle, pondering the Babylonian mysteries of ancient Kish, Theodore Powys lurked at the edge of his estate, writing extraordinary fables of English country life. His villages have quaint names — Mockery Gap, Folly Down, Madder or Dodderdown — and they crouch as snugly as any formula could demand in their welcoming folds of the downs. They also have many of the right constituent parts: the old church and graveyard, the pub, the cottages and the gnome-like local characters with their dialect and their traditional ways. The surrounding hills are so sympathetic to village life that they bend over to listen in on the villagers' conversations, but their contact with the idyll soon breaks, for what the hills hear is plainly inappropriate and they recoil in pink-faced shock.[11]

Theodor Powys's villages are indeed in shockingly decadent condition, full of viciousness, idiocy and violent instability. Repeatedly Powys likens their landscape to a book, but there's no security about the text. One interpretation slips into another as the village is tossed about on a seething confusion of allegory and symbolism. On Sundays Powys would walk up the lane to read the lessons in the church of St Nicholas, East Chaldon, but in his stories the biblical parables have escaped their holy enclosure and are running amok through the village, making it blessed one moment and damned the next. The water in the well suddenly becomes wine, and a lion wanders through the fields, scaring people to death. Sudden gusts of wind blow old ladies up against the wall, breaking their legs; and other helpless characters are abruptly lifted up to Heaven. The villagers are defenceless against these allegories, which ventriloquise them and kill them off with a perfunctory blow of fate when their purpose is served. Animals are sometimes ennobled on Powys's symbolic pasture, and people reduced to dumb and unknowing beasts caught up in a cycle of rape and perfunctory copulation in field or under hedge. Only the ducks on the village pond seem to possess the insight of properly autonomous characters. Powys's Bloomsbury admirers were inclined to play down the connection between the obscure village where he lived and his stories, which they hailed as the singular works of a dark and brooding genius. But while T. F. Powys was certainly a fabulist, this does not mean that his writing was fundamentally disengaged from the everyday condition of life on the Weld estate at that time.

Powys's villages can be places of apparently limitless power and subjection. An early story called *The Left Leg* follows the obsession of Farmer Mew, who feels compelled to possess everything he comes across. As he says to people who are already his servants: 'You have always worked well for me . . . Only this is not enough . . . This does not satisfy me; I must have more than this; I want to buy you; I intend you to be not my servants but mine — my own.'[12] Typically abject, the villagers feel flattered that anyone should think them worth a handful of coins, and they are soon competing for the honour of being purchased. Before its magical reversal, the story shows just how far Mew can go: raping and murdering his way through his village, laying claim to the standing stones, the butterflies and the very perspectives of the landscape. As one character puts it, ' "Farmer do swallow all." '[13]

T. F. Powys also had his own way with the often absent squire and his lush, depopulated park. In 1930, he published a story called 'The Key of the Field', which works a remarkable transformation on the distant but perfect figure of Squire Jar. The field in question consists of twelve acres of the richest pasture: an emblematic oak tree stands at its centre, providing a 'welcome shelter to the cows during the hot summer weather', and the whole domain is enclosed with high palings of the sort 'used by noblemen for their deer parks'.[14] As Powys writes, 'there was no better field in the whole world than this field'. The field once formed part of Squire Jar's garden, but the good squire, being a 'worthy man' who does not wish to keep the best of everything to himself, decides to grant its use to one of his tenants. The story tells of the trials of uncle Tiddy, the first tenant farmer to be given the key of the field by Squire Jar. Tiddy is plotted against by Grandmother Trott, who gets her sons to rape Tiddy's young niece Lily and, when she becomes pregnant, accuse poor Tiddy of incest. A little carefully directed gossip at the village well convinces Squire Jar's corruptible steward of Tiddy's guilt, and the key of the field is taken back and passed on to Grandmother Trott's son John. After a lifetime of hopeless pining, uncle Tiddy is finally taken into the field by Squire Jar where he lies down to die. By this time, the field has become decidedly Heavenly, and Squire Jar glows with the numinosity of God himself. Powys's fables map the hierarchy of the aristocratic estate with precision, showing the fine gradations of its descent: a chain of being that passes from the deified squire through his imperfect steward to the tenant farmers, and then on down to the village where it constrains the experience of every living creature, man, woman or beast. As Powys once wrote, 'Every civilised village is welded and held together by its middle.'[15]

This pastoral order informs many of Powys's stories, and it leaves the people at the bottom with little chance of forming an independent outlook: unlike Hardy's characters, Powys's are the ciphers of their circumstance: in them there are no reserves of humanity to pit against the injustices of history. Some of Powys's villagers may be innocents adrift in a world which is brutal and full of traps, but they are also ignorant, superstitious: creatures of hormonal caprice, and thoroughly adjusted to slithering about in the snake-pit of their village. The tenant farmers' sons strut around as the licensed rapists and studs of the village, while the village maids are often no more than willing or unwilling objects of their insatiable lust. It was one thing for Gamel Woolsey to write poems about 'trembling' on some 'grassy bed' under a leafy tree while her Luluising lover plunged on: a unicorn with his silver horn, a spear-bearing warrior who had finally found his sheath.[16] But for Theodore's village girls, who are mounted on mossy knolls under oak trees and tupped like the ewe-lambs to which Powys compares them, life was rather less poetic. God may appear as good Squire Jar, but he also has less beneficent manifestions. The farmer's son in *Mockery Gap* is also called God Simon: 'Often in the country a young farmer's son, whose parents are rich, is so fattened and reddened by praise and good living that he becomes a sort of man-god, spruce and verdant, and worshipped by all.' The same foul numinosity belongs to the two sons of Mr Mumby in *Mr Weston's Good Wine*, a loathsome pair whose behaviour, as we are told ironically, could only appear as 'most natural and proper to their kind, and no unpleasant hint or comment could possibly be made about such lively young gentlemen, who had each in the past ridden a winner at the local steeplechase, and had also been asked by Lord Bullman himself to drive a car to the polls at an election'.[17] Such also was Simon Cheney: full of 'unpleasant maxims and manners' but 'puffed and plumed with gross conceit' to make a 'fine Phallic symbol for the young ladies to admire'.

' "The other side of the hill" no longer existed' — so wrote Solomon J. Solomon, an artist and camouflage expert, describing the impact of aerial reconnaissance in the Great War.[18] There are no tanks in T. F. Powys's world, but the chalk hills that surround his villages — the very ones that H. J. Massingham was trying to raise up to the skies — were sinking all the time and the villages they had once isolated so effectively are filled with the apprehension of their own discovery. Typically, Powys's narratives are triggered by the arrival of an unexpected presence from the world beyond the lowering ridge.[19] The incomer may be a live ape washed up on the shore, a new fisherman who has no sooner arrived than the villagers turn him into a Christ-like symbol, or an apocalyptic monster which is part Beelzebub and part fossil come to life. In *Innocent Birds* the downs are still 'high enough to keep out the vulgar', but this is not the case in other stories. The ultimate vulgarity of modern advertisement is part of the redemption that Mr Weston, a salesman who is somehow also God, brings to the village of Folly Down in *Mr Weston's Good Wine*. Like the Shell lorries of that time, his Ford van is a mobile hoarding with advertisements on both sides; and the script it projects into the skies over Folly Down — and 'sky-writing' was the latest gimmick — announces a brand name as well as an approaching miracle. The cars sweeping into T. F. Powys's villages from the other side of those falling hills pass so fast that their drivers don't even notice the villagers mown down on the way through.

T. F. Powys also makes a great deal of the visual perspectives of his places. His villages are defined not just by lanes, buildings and chalky hills, but by powerful lines of sight. The squire and other well-placed individuals enjoy the privilege of not being watched in their activities, but this amenity is not extended to Nellie, a modest young girl in *Mark Only*, found in a field with only her slip on. In *Innocent Birds*, it is said that 'We can think of no place in the world that is more pleasant to watch in than Madder', and Powys frequently introduces a conflict between those for whom 'all life is but a looking' and others who maintain a practical relation to the place.[20] Farmer Cheney is upset at people who are 'always spying about in my fields'. Village girls are embarrassed by the tumescent state of the hills when they are empty or unpeopled, while visiting natural historians and walkers prefer just this sort of 'nakedness', studying it with indecent interest. Powys contrasts the pretty landscape loved by the visitor with the dark world that re-emerges at night to oppress the true residents. As he writes in *Mockery Gap*, 'the mere day time of prettiness departed with the town visitors, and now that they were gone the true look of the land, that had been hidden from them, came forth again to be seen by those who have eyes to see'. And at the centre of that 'true look' was 'the blackness of despair'.

In *Mockery Gap* (1925), the most formidable peering visitors are not trippers but members of the county field club — modelled as may be assumed, on the Dorset Natural History and Archaeological Society — whose destructive impact on the village of Mockery Gap is spelt out in close detail. The field trip arrives in a huge car, its learned members equipped with sticks and umbrellas, ready to observe the flora and fauna and visit 'places where old things might be found'. They stand about in threes, gazing out at the sea 'as if it had been placed there on purpose to interest them'. Their leading members, who come from high county families, discourse on the origins of rocks, the architectural qualities of the village church, and mount the scattered tumuli to pronounce upon 'the life-history of cliffs, valleys, hills and rivers'. The head of the party is Mr Roddy, a squire who is also a moving force at the county museum and has a fine collection of 'ancient monsters' that he has dug out of the earth with 'immense care and skill' and the assistance of his three gardeners. Roddy picks up a handful of shells from the grass and announces them to be Roddites, a variety that bear his name since he himself was their discoverer. This learned society is troubled by the attendance of a clueless newcomer, a wealthy young woman whose ignorance of field club protocol betrays a vulgar background. Miss Frances Ogle is an arriviste whose 'spying audacity' lacks the appropriate cultural refinement; indeed, she is a gossip who interrupts and is inclined to mistake distant sheep for clusters of ancient stones.

When the party finally arrives in Mockery, a village which had 'never been visited before so wholeheartedly by the learned', it emerges that the real damage is to be done by a Mr James Tarr, a true gentleman and leading light in the field club. The people of Mockery 'had lived for generations most patiently', tucked away in 'the ever-green valley of Mockery Gap'. Their village has its glittering stream, its vicarage and church 'settled meekly in the folds of the valley'. It has its pleasant wood that runs as far down to the sea as it can go 'without being uprooted by the waves' and contains a ruined church: 'the oldest in the country' which, 'even in this day when everything is discovered, except the peace of God (that none wish for)', has yet to be found by a visitor.

Here was another timeless Tyneham-like village which had survived for centuries without history, but it 'wasn't in Mr James Tarr's habit of life to leave well alone'. Indeed, he was 'the last gentleman in the world ... to allow any earthly paradise, where wild roses scent the air in June, to remain without ambitions as every real paradise should'. Convinced that the country people are 'ignorant' and 'low in the scale of being', he goes about giving the villagers what he considers to be 'a proper incitement to live'. And the best incitement of all is 'to hunt for something that was almost, if not entirely, impossible to be found'. He gives one formerly contented villager called Mr Gulliver a map of the world; he tells the glum schoolmistress that she will find a four-leaved clover which will cure all her woes if only she is prepared to search all the green fields between the village and the sea. He sows expectation among Mockery's children by telling them that one day their village will be visited by a rare kind of albatross called the Nellie-Bird. He tells the farmer that if only he digs deep enough into a tumulus he will find 'all the golden earrings that the concubines of the ancient Britons would wear so grandly'. Mr James Tarr goes around the village putting 'thoughts and ambitions into virgin hearts' and warning that 'I shouldn't be surprised if one dreadful day something might be seen.' He introduces restlessness and impossible aspiration into the village, and then his interfering party make their customary retreat: 'As soon as any village or tract of the countryside had yielded up all its ancient history, culled from the gravestones, its grassy terraces, and its silent valleys, to the prying eyes and hammer-taps of the grand and learned, then would these fine hunters, with one accord, as eagles to the carcass, crowd into the vicarage dining-room for tea.'

Metalled Road to Paradise

With the events of the Thirties, a new political commitment was also carried into East Chaldon from the other side of the hill. T. F. Powys once called himself a communist, but no one took him very seriously. His sister Philippa or 'Katie' Powys was also inclined to the revolutionary gesture and, for a time at least, was a member of the Communist Party.

But it was the famous lesbians of East Chaldon, Sylvia Townsend Warner and Valentine Ackland, whose political conversion was to prove most consequential. In 1939 Warner wrote an article for the *Countryman*, describing how she had come to see the miserable reality behind the rural idyll. Her first encounters with country life had been the conventional ones of an upper class child who 'went to the country' for family holidays. At that time 'meadows meant buttercups and white violets' while 'the village meant going to tea with kindly parishioners who had a great many flies in their palours'.[21] The country had been a 'place where mothers and aunts painted in watercolours' but there were contrary indications too. Sylvia remembers being sick after drinking milk she had seen come straight from the cow. One regular churchgoer lived in open incest with his daughter, and there was plenty of evidence to suggest that 'rape and brutality accompany the course of true love'. Young Sylvia was shocked by the 'indifference of public opinion' and 'the ignorant hopeless animal resignation' of the victims.

Among the writings that opened her eyes 'towards the likelihood that the English Pastoral was a grim and melancholy thing', she cites Crabbe's 'The Village', Cobbett's 'Rural Rides', *Piers Plowman*, the Hammonds's 'Village Labourer' and T. F. Powys's early novel *Mr Tasker's Gods*, which she had read in manuscript. She also mentions the anti-idyllic articles printed by *The Nation* under the heading 'England's Green and Pleasant Land'.[22] These were the anonymous work of John Robertson Scott, who had founded the *Countryman* from his retirement home in Idbury; and it was there, after renting a cottage from the Robertson Scotts, that Townsend Warner had first grasped how much a programme of educational and cultural activities could do to enliven a demoralised village. Idbury had been 'a melancholy little hamlet, full of picturesque cottages that had gone bad'. But Robertson Scott, who was well aware of the need to cut through the 'prettyish seeming' of country life as perceived by 'the week-ending classes' and to address the 'haggard reality' underneath,[23] was taking steps to revitalise the place. He and his wife were having a dozen cottages built, and leavening the village with events held in the church school: Edith Evans performed the death of Socrates; a string quartet came to give a concert; a skilled upholsterer showed what could be done with a worn-out old chair.

By 1930, when she was able to buy her modest cottage in East Chaldon, Sylvia Townsend Warner was 'exceedingly wary of that falsification of values which puts week-ends into sunbonnets and cares genuine regrets at any proposal to pull down a vermin-ridden, sixteenth-century nuisance and build a sound dwelling in its place'. The cottage she chose had 'no claims to be picturesque'. As she describes settling into East Chaldon, Townsend Warner puts the Marxist theory of base and superstructure through a green but resolutely anti-bucolic turn of her own. She had moved into the late Miss Green's cottage intending to be 'a week-ender', but the couchgrass in the neglected garden demanded a more sustained 'warfare with weeds', and by the time she had waged that battle together with Valentine Ackland she had decided to stay. She had planned to grow herbs and flowers, but she quickly realised that vegetables were a more worthy ambition for a true cottage gardener. This enthusiasm soon gave way to the mature realisation that the 'deeper gratification' is to be found in the soil itself: nothing could rival the satisfaction of a clean, well-dug and raked plot of earth. It was just the same with the neighbouring villagers. At first 'it was the flowers' that she enjoyed: 'the wisdom, the good friendships, the racy speech, the idiomatic quality of the English country worker — or the other flowers, the *fleurs du mal*, the twists and patiently-wrought vices that develop under thatch, the violent dramas that explode among green pastures'. Soon, however, she turned to 'the pursuit of more serious cabbage'. She became interested in 'the average amount of unpaid overtime filched from the labourer (he knows it right enough, but daren't speak); the average weekly mileage covered by the labourer's wife who fetches all her water from the well and carries all her slops to the ditch; the average yearly increase of thistles in the neglected pasture that once grew such fine crops of barley; the relative attendance at church and at inn; the average consumption of cheap and bulking starch foods, and the consequent spending on aperients; the amount of repairs done to cottages and the amount that should be done; the cost of milk to the combine and to the town consumer; the relative value of this same milk put into children and into umbrella handles; the average number of sleepers per bedroom and of rats per sleeper . . . '

Warner grew her flowers and vegetables, but her garden dialectic was not complete until she came to grips with 'the soil' from which her neighbours' misery grew. So she had come, finally, to recognise that 'the conditions which deform their lives, are more than Britain and the decay of British agriculture'; and, before long, she was 'glad to think' that many of her fellow villagers also looked beyond the confines of their own bewildered cabbage patch, and had 'come to know that the defeat of the peasants in Spain, defending their olive and orange co-operatives, is their loss, and that the new tractors swinging over the USSR collective farms are their gain'.

The awakening of this communist perspective is easily traced through Warner's literary writings. To begin with, she wrote poems eulogising the landscape around East Chaldon.[24] She expressed the conventional pleasures of wandering through 'scented acres/where haymakers/sharpen the scythe', and she had her poetic local types too: a promiscuous young woman called 'Black Eyes', and a sailor who consoles his anxious young love by comparing the sea over which he is about to voyage to the rolling landscape with its frothing hedges 'white with may'.

But the political perspective soon breaks in. In a poem called 'Green Pastures', she contrasts her own enraptured contemplation of a view ('O, I could lean/And look for ever/At such a scene!') with a brusque and more genuinely local response which sees the sublime pasture only as so much grazing: 'You're easily pleased if what you like/Best be a green field and a stone dyke!' In a longer poem entitled 'Peeping Tom', Warner confronts the idyll with a political fable of rural class struggle. Her Tom is a local labourer who, though he himself has grown out of the land, has no land 'for his own need'. Tom craves half an acre, and his want is soon known throughout the village. The local farmer, who is as malicious as he is powerful ('he in plenty/was rooted like an oak'), decides to play a game with Tom. He gives the miserable labourer the patch he craves, but he does so in a manner designed to punish him for his seditious ambition. The land is high up at the cliff's edge — a barren and exposed place where only weeds will grow. Tom's labours make no difference, and his aspiration for 'half an acre' becomes a village joke. Once the lesson is taught, the heartless farmer sacks him and reclaims his tied cottage.

Warner also set about the picturesque view of English country life in a long poem that set out 'to do for this date what Crabbe had done for his: write a truthful pastoral in the jog-trot English couplet'. Published in 1931, *Opus Seven* told the story of the gin-drinking Rebecca Random and her life in the village of Love Green. Rebecca's cottage had 'all things such as glad/the heart of those who dwell in town but would/spend weekends in the country'. With its thatch and large beams, it attracted artists and the passing Americans who paused to take its picture. Despite her own poverty Rebecca insists on growing flowers rather than food, prompting Warner into some ironical tut-tutting: 'Were but this realm/an honest Soviet, judgement would o'erwhelm/her and her trumpery, and the freehold give/to brisker hands.' Soon enough, however, it emerges that Rebecca's flowers, which are grown in the unromantically serried ranks of 'a countrified militia' are actually war memorials dedicated to the men of her family who died in the war leaving her to provide for herself ('Her kin all dead. Unpensioned, unallowanced . . . ').

The surviving men of the village had come back from the war to find only unemployment waiting for them, and the local pub is full of anger at the Peace. One night Rebecca starts drinking with a crippled Anzac war veteran. His grandfather had grown up in the area and, in the style of Tolpuddle, been transported to Australia for firing ricks. Having been raised on stories of England, he had found his opportunity to visit in the recent war. The disappointed Anzac expresses his disgust at the degenerate state of the old country he used to dream about: 'This silly sloppy landscape — what's the use/of all this beauty and no bloody juice?/Who'd fire a rick in these days?' As he continues, 'I've come too late/and stayed too long. Ruin can fascinate/a man.' Fearing that 'England is getting hold of me' he shrugs it off: 'Now I wouldn't give a damn/for England. She's as rotten as a cheese,/her women bitches, and her men C3's.'

Valentine Ackland's poem 'Winter' opens in a dimly lit world where there is 'no morning, no noon-day sun/And no light except half-light'. She and Sylvia lie 'clotted together in misery' like a couple of benighted peasants in pre-revolutionary Russia, demoralised by hunger and the slow 'drag' of rural time. And then 'we whisper together and the word we say is red'. In this spirit they rise up into the tasks of the new day:

> Red and angry as the sun will be when it rises,
> As the furnace-fires we kindle, as the fury which burns us,
> The Word unspoked in mind, soon to be spoken and heard
> Over screech of sirens when morning comes and the red sun rises.[25]

Alarmed by the rise of fascism in Europe, these thorough-going anti-idyllicists joined the Communist Party in the Spring of 1935, convinced that 'The choice for all who think and feel is already between fascism and socialism.'[26] They campaigned for, and visited, the anti-fascist forces in the Spanish Civil War. They worked for the advance of the Left Book Club, helped arrange screenings of the film *Defence of Madrid*, and sold copies of the *Daily Worker*. They visited a striking mining community in Wales, and helped to organise events in their own district: a peace march through Bridport, or a large rally in Maumbury Rings, the ancient amphitheatre at Dorchester, where Vera Brittain and George Lansbury were among the speakers. For a time, they were the centre of communism in Dorset.

Warner and Ackland applied their pens to the struggle too. Thanks to them the Weld estate became a source for the British left's view of the misery of rural conditions. Warner's poem 'In this Midwinter' confronted the nativity with hideous and doubtless also symbolic modern disease. A 'poison gas bomb let fall accidentally/On our uplands has blasted the penned pregnant ewes'; and the shepherds would find no 'Godling' with their sheep barren, except for 'foot-rot, lung-rot, womb-rot'. God had died, not as Llewelyn Powys imagined to make way for the superior religious impulse of individual poetic vision, but because man, 'having rationalised destruction inalienably . . . / Needs god no further'. The times were dark, but a future of comradeship, among those who were 'co-heir to the earth' still beckoned.[27] Warner also turned to the Weld estate for the material of 'an English fable' that ran along unwavering Party lines.[28] 'For some years,' she opened, 'the sheep on a certain estate had been increasingly hunted and worried by a pack of dogs.' The sheep, who were definitely the workers in this scenario, complained to the bailiff, who defended the dogs as only practising 'their privilege of Free Bite'. Soon, even the sheepdogs joined in this harassment so the sheep got organised, massing together in their own defence. Some had horns — 'as the old breed of sheep on this estate do have' — and were particularly effective when it came to charging the running dogs of capitalism. When the bailiff reappeared, called in by anxious tenants, his only response was to issue a Public Order Act stipulating that the dogs should not wear collars and that the sheep should not assemble themselves into a flock or, on any account, use their horns. He then 'went off to hunt, whistling the dogs to follow him. For he loved hunting above all things.'

It was as an ardent communist that Valentine Ackland started researching conditions in East Chaldon, writing her series of articles for *Left Review* and then retreating to the remoteness of Rats Barn, a now almost completely tumbled structure in an otherwise empty valley near Llewelyn Powys's house, to work on *Country Conditions*, a short book published by Lawrence and Wishart in 1936.[29] Ackland was contemptuous of the other Londoners or 'Intellectuals' who had recently 'discovered' the village. They may 'shut the gates and do no damage to the crops' and occasionally even 'take up a case of injustice and support the exploited'. But 'from the worker's point of view' their presence brings no consolation — except perhaps a bit of laundry for the publican's wife. 'These people,' as she writes, 'feel very bitterly about the slums in London, and quite bitterly about the state of their own country cottage, but if they feel anything at all about the other cottages in the village, they keep their counsel.'[30]

Ackland's country workers knew that they were the victims of the class structure, but they were sunk in isolation and, as could be gathered once their conversations in the pub had been stoked up a little, needed firm leadership from the Party ('We need to be told what to do. Rick-burning? What good's that? Set fire to the cottages? Where would we go? Burn out the landlords? What's the use, unless everyone does it . . .?'). Ackland reviews the rural scene to establish the prospects for drawing the rural workers into a 'United Front' not just with the farmers but with their industrialised brothers. She was confident that this strategy would 'gather in, I am sure, the vast majority of rural workers. It is what they are waiting for; what they are ripe for.' Yet, there were formidable obstacles, and these had to do with the basic forms of estate life.

Conditions had evidently deteriorated since the 1830s when agricultural workers still had the 'stubborn, independent spirit' to revolt against their condition: to fire ricks and ride with Captain Swing. 'The old independence' had been stifled: partly by the industrial revolution and the 'imperialistic stage of capitalism', which had combined to split the ranks of the working-class, focussing attention on 'the more immediately important industrial workers' and abandoning the country workers to 'political ignorance'; and partly by 'the bureaucratic system of distribution of responsibility' which meant there was no longer 'one hated figure to blame when the roof leaks or a man's eye falls on the rotting, wasting land: there is only a Ministry of Agriculture and Fisheries'.

Ackland chose some 'representative' types to illustrate conditions in her village. She told of the carter, Jack Ensor, and of Joe Talbot, an injured 'Permit-of Exemption' man whose 'exemption', far from sparing him the rigours of a full working week, appeared only to mean that he got paid less than the going rate. Her favourite ' "average" country worker' was Fred Dory, the exceptional hedger who had kept the insurrectionary memory of the old red jacket alive: he read the *Daily Herald* and refused to be cowed by the fear of victimisation that prevented other workers from chairing Labour Party election meetings. In general, the country worker was isolated and mute. Weekending 'Intellectuals' might harp on about the landworker's vocation for solitude, suggesting that he has 'unmatched opportunities for studying Nature', and has managed through his 'constant contact with the mother', to sublimate his needs and desires. But Ackland knew better, remarking that his isolation was aggravated by the fact that there were 'very few possibilities of leading a "social" life', while the amenities that did exist, like the nearby village hall, were 'almost entirely in the hands of the gentry'.

Ackland counts up the tribulations of village women, making do among the flies, fleas and slops: and of the children too, many of whom were obliged to walk over two miles to the nearest school: 'I have seen the walkers pass, wet and shivering with cold, the little ones straggling behind and the bigger ones yelling to them to hurry up. Boots squelching mud; thin coats dripping and hands and knees blue with cold. It is no joke for the mother, either, to have five or six half-drowned children returned to her at the end of the day; on the present wages it is not probable that a cottage household owns a complete change of all clothing for each child — even boots and socks are hard enough to find.'

She describes the bullying and inter-village feuding in the unsupervised lunch breaks. The little antagonisms that developed even between the youngest were all part of the fragmentation preventing country workers rising up together. Such were the obstacles that the Party would have to overcome 'if and when the labourers decide to "take steps" '.

In the uprisings of the 1830s, the tenant farmers sometimes seemed closer to their labourers than to the landowners, but this had changed too. Ackland remarks that the small farmers she has known have been 'steadily determined to support the people and ideas that must ruin them', and that they therefore 'appear to be the best possible example of capitalism in decay'. It was going to be hard to persuade the farmer that he was backing the wrong horse in putting his money on the gentry. For the old squirearchical system persisted: 'The farmers toady the squire and the squire toadies the farmers; they go out shooting and hunting together, and the squire makes pets of the farmers' sons and lends them his guns and his second-best horses.' The farmers have to put up with 'a great deal of impertinence from their betters', and they must also tolerate the damage done by 'the country gentleman's passion for game'. The situation was all the more pathetic since most of the farmers are 'still recognisably sprung from the working-class. Their accents and their rugged appearance make the gentry smile and chaff them; but they do not care because they are hailed as "good stout fellows".' So strong was this tradition of forelock-tugging deference that Ackland reckoned the labourer and farmer would only recognise the 'similarity of their positions' and their interest against the landowner 'as conditions grow steadily worse for them both'.

Ackland had no doubt that the landowner, a decidedly unGod-like figure in her book, was responsible for the dismal state of affairs in her village: 'The labourer badgers the farmer because cows stray through broken fences or the roof of a barn has fallen in; the farmer badgers the agent; the agent turns to the landowner, and there as often as not, comes the full stop. Either no attention is given to the matter at all, or else the agent is reminded that income tax and death duties and the expenses incidental to being a gentleman have taken all the spare money.'

It is not specified whether those 'incidental expenses' included the cost of archaeological digs in ancient Kish, but Ackland went out of her way to point out that it wasn't just absentee landowners who were at fault. Owners who live 'on as well as by their land' could also be 'deadly enemies' to struggling small farmers. They were inclined to indulge in the 'sport of idlers',[31] which caused tenant farmers endless problems; and where small farmers would suffer terribly, in a bad year, a landowner only had to ' "cut down on expenses", dismiss one or two employees, sell the extra hunter which used to be lent to the farmer's son, do without the motor car that was used to carry servants to and from the station, sell part of their shooting to a "syndicate" which includes themselves. In fact, put the burden on the workers and carry on as usual.'

Ackland ends her book with a glowing tribute to Stalin's collectivised farms, overlooking the absent kulaks and concentrating on the tractors and combine harvesters with which more and more acres were being drawn into cultivation, and the education programmes that had already turned millions of 'illiterate peasants' into 'educated citizens'. No tumbled down grassland there — but a workers' paradise with child benefit, crèches, libraries, student grants and eight weeks' annual holiday. Having read the Webbs' celebration, she was not inclined to join those critics who condemned the Soviet Union for its 'hypnotic reverence for machinery and mechanisation'.[32] Indeed, she concluded that 'There is little doubt that the farmworkers in Russia are beginning to live a truly civilised life, a life in sharp contrast with that of farm workers in any capitalist country in the world.'

Patching Up the Old Red Jacket

Ackland and Warner did their best to win their village for the struggle. They tried to organise a Chaldon Women's March on the Weld estate office over at Lulworth, but this intended protest against housing conditions never came off, apparently because, in a lapse towards the world of T. F. Powys, the women of West Chaldon had been divided by the activities of a local temptress called Blanche Rocket and could not overcome their differences sufficiently to combine against their exploitative rulers. So Warner, who had recently found eight dead rats in the village well, drove to East Lulworth with a bottle of the polluted water and made her protest alone.[33] They campaigned for the Labour Party during the 1935 election, organising a meeting for the candidate in the village hall, and using their Green MG to ferry Labour voters to the polling station. They took villagers with them as they went heckling, flyposting and demonstrating their way through the land: visiting Bovington Camp to stick anti-war notices on the tanks, or going up to London to attend May Day demonstrations – the latter trip being well remembered by Jimmy Pitman, the model for Ackland's unbowed farmworker who called down the red jacket on his own wretched abode. By this time Pitman had lost his slum cottage to Elizabeth Muntz, a Canadian sculptress who had bought it from the Weld estate for use as a studio; he and his family were living as Warner's tenant in Miss Green's cottage.[34]

Warner and Ackland also tried to revive the 'old independence' with a cultural programme. They initiated a book-lending scheme so that the citizens of their emerging Dorset Soviet could read the Hammonds, Engels and proletarian novels, which Warner judged to be all the better for 'a certain sectarian stiffening'.[35] They had no thought of reviving the traditional fêtes and harvest festivals but they did organise oppositional festivities. On 6 May 1935, they countered the village's official celebration of George V's Jubilee by running their own dance up by the barrows known as the Five Marys. Encouraged by the success of this event, which lasted much longer and was more exuberant than its rival in the village,[36] they organised further parties and dances, encouraging the village to boycott the parson and other representatives of class power and, for the first time in living memory, to 'run its own pleasures, without any interference from the gentry'.[37] The method was simple enough, as Warner once explained. They would hire the 'hideous' room that was available in the village, and not waste a penny trying to decorate it.[38] Cakes, sandwiches and lemonade were provided at minimal cost and soapflakes were sprinkled over the wooden floor to make a dancing surface. Children were welcome, so that mothers didn't get stuck at home, and no one was expected to dress up. The main thing, as Sylvia wrote to friends in the Party, was to 'have a band', since the wireless was 'so unadaptable'.[39] As the aim of these events was to open an independent cultural life for people who had, in Ackland's words, 'never, within memory, done anything by themselves, for themselves',[40] it would not have been appropriate to let the BBC set the pace.

Both women would late become regular contributors to *The Country Standard*,[41] a communist monthly which shared their enthusiasm for the red tractors of the Soviet Union, and for pouring vitriol on the upper class holidaymakers and rural preservationists who were so frequently 'appalled' by the sight of new bungalows while remaining regardless of the plight of rural workers.[42] In its first issue, *The Country Standard* condemned statutory bodies like The Pig Marketing Board and the Milk Marketing Board, as ramps for pouring money into the distributors' pockets, insisting that the time had come to 'fight these monopolies, these boards, these fascist methods of controlling industry'.[43] Surveying the doomed figures of traditional English husbandry — 'the horseman, the cowman, the shepherd, the labourer' — it insisted that these were 'skilled men who take a real pride in their own particular calling', and were quite capable of ensuring the success of 'a great scheme of national development for agriculture', if only the right one could be introduced.[44] Watching the harvest in full swing a couple of years later, Maurice Cornforth took a somewhat more metallic view, declaring the march of mechanisation undoubtedly a 'good thing', in that it 'increases the efficiency of production, and lightens labour'. And yet, under capitalism, the effect of machine methods was 'to throw farm workers out of a job . . . So what ought to be a blessing comes rather as a curse.'[45] A cartoon dismissed the whole National Government's agricultural policy as a 'War Machine', portraying it as a tank carrying the banner of 'Guns not Butter' as it rolls through a cornfield labelled 'The Power to Produce Plenty', while a redundant agricultural worker looks on, clenching his fist in simmering rural frustration.

Meanwhile, Sylvia Townsend Warner set about the official circulars and reports emanating from His Majesty's Stationery Office to reveal how badly 'our extremely urbanised government' neglected its responsibility for rural water supplies ('Not a drop to drink, nor a drop to wash with either, unless it is carried into the house in a bucket and carried out again as slops');[46] and then attacking the government's 'Blue books' to show how systematically agricultural workers were being robbed of their minimum wage and overtime money. An old Guild Socialist like H. J. Massingham could go on about crafts and the soil of Yeoman's England, but Townsend Warner insisted on calling agriculture an industry, and then passed certain judgement: 'I think there is no other industry in this country in which so vile a state of things obtains. In other industries wages may be kept down; but they are paid. In agriculture the wages are kept down; and they are not paid.'[47] She then asked Lenin's famous question: 'What is to be done?' Obviously 'the agriculture worker must no longer take it for granted that his employer knows how much to pay him, and pays it'. He should also join the union and organise his comrades, for 'very few farmers will care to dismiss a whole body of men'.

Ackland contributed crude propaganda stories designed to hammer home political points about the exploitation of the rural worker. She contrasted the wretched circumstance of the agricultural workers with the luxuriousness of the farmers who rise late for a breakfast served up on silver plate and then drive off for a leisurely day out. In case any slow readers missed the point she had one of her gentlefolk sing a line from a familiar children's song, and then adjusted the words: 'Call up your men, diddle-diddle, Set them to work, One to the plough, diddle-diddle, One to the cart. One to cut hay diddle-diddle, One to cut corn. While you and I, diddle-diddle, keep ourselves warm!'[48]

As war approached, people started to talk about Air Raid Precautions and the nation's long-suffering agricultural workers were now, so the *Country Standard* was quick to point out, expected to bow and scrape as the owners of their tied cottages — the very people who had failed, for generations, to make these dismal hovels 'proof against wind and rain' — came out to teach their labourers how to shove a sack up the chimney to make them proof against bomb blasts and poisonous gas. Maurice Cornforth was particularly incensed to read that the Dowager Lady Hanbury, wife of Sir Cecil Hanbury, the Tory MP for North Dorset, had converted the basement of their house in Kingston Maurward into 'a bomb- and gas-proof first-aid station' and was claiming, of her endeavour to make villagers 'gas-conscious', that 'they turned out better than for a Christmas tree'. It was 'a scandal that the safety of British country people should be left in the hands of a class' to which the likes of that patronising Dowager belonged.

Ackland and Warner pressed on with their Marxist barrage up into the early years of the war, although by 1939 the militant comrades of East Chaldon appear to have been using pseudonyms. They themselves had moved out of East Chaldon in August 1937, but 'Vanda Cook' was still there, pushing towards the Party's happy ending: 'Unity on the land would end the long history of the wretched squalid living and working conditions, would call a halt to the rot of the land, and would make this village and all others the happy, healthy, fertile home of British country people.'[49] 'Vanda Cook' reappeared during the war, asking 'What sort of government is this?'; and then going on to provide the answer: 'While the big landlords and farmers, the wealthy millers and merchants, pile up their profits and call for more and more war, the small-holder, the little farmer and shop-keeper and all the labouring folk in this country are squeezed dry.'[50]

'Jane Smith' had identical views. She carried out the same sorts of interviews with villagers who seem to have fitted the Marxist allegory just a little too perfectly to be true. There was young Mrs Turvey, a chronic asthmatic who sat in her damp and smoke-filled cottage while her Tom was away fighting the 'cruel war' that ought to be stopped: ' "It baint going to get us no place," she said, "no more than the last one did." '[51] There was Farmer Todd, 'an old Dorset man who loves the earth and toils all the day-lit hours and more to keep his little dairy farm going'. As a lay preacher, he was happy to deliver a sermon for the benefit of 'Jane Smith' when she came to collect her morning milk:

> A government chap up 'smorning telling me what to do wi' me grassland, 'e were. I says, 'I thought this was a democracy? You take yourself off, young man. It's your blamey government that ruins us farmers. Off with you! Democracy! S'pose you'll tell me that this is a democratic war to put down that Hitler? An' I'll tell you it's nowt but a Money Ramp. Aye, a war to keep money in the pockets of those as has it. You can't fool me.'

These were line-pushing articles, built up around the Communist Party's increasingly unsustainable position that the war was merely a dispute between imperialists, and that a 'People's Peace' would pave the way for revolution at home.[52]

There can have been little regret over at the Lulworth Castle estate office when in 1944, a German bomb fell near Miss Green's cottage in East Chaldon.[53] In his attack on the futility of the official Air Raid Precautions, Maurice Cornforth had observed that 'If a modern high explosive bomb fell anywhere near the average English village, windows would break, slates and tiles would come off the roofs, and many of the cottages would collapse altogether.'[54] Miss Green's cottage in East Chaldon gave itself up as conclusive proof of his point. As Warner wrote in a letter to Nancy Cunard, 'Our little house at Chaldon is gone, Nancy; the little stocky grey house that sat there looking so mittened and unperturbable.' There were no casualties. Jimmy Pitman had by this time been their tenant for some ten years, but both he and his wife May got out in time to escape serious injury when the red jacket finally descended on East Chaldon. As Warner wrote: 'The only decent cottage in that village, the only cottage kept in order, gone, while the hovels belonging to the Weld estate, God damnit, are untouched in all their filth, scarcely a bug shaken out of them.'[55]

Since Ackland and Warner had already moved on, this was really only a parting shot from the other side of the hill. We can leave with them, but not before joining Valentine Ackland to climb High Chaldon, the rounded green hill which is East Chaldon's primary landmark and observatory. Llewelyn Powys claimed it was possible to see Weymouth from the highest point on this hill but by the mid-Thirties Ackland was looking in the opposite direction. Gazing out towards Shaftesbury, some twenty-five miles to the north, she saw a rotting land, plain and unadorned, and smelt reaction in the evening air. There were stirrings where the chalk ridge of Cranborne Chase rises up at the edge of the Blackmore Vale; and they led her to fear that 'a split in the ranks gives Fascism its chance'.[56]

TWELVE

ORGANIC REVIVAL

> We'll have to establish some spot on earth, that will be the fissure into the underworld, like the oracle at Delphos, where one can always come to . . . some quiet house in the country — where one can begin — and from which the hiker, maybe, can branch out. Some place with a big barn and a bit of land — if one has enough money.
>
> D. H. Lawrence to Rolf Gardiner (1926)

SHAFTESBURY BEING an English hill town, and not the Italian one of long-standing comparison, it is quite possible to stand at the top of Gold Hill and see nothing but cloud and driving rain. The brochures have encouraged us to expect more than this. A cobbled lane should curve down steeply and the oak-dressed expanse of the Blackmore Vale should stretch out beyond the tilted and thatched roofs. Since this prospect is now most widely known as Hovis country, the wholesome smell of baking should suffuse the air. We might also expect to hear Vaughan Williams's Lark, not so much ascending as struggling to swim through syrup. But the rain dissolves this formulaic view, and the elements of the rural scene — soil, compost stooked straw and song — escape into the misted landscape where they take up unexpected positions of their own.

Gore Farm lies along the edge of that famous outlook, up the steep chalk escarpment from Melbury Abbas on the south-west heights of Cranborne Chase. It is surrounded by extensive mixed woodlands and quite undiminished by picturesque pretence. Beauty and utility seem to run together here. Yet, far from being a surviving fragment of Olde England of the sort that H. J. Massingham might have cherished, this landscape is evidently the creation of robust twentieth-century decision. Fontmell Down, another whale-backed turf promontory with magnificent views over the Blackmore Vale, may have been acquired by the National Trust, who maintain it as a rare stretch of unspoiled Wessex downland in memory of Thomas Hardy; but not before its unploughed turf had been thoroughly improved with methods advocated in the Nineteen Thirties by the modernising agriculturalist Sir George Stapledon: sprinkled with basic slag (a phosphate-bearing byproduct of the steel industry), enriched with scientifically improved grasses, and bisected at its most prominent point by a confidently enlarged shelter bed of trees.

Since the late Sixties, Gore Farm has been the home of John Eliot Gardiner, the conductor who also farms here along organic lines. The period instruments that feature in his orchestra, the London Baroque Soloists, are matched by those that stand in his barns and fields: an ancient reaper-binder and, at harvest-time, a combined threshing machine and reed binder brought in to thresh the old strain of Maris Wigeon wheat grown here, and to bundle the long reeds for thatch.

This combination of agriculture and music now extends back through three generations. The story begins with Balfour Gardiner, a composer of private means who was a friend of Percy Grainger's and also the patron of Frederick Delius. He discovered Gore Farm while out walking and bought it in 1924, when the baronial estates of Fontmell Magna and Iwerne Minster were being broken up and auctioned off in lots. It was a bleak and starvegutted place then, the buildings little more than a collection of stables that locals avoided at night on account of bad spirits. W. H. Hudson may have celebrated that famously 'ewe-cropped' downland turf as the living garment of pastoral England, but by the time Balfour Gardiner arrived, whole stretches had degenerated into rabbit-infested chalk scree. Advised by the Forestry Commission, Balfour began planting the desolated fields and upland slopes to timber, and was soon joined by his young nephew Rolf Gardiner, who took over Gore Farm as a 25-year-old in 1927. They continued through years of severe agricultural depression, planting over three million trees.

To begin with, Rolf Gardiner concentrated his endeavours in the fields rather than the woods, but he soon took over the afforestation programme. As a poet of the trees (his writings reveal a special fondness for words like 'sylvester') Rolf Gardiner was inclined to apply arboreal metaphors to human endeavour too. He was inspired by D. H. Lawrence's injunction that, instead of coming to terms with the mechanistic outlook of industrial civilisation, 'We must plant ourselves again in the universe.' Gardiner met and corresponded with Lawrence, and felt exhilarated when the great novelist seemed to approve of his plans for this corner of Wessex, remarking 'I think there's some sort of destiny in Gore Farm.'[1] Gardiner had his visionary side, but he was also a practical man. A skilled forester who had trained in silviculture at Dartington Hall, he planted his trees partly in order to provide shelter for livestock and cladding that would put an end to erosion, and partly because he was convinced that upland planting would help to raise a falling water table even in porous chalk. John Eliot Gardiner stands at a critical distance from his father's political vision but he observes that, on agrarian and ecological matters, Rolf Gardiner can still seem 'very contemporary and far-sighted'. That unconventional idea of achieving water catchment by planting trees on the chalk uplands was vindicated in the drought of 1976, when John Eliot remembers looking down over the normally lush Blackmore Vale and seeing it parched and camel-coloured, while up on the wooded heights around Gore Farm they had green grass.

Rolf Gardiner's curiously mixed legacy can be felt at Gore Farm, but if we are to bring it into clearer focus we must follow the path he knew as 'the Wild Way', dropping down from that isolated 'eyrie' on the downs to Springhead, which stands near the head of a sheltered combe where the Blackmore Vale runs into the rising chalk. For years, Gardiner had eyed this captivating place, with its courtyard of mill buildings and its large mill pond, from the downs above, and, with Balfour's assistance, he was eventually able to buy it into his estate in 1933. Accompanied by members of the Gore Kinship, a circle of comrades and acolytes that would soon be reformed as the Springhead Ring, he led an inaugural procession down the hill. There is good reason to imagine the party singing an ancient madrigal or canon as they kicked up white dust on the unmetalled upper Blandford Road, and made their descent through a depressed and bewildered landscape that seemed 'lost in a golden haze of dying tradition'. Rural England was 'drifting into dissolution', but Gardiner and his fellow pioneers were not distracted by the way 'wild nature cast a glamour on it'.[2] Convinced that 'the unfolding of a new order of human society might depend on the contribution of small exemplary bodies rather than on mass-movements',[3] they pledged themselves to restoring this piece of England 'from the herb to the hymn', as Gardiner liked to put it, creating a 'small local bulwark' against the 'disaster' of commercial opportunism and anarchy that had overtaken the land since the Great War.[4] They came bearing salt, earth, sulphur and lavender, and, on 3 September 1933, dedicated Springhead as 'a centre for the gathering and training of men and women for the weal of Wessex'.[5]

The idea, as members of Springhead Ring would retort when accused of hankering nostalgically after the lost age of the English yeoman, was to mend the clock and not just to put it back. Springhead would set out to 'rebuild a hill-and-vale economy along modern organic lines'. They would restore not just any old sheep but Dorset Downs to the slopes, and bring fertility back to the soil. They would revive rural industry, and use song and dance to bring season festivity back to the dwindled life of Fontmell Magna, and to recover the sacramental rhythm of the agricultural year. At Springhead, Dorset would have its harvest festivals again.

There was certainly a job to be done. Norman Oddy, a retired agricultural worker, who used to participate in folk-dancing and the Easter and Christmas plays at Springhead, still reveres the man who committed himself to the area at a time of terrible agricultural depression. People were leaving the land in droves. The rural schools were raising children for emigration to towns and cities, and of those who remained the lucky ones found work tarring the roads, or building military bases, while the rest languished, living off the pestilential rabbits and raising a pittance by scraping up moss to be sold as wadding to Covent Garden florists. Then Rolf Gardiner arrived, creating employment for thirty people in farm and forest work, and initiating cultural activities to overcome the stunting isolation of this moribund country life. Gardiner, explains Oddy with the caution of one who knows the sneer of eccentricity is never far away, 'saw the whole man'. He tried to revive the barter economy and heard the death of rural labour in the discordant sound of the chainsaw. 'How right he was,' says Oddy, referring to what has since been done with bulldozers in Chico Mendez's rain forest. Gardiner was 'a marvellous thing round here in those days': 'a little bit larger than life' and a man 'almost before his time'.

Gardiner's decentralising idea of rural leadership emphasised local responsibility and community service, but it was critical as well as unconventional and it is scarcely surprising that the Springhead initiative should have encountered some 'periods of reaction and a few difficult incidents' in the neighbourhood. In 1937, Gardiner stood for election to the County Council, displacing a retired general who, 'like the majority of councillors', had previously relied on apathy to ensure that he was elected unopposed, and who lost his seat despite the fact that his voters were zealousy ferried back and forth to the polling station by 'the limousines of the "County" '.[6] As for the mansions of the squirearchy, Gardiner judged these traditional centres of rural leadership to be shockingly decadent. He never liked to see country houses in military or institutional use but, like H. J. Massingham, who would later become his friend and collaborator, he believed that things had been fundamentally awry since the eighteenth-century enclosures, when the landowners had thrown in their lot with the urban merchant classes, spurning the people of the countryside who were their natural allies and responsibility, and allowing agriculture to become 'ancillary to sporting interests'.[7] Like the communists of East Chaldon, he reviled fox-hunting, less out of sympathy for the fox than because it showed the pitiful level to which the aristocracy had descended in pursuit of moneyed leisure. He loathed the pheasant as a 'foreign intruder' that had 'unmanned the responsible English squire to a childish degree'.

At a time when bodies like the National Trust were beginning to devise the schemes through which they would preserve some of the nation's beleaguered country houses as evocative symbols of a superior past, Gardiner was peering down the driveway with the contrary idea of turning these places into bustling centres of rural industry. Had he and his fellow rural revivers stood at the gates of Lulworth Park, they would have been less interested in the sham castle than in the practical possibilities of the stable block in front of it. It was their view that the aristocrats and big farmers should accept their responsibilities and become true leaders on their land: entrepreneurs of mutual aid, who would set up small co-operative businesses concerned with agriculture and rural crafts. As for the evacuated pasture around the church of St Andrews, they imagined going further than J. F. Pennie, the 'modern genius' of the Weld estate, who had only tried to keep the memory of that extinguished village alive. Gardiner and his circle hoped to reverse the damage done by the enclosures. They wanted the squires to start breaking their parks and fields into small holdings and resettling the land with new yeomen like those to be forged at the 'rural university' that Gardiner was determined to establish, with or without the help of a government intent on confining its 'Special Areas programme' to industrial regions, on the Springhead estate.

The men and women of the Springhead Ring were committed to organic husbandry, but they were like the mechanising communists of East Chaldon in being wholly opposed to the merely scenic view of country life. In 1929, they even sought to redirect the newly founded Youth Hostels Association. Determined to emphasise the 'rural aspect of hiking', they formed a Wessex circuit of 'Hiker's Lodges', based largely in farm buildings, through which they hoped to prove it possible to 'draw the urban hiker towards the land

and its inhabitants', and for the countryman to exercise his own hospitality. The YHA chose to stick with what Gardiner derided as 'chains of cheap lodging houses' and to establish itself as 'a spectacular organisation for the urban walker and cyclist'.[8]

Springhead is still there to cast its elemental spell. Originally a mill, the sixteenth and seventeenth-century buildings are grouped around a courtyard. A collapsing garage, built like a thatched pioneer's shack, still testifies to a mid-century ambivalence about the motor-car; and a small lake stretches back to a wooded bank under the downs where the chalk-filtered water of the Fontmell Brook trickles out over the greensand in seven much allegorised springs. The garden is no longer the musical grove it was when Mrs Marabel Gardiner was in her prime. The outdoor operas and masques that she used to produce here with the help of figures like Imogen Holst, Roger Norrington and her son John Eliot Gardiner are now distant memories, and time has also levelled the terraced beds shaped to echo the ancient lynchets on the down above. But there is still an orchard, a dancing lawn and an Italianate temple by the lake. It has been said that a classically landscaped aristocratic garden is a place where 'shit has no smell',[9] but Springhead would never have tolerated such a pretentious thought; as Rolf Gardiner himself once remarked, 'Manure is very nearly a fetish at Springhead.'[10] This was to be a garden of interconnectedness regained, where, through Morris-dancing ritual, sacrament and season, music itself would be brought back to earth.

Now owned by the Springhead Trust, founded by Mrs Marabel Gardiner after her husband's death in 1971 with the active encouragement of Fritz Schumacher of 'Small is Beautiful' fame,[11] the place is run as a residential centre available to the exotically mixed threads of the green cause. It is used for meetings by organisations like the Soil Association and the Other Economic Summit. One weekend may bring a Voluntary Services Overseas reunion; the next it may be filled with crop-circlers or Hasidic children from the Lubavitch School in London's Stamford Hill, who have come with their rabbi and banners announcing the coming of the Messiah.

The Springhead millroom is ornamented with environmentalist posters — one from Common Ground announces that 'We have deep roots in the Greenwood' and warns of 'the cult of the conifer' — and its electric lights are mounted like candles, on old wagonwheels. Upstairs, a small library contains books dating back to Rolf Gardiner's time: many works by H. J. Massingham and some by Henry Williamson; songbooks of Bach and Palestrina; Edward Carpenter on polytheism and *The Art of Creation;* David Irving's *The Destruction of Dresden*; early conservationist volumes with names like *Look to the Land* and *The Rape of the Earth*, and a book by R. Douglas Brown called *The Battle for Crichel Down.*

Rolf Gardiner died more than twenty years ago, but locals still gossip about the unconventional things this self-styled 'man of action' got up to at Springhead. Some recall the singing, folk-dancing and short-trousered ésprit de corps with an embarrassed cringe: 'dancing in purple knickers', as one calls it, quite inaccurately. Others remember how neighbouring landowners and farmers used to smirk at Gardiner's agricultural activities in the Thirties. They would describe Springhead as a place of 'muck and mystery', slapping their thighs as they joked coarsely that since organic husbandry is notoriously labour intensive, the real mystery was always who Gardiner would get to spread the muck: as if the many youth work-camps he organised were only cunning ways of securing unpaid assistance with this task.[12] Down in the Fontmell Magna pub a woman still puzzles at the memory of Gardiner coming to the village school when she was a girl there, perhaps for one of the Rogationtide processions he conducted with Bishop Lovett of Salisbury, and leading the children out into his woods, where he sat them on branches and encouraged them to sing, recite or just listen to verse. An older man tells of a boy before the war, who used to hide in a tree to ogle the maidens of the Springhead Ring as they came out to swim naked in the lake. It is still possible to find defenders of conventional morality who speculate, more pruriently than is convincing, about the 'Lawrentian' way in which Rolf Gardiner may have planted himself among the followers who revered him as a golden-haired young god.

Yet, as everyone associated with the Springhead Trust knows, a dark shadow keeps falling over the courtyard of Rolf Gardiner's memory. Standing by the old Paulownia tree, the present director of the Springhead Trust, Peter Hood, points to a pile of newly delivered paving stones and volunteers that the man who brought them had stepped out of his vehicle and asked, 'Is this where that Nazi lived?' After confirming that this was Rolf Gardiner's place, he had gone on to inform Hood, who had heard this one many times before, that Fontmell Magna never got bombed in the war because Gardiner had planted a large swastika in Fontmell Woods as a sign for

Hitler's planes. Gardiner loyalists try to dissolve this persistent lore by insisting that several bombs did in fact fall on the village, and that the woodlands were actually planted by Balfour Gardiner before the Nazi Party became a power on the German scene. But the canard persists. In some variations, it includes a secret landing strip.

The early years of the Second World War were certainly difficult for the Gardiners. John Stewart Collis, who came to work in Gardiner's woods in 1941 and soon discovered that it was impossible to sketch a church tower without being marched off as a suspected foreign agent, found his employer 'a lonely and embattled figure in the midst of many who are hostile or cold'.[13] Rolf Gardiner's daughter and literary executrix, Rosalind Richards, remembers her father's patriotic rage at being kicked off the Home Guard, and the way tongues wagged when a party of German prisoners of war were detailed to work on Springhead, and Gardiner greeted them in their own language.

Questions were asked about Gardiner, and not just in the village. His sister, Margaret Gardiner, well to the left of the political spectrum, was visited in London by detectives interested in ascertaining whether Rolf might be a traitor: she remembers the puzzlement with which they scrutinised the Marxist literature on her shelves, while she tried to explain that Rolf's interest in Germany had always been romantic — more concerned with hiking, music and agriculture than with politics. People excited themselves with the preposterous thought that, had Hitler invaded England, Gardiner would have stepped out of Springhead as the Gauleiter of Wessex; there were apparently vigilantes in Fontmell Magna who felt licensed to enter the Springhead house at night and poke about while the Gardiners, far from being bent over the standard Fifth Columnist's radio-transmitter, tried to sleep upstairs. Whispered suspicions followed Gardiner for the rest of his days: as he told Leslie Paul in 1951, labels tend to 'stick with the most unfortunate adhesiveness'. More than fifty years after the war, I listened as an elderly lady explained how she had been introduced to Gardiner in the Thirties. Quite blind now, she was still looking him up and down in her mind's eye, a mythical figure bent on recruiting her into his 'Dorset Nazi Party'; he looked just like 'The Sanatogen Man' as he stood there, erect, with blond hair and lederhosen.

These persistent accusations make no concessions to the complexity of Gardiner's situation in the mid-Thirties. They also release a great wave of remonstration from elderly people who remember Gardiner from that time. Sir George Trevelyan, who spent the post-war years 'metamorphosing' the old idea of the country house party to produce an adult education college in the National Trust's mansion at Attingham, Shropshire, and who is now well into his third decade as 'the grand old man of the New Age', rebuts Gardiner's whispering detractors. 'People will say anything.'[14] Rolf Gardiner was indeed 'a powerful-appearing man: Teutonic-looking, strong and very firm'. He 'marched in leather breeches and that sort of thing, and got people moving in movements'. He had extensive connections with 'the very best of the German Youth Movement', and wanted to build 'the true discipline of young people'. But Sir George is quite adamant that 'there was nothing of the Nazi' in Rolf Gardiner's make-up: indeed, that his German loyalties placed him among the enemies of National Socialism.

The point is underscored by Mary Langman and Ethelyn Hazel, who worked during the Thirties at the organic Pioneer Health Centre in Peckham, where they helped involve mothers in a vegetable-growing Women's Auxiliary Yeoman's Service. They remember Gardiner respectfully from the early days of the Soil Association (founded in 1945). Mary Langman defers to the judgement of Mrs Hazel, who remarks stoutly that he was 'a remarkable man' for whom one could only feel the 'very greatest respect'. However, she also recalls that the back-to-the-land movement of the Nineteen Thirties had a 'funny tinge' to it. The economic situation was desperate, and some 'very nice people' got mixed up in extreme causes: some drifting into communism, of which the doctors at the Pioneer Health Centre were sometimes accused, and some striking out in 'the other' direction.

Bell Tents in a Field

> In polyphonic music all parts have functions but they listen to one another and know when to make a stress and when to be in retreat. Is not this of the essence of political order?
>
> Rolf Gardiner (1933)

Anyone visiting Gore Farm in August 1934 would have encountered Sigvart Godeseth, a Norwegian whom Gardiner had first met at an International Voluntary Service camp in Wales. Godeseth farmed Gore organically, but as Gardiner's warden and guestmaster, he was also responsible for the semi-circle of bell tents standing in the field. The Springhead Ring's three-week

'Harvest camp' was like nothing the camping 'beaks' of Eton College had imagined even at their most utopian. As Gardiner wrote in a report written for the Minister of Labour and the York Trust, it brought together sixty-two young men and seven young women 'from different walks of life' to give them 'a direct experience of community by thinking, playing and working on the land'.[15] The event was designed to further 'the social education of young men in consequence of unemployment and rural decay'. Many of the twenty-one unemployed had been recruited from labour exchanges. The women were mostly teachers and social workers, but one farm girl was included. There were three public schoolboys, six university lecturers, two house painters, two miners, a brass engraver and a cinema operator. Twelve members of the German student movement were in attendance too.

As joint chief, Gardiner looked after 'policy and co-ordination', while responsibility for the 'ceremonial' aspect and for 'the education of the camp through artistic and ritual forms' rested with his long-standing friend, the poet Christopher Scaife. Springhead's camps aimed to meet the Depression by creating a 'reinvigorated stock of countrymen' from the unused material of the towns'. They were designed to create a sense of order, reverence and comradeship, while also 'emphasising the community in relation to its surroundings and its tasks'. Reveille was announced at 6.30 each morning with 'the rhythmic beating of a mellow-toned gong'. The participants would emerge barefoot from their tents and then run silently in single file, following the chiefs as they snaked in and out of the ring of tents in 'circular evolutions' — 'winding and turning in the rays of the rising sun' before drawing up in a semi-circle before the flagstaff.

Michael Pitt Rivers, the conservation-minded owner of the nearby Rushmore estate, attended these camps as an adolescent and remembers them still with affection and a little amazement. The flag of St George, its red cross augmented by a Wessex dragon, would be hoisted with due ceremony and the men would then greet the dawn by singing a German hymn: 'Hail the day, which in darkness lay . . . ' Breakfast would be served after a tent inspection, at 7.45. Everything was 'back to nature' — especially the bread, which was made from coarse ground wheat grown on the farm and had 'husks and all those other bits and pieces in it'. At 8.45, gangs assembled and marched off to work. They might be detailed to gather and thresh corn, plant trees, 'brush up' neglected woodlands or dredge the silted Springhead mill pond, preparing marshy land for the planting of basket willows, necessary if the rural industry of basket-weaving was to be revived. Yet the construction and administration of compost heaps was at the heart of the project. These would be built according to bio-dynamic methods learned in Germany — layered, with systems of aeration and, in some cases, even chimneys made of lengths of drainpipe.

After a sandwich lunch, 2.00–4.00 was left quiet for study and contemplation. There was singing at 4.30, followed by group work or rehearsals. A couple of hours would be set aside for lectures and discussion before the evening choral. Then the camp community would stand with linked arms in the farm courtyard, lit only by a torch, which the camp herald would extinguish immediately after the following words had been sung:

> The earth has turned us from the sun,
> And let us close our circle now to light,
> But open it to darkness, and each one
> Warm with this circle's warming,
> Go in good darkness to good sleep
> Good night.

Gardiner's camps were directed towards 'the recovery and tending of a tract of English country which shall support not only those who work there permanently but those who come there for training and preparation in the cause of the nation's renewal'. Manual labour was central, but since they intended to restore springs of action unbent by the Moloch of industrial capitalism, they also set out to overcome 'artificial distinctions' between leaders and led, and between manual and intellectual activity. Self-sufficiency was emphasised and responsibility devolved. Even so, Gardiner had to inform his funders that some of the unemployed failed to get the idea. Accustomed to 'the regimen of holiday camps' run by a government that didn't want to aggravate the trade unions by giving the unemployed real work to do, they found it hard to adjust to the more laborious endeavour of a Springhead camp. Indeed, some had to be sent home on their third day. Gardiner noted that the recruitment must be improved: his camps could only deal with men of 'promise, vitality, and eagerness' and could not 'undertake to break men in'.

Music, or rather 'the musical discipline of rhythmic forms' was essential. The movements used on the morning runs and during assemblies were 'drawn from the discipline of dance rather than military drill', and the camps were full of singing too. The beaks of Eton College may have considered resorting to Hackney songbooks in an attempt to enliven their camp fire at Worbarrow Bay, without, of course, 'Prussianizing' it. But the Springhead Ring were at once more ambitious and less xenophobic. Together with their German Master of Music, Dr Theodor Warner, they ensured that the rowdy, monotonous 'popular' songs brought in by the unemployed were discarded in the first few days. Helped by the experienced singers of the Springhead Ring, camp-members were soon signing parts of masses by William Byrd, folk songs set to instrumental settings, rounds and chorals, and passages of sixteenth-century liturgical music. They had been introduced to the statecraft of polyphonic song, which compels 'obedience and submission to an objective form'.

Gardiner and his leaders resisted the call for 'organised ball games' like football and cricket, suspecting these could only be 'negative activities' like the 'desultory' smoking, card-playing or football with which demoralised people try to 'kill time'. They also organised a library and evening discussions in the hope that the camps would restore 'a lost power of utterance' to the young unemployed men.[16] Each year the Harvest Camp would have a theme. It was to be Land Settlement in 1935 and Regional Reconstruction in 1936, but in 1934 the topic was 'the Tradition of English Social Leadership', chosen because the crisis besetting the country was at root 'a crisis of leadership'. In three discussion groups, leaders asked each participant to tell his life story 'as frankly and objectively as possible'. This strategy stimulated considerable interest and discussion as it revealed the remarkable difference between people's backgrounds. But Gardiner was disappointed to report that there had been 'practically no political tension in the camp', and that the unemployed 'shewed no clear political views or desires'. This lack of 'intellectual opposition' obliged the leaders, who had hoped that 'a vigorous clash of ideas would bring forth a more urgent sense of real needs', to lecture the participants.

The visiting German students, all of whom were National Socialists, stated that their ideal leader would be a man of 'soldierly virtues'. They then withdrew from discussion, saying they would prefer to listen as the English came up with their own definition. It may seem a pity that Gardiner hadn't invited Llewelyn Powys along to help out. He might have got discussion going by condemning Hitler's Nazis for their 'low born love of action' and suggesting that moral courage, surely far more useful than physical courage, was actually a quality of cowards: 'how far more admirable in every way are cowards. They can be counted upon to add to the refined amenities of social intercourse, and more trustworthy friends it would be impossible to find'.[17]

But Gardiner relied on schoolmasters, who had a different answer for those German students. Harold Greenleaves, who was still teaching at nearby Bryanston School when I was there in the Sixties, talked on 'Peace and War', but the real burden of exposition fell on Cecil de Sausmarez from Wellington College, who gave a series of talks proposing Alfred the Great as 'the prototype of the Great English leader'. Alfred was suitable because the camp took place in the middle of his Wessex kingdom and because the idea of a Saxon affinity between the English and the Germans was considered both 'natural and inspiring'. He had been a model of 'kingly initiative', and his example was used to elucidate the difference between true leaders and 'drivers of men' or those 'merely in authority'. Gardiner too viewed Alfred almost as an outward-bounder, a Kurt Hahn of the ninth century who took the path of frugality and self-sacrifice — sharing the life of his men, inspiring them by example and then, at a carefully chosen moment, leading them out to defeat the maurauding Danes.

The camp culminated in a harvest festival in which guests (including Ministry of Labour officials) were invited to attend performances of music, sword dances and the dramatised ballad of Robin Hood and the Butcher. The final event was a midnight hike. Having split into four groups and spread out over Cranborne Chase, the participants lit torches and converged on Win Green, the highest point in Wiltshire, where they lit a beacon fire, listened to speeches from the chiefs and sang the songs 'Full flaming fire' and 'Barbury Camp' — before marching back to their tents. The camp was closed, as it had been opened, 'by beating of its bounds, by the kindling of a fire . . . and by the speaking of lines from the English Bible'.

Agricultural Defence

> 'What a charming *leafy-looking, primrosy* valley this is before us,' said the lady. 'Fine country, maam,' replied the young farmer, 'and breeds some of the best cattle in all Dorsetshire.'
>
> J. F. Pennie on the Blackmore Vale
> as seen from a passing coach (1827)

It was not Springhead that Valentine Ackland had in mind when she looked north from East Chaldon and sensed the sour smell of fascism in the rural air — even though the man on whom her suspicions centred had visited Gardiner's 1934 Harvest Camp to talk about 'Race and Leadership'. Captain George Lane-Fox Pitt Rivers was an aristocrat of decidedly 'theoretical' bent. He owned the Pitt Rivers estate, which commanded a vast tract of southern England, and he lived at Hinton St Mary across the Blackmore Vale to the south-west.

When I drove across it early one autumn evening in 1991, the Blackmore Vale was still strongly aromatic, but it was only the smell of silage that wafted over the pasture, thickening into pungent pockets here and there. The mechanised fields were scattered with vast cylinders of rolled straw of a kind that would have done Stalin's collectivised farms proud, and I imagined Rolf Gardiner's disapproval as I heard the BBC's local radio station pumping American country music over the English acres that he had tried to revitalise with unaccompanied folk songs, motets and rhythmic country dances. The sun was hanging low over the misted horizon to the west: blood red, as Tex Ritter once growled, and going down.

The Blackmore Vale would have looked different in the Thirties. The woodlands may have been bright with rosebay willow herb, but they were also derelict, and smothered with thorns and brambles. There would have been empty cottages by the acidified and, in Gardiner's phrase, 'cow sick' fields, and demoralised agricultural workers struggling along on the bare minimum wage of thirty-one shillings and sixpence. The implements of traditional husbandry may be imagined discarded as the underestimated artist Thomas Hennell showed them, their 'wormy and twisted' forms left to rot by disused barns or in rough grass at the corner of a field.[18] Captain Pitt Rivers, who owned this land, and a host of villages besides, remains a much rumoured fellow and, like Springhead, his seventeenth-century manor house at Hinton St Mary can be approached along the leafy avenues of local speculation. Rolf Gardiner may be accused of having planted a swastika in his woods, but Captain Pitt Rivers is said to have planted arrows in the corn to guide the Nazi bombers. And here again there are those who reject the charge as 'absolute lunacy', adding that while 'you could write five novels' about this highly eccentric landowner, he 'couldn't have planted a crop' to save his life.

Yet the rumours persist. In the pub at Hinton St Mary an elderly man claims that the Captain opened a school in the village to provide for the many illegitimate children he had sired in the neighbourhood. Elsewhere, a former staff-member looks back aghast at the years she spent in the Captain's service. 'He was disgusting, really,' she observes with the deeply embedded disappointment of one who saw a long tradition of deference betrayed from above. She is adamant that the bricklayer once showed her where he had built a secret hole in the wall in which the Captain kept his radio transmitter. 'Everything was German,' she asserts, including his car and his dog. There was no shortage of swastikas inside the house either: she remembers them on the desk in the study, around the fireplace and woven into the hearth rugs. She recalls the Captain's habit of hiring high-stepping young ladies as secretaries in London, and also the reason for their hasty departure. Shortly after arriving, one of these comely recruits came down agitated in the morning, demanding that a lock be put on her bedroom door to protect her from the horrible old man who had turned up at her bedside in the middle of the night. It was more than any estate-worker's job was worth to grant her request, so she had no choice but to join the others who had already packed their bags and fled.

Valentine Ackland was most concerned about 'a certain interesting organisation' called the Wessex Agricultural Defence Association which was 'very popular with the local farmers' and 'steadily denied' that it had any association with the British Union of Fascists. Her suspicions were confirmed in February 1935, when the *Dorset County Chronicle* reported on 'significant movements' in the northern parts of the county. Members of the WADA — including the leader, Captain George Pitt Rivers — had attended a Blackshirt meeting in Sturminster Newton; and their presence was said to have 'given rise to statements connecting the two bodies'.[19] Pitt Rivers had also been present at the Dorchester meeting with which the BUF had recently opened its campaign in the county, and Sir Oswald Mosley had come down, in Autumn 1934, to address a meeting at the Tithe Barn Theatre in Hinton St Mary. The barn stands within the gates of the manor, and Pitt Rivers was certainly not just there as a disinterested host and squire.[20] That the policies of the BUF and the Independent Agriculturalists were remarkably similar at that time can be deduced from a letter by A. K. Chesterton of the British Union of Fascists, who wrote from London to contest the *Dorset County Chronicle*'s claim that fascism would fail to catch on in Wessex because it went against the grain of 'common sense'. Chesterton's rebuttal rehearsed Pitt Rivers's favourite arguments: 'Is it not "common sense" that the British standards of life should be safeguarded against mass production based upon the massed might of Oriental labour subsisting on rice? Is it not "common sense" that Britain should develop her vast Imperial resources and great productive power in order to turn out for Britons the goods for which there is a clamorous demand, and so abolish the anomaly of poverty in an age of plenty? Is it not "common sense" that the organised ramps of modern commercial civilisation should be transformed to socially useful purposes of the substitution of a planned economy in place of the chaos of laissez-faire conditions?'[21]

The BUF wouldn't give numbers but it claimed to have 'a very good following in North Dorset', and for a while there was speculation about 'a possible fusion' for electioneering purposes: indeed, 'the name of a very prominent landowner actively identified with the association' had even been mentioned 'as a possible "Blackshirt" candidate' in the next general election'.[22] Captain Pitt Rivers was clearly the man but by November 1935 he had put his urban Blackshirted friends at a little distance, preferring to stand for North Dorset as an Independent defender of agriculture. Indeed, by this time, the campaigning squire had made other changes too: the Wessex Agricultural Defence Association had been based in Sturminster Newton, only a mile or so down the road from his beech-lined drive, but he fought the election on behalf of an even more precisely localised outfit called the North Dorset Agricultural Defence League. Unimpressed by this shifting array of squirearchical fronts, Ackland noted drily that Pitt Rivers had won 1,771 votes in a four-cornered fight; she did not record that he had also lost his deposit, along with the Labour candidate who had polled 1,360 votes, or, for that matter, that the incumbent Tory, Sir Cecil Hanbury, had easily retained his seat with 13,055 votes.[23]

Ackland may seem to have overstated the threat, but something odd was brewing up in North Dorset during the Thirties. Captain George Pitt Rivers was the grandson of Lieutenant-General Augustus Henry Pitt Rivers, whose Victorian excavations on Cranborne Chase effectively inaugurated modern field archaeology. The Captain was also a colourful figure in his own right: a maverick aristocrat whose excesses strained the broad toleration that Wessex traditionally extends to its squires. Standing up in front of villagers in Motcombe, he declared that his battle was 'the same as William Cobbett's had been one hundred years ago — to fight not for the vermin who feed upon the taxes', but for 'those who work to raise them'.[24]

Valentine Ackland, who also invoked the memory of Cobbett for her communist cause, feared that Pitt Rivers and his accomplices would win the smaller farmers away from solidarity with their labourers, 'widening the breach' between them, and completing the isolation of the already 'neglected and oppressed' workers.[25] In the view of Pitt Rivers and his fellow Agricultural Defenders, the national political parties could offer nothing to Dorset's stricken agriculturalists, be they landowners, tenant farmers or landless labourers, except the continued subordination of their interests to those of the far more influential urban classes. As Pitt Rivers explained, 'this constituency can only be truly represented by someone completely independent of party domination. All political parties draw their support from votes in the large industrial areas and their members are powerless to voice the claims of the rural population.' The Captain hoped that the cause of Agricultural Defence would appeal across the traditional divisions of the class structure: 'We are starting the first movement in English politics which will unite all producers' interests on behalf of the industry as a whole and combine the interests of the farmer and the agricultural worker, as well as the functional landowner.'[26] Stressing that his supporters were drawn from all the established political parties, Captain Pitt Rivers hailed the constituents of North Dorset as 'Men and Women of the countryside' — even when they were jeering and trying to boo him off stage as the final results of the election were announced.[27]

Campaigning under the slogans 'Justice for Agriculture' and 'Agricultural Revival and Rural Prosperity', the Captain's men set themselves against 'all marketing schemes, quotas, deficiency payments and subsidies'. Like the communists of East Chaldon, they condemned the new marketing boards along with all the other machinery of State agricultural policy: 'we are fighting against all devices to cripple the initiative of producers without securing them markets in order to make profits for middlemen and importers of foodstuffs and to increase the vast army of officials'.[28] Yet in Valentine Ackland's opinion, it was the fact that tithes were still levied on much agricultural land — a tax that the communists of the *Country Standard* also opposed — that had 'given the Fascists their big chance'.

Pitt Rivers was surely right when he told the *Chronicle* that the uneven persistence of tithe rentcharge on agricultural land was anachronistic and unjust ('Why, every other industry has escaped tithes except farming . . . '). As the Chairman of the Wessex Agricultural Defence Association, which claimed to be the body most entitled to represent the interests of agricultural tithepayers in Britain, he ploughed his way through the statutes to build a formidable case against the 'parasitical' clergy who were growing fat on money originally intended for 'the relief of the poor', and against the Ecclesiastical Commissioners, for whom the word 'sacred' seemed to be 'an economic synonym for the word "sinecure" '.[29]

So the Captain went on the stump through the Blackmore Vale, clouding the air with his explanations of its sunken condition. He exchanged insults of the lowest kind with the other candidates, especially the Tories who despised the Agricultural Defenders as vote-splitting renegades. Lady Hanbury, the dowager wife of the incumbent Tory MP for North Dorset, insinuated that, as the owner of a far greater acreage than her own prosperous husband, Pitt Rivers stood to be greatly enriched by the abolition of tithes (a step, she warned darkly, that would only make it easier for a future socialist government to abolish rents). The Agricultural Defenders replied that Sir Cecil Hanbury's usurious commercial interests were such that he would profit handsomely from a slump in which surplus agricultural produce could be bought cheap — an accusation that was dismissed as 'a downright dirty lie'.[30]

The public meetings were rude and chaotic. As one close witness remembers, a lot of the farmers had decidedly Bolshevik sympathies, but came along because the Captain was the landowner. Pitt Rivers was no advocate of organic farming, so he didn't have that incredulity to face. But he was a notoriously bad speaker, given to overheated rhetoric and rabble-rousing. Once, he was questioned about his modest number of recruits. Replying along the lines of 'Rome wasn't built in a day', he reached for an illustration that seemed within the grasp of his audience: 'As you farmers know, you can put a bull in with a herd of cows, but you don't get results the next day.' The answer came quickly in that vale of mocking belly laughter: 'Yessir, but you expect to see a lot of satisfied faces.' Special measures had to be taken by Trelawney Reed, the Press officer for the Agricultural Defenders whose cottage under the hill at Farnham also provided William Joyce — who would later broadcast Nazi propaganda from Germany as Lord Haw Haw — with a base in the area. Having drummed up interest in London, Reed would meet journalists at the railway station, and then take them off to the pub, where he would ply them with free drink. When they were sufficiently legless, Reed would announce that although they had unfortunately missed the meeting, he had already prepared an account of everything that had happened there.

At least once during the campaign, the *Dorset County Chronicle* fell for the canvassing Captain's romantic charms. On 25 July 1935, it profiled him in frankly heroic terms: 'Captain Pitt Rivers is a landlord fighting for tenants' rights. He is a wealthy man defending poor men when they are attacked by officialdom. He is a squire with a fine old manor house that has an incomparable view across the lovely Blackmore Vale, who takes the part of the labourer in his village home against a policy which he declares has thrown hundreds of farm-workers out of employment in the last four years.' As for his vision of Wessex rejuvenated from the ground up, the reporter was entranced: 'In a prosperous farming community he sees also the salvation of the marketing towns of Dorset. When farmers ride into one of the Hardy towns jingling the money that once went to tithes but is now available for new machinery; when the worker's wife catches the carrier with a fuller purse because her husband works longer growing England's food; then the butcher, the tailor, the grocer, the bootmaker, yes, and some of "mine hosts" of Dorset, will share in the beneficient policy.'[31]

But though the *Chronicle* was briefly seduced, it had certainly been right to hint, a few months earlier, at the presence of something more alarming 'behind' his pronunciations. The squire preferred to canter about as an untrammelled Independent, rather than as the representative of London-based Blackshirts, but his enthusiasm for the more powerful European varieties of fascism shone through his utterances on diverse matters, starting with the General Election itself. As far as Pitt Rivers was concerned this event promised, at least before his own intervention, to be a stage-managed charade — a way of diverting public attention away from 'home affairs' and retaining the national government by concentrating political discussion on such 'international issues' as Mussolini's savage annexation of Abyssinia. Convinced that the real issue was the decline of English agriculture and the government's folly in 'giving away our home market to the foreign food importer at the dictates of financial interests', the Captain cited the 45,000 agricultural workers who had lost their jobs since 1931. This was reason enough to leave European fascism alone: 'What we feel very strongly is that there is no need for a single Englishman to turn his ploughshare into a sword because the Italian is fighting with the Abyssinian.'

Pitt Rivers didn't arrive at this telling combination of fascism and English agriculture by accident; he had been building up to it for years. As a young man, he had published a scholarly work called *Conscience and Fanaticism*, assessing such phenomena as 'cosmic suggestion' ('the force resulting from the accumulated suggestions or impulsions of aggregates of individuals'), and inventorising the oratorical techniques of fanatics and demagogues ('worthless and otherwise insignificant individuals' who knew how to play the collective mind).[32] He had followed this with a persuasive anthropological study, dedicated to Bronislaw Malinowski and based on a five year investigation of dying indigenous races in remote parts of the southern hemisphere, which set out to prove that, contrary to what missionaries claimed, 'contact' with European civilisation was the primary cause of the disintegration of native cultures and the depopulation that followed.[33]

But there was another side to this former Etonian, Royal Dragoons officer and Fellow Commoner of Worcester College, Oxford. The Captain may have been a robust autocrat who, in the words of one admirer, had 'nothing of the democrat in his composition', but he was also a thoroughgoing anti-Semite. In 1920 he had published a denunciation of the Russian Revolution, declaring that it had put the Russian people under the yoke of 'Alien Internationalists and Jews' who employed 'gangs of Chinese torturers' to maintain their rule, and then casting a contemptuous eye over his own country: an England which no longer saw any merit in 'a simple agricultural existence', having espoused the degenerate 'money values' of mass democracy and 'shop-keeping' and turned itself into 'one of the greatest lovers and entertainers of Jews' in the world.[34]

On returning from his travels in the mid-Twenties, Pitt Rivers devoted himself to the cause of eugenics, which he saw as anthropology applied to the cause of human improvement. Not to be entirely outdone by his eminent grandfather — acclaimed, in Sir Mortimer Wheeler's words, for having 'established the methodology' of modern field archaeology — the Captain claimed to have 'established the methodology of the science of ethnogenics'.[35] He became involved with the Eugenics Society, the International Federation of Eugenics Organisations and the International Union for the Scientific Investigation of Population Problems. He convened conferences in eugenics, sometimes using the old tithe barn at Hinton St Mary, writing about the importance of 'inbreeding' to healthy races (genetic defects are intensified and can therefore be eliminated through natural selection), and using the metaphors of rural husbandry to describe the degenerate condition of the modern British city — a deplorable hothouse in which he saw all too many 'weeds in the garden of marriage'. Pitt Rivers dismissed England's urban population as so many 'shiftless suckers on the productive community, those work-shy unemployables, who contribute nothing but a belly to be filled'. He gazed out in the direction of London, letting his eye wander over the walls and moat of his Manor House and up to the ridge of

Cranborne Chase on the horizon, and then, after imagining 'dole-fed' and 'dole-taught' masses from the city 'spawning wantonly' over his land, hoped that modern contraception would limit their disgusting fecundity.[36]

It was as a toiler in these fields of 'scientific' knowledge that our Independent Agriculturalist visited the University of Gottingen in September 1937, where he gave a speech regretting the extent of British support for the side that was 'opposed to all national aspirations'.[37] While the true English cause was easily reconciled with the German one as defined by Nazism, the country was now filled with influential aliens who would only mock it: 'Those who fight only for England and a greater England are contemptuously labelled "Little Englanders" by the international inheritors of an urbanized and semi-nomadic Euro-Asian stock.' Captain Pitt Rivers explained how 'the internationalisation of finance', which had so muddied the ancient springs of European nationhood, had taken place after the Napoleonic wars: this 'inspired conception' had been 'born in a Frankfurt ghetto' where it 'led to five brothers of the great banking house of Rothschild establishing the system' that would turn London into the financial capital of the world.

Pitt Rivers listed 'refuting politicians' as his hobby in *Who's Who* but, caper and strut as he might, the Captain was soon to be drawn up short; between 1940 and 1942 he was interned on the order of the Home Secretary, Herbert Morrison, under Regulation 18B. Released after a couple of years on the condition that he did not return to Dorset, he was back in the Blackmore Vale by 1945 — in time to inaugurate and sponsor the Wessex Music Festival, held at Hinton St Mary that October and intended to 'revive the cultural features of Wessex', with the help of the Arch Druid of Wales, who had walked to Dorset with a harpist in bardic costume; and also a white short-horned bull wreathed in chrysanthemums. The aim, so Pitt Rivers's assistant, Major Joyce, explained, was to recover the ancient festivities of 'Merrie England', and to get Wessex village choirs competing in the manner of the Welsh mining valleys: 'It is the revival of song that we are mostly after.'[38]

'English Food in English Bodies'

Pitt Rivers was not the only denizen of the Blackmore Vale who combined such repulsive attitudes with a patriotic commitment to the revival of

England's soil. Other frequenters of North Dorset – including Cecil de Sausmarez, who lectured at Gardiner's 1934 Harvest Camp on King Alfred – were associated with a curious cellular network called the English Mistery, founded by William Sanderson, an obscure ritualist who was convinced that 'the English race was on the verge of extinction', and that Freemasonry was 'the proper rallying point'. Constituted on Royalist, anti-democratic lines, the Mistery had a Council of Strength but voting was banned and authority rested with leaders. Sanderson's admiration of Yeoman's England came clothed in period anti-Semitism: usury was the cause of England's decline and to the extent that it had prevailed 'we have all become Jews'. A less accomplished eugenicist than Pitt Rivers, he also urged caution on the conjugal front: 'If a tall man from the plains mates with a woman of a short race of forest dwellers, incompatibility and unhappiness will be the result.'[39]

Sanderson was eventually deposed by his 'executive leader', the Wessex aristocrat Viscount Lymington, later the Earl of Portsmouth. Having sampled the Bohemian life, and found that 'there was no oblivion in the inns of Europe' with their 'ukelele frauleins' and their 'sentimental saxophones sobbing of adultery',[40] Lymington had returned to his ancestral estate at Farleigh Wallop, Hampshire, and committed himself to the cause of England's soil. By the early Thirties, he was striking back at the artificial society he had known in diverse European metropolises with a crude home truth: 'Minerals and dung in solution fused by human sweat: these are the foodstuffs of civilised man.'[41]

In 1936, Lymington relaunched the English Mistery as the English Array – a name of Gothic derivation that implied 'a militant response to duty', and had been used as a call of command by the archers at Agincourt.[42] The English Array had its network of Wardens and Masters, Keepers, Kin and Musters, and, as Marshall of the whole show, Lymington used its *Quarterly Gazette* to stipulate that 'the purpose of the British Subject . . . should be to regain, preserve and intensify all those attributes and qualities that appertained to English life and the English type at the most vigorous and flourishing periods of our history'.[43] The *Quarterly Gazette* would ignore the superficial attractions of the so-called 'News' and dedicate itself to the 'Olds' instead. Lymington expanded on this mission for the *New Pioneer*, the publication with which he replaced the *Quarterly Gazette* at the end of 1938: The 'heritage of the new worlds' opened up by the old pioneer had already been exploited in 'the fatness of easy money', so the new pioneer was 'the man who faces inwards. His is not the new world to conquer, but the old world to redeem.'[44] The compost heap offered a primary metaphor for his men: a 'fructification' of dead material that offered a revitalising alternative to the inorganic degradations of Commerce and the irreversible rusting of the metallic State. When women complained about being excluded from membership, they were informed that their place was in the home with the children, and reminded that what was good for the race was good for all.[45]

So the men of the English Array hoisted the flag of St George and set to work regenerating the 'English stock' so lost in the composite identity of modern Britain. They sang the praises of unpasteurised milk and the cottage pig — both threatened by the new marketing boards and health regulations of the centralised State.[46] They liked unburnt stubble fields and preferred to grow their runner beans up wands of native hazel rather than imported bamboo canes. They knew the difference between a block of council flats ('Birth Control Barracks') and a proper family home with flowers and children in the back garden. They condemned jerry-building and white bread in the same breath: 'as the Staff of Life, white bread is a broken reed, and a cruel deception to the very poor'.[47] They deplored tinned food, like the imported salmon featured in the thrifty recipes that Valentine Ackland contributed to the *Country Standard*, demanding 'English food in English bodies' and insisting that the 'product of our own and not alien soil have an intangible but very strong influence on British physique and stamina'.[48] Their country was like the ancient White Horse carved in the chalk downs in G. K. Chesterton's ballad: renewed by Alfred of Wessex, but subject to endless encroachment as 'the turf crawled and the fungus crept,/And the little sorrel, while all men slept,/Unwrought the work of man'.[49]

There is no reason to think that anyone in the English Array had ever heard of Tyneham, but their England (an ancestor of the one projected through the 1980s by Roy Faiers in his quarterly *This England*) was already an endangered valley tucked away in some remote fold of the chalk downs: a Hollow Land of remembered traditions and virtues to be approached along the untarred roads of nostalgic reminiscence. It was to this symbolic homeland that they came to bury their representative English craftsman, laying him to rest 'by the Domesday Yew and Norman Chancel', in a valley where 'No chemicals came . . . to kill the land and spoil the flavour of its yield for a few seasons of easy results.'[50] It was here that they stood among familiar hedges and fields, using rhyming verse to summon up the vanished husbandmen and 'Old Servants' who had made this 'heritage of homely things' before shuffling off the mortal coil.[51] It was here that they found the village of their grandfathers, remembered as a place of great vitality where 'the flail thudded in the tithe barn, and the blacksmith's hammer rang merrily all day through the village', but now dead as a modern plague village: its fields blighted by 'Agricultural Sickness'; the good timber trees felled for quick money while only 'tree weeds' like sycamore sprang up to replace them; the people devitalised by 'Council School education, or middle-class ignorant sentimentality'.[52] It was here too that they — or at least the archaeologically minded among them — could dig down into the rubbish dump of a cottage garden and find the story of England's degeneration in its layers: rusty tin cans at the top, and below that bones from the truer days when the cottager kept a pig and had no need of imported or bureaucratically distributed food.[53] The tanks had yet to arrive, but the men of the English Array were already picking the cold iron of commerce and the modern state out of England's native soil.

The Wessex cell of the English Array was known as the King Alfred Muster. Led by its Lieutenant, the Honourable Richard de Grey, it set about trying to spread its influence by forming gardening clubs in the villages. 'Reviving the English type' meant growing your own properly manured vegetables and 'securing a supply of stoneground wholewheat flour' so that the bakers in five parishes could resume 'making the bread of our ancestors'.[54] This problem became more acute during the war, by when the mantle of responsibility seems to have passed to Ralph Coward, who farmed in the Vale at Donhead St Mary.[55] In the first of his handwritten newsletters, he reports that wholemeal flour was unobtainable now that the local mill had been taken over by a larger miller, and that he had tried to form a Pig Club in the village 'but the international grocers still has plenty of bacon so he met with no success'. While reviewing the Muster's other ten or so members — reluctantly finding state employment or, if they were farmers, having trouble finding labour in competition with the nearby military camp — Coward lamented the 'bureaucratic control which sits on us everywhere and is not very inspiring'.[56] If the King Alfred Muster is anything to go by, the English Array was no match for the 'ultra-reactionary' secret society that the horrified latterday commentator imagines it to have been.[57] Surviving correspondence between Gardiner and

Coward reveals not a 'Dorset Nazi Party', but a couple of dreamy farmers coming to terms over some portable poultry pens.

From the Marshall's side, this was not for want of trying. The English Array appealed to the odd basket-weaving crank or 'refugee' from the modern world who 'accepted the cause for the sake of the company',[58] but he and his fellow leaders tried to stiffen the Array's purpose. At a camp in 1937, Captain A. M. Ludovici, a Nietzschean who had once been secretary to the sculptor Rodin, called the Array's attention to the growing discrepancy between the images normally evoked by the word 'England' or the Union Jack, and the prevalent realities. He observed that the traditional idea of England missed out the population of cities like London, Manchester, Sheffield and Liverpool, and also the stock exchanges and factories, preferring to dwell on the idea of John Bull 'placed in a setting of waving cornfields, green hills, and nestling red-roofed cottages'. He called on the English Array to fight resolutely for the 'transvaluation of values' that would halt the decline of the 'fast-vanishing Englishman' and overthrow the values that had produced the degenerate modern city; only then would 'pride be returned to the flag'.

Lymington, whose outlook resembled that of Captain Pitt Rivers in being a bizarre mixture of the utterly localised and the grand sweep, wanted a foreign policy too. He did what he could to bring the Array into line with his wider campaign as founder of the Council Against European Commitments, thereby raising rural parochialism to new heights: 'When a catastrophic hailstorm ruined completely a small area of Hampshire smallholders' farm crop no one, except for those responsible for local relief, worried about their lot or their children's lot'; and yet 'no sooner are the Czechs put within their ethnological boundary than our government makes a preliminary advance of £10,000,000 towards Czech reconstruction, and ... every sentimentalist in the country rushes to subscribe to the Lord Mayor's Refugee Fund'.[59]

Lymington's vision of 'ecological comity' was incubated in the foulest of cradles.[60] If the *New Pioneer* carried instructive articles on pruning gooseberry and currant bushes or advocating a 'Blitzkrieg' against rabbits on one page, the next would rush to the defence of Hitler, dismissing the Czechs as, in a Serbian phrase, the 'White Jews of Europe' and insisting that a war with Nazi Germany would benefit 'no one but the Jews and the international communists'. The average English farmer had always distrusted the 'slick higgler',[61] but Lymington added a simplistic idea of usury to produce a seething stew of anti-Semitic prejudice, demanding that Britain's borders should be closed to refugees fleeing Hitler on the grounds that London was already 'half a foreign city, where English faces were almost a surprise', and that this new 'Tide from central Europe' would only make matters worse.[62] In June 1939, Lymington was announcing how grateful the Balkan peasants were to Nazi Germany for ridding them of 'the moneylenders' ('from Poland to Bulgaria the peasant is in the thrall of the Jew').[63] He claimed to 'dislike' the Nazis' violent excesses, largely on the grounds that they made life very difficult for National Socialism's supporters overseas, but he had no doubt that the Nazis were 'justified in removing the Jews from all places of influence in national life, after the corruption and degradation which the Jews had brought about in the defeated and demoralised post-war Germany'.[64]

As the Second World War approached, Valentine Ackland would join the communist *Country Standard* in recommending that 'the big country mansions of the rich' should be 'taken over' and used as hostels for urban evacuees,[65] but Lymington's *New Pioneer* preferred the eugenic fantasies of Captain Pitt Rivers, whose pamphlet 'Your Home is Threatened' opposed evacuation of urban children as a 'treasonable' threat to the Englishman's liberty, bringing skin diseases and parasites 'both internal and external' to the countryside.[66] When war was declared Lymington wrote to tell Richard de Grey that it was not a true 'people's war' but a 'bloody folly' in which 'the only winners will be the Jews and Bolsheviks'.[67] The *New Pioneer* even came up with an anti-Semitic variation on the despised weekend cottage — condemning 'the alien (by blood at least!)' who had moved to the country and 'bought a farm in order to provide himself with a funk-hole from bombs'.[68]

So the torrent continued, a terrible warning of what can happen when a Wessex aristocrat derives a world view from the soil. Half a century later, we can only marvel at the fortitude with which Lady Evelyn Balfour laundered Lymington's books to produce the cleaned-up ecological vision on which she founded the Soil Association in 1945 to campaign for organic farming.[69] We should also be thankful to Mary Langman, veteran of the Pioneer Health Centre in Peckham, for her reminder that, even though the malnourished urban poor of the Thirties did present a sickly spectacle, the answer was to be found in decent food, useful employment and adequate healthcare, and not in any rural grandee's theories of racial degeneration.

THIRTEEN

NO SUCH THING AS A DORSET NAZI PARTY

> The English mind does not know how to distinguish between a wise man and a crank.
>
> Rolf Gardiner.[1]

THERE CAN BE no question that Rolf Gardiner moved in these circles. It was at a meeting of the English Mistery that he outlined his conception of music as 'the supreme political exercise';[2] and he became a friend of Viscount Lymington, who solicited articles from him for both the *Quarterly Gazette of the English Array* and the *New Pioneer*, inviting him to address supporter's meetings on Work Service Camps in order to lift discussion 'out of the good old hackneyed political lines'.[3] Yet Gardiner also had some reservations. In 1936, he informed members of the Springhead Ring that, while he felt entirely sympathetic to its ideas for agricultural reform and considered that 'the approach made by the Mistery was more in accord with the spirit which prompts the work of the Springhead Ring than that of any other political body in the country', he was still troubled by an 'over-intellectual formalistic attitude which is held in position by a stiff acceptance of doctrine rather than by roots in the soil of living experiences'.[4] This observation reflected his principal disagreement with Sanderson, the Mistery's founder, who was not interested in the work camps Gardiner saw as the vehicle of national renewal.[5] Once Lymington had taken over, Gardiner encouraged him to put the relaunched English Array on a more active basis, introducing team-building hikes for its leaders.[6] Gardiner provided the men of the King Alfred Muster with their wholemeal flour but he could not become more than a 'really near supporter' — due to his loyalty to the co-educational Springhead Ring, many of whom 'are unsuitable for the Array'. He hoped that the two bodies might collaborate in launching a 'Wessex Land Reclamation Service', and described their differences as follows: 'the Springhead Ring is a body of men and women concerned wholly with values and formed for the realisation of these values. It is a social and consultative group. I think the different names ARRAY and RING describe very nicely the differences of function: RING is essentially concentrated on a centre for the gathering and dissemination of inspiration and power. ARRAY denotes a battle front.'[7]

As for Captain Pitt Rivers, by 1936, Gardiner was expressing certain reservations here too. He had been 'approached many times by the Chairman of the Wessex Agriculture Defence Association and asked to join his organisation and play a full part in its development'. But while he resolved to support and work with WADA 'in every sphere where I believe its influence to be constructive and conducive to the regeneration of the Wessex countryside', he would remain 'guarded and critical at all points where methods of mass agitation are likely to be employed'.[8] It was almost certainly Pitt Rivers that Gardiner had in mind in 1942, when he dismissed an unnamed local landowner as 'a fanatical and mad eccentric who long ago alienated himself from county society'.[9]

These hesitations may well be insufficient to justify breaking with the tradition that now sticks an identical black shirt on all these 'fellow travellers of the right', but Gardiner's endeavour calls for more considered assessment — and not just on account of his early articulation of genuine ecological themes. His arguments with Pitt Rivers and the English Mistery reprise those that he also used to distinguish the German youth movement of the 1920s from the Nazi tide that overwhelmed it in 1933, and also, for that matter, from the roaming thugs of the Freikorps, with which he has also been unjustly associated.[10]

A Man of Action finds his Path

How did this passionate Englishman become so involved in European affairs? In a memoir written during the last years of the Second World War, Gardiner suggests that he had been fated by his own family background. His mother was part Austro-Hungarian Jewish and part Swedo-Finnish. Shortly after his birth in 1902, the family moved to Berlin where Gardiner's father, an eminent British Egyptologist, had been asked to collaborate on the preparation of the Berlin Hieroglyphic Dictionary. Until their European life was interrupted in 1914, the Gardiners would spend their summers with relatives, alternating between grandparents in Hampshire and the Baltic where their Finnish relatives lived.

Gardiner was schooled in England during and immediately after the Great War. Britain seethed with demagogic hatred for the land of the Hun, or 'Germhuny' as the rabble-rousing con-man Horatio Bottomley liked to call it, and it is not unreasonable to imagine Gardiner cherishing his European memories in the midst of that fervid patriotism. His sister Margaret remembers sitting on a Gloucestershire garden wall with Rolf — already a keen reader of Baden Powell's *Scouting for Boys* — and hearing village children identify him as the 'German enemy', but she doubts that his background was used against him in a serious way. A prep school in Winchester was followed by Rugby, which he hated, and left for progressive, co-educational Bedales, where he corresponded with J. G. Bergel, a friend he had left behind at Rugby. The seventeen-year-olds swapped verses and talked ardently about Flaubert, Zola and Selma Lagerlof. They shared an interest in country dancing, and enthused over the paintings of the visionary Irish patriot A. E. But young Bergel was rendered defensive by Gardiner's attack not just on 'the noble Arnold's prefectorial system' but on the whole public school system, and cautioned him about arguing with his new headmaster ('Bedales is . . . not a bear-house for the exploitation of novel or revolutionary educational ideas. Are you a socialist or an anarchist? You look more like the latter according to what you write'). He declared himself 'immeasurably disgusted' when Gardiner claimed that his sexual initiation had taken place when he was fifteen years old ('I did not think that such women were common outside books').

As Gardiner later recalled it, the immediate post-war world seemed like 'a black night with bright stars blazing above'. The survivors of the war-generation were too shattered to be of any use: Gardiner watched them drift off into the narcissistic morbidity of Bohemianism and the 'Jazz-libertine', leaving the country in the hands of the 'Old Gang':[11] Edwardian advocates of laissez-faire liberalism who, having profited very nicely from the war, had no interest in changing anything. Unimpressed by the atmosphere of 'scientific humanism' and 'Bloomsbury' intellectualism that he found at St John's College, Cambridge, Gardiner turned from this 'posthumous' England to seek out alternative inspiration. He was influenced by Guild Socialism with its 'Arts and Crafts' associations and its opposition — as expressed by H. J. Massingham, among others, in the pages of the *New Age* — to the 'metallic' machinery of the industrialised warrior state. He dallied with Major Douglas's idea of Social Credit, with its incipiently anti-Semitic hatred of usury; and he hailed D. H. Lawrence as the 'torch bearer' who had 'freed so many of my generation from the crushing imponderabilia of dead tradition'.[12] Gardiner identified very strongly with his generation — people who were innocent of the recent war, having been just too young to fight, but now had to repair the world it had broken.

Even Lawrence's words were not enough for Gardiner, who was also inspired by Charles Hamilton Sorley, a young poet who, before being killed in action, had decreed that poets should be 'men of action before they are men of speech, and men of speech because they are men of action'. It was in post-war Austria and Germany that he found his practical cause. Visiting Vienna as an eighteen-year-old in 1920, he found a depressing post-war city in which 'Everybody groaned; no one exercised initiative', and then set off for the Dolomites, walking great distances through the shattered Tyrolean landscape with a large aquascutum strapped to his back: pausing to help rebuild a remote war-shattered village; tripping over the skeletons of unburied soldiers in the snow and, when his money ran out, cutting off the bottom half of his Oxford bags and exchanging the valuable cloth for a meal.

Years later, Gardiner would describe himself as a 'barbed wire cutter' whose task had been to clear passages through the great coils of prejudice between Britain and Germany. But it was on that first protracted journey that he conceived the idea of reviving the tradition of the strolling English minstrels and players who had travelled through Germany in the sixteenth and seventeenth centuries: he would raise the spirit of Shakespeare's England and offer it to young Germany as a reminder of qualities 'higher than nationality'. Fired by this aim of breaking 'the spell of enmity and ignorance' between the two countries, Gardiner returned to Germany during successive vacations while he was at Cambridge. He wandered, by foot and fourth-class railway carriage, through those years of ruinous inflation and political ferment, an open-hearted young Englishman given to reparative gestures very different from those demanded by the Treaty of Versailles. When his passport was out of order he thought nothing of taking to the hills to cross borders illegally: he even had his life saved by the famous dogs from the monastery of St Bernard, while traversing the mountainous passage from Switzerland into Italy.

In September 1922, and despite strong opposition from Cecil Sharp and the 'academic oligarchy' in charge of the English Folk Dance Society, which barred its members from participating in a heretical venture that spurned 'traditional' authenticity, Gardiner scratched together a folk-dancing team and set off on the tour that brought him into contact with the German youth movement.[13] There were diverse youth associations or '*Bünde*', at that time, and Gardiner quickly recognised them as the post-war successors of the earlier Wandervogel, the inheritors of a romantic 'revolt of the soul' against 'suburban convention' and 'bourgeois materialism and complacency'.[14] The Wandervogel may have been dismissed as pagan and decadent as they took up their guitars and wandered out in search of the blue flower of the romantic poet Hölderlin, but Gardiner insisted that their soulful rebellion had been 'restorative and traditional' — disciplined in its repudiation of a 'degenerated Christianity which substituted sermons for worship and catechisms for consecration'.[15] The Wandervogel sought 'not a will o' the wisp, but reality; they sought a return to the roots of all values. They broke out of the suburbs and rediscovered Germany, the homeland.'

In the young Gardiner's eyes, the youth movement had an authenticity that ran far deeper than the merely bureaucratic arrangements of the Weimar Republic, and the only question was how a similar movement could be stimulated within the ruins of an economically far less straitened but culturally no less bankrupt Great Britain. While at St John's College, Cambridge, he took over the editorship of a journal called *Youth*, and used it to alert his generation to the existence of this new hero:

> Travellers in post-war Germany must surely have seen him, a youth of uncertain age, and probably undergrown, but of striking appearance, blue eyes, long flaxen hair, the skin clear and sun-scorched, drawn tight over the face muscles, the limbs bared, no stockings, shorts, open neck. You will probably meet him, ruck-sack on his back, with five or six companions of both sexes, one of whom will be playing a guitar or other musical instrument. And they will sing as they go, marching the town streets after dusk, or trudging a country road under a parching Saturday or Sunday afternoon sun.[16]

The Wandervogel was 'a much more romantic figure than the Boy Scout', and 'more of a realist too; he means business, not play. There is a terrifying earnestness in his eyes, a purpose almost grim with suffering, his whole body is taut with will, with the knowledge of a fate that must be lived through, he is a rebel, a rebel who rebels by intransigent constructive living, whose answer to every problem is the act.'

Believing that 'people are not merely born, they arrive', Gardiner opined that the Wandervogel came in from the near future; they were 'the people of the becoming', striding through the wreckage left over from an exhausted

9 Lulworth tank demonstration against mock castle, 1928?

GERMANY ACCEPTS PROPOSALS AT THE HAGUE

£1,000 PICTURE PUZZLE WEEKLY

Daily Mirror

THE DAILY PICTURE PAPER WITH THE LARGEST NET SALE

BEST HOLIDAY INSURANCE

HISTORIC CASTLE DESTROYED BY FIRE

10 *Daily Mirror*, 30 August 1929

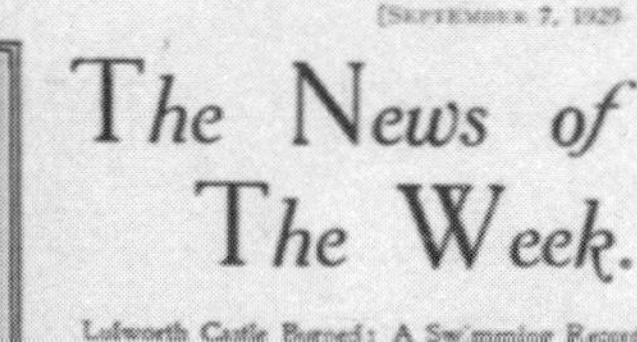

[SEPTEMBER 7, 1929

The News of The Week.

Lulworth Castle Burned: A Swimming Record: Mimic War on the Plain

WITNESSING A TRAGEDY: Mr. Herbert Weld watching his residence, Lulworth Castle, vanishing into flame.

THE GRAPHIC, September 7, 1929

ORDEAL BY FIRE

Dramatic Pictures of the Burning of Lulworth Castle

THE ROYAL TANK CORPS TO THE RESCUE

A tank, which brought a detachment from the neighbouring Tank Corps camp at Bovington, beside the burning building. The fire, which started in the upper storey, ate its way down until the beautiful Elizabethan mansion was a shell

11 *Left*: Herbert Weld watches his castle burn, *The Graphic*, 7 September 1929

12 *Right*: 'Tank' in the park, *The Graphic*, 7 September 1929

13 Llewelyn Powys holding Ankh at Chydyok, *c.* 1936

14 Valentine Ackland (far left) and Sylvi Townsend Warner (far right) at West Chaldon, *c.* 1935

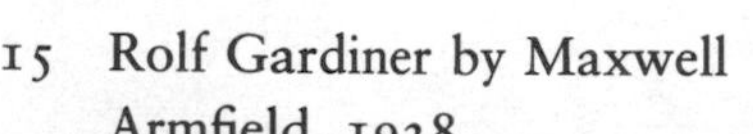

15 Rolf Gardiner by Maxwell Armfield, 1928

16 Rolf Gardiner at work, *c.* 1930

17 Springhead workcamp at Gore Farm, mid-1930s

18 Rolf Gardiner processing dancing team during the Yorkshire tour, 1931

19 Winston Churchill inspecting Churchill tanks at Arish Mell Gap, April 1942

20 Lord Hinchinbrooke, MP welcoming a deputation of Dorset Conservative women to Westminster, 1940s

past. The American and Russian peoples had only found different ways of colliding with the same 'iron wall: the ghastly impasse which lies in the complete mechanisation of the individual, the ruthless shaping of the individual living creature into a mere cog of the great grey machine En-Masse, servile Democracy'.

Turning their backs on Charlie Chaplin, the fox trot and the 'trash' of the urbanised culture industry, the Wandervogel's post-war successors took to the hills and woods, 'reviving the dance forms of their own soil, the songs, the dramas, the rituals'. Theirs was the winding green road that Gardiner would follow in his pursuit of an organic Third Way between American capitalism and Soviet communism. In those desperate post-war years, when almost everyone had to work and the distinctions of class and property were set aside, Germany had become 'culturally the most communistic democracy of the world'. He attended a festival of working-class youth in Weimar in 1920 where: 'A few thousand sons and daughters of the proletariat, representing Wandervogel organisations from all over Germany . . . came together to dance and sing, and play-act . . . to discuss and debate the problems of life and the day, and to listen to addresses, in which the names of Marx, Engels, Kant, Fichte, Hegel, Heine, Hebbel, Beethoven, Nietzsche, Mozart and Shakespeare occurred again and again.' This was all taken for granted in Germany, and it compared more than favourably with anything that could yet be expected of 'an assembly of Whitechapel youths and maidens'.

Gardiner surveyed the various German youth organisations trying to forge 'a new religious impulse' in the full knowledge of 'the limitations of language . . . the speciosity of dogma, the deadness of theory'. He described the right-wing and sometimes pessimistically Spenglerian associations to be found among the often 'wholly reactionary' university students; and he also noted the existence of a spiritualist strain that believed in 'religious regeneration anterior to political and social betterment'. The 'true crusading ardour', or so he thought in 1923, was to be found among the socialists and pacifists of the 'Arbeiter Jugend Berwegung' who 'do not merely abide by Marx and Engels, but rather stand on their shoulders and climb up into the future. They are in reality utterly antagonistic to the Bolshevik theory, which makes of every human being a screw in the machine . . . They believe in the sanctity of the individual, the perfection of the individual, through service and comradeship, and in the community, as diversity in unity.' And so they marched out in search of what one of *Youth*'s German correspondents called 'a new conviviality without alcohol and without smoke',[17] cheered on by Gardiner, who was inspired by the thought of them reclaiming 'something of the primal German soul, the soul of the Forest, something of the spirit of chivalry, of the wandering minstrel . . . '

Turning to the English situation, this romantic 21-year-old peered into 'the darkness which lies between this evening's twilight and tomorrow's dawn, in this interregnum of confusions of sickly pullulations, of feverish excitements and noisy tumults, wherein the air shall be lacerated by the raucous bawlings of false prophets, and the deathly moanings of piteous machine-mangled humanity'.[18] Against this tank-rolled vision of a world gone wrong, Gardiner called on his generation to spurn prudence as a 'deadly sin' and take courage as the axe with which to 'fell the thickening trees of sleep' and to cut through 'the corrupting, hardening, disintegrating forces of Death' all around. European civilisation was evidently 'crashing to its doom', and Gardiner, who saw it as 'a civilisation burnt out, hollow and futile', was all for letting it fall. The only hope was with the 'new world arising', which would put an end to the old polarisations of intellect versus instinct, word versus action, and slough off the abstracted idealism of the 'metallist thinkers of Bloomsbury and Cambridge'.

The 21-year-old Gardiner knew there were 'many millions of negative people in the world today'. These were the 'Robots' who had sold out to the 'mechanical utopia', or come to terms with 'the Caesardom of the great magnates' and enshrouded their God-like naked bodies in business suits made of 'good old English worsted'.[19] But Britain's younger generation should follow the Wandervogel out into 'Actionland'. As editor of *Youth*, Gardiner encouraged them to take a positive view of the 'cult of nakedness' espoused by the German youth movement, and also of eurythmic movement and the innovative youth theatre emerging from the Bauhaus. They were to recognise not just D. H. Lawrence and Walt Whitman among their prophets, but also Hermann Hesse, 'the hero poet of the German Youth Movements'.[20] Keen on progressive education, *Youth* was in touch with A. S. Neill, soon to arrive in Britain where he would set up Summerhill, but at that time only announcing that he had been obliged to leave Germany due to the political situation, and that he had recently reopened his free school in a mountain-top house in Austria: 'I expect Rolf Gardiner to be our first English visitor. He has that sort of insanity that finds joy in climbing a mountain . . . '[21]

Gardiner placed his hopes in the few thousand 'positive people' he knew to be scattered in 'self-supporting communities' that were 'springing up all over Europe today'. He imagined that, like the still rooted peasantry, some of these 'new monasteries' would survive 'the hurricanes of this wintry period of civilisation and become oases of light in the land of darkness'. The youth movements of Central and Northern Europe must build a new commonwealth — a federation of scattered colonies. The Germans had a head start, because it was in their country that the 'disintegration of civilisation' had gone furthest, but even insular old England was tottering 'at the edge of a precipice'. It was time to break through the abstracted geometry of Mercator's projection and regain the living world.

Across North Sea and Baltic

From 1923 until he broke off in 1925, Gardiner pursued this European vision as a kind of informal commissioner abroad to John Hargrave, the scoutmaster who had left Baden Powell and dedicated his own movement, Kibbo Kift Kindred, to the renewal of the folk life buried under 'Machine civilisation'.[22] Gardiner shared the aspirations of his new comrades in Germany as they marched out over the truncated borders of the post-war German state to make contact with German minorities scattered in Poland or Romania. He sympathised with their frustrations, admiring the resistant spirit in which they sang about General Degoutte and the 'nigger troops' that France had imposed on the occupied Ruhr.[23]

As an honorary member of the Deutsch Freischar, an elite within the youth movement formed in 1926 and dedicated to remaking Germany through the creation of 'a new aristocracy of character, bearing and spirit', Gardiner threw himself into a comprehensive programme that continued up through the dedication of Springhead in 1933. The organic vision he pursued in co-operation with youth movement centres in Scandinavia and Holland as well as Germany, implied a restoration of the countryside, but it also hoped to place a revitalised Germany at the heart of a community of North European nations united across the North Sea and Baltic. Gardiner imagined 'Celto-Germanic Christendom'[24] pressing back against the destructive forces of American capitalism and Soviet communism. Based on common Germanic culture, this North European federation would revive the spirit of the old Hanseatic League, embracing Denmark, Scandinavia, and also Baltic states like Estonia, Latvia and Lithuania, which had been settled by Germans centuries ago and now needed to be strengthened 'if Europe was not to collapse before the Soviet menace'.[25] It would include Britain, which should recognise that the Empire was coming to an end, and take its place in the 'new order' prefigured by the activities of the youth movement.

Even before Hitler came to power, there were critics who considered it dangerous folly to imagine German influence resurgent beyond the boundaries established by the Treaty of Versailles,[26] but Gardiner, whose vision had started out as a passionate variation on Guild Socialism with a diffusionist foreign policy attached, would reply that he was working towards 'unity in diversity', a polyphony of free states fostered from within by a new elite trained by the youth movement, and certainly not imposed coercively from the German centre. Even in the early days of *Youth*, there were indications that some activists failed to understand this distinction. In the summer of 1924, Heinrich Rocholl wrote from Germany that 'Pacifism is destroying every nation. We hate it as a womanish doctrine of fear and terror. We repudiate its devotees as homeless intellectuals.' He went on to suggest that 'The reconquest of the unredeemed territories in the south, north, east and west of today's little German republic is not a question of national prestige, but is inseparably linked with national unity, with a true German democracy . . . ' Gardiner acknowledged that this sort of argument was 'full of political unwisdom', but welcomed it nonetheless as 'a passionate gesture of health and virility'.

By 1927, when they put down their English roots at Gore Farm, Gardiner and his circle were committed to this idea of a Germanic revival led by a younger generation innocent of the Great War. Dedicated to the revival of Wessex, the Springhead estate would become a germ cell of the 'new order' stretching out across the Baltic. They set out to develop links that would work from the ground up according to the principle of 'interlocality', quite the opposite of centralised or bureaucratically mediated international exchange.[27] Devoted to the idea of 'Encounter' rather than Marxist fraternisation or pacifist reconciliation, Springhead would work alongside youth movement centres like the Boberhaus in Silesia, the Musikheim in Frankfurt an der Oder, and De Meihof outside Arnhem in Holland. Like Springhead, these centres combined musical and cultural activities with work on the land. Repeatedly, Gardiner likened them to the monasteries that kept Christian civilisation alive through the Dark Ages.

Gardiner adopted the two practical forms most characteristic of the

German youth movement. The cross-country expedition, or *Fahrt*, had been the *pièce-de-resistance* of the old Wandervogel, and Gardiner knew it from the early Twenties when he had marched across northern England with German youths from the Jungnationaler Bund dressed in velvet berets, corduroy shorts, and carrying eye-catching javelins. Members of the emerging Springhead Ring took to the hills in the same romantic spirit. Dedicated to 'the conquest of inertia', they would go 'Downland marching' in the dead of winter, gathering at a preappointed railway station with ruck-sacks, sharing out the responsibilities of cook, logman, bursar and chantyman, and then following their leader along the green droves past strip-lynchets, tumuli and downland 'castles' and up into that high country where 'the oldest Englands' had left their trace, and 'the dull curtains of mundane reality' could briefly be parted.[28]

Spurning 'all the hackneyed "national song-book" stuff', they would sing sixteenth-century canons, rounds or German marching songs as they went, exchanging songs with old shepherds in downland villages, and pausing, as they once did on the downs near Marlborough, to survey the bewildered orchard trees that marked the site of Snape, the extinguished village that was 'forty years ago the home of Wiltshire husbandmen', and to meditate upon the death of rural England.[29] These marchers struck out with the characteristically 'wandering step' of the German youth movement — 'an elastic onward springing from step to step borne on by the momentum of the column', which was certainly nothing like the 'machine-like swinging of your army sergeants' or the 'doleful trudge and wailing singing of your pack-laden English Tommy' (although Gardiner claimed to have pioneered the column of threes long before the British Army).[30]

Gardiner's work camps also owed their form to German example, right down to their emphasis on 'listening' and the restoration of a lost power of speech. He would later write that the Land Service idea was originated by A. E., the Irish visionary whose book, *The National Being*, urged the newly independent Irish state to develop public work schemes to unite the urban and rural populations in co-operation.[31] But the major influence was Eugen Rosenstock-Huessy, a Jewish Christian professor who, being impatient with the universities that offered nothing to a Germany that was already flying towards an extreme nationalistic solution to its post-war problem, put the idea into practice in a series of annual work camps at a youth centre, the Boberhaus in Silesia. The purpose of these events, the first of which was held in March 1928, was to generate common understanding and purpose among 'students, workmen and peasants of dangerously divergent political outlooks'. Gardiner attended, meeting Rosenstock-Huessy and his assistants — including Helmuth von Moltke and Adolf Reichwein, a communitarian socialist and rural educationalist Gardiner would later bring to Britain. These events were neither authoritarian nor fascistic in conception. Their aim was to repair the cultural fabric of a society that was breaking into political extremes,[32] but it was already too late; the project met considerable resistance from both left and right, and by the time of the last camp in 1931 the future of the Boberhaus was far from secure.

Having seen 'the university gone out into the wilderness', Gardiner brought the method back to England, where he imagined creating a 'reinvigorated stock of countrymen' from 'the unused material of the towns'. For a few years from 1932, he ran work camps in East Cleveland, creating allotments for the use of unemployed ironstone miners. The composer Michael Tippett, responsible for music at some of these events, is said to have been no more able than the miners to take seriously the atmosphere of 'nature worship, chivalry and woodcraft',[33] but Gardiner was undeterred by such disbelief. Following Eugen Rosenstock-Huessy's example, he knew that a work camp could be 'a rainbow arch under which the warring and dogmatic sections of a spiritually fractured society might gather and learn to heal themselves'.

Springhead was fiercely parochial — a proud word according to the creed of 'interlocality' — but its shared its vision with these predominantly German centres: a concern with leadership rather than mere authority, commitment to its 'landscape region',[34] an interest in regional self-government, folk culture, land settlement, and the broader political symbolism of polyphonic song — the latter enthusiasm being one that Gardiner shared most closely with Georg Goetsch of the Musikheim in Frankfurt an der Oder. Gardiner was much encouraged by the German visitors who helped him to imagine Gore Farm as, in the worlds of Dr C. H. Becker, Prussian Minister of Education during the Weimar Republic, a 'future pier' in an 'Anglo-German bridge', and the Springhead camps were rooted in this pre-Nazi exchange. In Autumn 1929, a fifteen-man detachment of the Silesian Jungmannschaft attended a two-week Harvest camp. They enacted the battle of Pentridge Hill — dividing into English and German parties that competed to capture this ancient site, without losing lives (represented by 'tails' worn from their belts). After working in the morning, they returned in the afternoon to hear a series of lectures delivered by Professor Eugen Rosenstock-Huessy, on the growth and character of English institutions. One evening Rosenstock-Huessy stood at the gates of Springhead and told Gardiner that he must 'someday come by it and make it the centre of an enlarged farm'.[35]

So Gardiner continued with his organic farming and forestry, looking up at regular intervals to condemn Leonard Elmhirst's much more heavily capitalised initiative at Dartington Hall as a model of 'How not to do it'.[36] Gardiner was dismayed by that whole antithetical project: its habit of beaming in disconnected metropolitan intellectuals and artists, its preference for industrialised methods of farming, the departmental bureaucracy of its Soviet-like Central Office with its many experts, and the lack of organic connectedness that could not be disguised by the endless humming of its machines. 'If I were an ironist,' as Gardiner wrote to Elmhirst in 1933, 'I should tell you that to your collection of experts you need to add an expert in social affection, an engineer in community joy. Something is holding you back and the suspense is camouflaged by talk about structure, costings and so forth. But plainly you have not yet evolved a technique of human initiation.'[37]

Too Much Blood, Not Enough Soil

Gardiner certainly had his own doubts about the rise of Hitler. As he would write in the last years of the war, he had been aware of a 'political fever' infecting the youth movement since 1929, and feared that, in the terrible rush of those impatient times, its project would be overwhelmed.[38] He gave voice to his forebodings in 1932. After declaring that 'Every nation to-day requires a form of Fascism to rescue it from the pitfalls of its own self-sufficiency'[39] — a phrase that is easily quoted out of context — he went on to condemn the varieties on offer as woefully inadequate. Of Hitler and Mussolini, he declared there was 'something hideously common, vulgar, mean in the expression': they were neither aristocratic, nor popular 'in the sense of peasant rebellions'.[40] Oswald Mosley's New Party was just as urban and middle class ('a pot-pourri of Mussolini, Hitler, Lenin and the public-school spirit stirred by Mr Wyndham Lewis will not cure the maladies of the British spirit'). The movement Gardiner wanted was 'not a spearhead like a fascist body' but something altogether more like a compost heap — an organic 'ferment which fructifies dead material'. Gardiner's vision was closer to what he called the 'Christian gnosticism' of the seventeenth-century poet Thomas Traherne: he wanted 'not the communism of the sect, but the communion of ordinary men and women in work and art, in their relation with birds, beasts and flowers, stars, trees and men'.

Gardiner would later describe feeling 'bewildered' when the Nazis took power in 1933, and an article he wrote at the time certainly provides ample evidence of confusion.[41] He warned against judging events in Germany in terms of a degenerated English idea of freedom, which seemed only to mean an 'absence of restraint'. In Germany, as he suggested naively, freedom implied 'free-willed subordination to leadership and service to the community'. Adamant that the Nazi seizure of power was 'not a coup d'état, but the result of organic growth' pioneered by the youth movement during the period of the Weimar Republic, he seemed unclear whether the Nazis were the hijackers or the more or less legitimate inheritors of that vision. The British journalists who filed wholly negative reports from Berlin were 'perforce liars': against them, Gardiner went so far as to describe the 'German revolution' as 'the spring of a new renaissance' which should benefit 'all the Germanic world'. The unemployed miners who visited Germany with members of the Springhead Ring may perhaps be forgiven their errors more easily. Reports describe them hesitating before singing the Horst Wessel song and raising their arms in Nazi salute. Some reckoned they would be happier living in Hitler's Germany than in depressed Wales, and one party even surprised the Führer by calling out 'Hip, Hip, Hooray' when they chanced upon him in the street.

Yet Gardiner also repeated certain objections: the Nazi Party was a 'mass party' devoted to 'demagogic and sensational' methods which had been 'abhorrent' to the earlier Bünde. As for the scapegoating of the Jews, Gardiner wrote that, of all the Nazis' 'many blunders', this was the one that had most infuriated the West. Declaring himself against Nazi race-hatred, he declaimed that 'soul was more powerful than race', insisting that 'Many Jews were and are German and European in the finest sense'. This didn't stop him blundering into his own misguided attempt to tell the sheep from the goats. It was, as Gardiner wrote in that same article of 1933, 'important to remember' that Germany since 1918 had become host to hundreds of thousands of Jews of the 'totally different' type that came from the Slavic lands. The 'restless' Jews of Berlin and Vienna had come 'with the smell of Asia fresh in their beards' and had not 'passed through the German cultural filter'. 'Without soil or craft traditions', these *Ostjuden* were 'sensational, analytic, clever . . . the eternal agitators and theorists of German society. They were behind every clever piece of art or literature: they were cosmopolitans and the promoters of Jazz culture.' Gardiner would later insist that his vision of a resurgent North Europe had been based on 'cultural' rather than 'racial' grounds, but when it came to the doomed 'Asiatic' Jews who Gardiner saw as the main beneficiaries of German decline in such places as Riga, the hedgerow between those close-lying fields was not thick enough to prevent him crashing through.

By February 1934, Gardiner was writing to The *Observer*, to insist that while he had, as reported, recently visited the University of Berlin to deliver a lecture in which he had compared Stanley Baldwin and D. H. Lawrence as representatives of England's pre-war and war generations, he had 'never suggested that Lawrence had fascist leanings. Nothing had been more repugnant to Lawrence than mass-movements; he looked upon Fascism and Communism alike with a certain disgust.'[42] Gardiner suggested that, in his ideas of leadership, community, discipline and power, Lawrence was actually remarkably similar to the pre-Nazi youth movement. He chided English observers for not noticing the difference between Fascism and National Socialism, which, despite its recent evincement of certain 'fascist traits', was at root based 'not on mass suggestion and mass-subjection' but on a communal kind of 'religious experience'. 'Anyone acquainted with the life of the German work-camps or of the finer contingents of the Storm Troops must realise that'.

The youth movement was barely to survive Hitler's accession to power. Eugen Rosenstock-Huessy immediately left for America, where he would eventually be hailed as a prophet of 'planetary service' and the New Age, and where ideas first developed in Silesia still influence rural development agencies working in the Caribbean and Central America.[43] In the Spring of 1933 the various independent *Bünde*, including the Deutsch Freischar, were extinguished and, as Gardiner would later remark, 'the spirit of the work camps fled abroad'. Springhead continued with its programme, but the German participants, who still came through the old contacts, were now National Socialists. The letters between Gardiner and Ludwig Lienhard, the student who organised some visiting parties, show Gardiner to have been highly critical of the Nazis' behaviour.[44] Writing in May 1935, Gardiner reminds Lienhard that when the Nazis 'destroyed' the independent youth movements in order to give 'unrestricted power' to the Hitler Youth, they had also 'stolen' the archives of the Deutsch Freischar, in which 'the whole history of English-German collaboration' was contained. The Springhead Ring had resolved to have nothing to do with the Hitler Youth from that point onwards, and Gardiner condemned the 'lies' with which they dismissed the earlier youth movement as romantic and elitist dreaming.

In public, however, Gardiner would be nothing like so forthright. Persisting in his vocation as 'barbed wire cutter' between England and Germany, he quickly found himself in trouble on both sides. In the German Press, he would rail against the anti-Nazi attitudes of the British political establishment, while also praising the achievements of the pre-war youth movement in terms designed to help his sometimes delicately placed German friends. The difficulties of this situation became evident when, at the request of Georg Goetsch, he wrote to Goebbels — 'innocently' and 'with whatever eloquence I could summon' — in support of the work of threatened centres like the Boberhaus and the Musikheim, only to find his letter printed as 'a piece of pro-Nazi propaganda in every newspaper in Germany'.[45]

Gardiner may quickly have found his way on to the Hitler Youth's blacklist, but news of his special pleadings in Germany was not well received in Britain, where he was busy claiming the Nazi revolution for the youth movement as he had known it. In February 1934, *The Adelphi*, a pacifist and socialist periodical edited by J. Middleton Murray, published an article called 'The Decline of the Youth Movement' by Leslie Paul, founder of the Woodcraft Folk. Paul described Hitler's accession to power as 'a triumph for the forces the Youth Movements had originally opposed'.[46] The freedom of expression or, in the words used by two generations, the 'right to live our lives in obedience to our conscience' had been snuffed out. 'Youth Movements had practised a very real equality between the sexes: the Nazi creed banishes women to the kitchen.' The 'instinctive pacifism' of the post-war German youth movements was outraged by the Third Reich.

Gardiner wrote back claiming that Paul had made 'the typical mistake of overstressing the lyric, romantic and individualistic aspect of the Wandervogel, and of underrating the epic continuity, classic consistency and essentially disciplined character of the *Bünde* . . . after 1918'.[47] The core of the movement had been political and nationalist in aim, rather than pacifist, and 'quite an astonishing number of Hitler's adjutants were previously Wandervogel leaders'. Gardiner asserted that, between 1919 and 1933, the youth movement had evolved 'a method of national training which was socialist not in idea but in action, and aristocratic in its ruthless self-selection and self-criticism'. He insisted that 'fundamentally the aims of this post-War youth movement and those of Hitler and his storm troops were the same' and that 'the young people of Germany are today National Socialist because they own a creed daily made manifest in action ... They are socialists in the primary sense: they are all poor and without class feeling, but they make a festival of poverty.' The really fundamental achievement of the Nazi revolution lay in its 'resuscitation of yeoman, peasant values as opposed to industrial, urban, manufacturing values'. Such was Gardiner's hope, and it led him to describe National Socialist Germany as if it was really just one vast work camp full of purpose, song and authority based not on 'despotic bullying' but on 'intimate, personal trust'.

Gardiner stumbled through the Thirties, a Morris-dancing boy scout who had dreamed of healing the industrial nation by increasing its 'coefficient of ruralicity', but who now found himself overtaken by storm troopers.[48] No matter how desperately he shook his kaleidoscope, he couldn't save his naive vision of a Northern Europe united through its common Germanic culture from the overwhelming totalitarian scenario of a Third Reich. Gardiner's letters to Lymington reveal how reluctant he was to abandon the idea that the 'real Germany' of his friends was still there, an 'organic ferment' which might yet break through the Nazi state to redeem the situation before another war broke out. In March 1939, he tried to reconcile the Nazi annexation of the Czech Sudetenland with his own dream of Germanic polyphony. Admitting that 'the Nazis are running great risks by forcing the pace and grabbing at time',[49] he still reckoned their task was to build up 'a federation or Commonwealth of Nations in Central-Eastern Europe'. Even at this late date, he struggled to understand what the Nazis had done with tanks in the language of basket weaving and wholefood, describing it as the only 'organic' solution to the problems of the area, but then conceding that 'There is always the danger that they may abuse their opportunities.'

Gardiner's correspondence of 1939–40 provides a vivid glimpse of the Springhead Ring and its associates coming to terms with the war. One member, now an RAF squadron leader, had just flown over Dorset in his Spitfire, and was thrilled to glimpse the blue and white of Springhead. Another writes from a gun emplacement on the Isle of Portland, relieved at no longer having to worry about money all the time and admitting that 'I never fail to thrill at the loveliness of the apparition of an enemy bomber caught in a ring of searchlights, a frail silver butterfly poised on the centre of a great golden flower . . . ' A young composer to be, who wrote from his RAF base in Scotland, missed singing Bach and Schutz motets, but was coming to terms with mechanisation nonetheless: the fall of Poland had demonstrated that 'spirit' was not enough and that 'all along it is the materials that have counted'.

Jimmy Edwards, the future comedian, found himself taking turns of duty next to an armoured car in Blackpool. Stuck among 'the scum of the nation' he could only dream of Violet, the old cart-horse at Gore. 'Did I ever make it clear to you that I thought the last camp I attended a failure? You remember: we were a small number, with four chaps from Oxford and a girl who nearly drove me mad. We weeded most of the time and the Oxons were determined not to work hard or enter into the spirit of the camp . . . ' An unimpressed young student rejected the whole work camp ethos as so much 'cranky idealism': there was 'nothing in Cambridge half as unreal as the crazily artificial traditions of Springhead'. A woman wrote from Bedford Park to complain that all the BUF offered a young man was the occasional Mosley oration and 'five or six nights a week in a smelly mews with a little Jew-baiting thrown in now and again', and to wonder why the so-called 'nationalist' organisations hadn't learned from Gardiner's example and set out to arouse 'the people's love and pride in their land, their songs and dances'.

One horrified correspondent counted up the likely cost of war in millions of lives but still saw no alternative but to 'crush' Nazism; and another wrote to say that while National Socialism is indeed a heresy, it demands a more 'organic' solution than the bloody extinction proposed by Cabinet Ministers. A literary man was in no doubt that the war was 'on our part . . . the last squirm of a spiritually bankrupt society'. His thoughts on the matter were not up to the moral standards of 'Elizabeth', who wrote from a farm in Gloucestershire to say that while she valued the music and the friendship of the Gardiners, she could go no further with the Springhead Ring. She had asked Gardiner to state clearly 'whether or not you believe in fascism as a form of government', and was still awaiting an adequate reply. Unimpressed by the anti-war line expressed in the bulletins of the 'Information and Policy' group, she took the view that Nazism 'necessarily oppressed religion and destroyed the culture of other races' and should therefore be 'broken'.

That these tensions could break out within Springhead's organic establishment was demonstrated by a letter from an intemperate young man who wrote to apologise for departing so precipitously before the planned end of his visit in April 1940 — a time when the war was at its most serious, and a great alarm was sounding about Fifth Column activity. Visiting with a party of Conscientious Objectors, he had come to blows with Mr Harold Woolridge, the Head Gardener. Woolridge had seen a lot by this time. He had managed to remain composed on the day when Balfour Gardiner turned up with Percy Grainger, who was dressed in the grass sandals, orange towelling shorts and string garters of his rational dress phase.[50] But conscientious objection was apparently by now more than he could take. One morning, when this fellow was walking to work with a colleague, Woolridge had shouted across the stream, calling them 'Bloody traitors' and when the pair only laughed at this, 'Hitler's number fifth'. That evening, Woolridge found his man putting his tools away and, 'without any provocation or even a conventional introductory argument, proceeded to hit me in the face and then to try and throttle me'. The victim was full of contempt for the 'unutterable stupidity' of his assailant, presuming that he suffered more from 'a surfeit of the daily Press than any deep emotional feeling'. But Gardiner conciliated, and the matter was allowed to drop.

Gardiner never really put his barbed-wire cutters down. Like his friend Arthur Bryant, he was with the appeasers right up until the outbreak of war. Yet by then the man who believed that true statecraft should resemble the harmonious condition of a Bach cantata, was in no doubt about Nazism. He had heard the elaborate contrapuntal songs of the Wandervogel taken over by the Hitler Youth and sung with a 'raucous, staccato bark of defiance' or replaced by the 'vulgar swing' of new songs in which 'Every line was barked out and clipped short in the worst super-metrical emphasis.' He had stood at hotel windows and worried as he saw the voluntary work camps of the Freischar being replaced by forced labour camps for 'Communists'. As for Nazi leaders like Hitler, Goebbels and Goering, Gardiner had watched these 'strikingly operatic posturers' in action at mass rallies and recognised them as figures from a hideously 'Wagnerian' nightmare.[51] While the patriots of Fontmell Magna ostracised Gardiner for his fascist sympathies, he was raging into his notebooks against the 'demagogic shamanism', 'megalomania' and 'fanatical impatience' of the Nazis who had corrupted everything. Too much blood, not enough soil.

Gardiner was, in his own words, 'mistaken and misguided'[52] in his assessment of the German situation in those pre-war years, but his insistence on the difference between Nazism and the youth movement of the Twenties found terrible vindication after the failure of the July 1944 plot against Hitler's life. Helmuth von Moltke, whom Gardiner had met as one of the 'rainbow men' assisting Rosenstock-Huessy with his work camps at the Boberhaus, was executed as the leader of the so-called Kreisauer Circle of conspirators. The same fate befell Adolf Reichwein, the rural educationalist whom Gardiner had met in the same connection and who is remembered by Sir George Trevelyan as a 'talented and beautiful soul'. For Gardiner, who had apparently been criticised by Reichwein for underestimating the sheer evil of Nazism, this 'desperate conspiracy' exonerated the ideals of the pre-Nazi youth movement, turning it into 'one of the few constructive alternatives to Hitler's chaotic tyranny'.

Tractors into Tanks

The composing rural revivalists of North Dorset were never entirely happy with the thought of metal touching Wessex soil. They disliked pylons and metalled roads and heard the clank of cold iron in the edicts of centralised state bureaucracy. They regretted tractors too — even if they were not all as intransigent as Gardiner's Norwegian warden at Gore, Sigvart Godeseth, who refused to exchange his horses for a tractor on the holistic grounds that the latter did not possess the capacity to produce its own young. They knew, as John Stewart Collis would later write, that the labourers had been 'exchanged for metal',[53] and they contrived their own allegories to demonstrate the point.

Shortly before the outbreak of war Gardiner's Springhead dancers teamed up with the Agricultural Workers' Union, under its Dorset leader, F. C. James, to revive the winter festival of Plough Monday. The men performed a sword dance in Dorchester, killing off the old year and conjuring fertility into the new, and Lymington 'stirred the meeting' with a speech in which he extolled the virtues of the wooden plough share, which had done less harm to the ground than the 'steel machines of today'. Lymington might have sympathised with the communists of the *Country Standard*, when they portrayed British agricultural policy as a tank crushing England, but he was no admirer of Stalin's collectivised farms; indeed, he took the opportunity of this Christian occasion to prophesy that 'the great multiple farrow tractors' of the Soviet Union would turn out to be 'engines of destruction and not servants of production'.[54]

These same themes preoccupied the men Gardiner involved in the wartime discussion group he convened under the name A Kinship in Husbandry — including Lymington, the poet Edmund Blunden, novelist Adrian Bell, H. J. Massingham, who had first met Gardiner in 1939 and hailed Springhead as 'the bud of the England to be',[55] and Arthur Bryant, the anti-laissez-faire Tory historian, who was now writing patriotic weekly articles on the war for the *Illustrated London News*. These advocates of 'return to husbandry' worried about the tractor, which took the song out of farmwork and was bad for the driver ('the position produces gastric ulcers'). They feared, with undeniable prescience, that the steel plough may have 'unfortunate ultimate effects on the soil'.[56]

As a member of the Dorset War Agricultural Executive Committee, Gardiner emphasised the advantages of hurdled sheep and recommended the formation of a county flock that would fertilise the depleted downs, and provide an apprentice scheme for shepherds, who would otherwise leave the land. He also argued for an ambitious post-war resettlement of Cranborne Chase, a 'densely populated region' in pre-Saxon times, but now only sparsely inhabited.[57] Drawing neighbouring landowners into various co-operative schemes, he informed them that the best way to inspect each other's holdings on the Chase would be on horseback, because 'motoring from point to point is always disjointed and the slower pattern of the landscape is broken up by fast locomotion'.[58]

Springhead continued to host work camps through the war, but Gardiner also made the most of the practical possibilities that came as the threat of war finally awakened the government to the importance of home agriculture. In 1939 he threw himself into the revival of the Wessex flax industry, developing a considerable enterprise at the then derelict Slape Flax Mill in West Dorset, and eventually becoming the government's agent for flax production in Dorset, Somerset and Devon.[59] Gardiner oversaw four hundred people, a small nucleus of experienced flax workers, augmented at harvest time by school children from nearby towns, factory staff, members of the Women's Land Army and even troops. He tried to involve this workforce in flax feasts, harvest festivals and country dancing, despite the preferences of the young women from London who liked 'crooning jazz songs' as they tugged listlessly at the flax, and whose preferred evening activity was the 'perpetual and frantic climax' of the loveless 'modern sex-dance', performed to the accompaniment of a 'rumba' — a machine-like, urban pulse that seemed 'demonish, goblinish and in every sense hideous'.[60] Gardiner had been working to create a craft-based 'vertical industry' which might support a 'regional guild' of growers, processors, spinners and weavers united behind the slogan 'Wessex fabrics from Wessex fields'. But the Home Flax Directorate was run as a 'centrally controlled munitions industry', bent on mass production, mechanisation, and apparently determined to 'socialise' flax in preparation for the establishment of a nationalised state industry after the war.[61] The bureaucrats won, leaving him no choice but to depart on the Ministry's terms in 1942.

The war lent speed to the Wessex plough, but it also brought a new 'accumulation of metal' to Dorset — the military one that Sylvia Townsend Warner observed on the coast in 1944.[62] By that time, there were tanks pouring south across the country in preparation for the Normandy landings. Some of those hell-bent drivers drew patriotic inspiration from the countryside as they passed,[63] but the non-serving rural revivers who looked back from the fields hardly allowed for this. John Stewart Collis describes how, as a self-made farm labourer, he stood in a just harvested stubble field in South-West England marvelling at the agricultural landscape with its 'eternal tale' of 'the order that does not break'. Unfortunately, his Breughel-like detachment from history was broken 'all day long and every day' by the Military, who 'dashed past in lorries, in jeeps, in tanks. The clatter of the tanks was something awful. They passed in long lines, these the chariots of our day, their helmeted riders aloft in the turrets. I sometimes lifted my hand in friendly salute, but there was not much response. The division between us was too great for communication. Only a thin fence, but what a gulf! On this side was life everlasting; and over there — History roaring past.'[64]

Collis also recalls the fate of Reggie, the woodman at Springhead, who found a bomb in the woods, presumably left by the 'practising soldiery' who were in the locality. Convinced that it was a smoke bomb, he took it home and started hammering at it in front of his two terrified young sons, until it exploded, blowing off his hands and killing him.[65] But long before this, Gardiner had seen the tank-drawn image of History in a Nazi rally. Visiting Germany in 1936 to investigate the agricultural policy of Walther Darré, whom he believed had 'honestly wished to restore to the peasantry an honoured place in German society', he attended the Harvest Festival at the Bückeberg, near Hamlin.[66] A million peasant farmers gathered on the hillside from all parts of the Greater Reich. Regional emblems were displayed alongside Nazi banners, and peasants in traditional costume danced on a great stage of garlanded poles. Gardiner watched as Hitler walked up a rising gangway through the adoring crowd. Peasants reached out towards him, and children crawled through the legs of SS officers to present him with gifts. Then, at the top of the hill, the Führer was given 'a magnificent Harvest Crown' composed of corn and flowers and grapes. Gardiner reported that Hitler looked more benign and 'rubicond' than his pictures normally suggested, and his speech was not that bombastic, even though the 'fanatical self-assertion' came through when he proclaimed that 'Germany was a "rocher de bronze" washed by the turbulent waves of Bolshevist chaos'. It was only towards the end, and in a 'brief, almost perfunctory expression', that Hitler thanked the Almighty for the fruits of the harvest. 'Whom do we thank?,' asked Gardiner. 'No mention of God or Nature; Oh No!' Instead Goebbels, speaking after Hitler, hailed the Party, and the National Socialist State. 'With this crude and materialist announcement, a million German peasants were told how to give thanks at a National Harvest Thanksgiving on the Bückeberg.'

And then the metal of Nazi power burst in to enact a 'giant spectacle in the landscape theatre of the plain':

> Modern bombers zoomed across the fields, their shining shark-like bodies gleaming with martial pride. Suddenly a village shot up in flames, and then another. Other planes chased low over the valley and parachutists fully armed with machine-guns, leapt to the ground. Through them charged helmeted motor-cyclists and tanks. A full-scale battle was now in progress between two forces: one making the assault, the other defending a bridgehead over the Weser. Self-propelled guns began firing against the bridgehead; the crackle of machine-gun fire and the thud of bombs joined in a thunderous tornado, whilst the air force zoomed and whirred to to and fro. The 'villages' were now great sheets of red flame and their illusory walls, of wood and canvas, toppled ignominiously into subsiding embers. The attack swept past the foot of the Bückeberg, and the defenders retreated before the pursuers to the bridge over the great river. Then all the sound was of the smacking in the wind of the scarlet Nazi standards, and the chirrupping of a single skylark high above the myriad crowd. As the latter roused itself from a hypnotised condition to sing the 'two songs of the nation', the mists thickened over the Nether-Saxon

> landscape and the rain began to fall. Germany seemed indeed threatened by the demonic cavalry of Hubris, chaos and doom.

On Gauleiters, Swastikas and the 'Teutonic' Nature of Fir Trees

Did Gardiner really wish to be the Gauleiter of Wessex as local gossip still suggests? With hindsight, he would describe the vision he had shared with the Deutsch Freischar as a kind of 'Regional Socialism' that would have avoided the centralised Mass State common to Nazism and Communism. He conceded that this system would still have demanded an 'all-powerful and protective central Authority' to 'displace the parliament of warring parties', wrest control of economic factors out of the hands of private interests and restore individual personal freedom within a secure state.[67] As the war proceeded, Gardiner retreated into a Royalist English variation on this brutally cancelled theme. Like Lymington, he concluded that the land, far from being nationalised by the state, should be vested in the Crown; and that regional committees should be set up with the power to 'confiscate' the land of owners who were too decadent to act as responsible 'trustees' and to pioneer the rural revival that would come through mutual aid.[68] The King would appoint 'regional commissioners' from among the landowners or farmers. They should not be elders but rather men in the 'prime of life' — matured youth leaders perhaps — and they should travel around their region 'mercilessly castigating every sort of bumbledom and red-tape, overlapping and compartmentalism, making government once more a direct, forcible and kindly benediction instead of an abstract curse'. Gardiner suggested that these commissioners might be called Dukes.

It is conceivable that, as an ecological Royalist, Gardiner might have been available for such office, yet this is not to say that he was ever a gauleiter in waiting. As he wrote,

> In what way would such a Duke differ from a 'gauleiter'? Surely in every way. A 'gauleiter' is the nominee of a dictatorial party which has captured the stronghold of the state; the Duke would be the personal appointment of the King, but he could be acclaimed or rejected by the total electorate of his region through a plebiscite held after his nomination and subsequently every three, five or seven years. This method of appointment from above and acclamation or rejection from below, is a very old device with good precedents in Anglo-

> Saxon history. It avoids completely the party flavour and demagogy of electoral methods, and at the same time safeguards the realm from the King's favourites.

Gardiner was dismayed to see the Nazi war machine turn even trees to its own twisted and metallic ends. Writing about forestry in the last years of the war, he opened with the image of Hitler's army advancing on Russia, and the 'rediscovery of wood' that fuelled it.[69] Wood derivatives fuelled and greased the trucks. The tyres were made from wood alcohol, and the explosives came from waste products of pulp mills. Plywood planes assisted, and the propaganda films were made of wood cellulose acetate. This was, he said, 'a colossal abuse of man's heritage', adding — once again — 'that it was time to restore the spirit of husbandry' and to recognise forests and rivers as 'the parents of civilisation'.

So we come back to the Springhead woods, and the swastika that Gardiner is said to have planted there. One key to this myth, as with so many others of the period, is to be found in an alarmed, nativist response to the encroaching modern state: this time the Forestry Commission, set up in 1919 and charged with ensuring that Britain never suffered a timber shortage of the sort brought on by German blockade. The new agency soon came under furious attack for the coniferous monoculture it was imposing where woodlands of hazel coppice and broadleaved standards formed the traditional norm. Many commentators were appalled by this innovation, including H. J. Massingham who condemned 'this worthy body' for turning 'the unique Breckland of south-west Norfolk into a parade ground for conifers, equidistant, each the spit of its brother and all of them set out in standardised rows as through the voice of Nature had just bawled "Attention!" '[70] The Douglas fir may actually have come from the North American Pacific, but in the minds of that post-war generation, it was soon spliced together with Sitka and Norway spruce to produce a reviled 'Teutonic' imposter. Planted in straight lines through block-shaped plantations, the new coniferous plantations were reviled as if they were squads of invading 'Huns' encroaching on English soil. So it was in the Thirties, when G. M. Trevelyan led the National Trust into battle against the Forestry Commission's plans to cover the English Lake District with 'German pine forest'.[71] There was no place for the State's conifers in what Kipling had hymned as the English 'ancientry' of Oak and Ash and Thorn.[72]

Gardiner saw this rather differently, having trained at Dartington Hall with Wilfred Hiley, the forest economist whose calculations were used to justify the Commission's commitment to coniferous monoculture. Hiley was then coniferising Dartington's woods, but while Gardiner shared his opposition to the preservationists who would 'mummify' rather than revitalise the English countryside, he struck out in his own contrary direction to pioneer 'organic' mixed foresty.[73] He knew about the 'semi-foreign, quick-growing species' of conifer, and he didn't approve the Forestry Commission's intention of covering the landscape with an unEnglish array of 'dark exotics'.[74] Yet he was sceptical about the idea of native stocks, remarking that 'it is as difficult to disinter the native forest skeleton as it is the foundation stock of the native race'.[75] For him, forestry was the difficult, multicultural art of blending species that would 'thrive in sympathetic support of one another and the whole', and there was no room for dogmatism on either side.

In Gardiner's view, 'the CPRE and the National Parks Commission have all along been too die-hard in their resistance to conifers, although I have striven to convert them to the wisdom of using pines, larches and spruces as pioneer umbrella crops under which slower-growing hardwoods may be economically and beneficially planted'.[76] At Springhead he had used Japanese Larch, Douglas fir, both Sitka and Norway spruce and Scots Pine, to foster an underplanting of hardwoods like beech, oak, and sycamore. 'Such dense silvicultural methods at first made the Forestry Commission experts raise their grant-bestowing eyebrows', but then they themselves adopted 'dapple-shade' planting with success; and Gardiner looked forward to the day when such methods would be used — as they have since — to diversify the Commission's monocultural plantations at places like Thetford and Keilder.

Gardiner knew that scientific forestry was Germanic in origin, pioneered by Heinrich von Cotta, director of the Forest Academy at Tharandt in Saxony in the early nineteenth century, whose method was to clearfell and then replant directly in order to obtain 'maximum financial return from fast-growing coniferous timber'. However, he also pointed out that Cotta had expressed reservations about the indiscriminate adoption of this system as long ago as 1820, and that German silviculture had been considerably adjusted during the twentieth century as it emerged that pure spruce and pine forests caused problems like those of 'extractive' agriculture: 'destruction by fires, pests, insects and infections; the deterioration of the forest soils by dessication or increasing acidity; the exhaustion of humus by exposure of the soil during the clear-cutting intervals'. German foresters had subsequently started opening the forest canopy to enable natural regeneration to resume, and derived felling and planting patterns that were closer to nature. The monocultural approach had been entirely abandoned under a forest law passed by the Nazi government in 1934, which 'forbids clear-felling, and re-establishes the mixed or uneven-aged forest as a general principle'.

Far from being too 'German' in its methods, Gardiner believed that the Forestry Commission's prostration before the altar of economic pragmatism testified to a regrettable 'Americanisation'.[77] It was 'by all continental standards' a hundred years out of date. Some of the Commission's present-day critics insist that the whole idea of 'forestry' is an unwelcome import, and that all one has to do to create a wood in Britain is fence off a patch of land and leave it to grow, but Gardiner was no advocate of 'reversion to haphazard laissez-faire'. His 'return to more natural methods' was a 'cultured, not a barbaric, process, deliberate rather than romantic'; and it demanded 'infinite skill and judgement'.

'He was strange, let's face it,' says Bill Seymour, former land agent at the Crichel estate, sitting in his house above Gold Hill in Shaftesbury and remembering Gardiner from the early Fifties. It is hardly a run of the mill chap who takes his eldest son to be christened on a bullock, but he was way ahead on forestry. Highly knowledgeable about diseases and soil, he was 'always very keen on amenity and aesthetics'. He surprised neighbouring landowners by planting conifers around a pylon to disguise it, and he was 'horrified' when anyone threatened to bulldoze an ancient mound. As for forest design, 'he always tried to break the contours and not have those solid blocks of conifer and, quite frankly, we didn't'.

Most of Gardiner's coniferous nurse crops have been felled by now, but some striking shelter beds remain, curving down across combes and bottoms, or bisecting the turf promontory of Fontmell Down. These may shock latterday conservationists with their assertive shape, but they were planted as evergreen tributes to the organic integration of agriculture and forestry, which he feared would never be achieved through the agencies of a state that had dismembered the countryside as it divided responsibility for the fields, woods and streams between different centralised departments. For Bill Seymour in the Fifties, Gardiner's were 'the sort of woods you learned from' — even if they hold no such lessons for the National Trust forester who recently looked at the shelter bed that Gardiner extended across Fontmell Down and regretted that the Whitebeam is the Swedish variety and therefore not of native stock.

There were German students among the many young people who helped Gardiner with his unusual woods, and he also used plenty of conifers of the kind that, for many members of his generation, symbolised both the regimented symmetries of the advancing state and the 'Nordic' enemy. Gardiner never set a swastika in his woods, even though these 'Germanic' constituents were apparently enough to support the rumour that he had done so. But he did, as his son John Eliot once showed me, plant one magical configuration of fir that still stands at the edge of a beechwood. Balfour's Circle is a ring of evergreen trees, each one of a different variety, surrounding the place where Balfour Gardiner's ashes are interred. Like Rolf Gardiner's broken dream of Northern Europe, it is not monocultural but full of disciplined variety: a green polyphony rather than a regimented design, a federation of individual entities rather than a Reich, a Ring rather than an Array. Gardiner, as John Eliot observes, was considerably better at woods than at politics and international affairs.

PART FOUR

The Scouring of Tyneham Valley (1943–61)

Even Sam's vision in the Mirror had not prepared him for what they saw. The Old Grange on the west side had been knocked down, and its place taken by rows of tarred sheds. All the chestnuts were gone. The banks and hedgerows were broken. Great waggons were standing in disorder in a field beaten bare of grass. Bagshot Row was a yawning sand and gravel quarry. Bag End up beyond could not be seen for a clutter of large huts.

'They've cut it down!' cried Sam. 'They've cut down the Party Tree!'

J. R. R. Tolkien[1]

FOURTEEN

EVACUATION

ONE SUMMER DAY in 1936, Mr Ralph Bond welcomed fellow members of the Dorset Natural History and Archaeological Society on a field trip to Tyneham.[2] He informed them that Tyneham Great House, which only the year before had been eulogised in *Country Life*,[3] stood on 'classic ground' near cliffs that provided a sanctuary for ravens and peregrine falcons, and that the entire estate was 'being treated as far as possible as a nature reserve'. Seven generations had lived at Tyneham since it had been acquired in 1683 by one Denis Bond — a member of Cromwell's Council of Staff but surely not, as Ralph's son, Major-General Mark Bond still hopes, a full-blown regicide — and there had been no disturbances since then. So deep were the still continuities of Tyneham that Ralph Bond could remark 'the house has had no history'.

Even then, the claim was only just true. Bond's father, William Henry Bond, had heard the tanks blasting away at Bindon Hill and joined Mr Herbert Weld in his unsuccessful protest. Tyneham House was still living by oil-lamp and candlelight in the early Thirties but the over-restored telephone kiosk that still stands in Post Office Row, proves that William Bond had lost one battle against the modern forces pressing in from the other side of the hill. Ralph Bond, who inherited Tyneham after his father's death in January 1935, tried to maintain the timeless traditions of the valley through the disturbances of the Second World War. In 1940, he became commander of the Tyneham and Steeple platoon of the Home Guard, forming it from scratch and turning it into 'an extremely efficient and practical unit'.[4]

As a naturalist, however, Ralph Bond was less interested in the booming of tanks than in the smiting of pigeons and the drumming of snipe. The papers he presented to the Dorset Natural History and Archaeological Society over these years betray not the slightest clue about the trauma engulfing his home. In 1941, he spoke on the subject of a 'specialised neolithic flint instrument' he thought might have been used as a 'limpet-scoop'. In April 1943, he gave a talk about Dorset bats, remarking that 'in the summer of 1938 my daughter called my attention to a bat in her room at Tyneham. This we captured and I was at once struck with the length and shape of the ears.'[5] On 17 October 1944, he read a paper on the fifty species of birds that nest in domestic gardens, observing that, however destructive the eighteenth-century Enclosure Acts may have been, it should be remembered that 'our familiar countryside' had developed as their consequence.[6] By that time, Bond himself had fallen victim to a different enclosure. His house, village and valley had been evacuated to make way for the Army, and he was living in a hastily requisitioned suburban box in Corfe Castle.

The Bindon firing range was first extended in 1939 when Arish Mell Gap was closed to the public without consultation with the Wareham and Purbeck Rural District Council. But the military occupation of Tyneham was a more gradual process that began early in the war. To begin with, it coincided quite happily with the dwindled condition of the village, which had suffered badly from agricultural decline. The Army came in, taking the empty cottages of already departed labourers and shepherds, and also spare rooms in some houses. One former villager, Miss Helen Taylor, whose father was woodman to the Bonds, remembers them going off to the front for about eighteen months before returning 'all bedraggled' to continue with guard duties along the coast.

The Royal Air Force arrived later to build a radar station on the limestone ridge between Tyneham and South Egliston. Known as 'RAF Brandy Bay', and surrounded by anti-aircraft gun emplacements, this installation was used to lay coastal guns on German E-boats operating in the Channel. Nissen huts were put up in the woods, and officers were billeted with the Taylors, one end of whose double cottage had housed a laundry the Taylor sisters ran for the Rector and the Bonds. The NAAFI girls slept in the schoolhouse, closed a number of years before the war on account of falling rolls, and ran their canteen in the village hall. When the Women's Auxiliary Air Force came to work at the radar station they were billeted in Tyneham Great House, three RAF officers having first met Ralph Bond to announce their intention of housing sixty WAAFs there. To begin with the Bonds stayed on, squeezed right down to a few rooms, but by Christmas 1941 they had lost even this modest hold on their ancestral home, moving in briefly with the Taylors before retreating to a more secluded gardener's cottage.

Pat Evans, a WAAF radio operator who came in 1942 found the house 'a cross between a barracks and a boarding school' with eleven girls sleeping to a room.[7] She remembers the weekly 'liberty run' to Wareham, with its cinemas and shops, and walking through woods scented by wild garlic, or joining the romancing couples at 'Beatie and Wynns': 'a primitive café run by the Taylor sisters 'where we sat by trestle tables, lit only by flickering oil lamps, sipping our tea or Camp coffee and relishing the occasional rare treat of a boiled egg'. She recalls the mahogany lavatory seat in Tyneham Great House; and also the dances at Lulworth Camp, where Glenn Miller was played by a 'superb' Army band. Such were the last months of the Tyneham valley, before the villagers and, a little later, the WAAFs too were kicked out to make an expanded practice ground for British and American tanks in the preparations for D-Day.

Towards the end of 1943, and on the ultimate authority of Churchill's War Cabinet, it was decided to evacuate the Tyneham valley and also the sparsely settled heath area that now forms the main long distance gunnery range to the north. In all 225 people are reported to have been affected: 102 properties including five farms and eleven small holdings.[8] The letters giving notice of eviction were posted on 16 November 1943. Signed by Major General Miller of Southern Command, they explained that 'In order to give our troops the fullest opportunity to perfect their training in the use of modern weapons of war, the Army must have an area of land particularly suited to their special needs and in which they can use live shells.' After stressing the care with which the authorities had searched for a suitable area, the letter continued: 'It is regretted that, in the National interest, it is necessary to move you from your homes, and everything possible will be done to help you, both by payment of compensation, and by finding other accommodation for you if you are unable to do so yourself.' The evacuation was to be completed by 19 December, and a special advice service would be available at the Rural District Council's offices in Wareham. The letter closed with a mollifying sentence: 'The government appreciate that this is no small sacrifice which you are asked to make, but they are sure that you will give this further help towards winning the war with a good heart.' Additionally, a War Department Land Agent is said to have notified evacuees that 'when the War Department has no further use for the property and it is handed back, you have every right to return to the property. It should not be assumed by you that because the War Department has turned you out, you lose the right of occupying the premises again.'

The evacuation took place under the cover of official secrecy; the only testimony in the local papers consists of advertisements for livestock and farming equipment to be auctioned in early December — with the auctioneer drawing 'special attention' to these sales and urging farmers from a wide area to attend in order to 'assist in the dispersal of the stock on offer'.[9] The few remaining farm labourers soon found work elsewhere and others moved in with relatives. But the responsibility for many fell on John Durant-Lewis, then Deputy Clerk of the Wareham and Purbeck Rural District Council. He had to organise the evacuation, moving families into whatever empty property he could find. He remembers having scouts in every village and every councillor on the lookout: 'Anywhere that I could find a couple of rooms . . . anything that was empty I requisitioned immediately.'

Durant-Lewis found the experience harrowing in the extreme. Forty-five years later he described it as 'a dreadful thing to happen to them, and it was a dreadful thing to have to do'. Two Ministry of Health inspectors were sent down from Reading to lend a hand; and he also had the assistance of three senior ladies from the Women's Voluntary Service, who helped the evacuees pack and 'accustom their thoughts and ideas'. Repeating that this was 'the worst job I ever had', he explains that all those interviewing the displaced people were 'given the same story to tell'. Villagers were told that they must be out before Christmas, and reassured not just that they would be found other accommodation, but that they wouldn't have to pay any more for it. The whole operation was very 'hush hush', and it seemed especially cruel because of the timing: indeed, many people seemed more shocked by the fact that they had to leave just before Christmas, than by the loss of their homes.

Mrs Evelyn Bond, the wife of Ralph, was among the local WVS organisers who helped. Remembered by Mrs Durant-Lewis as 'a saint', she worked hard for her distressed villagers and 'found a lot of empty houses and vacant property in Purbeck'. It was she who informed the other evacuees about the government pledge promising them the right to return. Her sister-in-law, Lilian Bond, was later told by two separate families that Mrs Evelyn Bond had, 'by express request of the authorities', gone round the houses on the same day the notices arrived, 'to persuade the inhabitants of the necessity of evacuation and to promise that if they would "go quietly" — so to speak — they would be brought back to their homes immediately peace was restored'.[10]

So, in that bitterly cold winter the people of the Tyneham valley gathered up their things and, after waiting many hours for lorries that often didn't come due to flu and other difficulties, left the valley that they didn't necessarily know was blessed. Winnie and Beatie Mintern were horrified to be taken from Worbarrow Bay to a requisitioned house on a main road in Upwey next to the Station Hotel. Margaret Bond, who drove them there, recalled how they 'cried out in horror' when they saw the location: as strict Christians, they 'could not and would not live next to a pub'.[11] Jack and Miggy Miller ended up in a condemned stone cottage in Langton Matravers. On arriving at this bronchitic slum, Miggy refused to allow the lorry driver to unpack their things so that he could reuse the cases, saying that she was going to keep everything in cases until she was moved back to Worbarrow. Jack was found upstairs a few days later, wandering around helplessly with a washstand saying 'Where do'e want this put?' Mrs Virtue Gould had most of her crockery smashed while being transported in an old tin bath tub — her son, John, who was serving abroad at the time, observes that no amount of money can compensate for that kind of loss. Some of the older evacuees died of shock: 'The movement killed 'em. That's for certain.'

Tipped so precipitously out of their valley, some found it impossible to adjust. Charlie Miller, who was in his nineties, had flu when he and his wife Harriet were carted off to an old cottage in Stoborough — hastily cleared of the ladders and painting equipment that had been stored there. Helen Taylor, who visited them, remembers finding Mrs Miller impressed by the electric light put on the stairs for them; but bedridden Charlie was so terrified by the blaze that he shouted anxiously down the stairs, 'Put the light out down there, Harriet, you're going to catch the house afire!' Charlie Miller settled down enough to be entertained by the sight of traffic going by, but he didn't survive the evacuation by long; and neither, according to Margaret Bond's letters, did Mr Cleall, the road man, who died of pneumonia, caught as a result of the upheavals — much to the distress of his wife, who 'went off her head when the news came and was taken away'.[12] Mr Longman of Baltington Farm, the tenant who had rented his field to the Eton scouts, died soon after the removal — his heart broken, so Margaret Bond remembered it being said, by the sight of his cattle being 'sold off for a song at a hasty auction'.

The Bonds suffered their losses in a spirit of patriotic resignation. They could have complained about the absence of lorries, which left them no choice but to cram valuable clocks and other furniture into the cellar and to pile priceless old books into the granary, where they would soon moulder away. But when Evelyn Bond finally made her plea for special consideration, she did so on behalf of the whole village, writing the moving note she pinned to the church door before leaving: 'Please treat the church and houses with care. We have given up our homes, where many of us have lived for generations, to help win the war to keep men free. We shall return one day and thank you for treating the village kindly.' And then, having gathered up some 'very frightened' hens and 'Tipper', the kitchen cat that Ralph Bond refused to have put down, she joined the evacuees she had already counselled out of the valley.

From her hastily white-washed new house in Corfe Castle, Evelyn Bond turned to help the Taylors, who were almost the last to leave Tyneham: finding the cramped house into which they moved with their elderly father within hours of the deadline's expiry, and later securing them a more adequate bungalow called Sunnymount next to her own temporary residence in Corfe Castle. Helen Taylor remembers Mrs Bond urging them to break in with a table and chair to establish occupancy while the requisitioning order was sorted out. 'Well,' thought Helen Taylor, 'it's safe enough 'cause he's a magistrate if we get into trouble.' And all the time Mrs Bond was promising that this would only be an interim measure, and that 'we shall go back in another two years or something like that'.

Dining Out with the Lord Chief Justice and Tyneham's last MP

On 5 May 1947, after a famously severe winter in which the many troubles of Clement Attlee's austerity-ridden Labour government had been aggravated by unprecedented levels of snow and floods, a group of hardened survivors known as the Society of Dorset Men gathered at the Connaught Rooms in Bloomsbury for their annual dinner.[13]

The President of the Society was the Tory Lord John Jestyn Llewellin, PC, CBE, MC, TD, DL, who had been Minister of Food during the last two years of Winston Churchill's wartime coalition. He welcomed members and their guests one by one in the antechamber; and the assembled company then proceeded into the dining room 'to the festive strains of the Raymond Davis Orchestra which discoursed sweet music throughout the evening'. After the meal, Lord Chief Justice Rayner Goddard rose to welcome 'My Lord President, my Lords, Ladies and Gentlemen, my Zonnies'. Having deplored the industrial-looking cheese on his plate ('something white ... made by Tom Walls or someone of that sort') and observed, at the expense of the stricken Labour government, that 'To come to a dinner of Dorset men and not be able to have blue vinney is austerity indeed,' Goddard went on to apologise for the fact that, far from being a Dorset man, like Lord Llewellin who lived in Poole, he was actually 'a Wiltshire man, and you can call me a moon-raker if you wish (laughter)'. In mitigation, this famously bullfrog-faced judge, who had been appointed Lord Chief Justice by Clement Attlee only the year before, reminded the company that he had spent 'many a happy holiday' in Dorset and, indeed, that he had served seven years as Recorder of Poole. No doubt some of the Dorset Men who applauded remembered the battle he had fought against the tanks on Bindon Hill, stepping out of his West Lulworth house to join ranks with other late objectors like Herbert Weld and Sir Alfred Fripp.

So the peroration began: 'Dorset, our County. What better county is there? I believe I can claim to know every lane in it.' Goddard hymned the attractions of the 'magnificent sea-coast — Swanage Bay, Worbarrow Bay, Lulworth Cove and Weymouth Bay ... ' Then there was the 'Great Heath', immortalised by Thomas Hardy, and Sherborne — 'The Abbey, the School, the Cross'. All this, as Lord Goddard exclaimed, 'reminding us of England as it once was and England as we should like to see it again'.

Goddard himself embodied one English stereotype all too well. He was notorious as a judge of traditional English twist: a monstrous hanger and flogger whose victims came to include Derek Bentley, and who is said to have taken such pleasure in his work that his clerk was accustomed to packing a spare pair of trousers because he knew that Goddard 'always had an ejaculation in his pants when sentencing a youth to be flogged or hanged'.[14] But on that evening in May 1947, he kept to lighter matters. After hymning the Dorset landscapes that had refreshed him in his none too taxing legal duties as Recorder of Poole, the Lord Chief Justice selected an after-dinner joke from his ample collection. Passing over his old favourite, in which a barrel organ outside Winchester Assize broke into the Eton Boating Song, 'We'll all swing together', as soon as Goddard had condemned three men to the rope, he chose a less memorable example on the perennial theme of the thick-headed Dorsetshire yokel. He then proposed the second toast: 'So I give you "Dorset, Your County" — and my County from long association.'

This was drunk with 'tremendous enthusiasm', and it was then the turn of Tyneham's MP, the Right Hon Lord Hinchinbrooke, who launched into a condemnation of the military occupation of Purbeck. As Lord Chief Justice, Rayner Goddard was hardly in a position to renew his old battle with the War Office, but Hinchinbrooke was under no such constraint. Indeed, that evening he would take the standard from Lord Goddard, and lead the assembled Society of Dorset Men straight into the Tyneham valley, where he would array them against the military State.

Once described by Michael Foot as 'the most formidable of Tory die-hards'[15] and still remembered by one Purbeck quarrier as a 'resident of the last ditch', Hinchinbrooke had been MP for South Dorset since 1941, having taken over unopposed when the previous incumbent, Viscount Cranborne, was elevated to the House of Lords as Lord Salisbury. He liked to ride out over down and heath to meet voters on horseback. This approach seemed suited to the constituency: 'It is much easier,' as he later observed, 'for going across land to talk to farmers and farm labourers without getting covered in mud.'[16] His first campaign, which won him South Dorset on a much reduced majority in the 1945 election, is remembered by Neal Ascherson, then at the Old Malthouse, a preparatory school at Langton Matravers in Purbeck. The headmaster, Victor Haggard, warned his boys about the catastrophe that would follow a Labour victory. Then as now, the Old Malthouse is only separated from an adjacent state school by a high stone wall, and if Labour won they would surely tear the wall down and put a brutal end to the world as that shielded community knew it. Being a friend of Lord Hinchinbrooke's, Haggard didn't hesitate to enlist his senior boys in the last-ditch defence of English culture that his election campaign represented. They were briefed to visit houses in the nearby quarrying village of Worth Matravers, asking people whether they wanted a Conservative taxi or a Liberal taxi to take them to the polling station. As Ascherson recalls, the boys knew they had been put up to something disreputable, not least because the villagers saw straight through this trick question and despatched them with impressive rudeness.

Hinchinbrooke was no Tory dullard. The son and heir of the Earl of Sandwich of Hinchinbrooke, Hertfordshire, he had been educated at Eton and Trinity College Cambridge and then worked for two years as a factory hand in Woolwich before joining the boards of various telecommunications companies and becoming private secretary to Stanley Baldwin in 1932. He quickly distinguished himself as a free-thinking firebrand within the Conservative Party. A member and sometime chairman of the Tory Reform

Group, he wanted to dissociate modern Conservatism from the 'Liberal laissez-faire capitalism' which, before the war, had been allowed to 'run mad with results that lie on every side'.[17] Appalled to find the arteries of the Conservative Party choked by beer and whisky, 'money that is "hot" and running', share certificates and trash journalism, he hoped to cleanse his party not just of the 'mechanical politicians' whose defence of the status quo was a self-interested stand for their own 'miserable attainments',[18] but also of the Whiggish financiers and speculators who were 'creeping unnoticed into the fold of Conservatism to insult the Party with their votes at elections'.[19] The *Daily Worker* had its reservations about 'the arrogant, aristocratic Viscount Hinchinbrooke',[20] but many colleagues in the Conservative Party were also worried by this 'dissident' who insisted that the Modern Tory should reject Individualism as 'a philosophy in which the citizen has few duties in society', and set itself against 'the incubus of finance and the control of big business'.

The Conservatism of Tyneham's last member of Parliament was more like a familiar and intuitively known landscape than an abstractly conceived political ideology: like that of Stanley Baldwin, it was rooted in an unmodernised glade at the back of the wellborn English mind: a crouching vale of Christian virtues that had somehow escaped the rapacious 'money barons'. For Hinchinbrooke the stream of Tory inspiration flowed out of 'the compact world in which we lived until a generation ago — in which the parish constituted the surroundings which a man knew and loved as his home — the secure base from which he launched forth into adventures of body and mind and to which he returned at the end of his days'. Unlike Socialism, with its doctrines and its call to mass action, his Toryism was an organic thing: a 'way of life' and an 'attitude of mind' best described with the help of a large and metaphoric English oak.[21] It aimed at decentralisation and had an instinctive desire to 'disperse the crowd'. It sought to 'preserve all the best elements of English life', cherishing 'variety, independence, and distinction'.[22]

Hinchinbrooke kept a worried eye on the destructive forces advancing from the other side of England's native hill. His singular political credo was not to find its most epigrammic expression until March 1953, when he wrote to the *Daily Telegraph* to suggest that landowners and foresters should do something about the ivy gaining a symbolic hold on the beeches and elms of South-West England: 'Good work can be done by one man in half a day, with a light slasher.'[23] By then, Hinchinbrooke was finding 'encroachments' everywhere — so much so that slashing had become his full-time job. He had long since warned of 'the creeping shadow of Left Wing thought that was drawing across the whole countryside',[24] but he had taken a swipe at ribbon development too, declaring the 'cracking walls and rotting timbers' of its bungalows to be 'sickening evidence' of 'a capitalism and a financial system that has atrophied our minds and debased the loftiness of our conceptions'.[25] He had counted up the machines — bulldozers, dehydrators, tanks, harvesters and concrete mixers — with which modern science was stretching out the 'compact world' from which true Tory virtues derived, and which he feared would be shattered by developments to come.

During the war, Hinchinbrooke had declared the modern Tory 'hopeful of planning', which he regarded as 'a grand design to bring the aims of man into a true relation with the aims of the community'. As a leading member of the Tory Reform Group, he had welcomed the Beveridge Report as the 'essence of modern Toryism'. In 1943, he had predicted that the Conservative Party would face dramatic defeat unless it committed itself to 'a re-education of the national mind in moral and spiritual values'.[26] Proved right by Clement Attlee's landslide victory in 1945, he observed that the war had thrown 'the rose-covered Beveridge cottage into stark relief' and, in the absence of sufficient Tory reform, the 'planning Excalibur' had been seized by the Labour Party, which was now building the authoritarian 'State Leviathan'.[27] While awaiting the reaction that would eventually come, the Conservative Party should recognise its role as being to 'sharpen the instruments of deceleration'.

By 1947, when this outspoken 41-year-old Viscount stood up before the Society of Dorset Men to respond to Lord Rayner Goddard's toast, he had retreated some distance into the liberal camp. In 1945, his condemnation of the National Savings Scheme had filled the Dorset papers with letters from outraged voters who could barely believe his objection to the principle of the state raising money to fund post-war reconstruction.[28] There had been further controversy, when he attacked the Labour Chancellor, Hugh Dalton, for removing two million of the lowest paid workers from all income tax liabilities, arguing that all people should pay tax in order to know their responsibility for public policy, and that entrepreneurs who actually earned their income should be taxed on a more favourable basis than rentiers and stockmarket speculators who did not.[29]

Hinchinbrooke trotted through his constituency, telling voters that, while it was indeed 'the duty of the strong to aid the weak', Stafford Cripps was 'a menace' and 'there was not a soul in this country who did not feel, in some sense, that he was in a kind of strait-jacket'.[30] In the early years of the Cold War he broke with the party line to insist that the Hydrogen Bomb was 'no answer to Communism'. Britain should oppose the Soviet Union not by developing superior weapons of mass destruction, but by 'a great social and economic effort' which would demonstrate the absolute superiority of western democracy by peaceful means.[31] England's role, as Hinchinbrooke explained at Weymouth Grammar School Speech Day, was 'not to terrify the world with power, but to inspire'. Despite the losses of two world wars, 'we are still paramount in the moral and spiritual field'.[32] Against McCarthyism, the member for Tyneham urged 'a spiritual reply to the Communist system'.[33]

Such was the 'dissident Tory'[34] who, that evening in Bloomsbury, hailed the Lord Chief Justice as 'the prime after-dinner speaker in England', insisting that his evident 'appreciation of the countryside of Dorset' made him a true adopted son of Dorset, as he himself was. And such was the vision of England that prompted him to rally the Men of Dorset against the dire threat facing their county:

> There is a task which confronts all the sons of Dorset in the coming year . . . You spoke of our coasts belonging to us. Is that really so? The part of Dorset I love best, extending from Corfe to Lulworth, is bound like Andromeda to the rock. The War Office dragon is breathing its fire and smoke over her, and we like Perseus, must go to her rescue. There were two occasions in history when the sons of Dorset rose in defence of her coasts. At the time of the Napoleonic menace, so wonderfully depicted by Thomas Hardy in The Dynasts, every man leapt to his allotted post in order to defend her shores, and again in September 1940, when the alarm was once more given. In both cases the alarm was unfounded. But we must not allow it to be said that Dorset men only move to action when the alarm is false. Today there is an urgent alarm — Southern Dorset is gradually being turned, by an insidious process, into a military encampment — and the project will be backed up by all the mercenary and commercial forces which come in its train.

He closed this call to arms with a remark that stands as a classic expression of a strain of Tory conservationism that barely survived the Eighties. Looking over towards Purbeck, he saw the valley of English patriotism being crushed by the tanks of an all powerful state bent on usurping the nation's name. 'What is the use of a great standing army and fleets of aircraft if the source and inspiration of patriotism is lacking through the spoilation of our countryside?' Burke had once declared that 'the thing which inspires valour in the army is nothing more than the love of the people for their country and their attachment to its institutions'. 'I sincerely hope,' as he concluded, 'that we shall have the support of every Dorset man is ridding our lovely countryside of the shackles of the War Office.'

There was applause before Mr Thorpe Bates, a well-known baritone whose Dorset connections can safely be assumed, gave 'fine renderings of songs like "The Crown of the Year", "Praise o' Dorset" and the old drinking-song "Away, dull care" '. But the symbolic outrage that was Tyneham demanded action. As Lord Llewellin promised: 'A number of us, at the local enquiry, are going to put up a good fight against this.'

From Churchill's Pledge to Attlee's Betrayal

The suspicion that the military might be planning to hold on to its greatly expanded firing range was being voiced before 8 March 1945, when VE Day marked the end of the war in Europe. The ban controlling civilian access to the southern coast had been partly lifted in July 1944, but this was not enough to prevent England's most ardent letter-writers rising up to protest against the perfidy of a War Office that apparently intended to keep its requisitioned land in Purbeck.

The Wareham and Purbeck Rural District Council made its first representations in January 1944, asking that areas taken over by the War Office should be 'restored and made available to the general public at the earliest possible date after the cessation of hostilities'.[35] A year later the members, who included Ralph Bond — elected as councillor for the parish of Tyneham in October 1944 — were expressing 'great concern' lest some purely emergency war measure should result in many people permanently losing their homes and the general public losing access to 'some of the most beautiful coastal districts of England'. This judgement was shared by the members of the Dorset Natural History and Archaeological Society, who, in February 1945, passed a unanimous resolution expressing 'grave alarm' at 'the possible retention after the war by the Service Authorities of areas in the Isle of

Purbeck'.[36] Since Ralph Bond was on their committee too, they wisely added that it was on the grounds of 'public interest and the Nation at large' that they demanded 'the earliest possible restoration and the maintenance intact of this outstanding beauty spot'.

By May 1945, when the requisitioned area had been redesignated the East Holme Range and permanent roadbarriers had been put up at Steeple, Major F. Holland Swann, the Chairman of the District Council who himself lived in Steeple Manor, was riding out at the head of a newly initiated 'Hands Off Purbeck' campaign. That July, the month in which Attlee swept Churchill out of Downing Street, he wrote to *The Times*, protesting that while an obelisk had been erected on Slapton Sands to mark the sacrifice of evacuated villagers who had already been given leave to return to their homes, no thought had apparently been given to 'the unfortunate inhabitants of the Isle of Purbeck who were evacuated from their homes at the same time'.[37] As for the threat of permanent expropriation, 'this should not be permitted and my council appeal to all who are able to help them to resist this encroachment'.

By 5 October, a local reporter confirmed that large numbers of troops were 'still engaged in works' on the expanded gunnery range, and the traveller proceeding towards East Lulworth from West Holme across the heath range would find 'for a distance of a mile and a half, the narrow, winding county lane has been replaced by a concrete highway, with concrete roads and tank parking grounds leading off from it'.[38] Ammunition dumps lined the road, and there were 'frequent warning notices against smoking, loitering, parking, and wandering on to the battle area, where there are "no regular lines of fire" '.

Wareham and Purbeck Rural District Council resolved to send a deputation to Whitehall, authorising expenditure of £20 to cover the costs of the party that would take the 'Hands Off Purbeck!' committee's case up the well-travelled road to Westminster, where it would be placed before the Secretary of State for War. A decidedly upper-crust affair, the deputation included Major Swann, Lord Hinchinbrooke and two other Dorset MPs. Lord Cranborne was there as the former Tory MP for South Dorset and so too were Lord Ilchester, and Mr J. W. G. Bond, landowner and director of the company that quarried ball clay from the heath now lying within the requisitioned area. The County Council was represented, as were national agencies like the National Trust, the Council for the Preservation of Rural England, the Co-operative Holidays Association, and the Standing Committee on National Parks. The whole occasion seems to have been exceedingly well-mannered.[39] The minister insisted the matter would have to be considered from 'the national viewpoint', but he was found to be 'exceedingly pleasant' and promised to visit Dorset in order to take a look for himself. As one delegate concluded, 'although he didn't say anything definite, I had a feeling of hope'.

Much of Purbeck would indeed be released, but the War Department was not to be budged from Tyneham. There was considerable disappointment in the House of Lords. Lord Salisbury declared that there were 'conclusive reasons' why the Tyneham area 'should be returned to the purposes for which Nature ordained it'.[40] It was, as he explained, 'one of the most lovely and unspoiled stretches of country in the south of England and was visited before the war by many thousands of town dwellers who found rest and mental refurbishment from their labours'. An undertaking had been given to the local inhabitants and this raised 'very broad national issues since it involved the good name of the British government'.

By February 1947, Tyneham was on the list of seven 'contentious areas' where the military authorities were still holding out against the return of requisitioned land. Some compromise may have been possible on Dartmoor, but Prime Minister Attlee told the House of Commons that 'As regards the Purbeck area, comprising 6,940 areas, no reconciliation of military and civil interests has been found possible', promising only that 'a public local inquiry would be held before a decision on the retention of this range is taken'.[41]

As had happened over Bindon Hill in the Twenties, this local altercation was amplified by a variety of national commentators. For C. E. M. Joad, Tyneham was among the 'downlands hacked and mauled by tanks and guns' that Labour's new Ministry of Town and Country Planning should set out to restore.[42] He opposed the recent closure of roads in the area, repeating the words of a correspondent: 'If there are some to whom the names of Arish Mell, Worbarrow, Brandy Bay, Flowers Barrow and Steeple are music, I can only hope that they can make their protests heard in time to prevent the War Department from going ahead with its plans to turn that isle of refreshment for the soul into a permanent battle range.'[43] Writing from well to the left of this 'Brains Trust' boffin, Douglas Goldring also objected to 'War Office land-grabbing', because it proved that the 'armour-plated' politicians in Attlee's Cabinet had, 'ever since the nominal end of the war', been 'more or less openly planning for a renewed outbreak of hostilities' — this time in alliance with the United States against the Soviet Union.[44]

H. J. Massingham had lost a leg by now, but in his mind this 'downland traveller' was still stepping out over megalithic chalk heights. In May 1947, he visited Dorset, and found the green rings on Eggardon Hill quite deserted, which he considered proof that 'Solitude is intolerable to an era that works and plays, thinks and acts on the principle of the storm.'[45] At Slape Flax Mill near Netherbury, he found Rolf Gardiner's roughly nationalised revival of the Wessex flax industry closed and quite 'stamped out' by the Labour government. As for the Isle of Purbeck where Massingham stayed with his friend, Arthur Bryant, it had been 'captured from England by its own Army'. Driving into that Hollow Land, Massingham found decay and desolation 'written upon the land-surface in the modern scrawl. Ribbon development, surburban sprawl, pylons, the ruins of woodlands, the litter of our civilisation and the violations of the military are everywhere. In the Isle of Purbeck, farmlands are choked with weeds, farmhouses falling to pieces, wilderness is creeping over a region that was once the Canaan of the south.'

Already recommended for 'reserve' status in the 1945 Dower Report on National Parks in England and Wales, Purbeck had by this time also been singled out for conservation by the National Parks Committee of the Labour government's new Ministry of Town and Country Planning Committee.[46] But the government countered grey prose with grey prose, and the case for conservation was no match for the White Paper on 'Needs of the Armed Forces for Land for Training and Other Purposes', published in December 1947. Without specifically mentioning deteriorating relations between the Soviet Union and the West, this offered cogent reasons why the forces now needed twice as much land as before the war. It also included a carefully placed paragraph designed to pre-empt the imminent public inquiry over the tank ranges in Purbeck and, in particular, to defuse the ticking bomb of Churchill's pledge: 'In the case of some of the proposed training areas ... it has been, or may be represented that pledges were given that persons required to leave their homes would be allowed to return at the end of the war. The government accepts the fact that pledges of this kind were given or understood to be given and it will not therefore be necessary to press the point at public inquiry.' In cases where the pledge could not be honoured, special assistance, 'over and above the compensation provided by the relevant statutes', might be forthcoming.

On 25 February 1948, Brigadier N. W. Duncan, Commander of the Royal Armoured Corps in Dorset, attended the Annual General Meeting of the Dorset Council for the Preservation of Rural England, to introduce the arguments he would shortly put to Attlee's promised public inquiry.[47] The expanded Lulworth ranges were essential to the 'professional efficiency' of the army, without which the lives of soldiers would be 'squandered to no purpose'. Perhaps, as some had suggested, the development of nuclear warfare would 'revolutionise present conceptions of land warfare', but it would be a foolish man who kicked away his crutch until he was certain that it had been replaced by something else.

Duncan stopped short of describing Tyneham and its blasted heath as a nature reserve, but he did suggest that things could have been worse under private ownership: 'In some sense I can claim that the Army, nuisance though it is in the way that it occupies land of which you would willingly see it dispossessed, does ensure that the land is not disfigured by the erection of unsuitable houses and the creation of new towns which further reduce the already restricted open spaces.' But the Dorset CPRE was not to be fobbed off so easily. An influential member, Rolf Gardiner 'deplored the physical destruction which was going on', and asked 'Could not the land, or part of it, be put to a practical use and the creation avoided of an appalling wilderness?'

Moving in to Tyneham Close

Once again, this passionate argument was squeezed into the disillusioning labyrinth of cold iron tubes that is the official public inquiry procedure. Held in Wareham's Masonic Hall over two days in March 1948, the inquiry was conducted for the Ministry of Town and Country Planning by Sir Cecil Oakes CBE.[48] On the first morning, the case for the War Office was put by Brigadier Duncan, assisted by Colonel Blain, Commandant of the gunnery school, who had brought along maps and a model to demonstrate the absolute impossibility of surrendering the range. Referring to the White Paper, Duncan admitted that pledges had been given — 'that fact is not in dispute' — but then went into a rapid fire recitation of the many reasons why they were now beside the point.

Lord Hinchinbrooke put up a colourful show against the forces of bureaucratic realism. 'From the time of Oliver Cromwell we have resented having the military quartered on us,'[49] he said, emphasising, with a sheepish eye on the pragmatic interests of his voters, that the camps at Bovington and Lulworth were, of course, 'welcome establishments in the constituency'. Loudly insistent on the 'broken pledges' that the government and its hirelings were now trying to sweep under the carpet of history, he described visiting the evacuated area in November 1943, when 'the belongings of the people' were already piled high ready to be carted away. Like Evelyn Bond, he had reassured uprooted villagers that the evacuation would only be temporary. It was his word, as well as Churchill's, that the Labour government now proposed to betray:

> I walked into a cottage and found an old woman weeping. She said 'This is for the war, isn't it?' And I answered, 'It is for the war.' She asked, 'Will they let me come back after the war is over?' And I said, 'Yes. If they don't let you come back we will fight for the right.' That is what we are fighting for today.

Hinchinbrooke's assertion of English principle against mediocre political pragmatism was supported by Revd H. C. Money, the last rector of Tyneham, who spoke for his scattered parishioners: 'They definitely feel that if the area is retained by the War Office, they have been lied to and let down.' This left Ralph Bond free to concentrate on the insult to his forebears implicit in the emerging 'tanks are better than caravans' line of argument. Repudiating the suggestion that the Army was actually 'preserving' his valley from exploitation, he insisted that his 'predecessors had resisted the encroachment of civilisation in so far as it was associated with the building of week-end cottages'.

J. Scott Henderson KC, representing the objecting local authorities, claimed that the Tyneham valley was vital from the 'town and country planning point of view'. The area had been preserved 'by the public spiritedness of landowners and by the public activities of the planning authorities', and now along came the War Department saying: 'Thank you very much for keeping this as a natural preserve, and it now suits our purpose and we will take it over.' The only objector who was not prepared to argue for full-scale military withdrawal seems to have been Captain C. Diver from the British Ecological Society, who hoped for better access for scientists but declared himself unwilling 'to stand here and say that the Army must get out because there are some interesting populations of rare insects on the coast'.[50]

A War Office official would later look back at the 1948 Inquiry and remark, with those broken pledges in mind, that 'everything was quite rightly thrown at the War Office, including the kitchen sink'.[51] There is little sign of this in Sir Cecil Oakes's never officially published report to Lewis Silkin, Labour's Minister of Town and Country Planning — except perhaps in the eagerness with which he too tried to declare those increasingly symbolic English promises beside the point: 'Brigadier Duncan on behalf of the War Department referred to the pledge understood to have been given that disturbed residents would be allowed to return at the end of the war; consequently no need arose to discuss this aspect of the problem . . .'

Having ruled out the moral case that seemed so overwhelming to many of the protesters, Oakes and his anonymous civil servants weighed up the pros and cons of the present status quo. Beauty, Science and Agriculture were at stake, but the most serious loss was the one threatening the 'long established flourishing and valuable industry' devoted to extracting the raw material of the new welfare state from the now militarised heath to the north of the Tyneham valley. There were only three known workable deposits of ball clay in the country, said Oakes, and the articles made from this material were essential to the nation: porcelain for electrical industries, crucibles for the non-ferrous metal industries, sinks and lavatory bowls for the domestic household. The ball clay, quarried by Ralph Bond's cousins over at Creech Grange, was 'quite vital', not just to 'the maintenance of our position as a manufacturing nation' but also, as Oakes added with an eye to the priorities of the Labour government, 'in connection with the government's Housing programme, which is of quite indefinite duration . . .' and would be followed by the expanding Education and Health Services, which in turn would demand mountains of ball clay too. Oakes was in no doubt that the quarrying of this material from the heath was 'essential for the contentment of the people'.

That was how things threatened to fall out in 1948: tanks against the council houses, schools and hospitals of the welfare state. Oakes appreciated that 'the conflict of interests is deep and serious', but he noted that the Army had already made arrangements to allow for quarrying to continue at times when firing was not in progress. So the Ministry of Town and Country Planning advised the Under Secretary of State for War that the requisitioned area could be compulsorily purchased on certain conditions. Ball clay quarrying was to be facilitated, fishing boats were to be given access to coastal waters in the mornings, and maximum possible use was to be made available to the farmers with an interest in the area. Proper public access should also be given 'as soon as safe and practical' to the Whiteway, Worbarrow Bay, the ancient monuments on Bindon Hill, Flowers Barrow and to Tyneham, both the village and the house. As for the evacuees, Oakes advised the government to compensate them 'as liberally as may be found possible' with 'exceptional grants'.

So the symbolic promise, already mythologised as 'Churchill's pledge', was broken by Attlee's Labour government. On 16 July 1948, Lewis Silkin, the Labour Minister of Town and Country Planning, came down to announce the Labour Cabinet's reluctant decision to retain the Tyneham valley permanently.[52] The government accepted that 'there was a definite pledge given to the people'. But regrettably the world had changed enormously since 1943 and the future suddenly seemed full of tanks:

> No one imagined we should have to begin preparing for a fresh war. As we all know, we have only to look at our morning papers to see the unexpected happening. Nobody can guarantee that we should be at peace this time next year ... For the first time in the history of this country, at any rate for many hundreds of years, conscription has been introduced in peace time. All parties of the State are in agreement with it. Training implies having the necessary land on which to train.

This preamble lent the intended sense of inevitability to Silkin's reluctant conclusion: 'The pledge which was given in good faith to the people of this area cannot in the circumstances be kept.' The village that had alread 'died for D-Day' was going to have to die all over again for the Cold War.

This left the outstanding question of what was to be done for the evacuees, and here at least the Labour government would do its decent best. As 'a trustee in the interests of those who have been displaced', Silkin stated that 'the duty of government so far as is possible is to put people in as good a position as if the pledge had been carried out'. It would be impossible to do that absolutely: 'Some people have sentimental ties to a particular area, having lived there all their lives and their ancestors before them. No government can reinstate that sort of situation.' But it should be possible to find people something equivalent to what they had before. This was the Labour government's promise — as emblematic in its own way as

'Churchill's pledge' — and it was to be applied to tenants as well as owners. The government had arranged for the Ministry of Health to authorise sufficient materials and labour to enable the Rural District Council to build the necessary houses, so that they could be let at 'roughly the same rents' as people had paid before. This scheme was intended to ensure that people already waiting for council housing would not be 'baulked of getting a house at the expense of the displaced persons'.

'Put not your trust in princes — or politicians,' so concluded the *Dorset County Chronicle* of the Churchillian pledge that had now been 'repudiated' by a Labour government.[53] The news came as 'a bitter disappointment' for those who had worked so hard to win the release of the area.[54] 'Just one more disillusionment,' said Mrs E. A. Leaver of Corfe Castle. As honorary secretary of the 'Hands off Purbeck' campaign, she had received letters of support from all over the country, and the loss of Tyneham might still only be the thin end of the wedge: 'We have no guarantee there will be no further encroachment.' Gloomy resignation also descended on the spirit of Revd H. C. Money, the former rector of Tyneham, who had made the most, during the battle's first years, of having heard John Strachey, Minister for the Army, say 'I think we'll keep it', as the two of them were walking along the recently mine-cleared beach at Worbarrow Bay. Remembered for 'his vehement plea at a public meeting to "boot these vandals out" ', Money now felt obliged to modify his attitude 'in view of present circumstances'.

So the valley was left to wander. By September 1949, when *The Times* passed this way again, its special correspondent declared that the people had 'given up the fight' since the public inquiry went against them, and were now busy 'salving what they can'.[55] The compensation was generally considered fair, but there were still some 'perverse people, particularly among the visitors, who regard lovely pieces of countryside as part of their national heritage'. Seventeen warning notices protruded from the hedge along the road from Lulworth Camp to East Lulworth, and the whole scene was littered with discarded corrugated iron, lumps of broken concrete and new concrete roads. As for the Tyneham valley, 'surely one of the most exquisite little sanctuaries in the south of England', a photograph taken from a vantage point close to that used to capture the idyllic oats harvest in 1929, showed 'an abandoned valley in Dorset', with empty farms, overgrown fields of reverted pasture, and unkempt hedges. Converted into an overshoot or 'safety area', Tyneham was 'fast becoming a wilderness'. Shells had already gone through the roof of the fourteenth-century church and

Tyneham Great House was no longer thriving under the military care that had been so generously commended by both Sir Cecil Oakes and Mr Ralph Bond at the inquiry eighteen months previously: thieves had stolen the lead from part of the roof, and pools of rainwater were forming inside.

So the people of Tyneham were settled into permanent exile. Some former tenants stayed on in temporary billets that were now bought by the council with money provided by the War Office, but a significant number made the journey from one classic English archetype to another. Shaken out of that famously 'unspoiled' village, they were rehoused in a small specially built council estate in Sandford near Wareham. Originally part of Keysworth Drive, this was renamed Tyneham Close after the prefabs had given way to more permanent structures — not exactly 'rose-covered Beveridge cottages', but small, low-rise blocks and bungalows of red brick rather than the Dorset stone preferred by Lord Hinchinbrooke. The natives of Tyneham had moved from the timeless valley of English tradition to the fully-fitted modern convenience of the welfare state: hot and cold running water, lavatories, sinks, and baths too — all, no doubt, made from ballclay quarried, under special dispensation, from the blasted heath.

Did they still feel traumatised? Mr Durant-Lewis refers the question to his wife Margot, who had the job of visiting them every week to collect their modest rents. Retracing her old itinerary, through that scattered and hastily requisitioned collection of old farm buildings, coastguard cottages and former holiday homes, she tries to recapture their abruptly relocated inhabitants: the woman from Monastery Farm who was happily settled not far from Coombe Keynes: the retired musicians who had played in national orchestras but were now only remembered as 'the two odd women with a dappy brother'. The Millers of Worbarrow Bay had been 'really heartbroken', but the majority of evacuees were content, once they had got over the undoubted shock, and probably also pleased to lead a less isolated life than they had known on the heath or in the prehistoric bowl of the Tyneham valley. There is no reason to think that Tyneham Close was an unusually mournful place.

John Durant-Lewis confirms this. 'I think once they'd got over the shock . . . they were quite happy, ninety per cent of them. Not only that, they didn't want to go back.' And yet he himself had been permanently affected by the trauma. When I met him in 1990, he was still working to uphold a promise: not Churchill's irretrievably broken pledge, but the lesser undertaking that Lewis Silkin had given the evacuees on behalf of Attlee's Cabinet. It had been stated that the alienated villagers would be properly rehoused 'at no greater expenditure to themselves than that to which they were committed at the time'; and Durant-Lewis understood this to mean that they would be able to live the rest of their days in a compensatory timewarp: their timeless valley still hedged against history, even though removed from its expropriated fold in the downs and transferred into the soft grey blanket of the welfare state.

But then, some forty years after Attlee's Cabinet had given this pastoral undertaking, he discovered 'a great injustice' had been done to one of the last surviving villagers. Some time in the late Seventies, Helen Taylor's accommodation charges were considerably increased by the council. Miss Taylor would never have complained, but when Durant-Lewis found out he wrote to the rural district council he had once directed. Unfortunately, it was not just the Tyneham valley but the whole landscape of public administration that had been taken over since that Arcadian settlement was offered. As a 'clerk' who would never have dreamed of strutting about as a 'chief executive', Durant-Lewis may have built up a thrifty and effective council machine; but when he took the memory of Attlee's promise into the gleaming palace of privatising bureaucracy his council has since become, he was told that it wasn't on, and that the council had been incorrect to accept such an unrealistic agreement in the first place.

Forty years later, the survivors of Tyneham's organic community were still inclined to grumble about the arbitrary aspect of the state bureaucracy that had launched them into the new world. They muttered about the inequities of the compensation: one born and bred Tyneham villager was working at sea at the time and got nothing, whereas a recently arrived tenant farmer, a useless fellow whose only achievement had been to replace most of his workers with a tractor — and who was already under notice to quit — came out of the valley quite handsomely. Miss Margaret Bond remembered how the mother of a newly employed milkman was awarded £1,000 after claiming that she could have taken in summer guests by the dozen (something that the Bonds would never have allowed). Not bad compared with the £30,000 eventually awarded to her brother Ralph for Tyneham Great House, the village, half the valley and all those centuries of ancestral history.

If there was one person who stood above petty carping, it was, according to all testimonials, Ralph Bond himself. As their son Mark recalls, 'the breaking of the promise' really shocked Ralph and his wife Evelyn, but they bore their troubles with stoical dignity. Throughout the upheaval, Ralph pressed on, whether as councillor, Justice of the Peace or regional adviser to the Nature Reserves Investigation Committee, the pioneering wartime body which recommended that the state should assume some responsibility for the conservation of plants and wildlife. He served as High Sheriff in 1945 and, in 1946, moved from temporary accommodation into a large house called Moigne Combe near Dorchester, inherited on the death of an uncle. He also continued as a committee member of the Dorset Natural History and Archaeological Society. In 1949 the dispossessed squire of Tyneham, who had already drawn up a map recording the ancient names of Tyneham's fields for the Society's library, pointed out that the Tree-Creeper had all but disappeared from the Sherborne area after a cold spell, and regretted that there had been no takers for a county essay prize on 'The Influence of Local Materials on Dorset Buildings'.

In 1950 he was elected President of the Society, an organisation to which he had belonged since 1904, and which gave also refuge to almost all that now remains of Tyneham Great House. By 1951 the Ministry of Public Buildings and Works had reluctantly resigned itself to 'the survival of the house in a survey record only, and to its final abandonment'. Some relics were removed to the County Museum in Dorchester: seventeenth-century heraldic glass, which can still be seen set in the windows of the Society's library; and the oak panelling lining what was once the curator's spacious office upstairs. Ralph Bond was mortally ill by the time these fragments were properly installed in their new home, and they became his memorial. As for the compensation, this only arrived in 1952. General Mark Bond speaks of receiving it with one hand and then handing it back in payment of his recently deceased father's death duties. He has never been inclined to see the amount as generous.

Ralph Bond had died from cancer earlier that year — aged seventy-two, and young for the Bonds of Tyneham who, in the pre-war words of *Country Life*, had 'a remarkable record of longevity'. There was speculation that his sadness over the loss of Tyneham may have hastened his decline. One friend remarked, 'I know the ruin of Tyneham has hurt him terribly', but nobody was anything like so sure as *This England* would later be that he had died of a 'broken heart'.

The memorial booklet produced by his sister Lilian is full of tributes. As she wrote, 'Ralph seemed incapable of harbouring resentment though, during his latter years, he suffered many injuries and injustices great and small. I believe he felt the injustice and ingratitude and venomous attacks as keenly as did we who felt them for him, but I never heard him speak a bitter word or say a harsh thing of the individuals at whose hands he suffered. While fighting doggedly for the rights of tenants and poor neighbours, he would not fight for himself or seek to claim his own.' Former tenants remembered him as 'that perfect gentleman and squire'. They praised the spirit in which he had endured 'the ravishing of his old home by the War Office'; they remembered how Ralph only 'smiled, and did his best to encourage his tenants to try with him to make the very best of a bad job'. Lord Hinchinbrooke paid his respects too: 'I have felt that, behind Ralph's gay skepticism about our present social and moral values, there was a deep hurt . . . One occasionally asks oneself just why our modern age should take revenge on those of Christian charity and complete friendliness to all who are guilty of no political, economic and social sin.' Once a lovely Dorset village, Tyneham was now the name of a grievous wound torn in the national character by the modern State.

Crichel Down: Signing Off on Chalk

For a time at least, Hinchinbrooke would stay true to the memory of that virtuous valley. He had been loudly unimpressed when Silkin informed the Commons of the government's decision to retain the area requisitioned in 1943, wanting to know whether Silkin knew that his decision had been 'protracted for three years, and that great hardship and suffering have been caused to my constituents'.[56] He rejected the claimed £4 million cost of relocating the firing range as a 'complete falsification' and, noting that the decision had been delayed into the early months of the Cold War, put a further question to Lewis Silkin: 'Is he further aware that he has produced this decision, perhaps by design, at this particular moment of international tension so that public opinion is likely to support the view which is acceptable to the Generals in the War Office?'

Hinchinbrooke was not a man to be bullied into line by the party whips, and neither would he be intimidated when, in the early Fifties, his constituency party in South Dorset passed a vote of no confidence in him. As an 'individual' and independent thinker threatened by a 'party machine' that was, in its own way, proving as destructive of English values as the bureaucracy of state socialism, Hinchinbrooke saw no alternative but to abolish his constituency party — which he did forthwith, calling his own meeting at the Alexandra Gardens Theatre, and using it to set up 'a new edifice of Conservatism in South Dorset'.[57] Hinchinbrooke emerged triumphant from this local coup, and his new party, distanced from the shopkeepers of Weymouth and properly reconnected to the seats of the old squirearchy, was chaired by Colonel Sir Joseph Weld, of East Lulworth.

But the case for Tyneham proved hard to uphold. Hinchinbrooke may never have doubted that the organic qualities of the Tyneham valley offered a far superior answer to the communist threat than the metal tanks to which it had so foolishly been surrendered, but it was not easy to maintain this position. When, shortly after Easter 1988, I went to Mapperton House in West Dorset to meet Mr Victor Montagu (for that is what Hinchinbrooke became after renouncing his peerage in 1964 in order to stand, unsuccessfully, for the Commons on an anti-Common Market platform), he remembered how the Army didn't want the local MP 'rattling away' in politics, and showed 'hostility and fright' at the thought of him joining the campaign. Gazing out through ancient English glass at the floating sight of children playing on lawns outside, he remembered drawing 'boos not cheers' when he spoke against the War Office's retention of the valley and heath.

Tyneham was irrevocably lost, but the poignancy of Churchill's pledge was only intensified by that sad historical fact; and Hinchinbrooke was among the Dorset men who used it again in their successful struggle to drive the 'State Leviathan' off a 725-acre patch of land at Crichel Down near Blandford Forum, in the north of the county.[58] In 1938, this tract of chalk downland had been acquired from three owners, without the use of compulsory powers, and turned into a practice bombing range. After the war, it was cleared of bombs and transferred to the Ministry of Agriculture, which converted it into a model farm on which new, industrialised methods could be demonstrated, and then prepared to lease it out to a tenant farmer. However, Lieutenant-Commander George Marten, who had married the heiress to the Crichel Estate in 1949, decided that he would like to buy the land back. So he and his agent, Major William Seymour, launched a campaign for its release. Their battle against usurping state bureaucracy was supported by many farmers, landowners and estate workers in the nearby villages roundabout, including Rolf Gardiner and others who had supported the King Alfred Muster of the English Array. The protest meeting in which Marten declaimed 'now is the time to stand',

and 'never in 100 years will ordinary country people like ourselves have a better case against the State', was chaired by Ronald Farquharson, who before the war had crusaded against tithes with Captain Pitt Rivers and the Wessex Agricultural Defence Association, and who had once, as his brother Peter recalls, been presented with a swastika by William Joyce (aka Lord Haw Haw), an emblem with which he enjoyed shocking acquaintances — until the War broke out, when he got rid of it very quickly.[59]

At Crichel Down, as at Tyneham before, the complex facts of the case were overriden by a simplifying fable of state encroachment on ancient English rights. The public inquiry, held in April 1954, was conducted by a picaresque barrister apparently more concerned to vindicate this myth and to deride what the *Daily Mirror* called the 'tin pot Napoleons' of Whitehall than to understand the administrative decisions involved. On this occasion the wartime pledge was said to be embodied in a law passed by the coalition government in 1941 (i.e. some years after the unenforced purchase of Crichel Down), which specified that agricultural land could be taken over on the condition that it was offered back to the original owners within five years of the end of the war — as long, that is, as the Minister was satisfied that it would then be efficiently managed.[60]

At Tyneham, Churchill's pledge had been permanently broken by Attlee's Labour government, but the anti-bureaucratic crusaders now found themselves tilting at a different target. Initially aimed at Labour ministers and their civil servants, their lances did not actually strike home until after Churchill had led the Tories back into power. So it was Churchill's own Minister of Agriculture, Sir Thomas Dugdale — generally agreed by the defenders of Crichel Down to have been a decent sort of chap — who felt obliged to resign in 1954 after accepting responsibility for the conduct of his civil servants. Crichel Down put the writing on the wall for the reforming post-war state, but it also established 'the Crichel Down rule', which for decades would be said to bind the government, when it sought to dispose of no longer needed requisitioned land, to offer it for sale back to its last civilian owners or their successors: a precedent that was to have a decisive influence over later chapters of Tyneham's story. It wasn't just the trees that were taking over in Dorset's forbidden valley, as suggested by a reporter for *Illustrated*, who followed some of the villagers on their summer pilgrimage back to their former homes, and concluded on 13 September 1952 that 'The villain was the Cold War'.

FIFTEEN

THE POSTHUMOUS CHARMS OF ENGLAND'S LAST DITCH

> 'This is worse than Mordor!' said Sam. 'Much worse in a way. It comes home to you as they say; because it is a home, and you remember it before it was ruined.'
>
> J. R. R. Tolkien

THE POISONOUS RAGWORT was worry enough for the neigbouring farmers but as Tyneham disappeared behind the wire it would also be overgrown by legend, becoming a place of timeless perfection from the moment history reached in to destroy it. No sooner had it been permanently sealed off — initially without the limited public access promised by Lewis Silkin — than the romance of 'The Tyneham Valley' took off into such exotic flights that one former villager protested grumpily that there had never even been such a place: 'It is the Purbeck Valley, and Tyneham occupies a very minute part of it.'[1]

After the Attlee Cabinet's decision of 1948, Tyneham's tributes were woven of barbed wire as well as creeping ivy. To begin with at least, they had something of the 'Neo-Romantic' character revealed by other intertwining works of that time: Michael Powell's film *A Canterbury Tale*, or novels like Evelyn Waugh's *Brideshead Revisited* (1945), Jocelyn Brooke's *The Military Orchid* (1948) and John Lodwick's *Peal of Ordnance* (1947) in which purloined military explosives are used to blow up national monuments like the Albert Memorial. At Tyneham, the 'Scouring of the Shire' had already happened — a decade before Tolkien wrote it up in *The Lord of The Rings*.

The journalistic descriptions of the forbidden valley started to appear shortly after Lewis Silkin had declared the extension of the ranges permanent. Always inclined to an excessive use of metaphor, they describe visits with a military guide who was already as adept as any sapper at defusing objections. One of the first reporters to enjoy this military helpfulness was quite turned around by it. Ronald Palmer's article, which appeared in the *Bournemouth Daily Echo* on Wednesday 21 June 1950, paired Tyneham with Arne, near Poole Harbour, describing both as villages that had 'Died for D-Day'. Having found Arne deserted and broken, its emptiness rendered all the more palpable by the din of birdsong, Palmer drove over to 'lovely, lonely Tyneham where the Romans lived'. He paused on the chalk heights above to survey 'the loveliness that is Worbarrow Bay' and then descended into the village, where he found a line of cottages 'almost covered in trees and nettles', and 'a battered telephone box' which stood outside 'the stone and foliage of what was once the village store'. He heard the village tap dripping in the silence, and respectfully recorded the biblical legend carved in the stone beside it. The Church of St Mary was guarded by great coils of barbed wire, but inside an obliging soldier lifted a hurricane lamp so that Palmer could transcribe the departing villagers' poignant message.

Palmer knew that 'Dorset has protested against the Army' but, even though his journey was punctuated by the throbbing of distant machine-gun fire and the sudden appearance of an armoured car, he was convinced that 'the indictment for vandalism is not against the soldiers but against the thoughtless public'. He had stood in the lounge of 'the luxurious gunnery school at Lulworth' and watched through the window as a target tank moved slowly across the range with shells bursting beside it, a sight that prompted him to the militarily assisted observation that 'You cannot feel anger against the soldiers, who are treating with reverence the land they occupy; whose officers are as careful of their heritage as the most conscientious land agent, who repair delicately the damage done when a shell ricochets and hits a building.'

Two years later, John Gale visited Tyneham for the *Observer*.[2] By this time, 'the small Dorset village of Tyneham has been dead nine years, stripped of human life as though by plague'. The village was now only frequented by the wind — 'an idle tenant, slamming doors with a ghostly hand, heedless of the scores of rabbits that ripple the nettles, thick about the buildings'. The old church was 'ringed with barbed wire', its graveyard 'watched over by the rotten stump of a great elm', and its windows boarded up after the stained glass had been removed for safe-keeping. He too was shown the villagers' pathetic message, pinned on the pew above a mouldy hymnbook.

Tyneham House was found deserted among noble trees, its windows 'grotesquely blindfolded with sheets of black corrugated iron' and the garden 'run wild amid barbed wire'. A tawny owl completed the Gothic scene, dropping from the eves of the empty house as Gale and his guide approached. Down at Worbarrow Bay, Gale found an 'elemental' world from which all human content seemed suddenly stripped. He saw a mine-blasted boathouse, its metal roof 'torn and crumpled into some primeval shape', and a cow's skeleton among clots of oil on the beach. Gale remarked that the evacuation had been worst of all for the fishermen, mentioning two brothers, both over eighty, who had been sent to live inland. They had been 'lovely men, from a family strong about this coast', but they hadn't fared well when 'torn from their roots' in this wild place. One had died almost immediately, while the other had survived until just a few months ago: 'with his going, the land at Worbarrow, indifferent to the mutter of the guns and the impact of hot metal, seems to have decided to rid itself for good of the traces of man.' Gale swept the hilltop rings of Flowers Barrow into his terminating flourish, 'even the remains of a Roman camp on the highest cliff are now rapidly crumbling into the sea below'.

Ostensibly based on a single visit, Gale's article was actually founded on a far deeper familiarity with the Tyneham area — as became apparent when he incorporated its text into his autobiography, *Clean Young Englishman*.[3] Here Gale reveals that he spent his summer holidays at Worbarrow until 1939. His father rented Sheepleaze from Warwick Draper, and Gale remembered the glinting crystalline stone of that house, the floors of scrubbed white deal covered with rush mats, and the rough bed-sheets with their smell of lavender. He had enjoyed the fishing, canoed around Worbarrow Tout and played tip and run where Constable had once sat to paint a watercolour that his father eventually bought. Gale experienced his first erotic awakening here when he became infatuated with his younger brother's nurse, but his great pride had been to gain the grudging respect of Jack Miller, the elderly fisherman who had been the undisputed 'King' of Worbarrow: 'In this house I was as happy as I have ever been.'

The Tyneham valley had a special place in Gale's personal mythology. In writing of its reduction to a deadly wilderness, he was alluding to the disintegration of his own life. The shells and wire which had destroyed that recollected landscape came to echo the depressive episodes he began to suffer in the later Fifties; they found their equivalents in the shock treatment and drug therapy with which doctors had attempted to improve his mental state. For Gale, who took his own life in 1974, Tyneham was a fragment of emblematic scenery on a perilous cliff path: a before-and-after tableau that seemed to echo the story of his life.

Tyneham's lost valley gained subjective depth from John Gale, but it was Sir Arthur Bryant, the Tory historian and former member of Rolf Gardiner's A Kinship in Husbandry, who really inaugurated Tyneham as the valley of lost English causes. Then at the height of his fame as the best-selling historian who had rallied England's imperial past in the war against Nazi tyranny, Bryant was living at Smedmore, the Elizabethan mansion near Kimmeridge just over the limestone ridge at the eastern edge of the Tyneham valley. On 7 May 1949, he had devoted his column in the *Illustrated London News* to a story in which Tyneham appeared as an emblem of England in those immediate post-war years.[4] It was St George's Day and Bryant was at home in the exquisite house he had recently leased from the Mansell family and which was itself only just emerging from military occupation. The last light was glowing 'pink against the jagged contours of Gad Cliff', and England's historian was meditating on the 'indescribably beautiful' day now drawing to a close. He had spent much of it in the walled garden, where wisteria cast 'thick sprays of deep mauve' over sun-mellowed brick. He had sat there 'hour by hour, in the checkered patterns of shade and sunbeam', collecting descriptions of 'England as she was in the aftermath of the Napoleonic Wars'. The yews and ilex at the foot of the garden were 'veiled with the nearer shimmer of pink and white blossom' and 'the sound of distant gunfire reverberated' over the whole entrancing scene. Bryant may not have known it, but this was the house and garden over which Mary Butts had superimposed the racially threatened ancestral home of Felicity Taverner.

As Bryant worked on, trying to 'repaint' an England he had never seen 'for the information of those who had also never seen it', he felt a profound and unexpected sadness grip his heart. He was 'sad at the thought of so much that was lovely in England lost for ever, of her people imprisoned for so long in mean streets and amid mean, ignoble surroundings and subjected to a thousand mean, vulgarising influences; of the dangers which faced her in a world she once controlled but which has of late passed beyond her control'.

It was doubtless 'foolish and ungrateful' to allow such melancholy thoughts to darken his paradise and, in an attempt to dispel the depressing cloud, he left the garden, with its thrushes and blackbirds darting about 'under the Kremlin-like eyes of a watching cat', and set off for an invigorating afternoon walk. Like Joan Begbie and other allegorising strollers before him, Sir Arthur let his dog lead the way. Striking westwards, he joined the path along the rising cliff that Mary Butts had adopted as the rim of her

'Hollow Land'. His spirits lifted as he glanced round to see 'a blue sea on one side, a lonely valley with a minute church tower flying the flag of St George on the other', but his walk had only just begun. The white and brown terrier led him up on to the 'bare open down, with its springy turf'. Bryant was on the high ground, with 'only the grass and sky and a solitary white sail in the bay, the first I had seen since the winter'. Yet Disenchantment hovered, with full dramatic licence, in the wings. After striding over a few broken fences, Bryant was suddenly awoken to the fact that he had drifted on to 'one of those no-man's-lands which Englishmen of my generation first encountered in Northern France and Belgium in the first war to end wars more than thirty years ago, but which now, with the march of human progress, have become, in so many formerly quiet and beautiful places, a permanent part of our landscape'.

Bryant's account of wandering, all innocent, on to a tank firing range is no less contrived than was Joan Begbie's pre-war encounter with tanks on Bindon Hill. The reader of the *Illustrated London News* was invited to imagine the striding author grieving over the fact that England had become 'so crowded and overpopulated' and then, right on cue, to see his pace quickened by the 'vicious whistle and kick of a shell' soaring overhead. After allowing himself the conventional rude awakening ('realising that I had unwittingly wandered into the outskirts of a battle area, I retraced my steps'), Bryant walked further into 'that little corner of England now for ever forbidden to Englishmen', until he arrived, as if by pure coincidence, at 'an old house in a little wood':

> Its doors and windows were nailed up with black match-boarding, its stone roof was overgrown with creepers and brambles, owls and bats nested in its ivied trees, but its beauty, made by successive generations of English craftsmen through four centuries, still survived. It was strange to think that mine might be one of the last appraising eyes ever to see that beauty, loved by so many and now doomed. A few more years of the present neglect and nothing will remain.

As he gazed at the forbidden ruins of Tyneham House, Bryant saw everything that was wrong with England. Not just a broken governmental promise, but a false financial calculation that was destroying the country: 'It seemed ironical that the reason given by the Government for its breach of faith to the people who once lived in this ravished corner of England was that the capital cost of the wartime military "installations" made it impossible for the Treasury to authorise their removal elsewhere. I could not help wondering about the capital cost of the ancient home and breeding-ground of good Englishmen now sealed off for ever from the use of present and future generations.' Bryant lifted the sight of that disintegrating ancient house into his wider polemic against dominant financial values: 'The economic arguments we use to justify our barbarism are false arguments, for our economy is based not on enduring wealth — the wealth that enriches men from generation to generation — but all too often on the opportunities it offers for the quick exploitation of the passing hour: for the contractor's profit, the middleman's rake-off and the labourer's job shuffled through as quickly as possible for the maximum cash return obtainable.'

It was 'this loss of ancient English values' that had saddened Bryant through 'this most beautiful of St George's Days'; but as he closed his article that evening, now back in his ilex tree bower at Smedmore, the slanting light of the setting sun reached in to restore his true sense of proportion. In this house too there had been long military occupation, but even the weeds that Bryant had failed to eradicate after nine months of 'ceaseless battle' now seemed to glow in the perfect light of Eden. 'The loss is still there, though we may ignore it, staring us in the face: tragic, feckless, eroding. Yet side by side with it is something which redeems and transcends it. I thought, in the glorious twilight of this St George's Day, of the great company of Englishmen who during six bitter years gave to their country and the high cause of man all they had to give, who battled in these skies, endured the blitz, suffered, wrought and triumphed in desert, ocean and jungle, who went out — some of them from this very garden — and crossed the seas on D-Day to inscribe on England's shield an imperishable glory, and died, many of them, that their country and all it stands for might continue.'

For Arthur Bryant, the requisitioning and destruction of that small Doomsday village symbolised a wider betrayal. Like Lord Hinchinbrooke, England's historian had long been ready for this vale of extinguished virtues. Back in the Twenties, he had written that the cause of 'preserving rural England' was close to the very heart of Conservatism. Following the example of Stanley Baldwin, he had associated Toryism with 'home-smoke rising in the valley', and deplored the modern history that had deprived the plain Englishman of this happy pre-industrial inheritance and dumped him down in the 'grey land of the coal truck and the slag heap'.[5]

If Bryant could imagine Tyneham as a forgotten corner of England that had somehow escaped the traumatic consequences of enclosure and urbanisation, this was partly because he treated it as a repository of the organic vision he shared with Rolf Gardiner, H. J. Massingham, Edmund Blunden and other members of A Kinship in Husbandry. To stand with them was to oppose the priorities of a modern society that 'persistently puts last things first and first things last: industrialism before agriculture, technology before life, acquisition before function, chemistry before nature and the State before God'.[6] Tyneham had been snuffed out by the Army, but it still represented the lost England in which that reversal had never taken place.

The story of the broken pledge could hardly have had greater resonance in Bryant's mind, and it was not just for effect that he likened the militarised Tyneham landscape to the battlefields of the Western Front. Bryant had long since associated the Great War with a terrible breach of promise: a trench-born vision of national renewal, brutally betrayed by a political establishment made up of those hard-faced men who looked as if they had done very well out of the war. Entitled 'Crumbling Heritage', the chapter telling this story in *English Saga 1840–1940*, Bryant's bestselling book of 1940, deplores the circumstance under which the 'simple fighting men' returned to the homeland only to have their hopes dashed. The vast majority of these men went out into the 'troglodyte' world of the trenches from drab urban streets but they had, according to Bryant, come back as reborn Yeomen — sustained by patriotic visions that spurned the nineteenth-century city, reverting instead to older ideas of 'roses round the door and nightingales singing and the sound of the rooster':

> Put to the test the slum boy, made man by ordeal of battle, had acquired an atavistic memory of the things he had lost. He wanted a home he could call his own, with perhaps a garden for vegetables and flowers, a regular job of work in which he could take pleasure and pride, security in his livelihood and the self-respect that comes from status and a fixed place in society.

For Bryant, every returning soldier had disembarked with an acre of the Tyneham valley in mind, but the rebuilding of England according to the visionary lights of 'Blighty' was not to take place. Instead the nation sank into the morass of bitterness and strife that was the vicious legacy of nineteenth-century laissez-faire economic policy. 'There were constant strikes and lock-outs, and violent speeches in which Britons in the public eye called each other tyrants, bloodsuckers, murderers, firebrands and red revolutionaries ...' By 1921 many of those war-made Englishmen were eking out the most wretched of subsistences on the dole: 'The nation to which they had returned was built not in the image of their apocalyptic dream but in that of the utilitarian labyrinth of the money-changers from which they had gone forth in 1914.'[7] Even the beauty of her countryside, which Bryant knew to be 'an irreplaceable and spiritual heritage', had been subordinated to private gain.[8]

This national tragedy found its allegorical reprise in the fate of Tyneham after the Second World War. The industrialised capitalism of the nineteenth century had generated great power and wealth, but it had also 'blinded civilisation to the essential difference between profits and real wealth'. Those who 'set out so gaily along that glittering road of accumulation' had been blind to 'the moral truth ... that greed always over-reaches itself'. People might whisper accusations of treason about certain members of A Kinship in Husbandry, but the year before he joined that organic discussion circle in 1941, Bryant had already hurled the charge back: 'It is as high a treason to undermine public morality and endanger the safety of the commonwealth for the sake of profits as it is to trade with the enemy or sell military secrets. In time of war nothing can save the State but the character of its people. The man who for selfish ends undermines it is the real fifth columnist.'[9]

There was another reason why Bryant's organic England had apparently shrunken down to a small forbidden valley in Dorset by the time Nazism was defeated. Bryant would be much honoured for his patriotic commentaries through the war, but he too had been guilty of a deeply flawed assessment of the rise of National Socialism. The point is not just that he had been on the side of the appeasers at the time of the Munich crisis, supporting Chamberlain's efforts to establish 'man-to-man' contact with Adolf Hitler. He published *English Saga* in 1940, but that was also the year in which he chose to issue *Unfinished Victory*,[10] a book written considerably earlier in which he tried to disentangle the true cause of the new Germany. Here Bryant condemned the punitive Treaty of Versailles, which he had seen dismembering the German nation and destroying its economy — while British politicians rattled on about squeezing 'Hunland' like a lemon until the pips squeaked. But he also went a long way with the Nazis, dismissing the Weimar state as a 'mere mechanism for preserving the capitalist status quo', and casting a eugenical eye over the 'slums of the capitalist industrial cities, where the least happy products of every race were allowed to mingle and breed indiscriminately in enormous masses'. Bryant declared Nazi anti-Semitism to be 'revolting and sickening', but his explanatory account of Jews profiteering on the disorders of inflation, taking over the professions and newspapers, manipulating popular forms like the cinema, and turning culture into the lucrative playground of their own avant-garde and pornographic tastes, is not so easily distinguished from many other views from the road to Auschwitz. Bryant tried to suppress this book after the war — he is said to have bought up copies to destroy them. And that same embarrassment surely increased the poignancy of Tyneham's 'forbidden land'. The barbed wire that stood between Bryant and his lost English utopia was also the thread of complicity that revealed the shakiness of his claim to conceive of nationality in terms of 'culture and creed' rather than race.

A Tribute to Angels

Embracing Tyneham as the symbol of a nation that had gone to war against all that was best in itself, Bryant found no shortage of visionary stuff to project over the forbidding wire. Tyneham represented true Christian values, self-sacrifice, the disinterested idea of service, the patriotism that over-rode merely political divisions. In 1956, Bryant contributed the foreword to an elegiac book called *Tyneham: A Lost Heritage*, which gave apparently incontrovertible proof that these qualities really had belonged in Tyneham's valley.[11] Its author, Lilian Bond, was the sister of Ralph Bond, the last resident owner of the valley, whose memorial volume she had compiled in 1952. Born in 1887, she had grown up in Tyneham Great House, leaving after she married in 1914, and her book drew on those distant Edwardian memories to create the prelapsarian portrait of Tyneham that, for decades, was to stand at the centre of its posthumous cult.

Bryant set the scene by describing Purbeck as 'a kind of inner shrine of coastal England — perhaps its oldest inhabited corner, for long one of its most solitary, and still, despite the continuing depredations of war and the War Department, one of its most beautiful'. All three of Purbeck's manor houses had suffered during the war. Encombe had lost its great trees but was still lived in by the family that had built it. Smedmore was now restored thanks to 'a long labour of love in which the author played some part'. But 'the hardest fate of all' had befallen Tyneham, 'with its exquisite village and Worbarrow Bay — surely the loveliest in England'.

By this time, Bryant had converted the story of Tyneham's evacuation into a much simplified fable of betrayal. He recalled the military takeover, the self-sacrifice of the villagers, and the 'lamentable breach of faith' perpetrated by the post-war Labour government. As for Churchill's pledge, he suggested — and I have found no evidence to suggest that any such thing happened — that it had been dutifully written out and posted in the village. As he wrote, 'The notice board which during the War years, recorded the Nation's promise to restore to those whose forbears had made them the homes in which they had been born, has been removed by Authority.'

Remarking on the lasting fascination of her extinguished homeland, Lilian Bond reports having found 'friends of Tyneham' all over the world: 'On numberless occasions, in places far from Purbeck, I have met chance acquaintances who, when the talk has turned on Dorset, spoke of one corner of it which they had "discovered", a corner so remote that they thought it hardly likely I should know its name. The spot they knew and loved was, almost without exception, Tyneham.' Hilaire Belloc had once remarked that 'the corner of a corner of England is infinite and can never be exhausted', and *Tyneham: A Lost Heritage* was published with those words emblazoned on its cover.

Bond remembers the Tyneham valley as a place of unique variety and distinction. There was 'healing' in the air and 'a ride along the hills to Chapman's pool' involved the opening of seventy gates. Every flowering plant was named and known, and there was a local dialect to suture the human intelligence of the valley to its soil. The shop in Post Office Row was full of bacon and licorice, and parcels could safely be left at the roadside, in the sure knowledge that they would remain there until the person to whom they were addressed walked up the field track to find them. Such had been the honesty of the valley that, as a child, Lilian Bond had been puzzled by the history teacher who found it worth remarking that, in King Alfred's England, a woman wearing all her jewellery could walk alone from one end of England to the other and never be molested.

As members of the old Dorset gentry, the Bonds had been happy to fall a long way short of aristocratic decadence; and their house was an organic composition of thrift and grace — right down to the lichens which gave an everchanging seasonal aspect to the mellowed Purbeck ashlar of its walls. Bond recalls the peaceful library, suffused with 'that mellow scent of ancient bindings'; the log-fires and the many games that had been handed on from one generation to the next: 'old ivory chessmen exquisitely carved, a box of fish-shaped counters cut from mother of pearl, a solitaire board rubbed bright by years of handling. The interior of that ancestral home was unimpaired by contemporary ideas of period decor:

> I still remember Detmar Blow's delight on his first introduction to the accumulated contents and shabby interior of the house. He had so often been required to furnish country houses 'to a period', with all the landmarks of successive generations' tastes obliterated, that he hailed with relief the evidence, at Tyneham, of centuries of domestic history.

As for the staff, Lilian Bond's book is scattered with tributes and posthumous character references: whether they be for the much-loved nurse from Durham or the Shakespeare-loving Russian governess, with her four languages, her pince-nez and her habit of practising operatic airs as she paced up and down the Coppice Walk.

Tyneham's was a valley of making-do, in which outdoor games were imaginatively contrived out of rabbit skin and bent sticks. The garden was filled with ancient roses, melons, yuccas and prodigious exotic shrubs, each of which was still associated with the ancestor who had planted it. The famous Victorian orange tree had been killed by gnawing mice in the early years of the century but the gooseberries came in almost every imaginable variety: 'The one kind happily unrepresented was the big, smooth, watery and tasteless fruit which swamps the market now.'

Tyneham belonged to an age of unshrunken distances, and the world on the other side of the hill remained far, far away. This made for self-sufficiency, but it also gave special interest to the travellers who would come to the village: Italian organ-grinders with their monkeys in red coats; wandering actors; gipsies in bright head handkerchiefs with lace and ribbons to sell; Greek or Pyrenean showmen who were then still allowed to travel country roads with 'poor dusty, footsore bears'; and the 'sad and gentle hurdy-gurdy man', surely the last of all his race, whose hushed and melancholy rendering of 'The Farmer's Boy' had echoed from the walls of Tyneham House, 'like a snatch of music from a long-dead past'.

Lilian Bond recalls the 'bright' rasp of whetstone against blade: 'the soothing sounds of scythe and mowing-machine in the summer term, the brushing of crisp leaves on autumn days, and the chink of hoes on gravel paths', all mixed up with the 'small talk of rooks', and the continuous chime of sheep bells. As for the noise from the saw-pit, 'the rhythmic sighing of the blade drawn down through the wood was one of the many peaceful sounds of Tyneham'. While the valley tinkled and sighed, its local polyphony was augmented from afar. There was the drumming of snipe on the heath, the wild cry of curlews; and, just at the edges of audibility, 'the liquid sound of Lulworth's sixteenth-century bells', or the 'charm' of the Kingston peals, 'no louder than the tinkling of a musical box'.

Despite a tarred track from the house to Rookery Wood and also an old iron target set against the hillside at Worbarrow, where the coastguards would practise with their rifles and revolvers, Tyneham was the opposite of a metallic place. Every field was named — Three Acres, Long Mead or Eweleaze, which on an autumn morning would be 'covered by a rippling sea of gossamer, broken by milk-white waves of cobweb-covered tufts of grass' and as translucent as finely spun glass. Thanks to the natural ecology of God's Creation, 'there had been no need of artificial fertilisers and no pests requiring chemical insecticides attacked the crops'. The wind brought in unwanted seed from neighbouring farms but Lilian's father William could not pass a weed without uprooting it from the soil of his valley and 'his score of spudded weeds over many years must have mounted up to millions'.

The valley was a 'sanctuary for all wild life' — one in which the 'balance of nature' looked after itself: the rabbit population was regulated by foxes, badgers, stoats and weasels, ravens, peregrines and buzzards; and Tyneham was 'equally free from rodent and insect pests. Red squirrels had been common and protected in the earlier years', but even after their disappearance, Lilian Bond was confident that 'the sinister grey tree rats never found their way to Tyneham'. Indeed, Tyneham was a paradise for birds. Ditto for wild flowers, which thrived due to 'a long tradition of protective policy' extending right down to the woodmen who were ordered to spare the wild flowers as they trimmed the banks of lanes. This tradition of organic husbandry was extended to the villagers themselves: Lilian Bond describes how her father spent a remarkable proportion of his income on wages. There were frequent financial crises and the money could have been employed in other 'far more satisfying ways but he and his like were still old-fashioned in their view of their responsibilities'.

The constitution of Tyneham was, doubtless, irrational: 'To one accustomed since his childhood to the centralising, mass-directing policies of the brave new world, the whole conception of exclusive interdependence in a small community must be barely comprehensible.' But like other country squires, her father would never have thought of worshipping at the shrine of monetary values:

> To him the place was a trust, a piece of England to be kept intact, unspoilt and handed on in at least as good a state as that in which it came to him, and the primary charge upon his means was the employment of the families on his estate. It might be thought that he had no need of so many dependents but, rightly or wrongly, he believed that they were in need of him.

Tyneham's was a close-knit, church-centred community, but not an egalitarian one of the kind imagined by the new parson who, at a party, once put Lilian to sit next to Mr Taylor, the embarrassed woodman, on the mistaken assumption that 'it would be wonderful for everyone to mix together'.[12] This was a community of vivid differences, defined by character and vocation. Belonging to a time 'before all men and women were compressed into an anonymous mould we claimed our privileged place as members of a family, a parish and a district'. Tyneham existed 'before domestic service was "degrading", and servants thought no shame of following their age-old calling with its honoured traditions'. Conditions might strike modern readers as spartan, but the standard of ease and comfort was lower all round, and employers too 'cheerfully did without a number of refinements now considered necessary in the smallest council house'.

Bond's tribute is threaded with references to the ruin caused by the 'army of occupation'. Many of Tyneham's old trees — elms, carefully sited copper beeches, the avenue leading up through the woods to the Ocean Seat, the windswept old thorn-tree down by Worbarrow Bay which had been 'a play thing for the young of many generations' — were set upon and 'hacked down for firewood'. The house was sorely treated. Some months before the evacuation, an old mullioned window with ancient roundels in the Chintz room had been broken, together with a stained glass window in the library below, by WAAFs climbing out of a gable window on rope ladders in a fire drill. Nothing was done to protect the windows below, and the damage went unreported, so that the broken fragments of stained glass were lost before Ralph Bond could gather them up.[13] They had also made short work of the garden. The old fan palm (*chaemoerops fortuneii*), had survived many winter gales, but the WAAFs 'beheaded' it to make a party decoration for their mess. The most delicate and least transportable furniture, hastily stored in the cellar, was doomed once the Air Force lorries had flattened the surface drains outside the house, causing the cellar to flood. The wrought iron gate in the archway between the two walled gardens also 'suffered sadly at the feet of WAAF's and soldiers climbing the wall into the garden when it was out of bounds'. As for the scarce supply of 'pure and sparkling' water available from the village tap by the church, a delicate ecology of reservoir pipe and scriptural inscription which had always demanded the most careful husbandry, the RAF simply wiped it out, tapping the pipe down to that village spring, and leaving the village without water.

Lilian Bond's book is a threnody to an idealised world gone down. For her the twinkling lights of Tyneham shone against all 'the centralising, mass-directing policies of the brave new world'. Even the horse-drawn brougham carriage was filled with contrary wisdom: built to last for generations and cheaper to run than a car, this supposed symbol of extravagance showed that neither rust nor obsolescence had been among the principles governing the Tyneham valley. Children still walked through the world, understanding things that could never be grasped by their 'bus-borne' urban equivalents ('What can you know of England who only know its well-tarred roads and asphalt play-grounds, robbed as you are of your country heritage?') As for the 'strong individuality' of the 'Tyneham dwellers', if 'long connection to the land produced stability and strength of character', it had also innoculated them against the 'odious tyranny of class distinctions' so prevalent in towns, and the snobbery — 'both ordinary and inverted' — that went with it. The Tyneham dwellers had never counted their hours like industrial wage-slaves; and their 'rich and pithy' speech, which combined the 'dignified, plain English of the Bible' with a local dialect in which cows 'bleared' when they would have lowed elsewhere and sounded L's stuck out stubbornly to interrupt the flow of words like 'calm' and 'palm', was far superior to the 'genteel and colourless' standard English of the BBC. It was 'strange that speaking with a Dorset intonation is accounted "common" or "uneducated" while transatlantic vulgarisms or the mincing accents of "refainement" pass for culture'. Tyneham dwellers may have been without 'any education according to popular standards', but they had 'better furnished' minds than many Board School children, whose schooling 'had to a certain extent replaced their native sense and personal judgement'. Holding up the valley against the advancing Forestry Commission, Bond took a stoutly nativist line: 'The average Englishman nowadays prefers some oriental midget to his own magnificent native timber. It seems that, in a very few more years, the only specimen trees left in the country will be foreigners, the only woodland vast State forests of Teutonic trees, where no bird sings, or even cares to fly, no wild flowers grow and where a forest fire is a perpetual menace.'

Lilian Bond refused ever to revisit the valley after the expropriation of 1943, spurning such 'public access' as the Army would come to allow, preferring the distant hope that 'perhaps the tide may turn again and disregard for much that went to the nation's making will give way to a grateful recognition of the stock whence we are sprung'.[14] Her remembered village is in many ways the reversed image of East Chaldon as Valentine Ackland described it in *Country Conditions*; the spartan virtues of one being the injustices and deprivations of the other. When Bond wanted a world-view to justify her memories, she could think of no one better than the late H. J. Massingham, 'that doughty champion of the countryman', whom she quoted as follows:

> the real, fundamental division of our times . . . is not between political parties nor between conflicting ideologies nor even between nations . . . The real division is between rival philosophies of life. The one believes in exploiting natural resources, the other in conserving them; the one in centralised control, the other in regional self-government; the one in conquering and the other in co-operating with nature; the one in chemical and inorganic methods imitated from those of the urban factory and the other in biological and organic ones derived from the observation of nature as a whole; the one in man as a responsible agent with freewill to choose between the good and the bad, the other [in man] as a unit of production directed from above by an élite of technologists and bureaucrats; the one in the divine creation both of man and nature, and the other in man as self-sufficient in himself, with nature merely as the means for extracting wealth for himself. The one philosophy is dominant and possesses all the power but the other is in possession of the *truth*.

Tyneham Against Nuclear Power

When was the Tyneham of Lilian Bond's description? Some readers, including former 'Tyneham dwellers', have wondered whether such perfection can ever have existed on earth; and at least one correspondent, who questioned the status of Churchill's increasingly mythologised pledge, had to be referred on to Sir Arthur Bryant.

Rolf Gardiner, however, who was among the first and most ardent admirers of Lilian Bond's book, was not a doubter. The memory of the German Youth Movement may have been drowned in blood, but Springhead was still dedicated to the cause of rural revival; and its owner recognised Lilian Bond's Tyneham as a place after his own romantic heart. Her book moved him to write a poem in which he marches through that promised valley on archaic stilts, trying hard to pull some future inspiration from its remaining internal rhymes:

This tender book which bravely shook
With smiling love the tears away,
Now makes us look where we forsook
The wisdoms of our yesterday.
So by the dint of many a stint
God weaves Earth's magic web anew.
And pearly glint shows many a flint
To hold a gossamer peace of dew.[15]

This verse tribute was accompanied by a note describing Lilian Bond's book as 'A classic record of an English country house and estate', and offering another less than accurate version of the story of the broken pledge: 'Tyneham, near Lulworth Cove, one of the treasures of Dorset, and the home of the Bond family for generations was commandeered by the War Department in 1939 and despite promises of its return after the War, retained as a Gunnery Range and destroyed.'

Gardiner also wrote this new soulmate an admiring letter of recognition explaining that her book had been 'a comfort and a wonder for me all this winter'.[16] As a hard-working farmer and forester, he had been able to absorb only a very little at a time but he hopèd she might find some 'small consolation' in having 'such a slow sipping reader'. He had never been to Tyneham, but 'through your pages I have come to possess it in minute detail and completeness . . . ' Unusually, Gardiner found words failing him:

'I cannot tell you how much I love and esteem your book and all that it stands for.' He singled out the last lines, in which Lilian Bond rose up to defend the extinguished traditions of her late brother's valley:

> The English squires are riding to the sea. Most of them have already passed from sight and, such is the power of town-dictated mass opinion, their going is regarded with indifference if not with satisfaction and ill-informed abuse. Perhaps there is no place left for them in a slick and glossy world where getting on and getting rich are the main objectives and where values must be reckoned by a monetary standard. The land they loved, for which they sacrificed so much, the land to which they and their followers gave such loyal service, knows them no more. It is, for the most part, left to the tender mercies of the opportunist, whose only use for it is to strip and exhaust it for the sake of quick returns.
>
> It cannot be that the centuries of faithful care and toil have been in vain. A day must surely come, and may it come before it is too late, when saner principles will reassert themselves and the wise and self-denying service of our forefathers will have its recognition.

This closing 'peroration' was, so Gardiner wrote, of 'a classic nobility and soundness'; indeed, it should be 'engraved on stone and set up amidst the wreckage to rebuke our age'.

When phosphorescence lit up Worbarrow Bay at night, native 'Tyneham dwellers' used to say that the sea was 'bremming'. They could hardly have named the irridescence with which every detail of their evacuated valley would come to shine in the eyes of its post-war devotees. Like Hinchinbrooke and Bryant, Gardiner adored the memory of Tyneham as an organic community that had escaped mechanisation, laissez-faire economics, and the centralised bureaucratic State. Yet by the time he came to it, the valley had the additional virtue of never having gone nuclear.

When Gardiner told Lilian Bond how her book had 'sustained him' through the recent 'battle of Winfrith Heath', he was referring to the unsuccessful campaign that he and other objectors had waged against the government's proposal to establish the 'Atomic Energy Authority Technology Establishment' that now stands on Thomas Hardy's much-assaulted heath just across the Frome from the Royal Armoured Corps Headquarters at Bovington. This latest threat had forced its way on to the Dorset CPRE's agenda by the AGM of 1956. Determined, as he once put it, to 'frustrate the encroachment of the atomic serpent',[17] Gardiner had taken immediate steps to stiffen up the Dorset CPRE, fighting the case through the County Council, where the argument was overwhelmingly lost in November 1956, leaving him to pen a Cassandra-like epistle to the *Western Gazette*, in which he remarked that 'those who listened to the debate in the County Council on the Winfrith project last Friday heard their elected representatives selling Dorset at a bargain price'.[18]

Spurred on by Gardiner, the anti-nuclear objectors formed a 'Dorset Land Resources Committee' to speak out for 'the movement which has pressed for a public inquiry', and sought to defend Dorset as a 'small-scale' county. Untold consequences might follow if the nuclear establishment really started drawing off as much as 11 million gallons of water daily from Dorset's still unmeasured supply; and 3,000 new houses would have to be built, which would surely damage the holiday trade. As for the radioactive effluent that would be piped out to sea through Lulworth Park and Arish Mell Gap, it was 'an appalling thought that the remaining free coastal area of Dorset may be contaminated'. Gardiner and his fellow objectors ('We, the undersigned') had urged vigilance all round: 'We must watch lest material prosperity induces neglect of the spiritual values — beauty, peace and freedom.' At the public inquiry, which extended over three days from 8 January 1957, Gardiner stood on the same side as the leading pre-war communist of East Chaldon, Sylvia Townsend Warner, who told of having received letters from all over the world objecting to this attempt to site 'an industrial project in the middle of this historic landscape'.[19]

Writing to Lilian Bond about the unsuccessful struggle, in which he had taken it on himself 'to fight for the long-term values to the bitter end', Gardiner used her own words to deplore 'How shamefully our leading men failed us. I was sickened by the "slick and glossy" values that prevailed . . . opportunism and self-interest and fear of unpopularity now lead men into a mean cowardice which dastardly betrayed our Dorset dear.' Gardiner told how he had used the memory of Tyneham to stoke the fires of resistance, buying an extra copy of Lilian Bond's book and giving it to Peter Rawlinson QC, briefed to present the Dorset Land Resources Committee's objections, so that he should know exactly what he was fighting for. He signed off by re-emphasising his enthusiasm: 'I cannot tell you how much I love and esteem your book and all that it stands for. For over thirty years I have striven against all the tides of our time to remake my own little corner of North Dorset, to restore it from herb to hymn . . . Perhaps the fact that we took over a dilapidated derelict landscape and began to rearrange it with toil and imagination and love rather than with money and machinery may eventually encourage others to take heart and do even better.'

Bond welcomed Gardiner's letter: 'I often feel that I am an anachronism and there can scarcely be anybody left who cares for the vanished past as I do.' She too had been 'sickened by the "atmosphere" at the Winfrith Heath inquiry . . . How the Dorset County Council can go on putting faith in the word of Ministries and continue to truckle to them I cannot understand.' She added, 'What a loss H. J. Massingham is to the cause of rural England and I am glad that his mantle has fallen upon you and that you wear it in Dorset.'

The County Shakes Down

Tyneham had taken another symbolic fall at Winfrith, but the actual expropriation was brought to a head in December 1959 when the Ministry of Transport published a draft order under the Requisitioned Land and War Works Act, which would permanently stop up over forty footpaths on the range area. Sensing this to be the final alienation, the county and district authorities protested, together with environmental and amenity groups. So, once more, *The Times* sent a reporter down to capture the familiar special effects: 'Sherry glasses jingled, furniture shook and windows rattled. Explosion after explosion shook the lovely Dorset village of East Lulworth . . . '[20]

Such was the level of objection that the government announced a public inquiry — this one to be conducted in Dorchester by the members of the independent War Works Commission on 11 January 1961. So the letter-writing vigilantes took up their pens again, bombarding the Commission with explosive condemnations. A *Daily Telegraph* reader denounced the proposal as 'monstrous', and wondered why the 'southern and western counties of England' should be the Army's victims every time: 'I have a shrewd suspicion it is because of a desire to be within easy reach of Lords'.[21] An expatriate gentleman wrote from Malaya: 'To me it seems inconceivable that what I might call the "British way of life" will tolerate a situation in which the public can only visit one of the most beautiful stretches of coastline in the world at Easter, or August Bank Holiday or on Christmas Day or Boxing Day . . . I am sure the county of the Tolpuddle Martyrs will not suffer such a gross abuse of Authority . . . '

Most of the military arguments were carried over unchanged from the 1948 inquiry. Brigadier R. N. Harding-Newman repeated the holistic creed of tank-training, explaining that if the gunnery school didn't get exactly what it wanted at Lulworth, the whole RAC establishment might have to leave Dorset — with dire financial consequences all round. The Commanding Officer of the gunnery school showed photographs of the twelve 'unexploded missiles' — each one marked with a little upright stick — he had found in a sample stretch of eighteen square yards on the northern flank of Bindon Hill. Referring the inquiry's attention to a close-up of a beautifully posed unexploded shell sticking out of the turf, he declared himself 'of the opinion that this would be a very tempting object for anyone to pick up', and then went on to expound on the phenomenon known as 'sympathetic detonation', explaining that a blind shell could be set off by 'vibration in its vicinity': a passing Dorset naturalist would certainly be enough. If the public were to be given access to the ridge of Bindon Hill, 'it would be necessary either to make a permanent path of a metalled nature or else to keep the whole hillside permanently burnt off'. So much for the conservationists' precious downland turf and the ancient green roads.

As in 1948, the War Office had already tried to sweep aside the question of Churchill's pledge — admitting its existence, but only in order to place it beyond the bounds of legitimate discussion. Prior to the inquiry a spokesman had told the Press, with obviously pre-emptive intentions, that the undertakings given in 1943 had been given without permission.[22] And on the day, Mr Turner of the War Office dismissed all mention of pledges, observing that 'This is not a matter which should be discussed at this inquiry.' He was supported by the impartial chairman, who remarked that the promise given in the past was 'merely a political promise' — as if politics was a mere shadow play performed by a succession of fleeting parliamentarians who strutted their stuff on the enduring boards of the bureaucratic state, and then vanished back into obscurity.

It is true that, by this time, some formerly stalwart upholders of Tyneham's vision had indeed wandered off into a fog of grey realism. Lord Hinchinbrooke had fulminated about the broken pledge twelve years previously, but he was now more resigned. He had written to John Durant-Lewis, Clerk of the Wareham and Purbeck Rural District Council, explaining that he 'went into all this very closely with the Ministry about six months ago and, to the best of my knowledge, the problem is, for the time being at any rate, satisfactorily solved'.[23] This statement was greeted with dismay by Colonel Joseph Weld, who declared himself surprised to hear that 'apparently Lord Hinchinbrooke thought everything in the garden was lovely'.[24]

As chairman of the rural district council, Colonel Weld stood firm. His opposition to the War Office was supported by a detailed memorandum in which Durant-Lewis reviewed the history of the gunnery range and concluded that 'It is obvious that the present proposal is not just a further restriction of public rights, but rather a complete and utter destruction thereof.' So the squire of Lulworth counted his way through the string of broken promises that had attended the firing range since the first battle of Bindon Hill in 1923. The War Office had undertaken to vacate the site by the end of September 1929. They had promised to protect the movement of fishermen and the public when Arish Mell Gap was absorbed in 1939, and to remove restrictions once firing was finished. The pledge of 1943 had been dishonoured, and so too had Lewis Silkin's 1948 assurance that access to Worbarrow Bay would be provided after firing was finished. In this situation his Council considered that 'no reliance at all could be placed on assurances or promises and that once the War Department had been accorded the powers of closure, they would sooner or later be applied to the fullest extent. The rights of access must therefore be legally safeguarded. Nothing else would do.' As he sat down, Colonel Weld was in a good position to consider a sad and little acknowledged fact about public administration: organic landscapes may seem timeless to their defenders, but State bureaucracy, which takes inertia rather than morality, truth or beauty as its own Iron Law, can outlast them all.

Other signs of public impatience remain in the transcript. When her moment came, a certain Mrs Cawley explained that she was speaking out for a public that was losing its confidence in democratic procedure. She had conducted a straw poll in the high street of her Surrey village, and was worried to hear people speaking with 'resigned indignation' of the pointlessness of attending a public inquiry, presumed to be stage-managed by the government and really 'just an opportunity to blow off steam'. Then she went straight over the top:

> Ten years ago, when I was an individual person and had not a family to think about, my brother and I were walking along the coast here, and coming along these paths and seeing the red flag up we said, 'what right have they to take this lovely part? It isn't war time now' — and it wasn't — 'They shouldn't take this away from us; this belongs to us, not to them', and quite deliberately we walked across these blessed ranges — and I wear the scars where the things came along. You may consider that irresponsible but he was a school master and at the time I had quite a responsible job. We aren't irresponsible people. It was a strong personal objection, and I don't see how much more strongly I can put it. He and I were quite right to be shot to pieces in order to draw attention to this monstrous abuse and alienation of our rights.

Mrs Cawley stopped short of showing her wounds, but as chairman of the inquiry, Sir David Parry QC knew how to despatch an emotional woman with a withering aside ('You have certainly indicated a depth of feeling in the matter'). Mrs Burrows from Purbeck also tried to speak on behalf of 'the ordinary members of the public'. 'We should like a little of our county handed back to us,' she said, observing that the attitude nowadays was 'What's the use of doing anything about it?'

And so the inquiry was closed. Parry declared himself relieved, admitting that 'before we came here we were very much afraid that we might have to have the hand of the law, as a policeman, to protect us, or do something of that sort'. 'Not in Dorset,' replied the barrister for the objecting County Council. And then, Parry moved on to other matters while the civil servants drew up the letter in which he would give the War Office permission to close the contested footpaths — on condition that access was provided to Tyneham and Worbarrow Bay during block leave periods. Colonel Joseph Weld had put up a good fight, but he had known the battle was lost as far back as 1952, when he arranged for the bones of the Trappist monks buried at Monastery Farm to be exhumed from their noisy patch of ground near Arish Mell, and transported to Mount St Bernard in Leicestershire, where they were laid to rest in properly consecrated Catholic soil.

PART FIVE

Slugging it Out with the Tyneham Action Group (1968–75)

In fighting for the freedom of Tyneham and its sea coast and the fishing grounds, we are fighting for something greater. We are fighting against a mindless mechanical monster which threatens to rob us of those few things which make life worth living. As we can all see for ourselves this monster tends to grow larger all the time, and must be contained if we are to have anything left.

Tyneham Action Group Newsletter, November 1970

I like these Muggletonians, but it is clear that they were not among history's winners.

E. P. Thompson

SIXTEEN

MAY '68 – THE DORSET UPRISING

> Initiative is a dangerous word. Those who use it may find themselves unpopular. The herd-mind seeks safety in numbers. To depart from a current line of expression or action is to be marked out among one's fellow-men. It means being reviled and often accused of the worst possible motives.
>
> Monica Hutchings 1951[1]

IT MIGHT HAVE been 'the events' in Paris or Bonn, or the wave of student occupations then surging through British art schools and universities, but the 'militant resistant movement' that concerned the *Daily Telegraph* on Saturday 18 May 1968 had actually broken out in South Dorset, where activists were determined to awaken the dormant 'campaign for the removal of the Army from the Purbeck hills'.[2] Less genteel than their predecessors, these new agitators promised to launch a really offensive assault at a meeting in a Dorchester church hall later that day: the rallying cry was an uncompromising 'Surrender Purbeck'.

The accompanying photograph showed the derelict cottages of Tyneham's Post Office Row, with that already much depicted telephone box standing chipped and battered in front of them. The 'new note of militancy' that was creeping into the 'well-worn campaign' threatened to blow not just the Army out of the Tyneham valley but also the nostalgic Old English fug that earlier partisans had brewed up there. The ardent young man who had called this meeting said he wanted to 'advocate positive action' and had already received about a hundred letters of support. He described Tyneham as 'the worst case of military rape in the country' and talked of mustering an 'Armada' to land on the shores. *Telegraph* readers may not have been wrong to detect a hint of regret in his reassurance that 'We would, of course, only be armed with banners.'

Country Life is not known for its advocacy of trespass and fisticuffs, but it still helped to fire this unexpected renewal. Two years previously, it had revisited Tyneham and published an unusually hard-hitting condemnation of the 'appalling act of desecration' perpetrated there since 1935, when it found the valley 'happily . . . almost entirely unspoilt'.[3] Illustrated with before and after photographs, this article denounced 'the Rape of Tyneham'. The grey gabled manor house which had once epitomised 'the heart of England', stood overgrown and shuttered, and the cottages were shelled. Affronted, *Country Life* now suggested that 'an uninformed foreigner might well suppose . . . that the German army had succeeded in landing on the Dorset Coast'. It was surely time to rescue Tyneham from its 'present pitiable condition'.

Tariq Ali, a leading firebrand of May '68, was busy that month in London, launching the Trotskyist paper *Black Dwarf* and joining other student leaders on television to advocate the abolition of money and the expropriation of private property. Yet he too had done his bit for the remote English valley where that expropriation had already been carried out.[4] Ali had heard about the 'village on the ranges' while working for Michael Heseltine on *Town* magazine in 1966. As one of the principal organs of 'Swinging London', *Town* had no interest whatsoever in turning the clock back. Nevertheless, when Graham Finlayson's mournful photographs of Tyneham arrived in the office, Ali recognised that this story could appeal to his metropolitan readers too. So he commissioned writer Michael Frenchman to go down to Dorset and follow the 'dwindling number of former inhabitants' as they made their 'once a year' pilgrimage into the forbidden wilderness.[5]

So the day came, in December 1966, when *Town*'s urbane readers turned the page expecting another article by Tom Wolfe, and found themselves following only a few steps behind as 'the Natives return to what were once their homes in this valley just beyond Thomas Hardy's Egdon Heath'. They picked their way down a village street said, with considerable journalistic licence, to be 'pockmarked by exploding shells' and past once charming cottages on which 'the scars of the Invader' were only obscured by Gothic overgrowth. Michael Frenchman invited them to savour one lugubrious attraction after another: 'Great folds of cancerous moss have replaced the window glasses . . . cruel spiked trees crouch with their shell-scarred branches to the ground in desperation, like surplus props from Macbeth's blasted heath.' He led this fashionable crowd down a distraught country lane to the Elizabethan manor house where his most shocking revelation awaited.

After the public inquiry of 1948, Sir Cecil Oakes had insisted that 'a tribute of praise' was due to the Army for the 'extreme care' it had taken to safeguard Tyneham House; and Lewis Silkin had assured the House of Commons that this ancient English building would be safeguarded by the War Office. Eighteen years later, a Ministry of Defence spokesman informed Frenchman that, while the house had never been adopted as a target, it was nevertheless now in such bad condition that 'we are discussing the possibility of pulling it down . . . it is a closed book. It is too late in the day.'

Tyneham House had been a 'scene of banquets, parties and weddings', but now it was only 'a facade with nothing inside'. The windows were still securely boarded, but it was uncertain whether this was to keep vandals out or to stop people seeing 'the terrible havoc' that had been wrought 'by shell fire and delay'. The Army had allowed thieves to steal lead from the roof, and the rot had set in long ago. Doors that once led into rooms whose unostentatious elegance had been so fondly remembered by Lilian Bond, now creaked open on to a void that was 'silent in death except for the whirring of pigeon's wings'. The house was 'a dying monument' to what John Betjeman had denounced as 'the smooth, duplicate, words of civil servants and the wanton destruction by the Army of a part of England they are paid to protect'. Even the signs of wartime occupation were fading: a notice warning 'Water unfit for drinking', and a latrine extension on the old Brewhouse signed 'WAAFS only — NCOs'.

The pictures confirmed this impression of a deeply stratified rural scene that had been sufficiently violated to appeal on London's King's Road. They put on a weird light show as the sun reached in through holes in the roof and sent bright stroboscopic shafts down into the dark 'scene of devastation' that had been Lilian Bond's perfect childhood home. They caught the evening light as it died over the gaunt ruins of Sheepleaze, the stone house that Warwick Draper had built on the cliff-top at Worbarrow Bay in 1910, and which had survived unmolested until recent shellfire 'wrecked the roof'. They revealed the forsaken telephone box with its ornamental finial fetchingly aslant, and found poignant juxtapositions throughout the reverted valley: giant hog-weed superimposed against forgotten Elizabethan gables; a battered Victorian hip-bath rusting next to an ancient stone arch; the turret of a dead tank with its barrel hanging down like a mortified elephant's trunk . . .

As for the returning villagers, they looked seriously bewildered too. Over the years many journalists have described them as 'pilgrims' and shown them wandering photogenically back into that forbidden land of origins, but *Town*'s photographer was more inclined to portray them as if they were an archaic species of wildlife engaged in strange rituals connected with mourning. The behatted Taylor sisters, Helen, aged sixty-nine, and Elizabeth, aged seventy-four, were shown, bending down over their mother's broken tombstone. The younger John Gould was also pictured in somewhat gnome-like position, craning wistfully through 'the open doorway of his childhood home now but a shell'. The village may long have 'crouched' in its scenic valley, but it took *Town* magazine to recognise the bending of former Tyneham dwellers as a behavioural quirk akin to the smiting of pigeons and the drumming of snipe. These stooped and Hobbit-like figures were the last of 'The People' and their cause seemed antediluvian and hopelessly lost. 'The Enemy' that marched into their enchanted Shire twenty-three years ago, had not surrendered so much as 'an inch of ground' of this 'Occupied Zone' and there was nothing to hint that it might do so in the future.

Frenchman tried to find some consolation in the ruins. Worbarrow Bay was littered with 'tar, old shell cases . . . and the usual debris of an assault beach', but at least there were 'no beach huts, no iced lollies, no hamburger stalls'. He even ventured to suggest that 'The Enemy' should be thanked for the fact that up until now, as *Town* was well placed to declare, 'the "swinging" world had passed Tyneham by'. But the destruction was altogether too much and Frenchman sounded the Last Post: 'Tyneham will become just a phantom village, to be talked about but never seen. Only a name, Tyneham.'

Introducing Mr Legg

For *Town* magazine, the battle for Tyneham was already lost. But Rodney Legg, the 21-year-old journalist who set out to revive the campaign two years later in 1968, was not prepared to settle for such a pathetic outcome. 'Talking has got us nowhere,' he declaimed. Legg's uprising was supported by Monica Hutchings, an older writer who resided near the ranges in Church Knowle. 'It's like living on the edge of a battlefield,' she told the *Telegraph*: 'the windows rattle and the house shakes when they are firing.' Claiming to have been fighting this campaign since 1948, she now stood with Legg because 'it is important that we should not give up'. Further support was said to come from Mr Durant-Lewis, Clerk to Wareham and

Purbeck Rural District Council, and a veteran of earlier struggles. The *Telegraph* quoted him as saying 'I wish these people luck.' In the past, his council had 'tried every constitutional means to dislodge the Army and failed. We have learnt to live with the noise, but we still think it was a dirty trick not to return the land as promised.'

Rodney Legg had been exercised about the Lulworth ranges for some time before this intervention. A couple of years previously he had written an article for the *Countryman*, urging that Tyneham should be given to the National Trust to mark the twenty-first anniversary of the end of the Second World War, and another for The Society of Dorset Men's magazine, 'a stuffy annual called the *Dorset Year Book*', which declined to print it. Lord Hinchinbrooke's call to arms had been acceptable twenty years before, but Legg was a child of the sprawling conurbation known as Bournemouth, and hardly the type to enjoy blue vinney, port and the beautiful thought of Bindon Hill with the likes of Lord Rayner Goddard.

Legg, however, was not to be deterred. Giving up his job as a reporter on the *Basildon Standard*, he returned to Dorset determined to use his modest savings to launch a proper county magazine. In December 1967, the article that had been rejected by the *Dorset Year Book* was published, under the heading 'Surrender Purbeck', as the opening editorial in the first issue of *Dorset: The County Magazine*. The government was planning reductions for the armed forces, but local agitation against 'the worst case of military rape in the country' was sadly lacking. Legg itched for action:

> If this was some Celtic fringe of the country there would be bomb incidents and other colourful demonstrations. I am not advocating that type of militant action in Purbeck (it would be sedition if I did) though this would immediately solve the publicity problem. Some expression of feeling is necessary — we have not even managed to paint 'Surrender Purbeck' on a wall. It is time, belated yes, to form a Tyneham Action Group to end the indifference and silence which is golden for those in authority who refuse to acknowledge a wartime pledge.

Supportive letters certainly arrived by the dozen — even if they didn't quite add up to the hundred Legg would mention to the *Telegraph*. Some merely recited pathetic memories but Patrick Dingle of the Bournemouth Symphony Orchestra suggested that 'a march through the range might be possible'.[6] Mrs D. E. Wells-Furby testified that she had 'often advocated a sit-down strike before the gates of Tyneham'. She wished Legg luck with his Tyneham Action Group: 'Let's make trouble with a capital T.'

Monica Hutchings had also made contact early on. In a letter dated 6 December 1967 she told Legg 'I think together we may do some good and rout the forces against us. Though I am told that you can't fight the army and win. To this I say remember Dreyfus (not to mention Crichel Down).' So too did Michael Pitt Rivers, the landowning son of Captain George Pitt Rivers of Hinton St Mary, who was also, thanks to John Betjeman's encouragement, the author of a revised edition of Paul Nash's *Shell Guide to Dorset*, published in 1965. Pitt Rivers had declared it 'intolerable to Dorset people' that the War Office should still occupy the stretch of 'glorious coastline' at Lulworth, leaving 'the little village of Tyneham' abandoned and derelict.[7] He now wished Legg 'Best of luck with the Tyneham Action Group'. Described rather drily by Legg as 'another prominent landowner', Rolf Gardiner also offered 'Congratulations on your bold initiative and all good wishes for true success'.

This assorted group of Dorset volunteers promised to be more militant than any of the civilian forces that had been mustered against Dorset's tanks before. Yet it would be quite wrong to conclude that Legg started out as Dorset's answer to Danny the Red. Indeed, his interest in 'direct action' derived not from the left at all.

Legg had joined the League of Empire Loyalists as a fervent fourteen-year-old patriot in 1961 and, over the next seven years, became one of its main political activists. Looking back on this confused period, he recalls how as a schoolboy he had read that the League was ailing in the *Daily Telegraph*'s Peterborough column, and promptly gone up to its offices in Westminster and volunteered his services. The League had been founded by A. K. Chesterton, a sometime Shakespearean scholar who had won the Military Cross for bravery in the Great War, and who later threw in his lot with Oswald Mosley and the British Union of Fascists, for which he edited *Action* magazine and on whose behalf he wrote letters to the Dorset press during the time of Captain George Pitt Rivers's anti-tithe campaign. This hoary old anti-Semite pioneered disruptive, publicity-seeking forms of intervention that pre-dated those of May '68. His activists specialised in such antics as sending Jomo Kenyatta a bag of sheep entrails; or impersonating Archbishop Makarios, the hated champion of Cypriot independence.

Legg had joined when the League 'like its subject was in its dying days', and travelled around the country as what he now calls 'a bit of political froth', harrying and heckling Prime Ministers. In 1964 he was pictured on the front page of the *Sunday Telegraph*, being silenced at the Young Conservatives' annual rally, which he had interrupted to denounce Alec Douglas Home as the betrayer of Cyprus, yelling 'Empire Loyalists say Stand by the White man in Rhodesia.' The adolescent Legg made more headlines at the 1965 Labour Party conference, pulling a Union Jack from under his mackintosh just before the assembled comrades stood to sing 'The Red Flag' and shouting 'Empire Loyalists say this is the flag which stands for British loyalty — not the red flag of Communist tyranny.'

This episode came to a close soon enough. As Legg later reported, 'not only were we running out of money but the name was ceasing to be credible . . . the title was anachronistic. Political realities had made the name a joke.'[8] But Legg had also seen the league infiltrated by fascists like John Tyndall and Martin Webster, who hijacked it as a vehicle for the emerging National Front. What Chesterton had conceived as an 'elite' movement was taken over by a bunch of overtly Nazi thugs who indulged in 'chanting' of the sort he abhorred and displaced the old League members, some of whom were evidently horrified by the new stories in which loaded revolvers, Nazi salutes and homosexual misdemeanour featured prominently. Legg opposed this infiltration and walked out on the disintegrating League shortly before he found his next cause in the lost English valley of Tyneham. He may have turned his back on the politics but his experience of A. K. Chesterton's style of 'direct action' would serve him well in the years to come.

The Tyneham Action Group is Formed

Forty or so would-be Actionists turned up for the inaugural meeting, held on the afternoon of Saturday, 18 May 1968 at the Moule Institute in Fordington: a part of Dorchester known historically for its slums, its ale-houses, and its denizens' timeless resistance to enlightened reform, whether it be that of the post-war welfare state's planners or of the early seventeenth-century Puritans who tried to turn Dorchester into a 'City on a Hill' after the great fire of 1613.[9]

Rodney Legg opened the meeting by reminding everyone of the story of Churchill's broken pledge.[10] The government had freely accepted that pledges were given in 1948, but 'enough time is now gone for even the existence of an official pledge to be disputed'. Indeed, even Brigadier Mark Bond, who had once stood to inherit 'the late Tyneham House' from his father Ralph, had expressed doubts as to whether the pledge of Tyneham mythology was ever actually given — a claim he had later withdrawn after finding a copy of an official letter referring to the return of the evicted 'at the end of the present emergency'. So the campaign's revival began with an emphatic reminder: 'There was a pledge. It was broken. The facts are on our side.'

Legg rejected claims for the Army as 'the guardians of beauty', describing them as 'the alien occupation force which has stolen and wrecked our own countryside'.[11] Tyneham House had been 'the symbol of peace'. So, for the shamefaced military authorities, there could be no question: 'It had to go.' As Legg explained, 'removal of symbols is a first step to eradicating the memories they stand for'.

Since Tyneham was now 'devastated', there could surely be no question of fighting, as agitators had done in the late Forties, for the area to be returned to the former occupiers on the assumption that life might be resumed where it had been left off in 1943. Such 'genuine honouring' of the pledge was no longer possible and Legg recommended instead that the new campaign should aim to have 'this superb stretch of English coast line' given to the National Trust. He spoke not just of Tyneham, but of the entire five mile stretch from Kimmeridge over past Bindon Hill to Lulworth Cove.

Since 'an essential part of the campaign is to make the Army feel uncomfortable, unwanted and embarrassed', Legg hoped that the Group would recognise that 'militant action, just inside the framework of the law, is called for'. There were, he suggested, unextinguished public rights to be on the foreshore between high and low water mark, and it would surely be possible to muster six boats at Lulworth Cove and land an 'Armada' of fifty invaders at Arish Mell Gap. A cavalcade of cars could be organised to go down to Tyneham on Summer Bank Holiday Monday, or the Tyneham liberationists might use wire-cutters to snip symbolic sections of barbed wire. Conceding that 'our actions cannot be so extreme that we are branded as a band of anarchists', Legg threw the meeting open to ideas: 'Together we must find ways in which all our supporters — I alone have heard from a couple of hundred in the last two months — can join together in forming an efficient resistance movement to force the belated surrender of Purbeck.'

There may well have been some clapping at that point, but there were certainly also some raised eyebrows on the floor. Who was this swarthy 21-year-old who had arrived in the county and, by means of an upstart magazine, commandeered one of the county's most cherished lost causes and forced it once again into the national media? Legg also had things to learn about what went to make up an environmentalist campaign. He had expected a gathering of concerned but so far uncommitted people drawn by the publicity he had created, but, as he looked out into an expectedly grey-haired assembly, he realised that he was actually facing 'a pre-existing local interest group', the members of which had already met to plan their response to his unexpected initiative.

Central to this group was Monica Hutchings, who followed Legg's introduction by showing colour slides of the forbidden range area. In her fifties by this time, Hutchings had some reputation as a Wessex author — of autobiography, topography, animal stories, romantic and historical fiction. The resourceful daughter of a 'gentleman's gentleman' or, in plainer terms, a butler whose drinking habits had led to successive dismissals and hasty relocations for his family, she had grown up on the hoof.[12] Having left school at fifteen without a single qualification, she had worked as a domestic servant and a dormitory maid in a preparatory school, before installing herself on the Dorset-Somerset border, where she had rented a remote 'Keeper's Cottage' in a meadow of buttercups and daisies, and embarked on her life as a writer.[13] A silver stream of alarming newsreels about Europe ran through the Yeovil cinema where Hutchings worked as a 'chocolate girl', but one day this young rhapsodist had walked out to find three Nazi bombers skimming her beloved woods and fields 'like huge black bats against the luminous sky'. She became adept at running for cover in an old tithe barn as machine gun bullets spattered the hedgerows and the crump of falling bombs set the cart-horses 'careering like young tanks' around the meadow.

Hutchings had watched as the war brought the military base into the countryside, and she was also among those who, in the later Forties and early Fifties, protested against the continued presence of the war machines that had 'replaced the sheep on the downs'. She joined the campaign for Imber, the Wiltshire village lost to the Army on Salisbury Plain,[14] and for Tyneham too. The opening shot of 'The New Face of Britain', a film she made with Tony Essex, showed a notice stuck up near Tyneham by the 'Hands Off Purbeck!' campaign: 'We, the People of Purbeck, Need Your Help.'[15]

In a magazine article written at this time, she had followed the road over towards Tyneham from Swanage, describing how the hedges bristled with instruction.[16] The road to Tyneham was closed and the road to Wareham via Creech Hill was open, and both were unfit to be used by vehicles with seats for more than twenty-six persons, or sixteen persons, or ten persons: each successive notice pulling more seats out of an imagined charabanc as it made its controversial way along the leafy lane to Tyneham. Near Major F. Holland Swann's manor house at Steeple, she had seen a green and white sign posted by the citizens of Purbeck, who wanted wayfarers to know that within the prohibited area beyond were 'farms, homes, whole villages, where people had lived for generations'. Beyond that the roadside started to splutter with official warning: 'Keep Out', 'Danger! Battle Range'. 'You have been warned', and 'There are Bombs and Unexploded Shells Inside — They can Kill You!' Hutchings drove on through this barking wilderness, passing 'Barrier Ahead' and 'Battle Range. Firing over Road'. What a welcome to travellers! she had thought as she spurred her old Wolseley up to the chalk ridge of Povington Hill, only to find the old Whiteway to East Lulworth closed and yet another battery of notices banging away on the theme of Keeping Out or Getting Oneself Killed, and announcing that 'Worbarrow Bay is Mined.'

Some pictures in Monica Hutchings's slide show, which would soon enough grow in to a full hour-long exposition of 'Purbeck the Unseen', reprised the old themes. But even though she denounced the destruction of Tyneham House as the greatest of the Army's 'crimes',[17] Hutchings placed her strongest emphasis on the plight of the animals living on the range. Hutchings had always loathed blood-sports, but neither for the same reasons as Rolf Gardiner, who deplored those rustic pursuits as a sign of degenerate rural leadership; nor for those adopted by Valentine Ackland, who had found yet more evidence of the decadence of the rural class structure in the indifference with which drunken aristocrats churned up the fields of their deferential tenant farmers. Hutchings objected out of sympathy for the quarry, and she did so with the vehemence of one who believed hunting and war to be branches of the same evil.[18] In *Man's Dominion*, a book that she co-wrote with Mavis Caver, who would later become Vice-Chairman of the Tyneham Action Group, Hutchings compared the infernal racket of the firing range with the 'noise, commotion and uproar' she had once heard a party of otter hunters bring to a quiet river bank. Indeed, she observed that 'often the backbone of any hunting fraternity are Service people' and condemned hunting not just as 'organised torture leading to murder' but as 'both a rehearsal and a substitute for war'.

Shortly after moving to Purbeck in 1965, Monica Hutchings and her farming husband had been alerted to the dire condition of the scrub ponies living semi-wild on the range. As part of their campaign to 'get help for the animals of the Tyneham valley', they trespassed widely over the range, drawing up a casualty map on which they recorded such findings as 'dead cow below cliff, pony dead with shrapnel wound, dead foal in pond, dead mare in pond, two dead cows in barn, dead sheep, dead cow in bedroom of house'.

Hutchings looked forward to a better world in which wild animals would not have to live in 'constant apprehension and terror'. But the Tyneham valley of her slide-show fell far short of that Franciscan state of perfection. Its telling sights included a young deer with its leg severed by the thin wire used to guide Malcara missiles and then left draped over the valley, a struggling guillemot hung by the leg in the same Satanic cobweb and a hopelessly entangled lamb too.[19] It showed Gad Cliff, where England's mountaineers had practised for the conquest of Everest, deserted by the fulmars and peregrines since 1967, when the firing of guided missiles began in earnest. As for the badger colony near Tyneham Great House, Hutchings had discovered its fate only a few weeks before the inaugural meeting. Visiting this 'ancient set' on a public access day over Easter 1968, she had found holes blocked, terrier paw prints and boot marks, and heavy cudgels lying about the place: 'Those badgers were not near livestock or poultry . . . and now they had been dug out and destroyed.'[20] And all because the Army officers, who enjoyed unofficial use of the range as a private shoot, thought the badgers might disturb nesting pheasants.

The third speaker at that inaugural meeting was an older veteran of the 'Hands Off Purbeck!' campaign. Rolf Gardiner had by this time achieved considerable standing in the County. He had recently finished a ten-year stint as chairman of the Dorset CPRE, and he had also just completed a year's service as High Sheriff to Colonel Sir Joseph Weld's Lord Lieutenant. Springhead had burgeoned as an influential centre of the early music movement, with both Roger Norrington and John Eliot Gardiner (who, four years previously as a history student at King's College, Cambridge, had formed the Monteverdi Choir in opposition to an ossified choral tradition that reduced everything to the same 'Victorian slush') working there on masques, operas and other performances in the garden. Rolf Gardiner participated in this activity, singing in fundraising concerts for the Dorset Historical Churches Trust in places like St Andrew's, the isolated church in the park at East Lulworth, and acting in dramatic events at Springhead — where one sceptic claims to have seen him dressed up as St George, charging down to the lakeside on a white horse and leaping into a boat that promptly sank.

Yet Gardiner was also something of an *eminence vert* by this time. Still uncompromising in his condemnation of 'petrol England',[21] he was busy promoting the new kind of 'landscape husbandry' he considered to be urgently necessary since mechanisation had rendered the traditional look of the countryside agriculturally redundant.[22] He was in touch with Fritz Schumaker and his colleagues at the Intermediate Technology Group, and he continued to pioneer his ecological ideas on lands owned by his family in Malawi: reafforesting overexploited land, building village-style settlements to counter peri-urban sprawl, and then coming home to commend his fellow share-holders for their commitment to a higher, if less immediately profitable, project than that of the conventional expatriate 'extractor'.

By 1968, Gardiner's vision may often have been expressed in terms closer to Rachel Carson's influential condemnation of pesticides, *Silent Spring*, than to the organic injunctions of D. H. Lawrence, but there were still whispering dryads in his trees and the influence of Rudolf Steiner remained strong too. Gardiner had metamorphosed the 'new order' he had once imagined with the pre-Nazi German youth movement into the 'post-modern' New Age he would announce later that year in a harvest-thanksgiving sermon, delivered from what he and H. J. Massingham had long ago agreed to be Dorset's innermost pulpit at Cerne Abbas.[23]

Gardiner's address to the nascent Action Group leaves no doubt that he still saw Tyneham as a place where organic England could be won back from the metallic grip of the centralised state. Comdemning the Army's retention of the Purbeck ranges as 'a national scandal and an example of bureaucratic infidelity at its worst',[24] he announced that 'a heathland of Dorset is being demolished field by field, house by house, tree by tree, rock by rock'. It had been reaffirmed that the Army were staying on indefinitely but Gardiner reckoned that 'in these days of kaleidoscopic change this can be suddenly reversed. It could happen that any day a top-level defence decision could lead to the ranges being closed.' And what would happen then to prevent the land being 'parcelled up among developers and other "vultures of rural substance" '? Without explicitly disagreeing with Legg, who had put the case for National Trust ownership, Gardiner urged, in the spirit of Crichel Down, that 'the land must be offered back to the original owners'. It would then have to be cleared of 'missiles, debris, ironmongery' — a laborious task, as he knew — and 'rehabilitated, not merely scenically, but biologically, by replanting of hedges and trees, by cultivations and rebuilding'.

Legg had talked about Armadas and symbolic wire-cutting, but Gardiner recommended that the Tyneham Action Group should be content to win the agreement of the former owners, and then 'employ a consultant with a team of experienced surveyors and designers to make a landscape plan for the valley — to redesign it for agriculture, forestry, nature reserves, and, above all, for beauty and recreation of the sort desired by lovers of Dorset scenery and solitude'. When completed, the plan should be deposited with the County Council to provide 'something to go on' in the event of Tyneham's release.

Such was the meeting at which the Tyneham Action Group was formed. Legg was elected 'honorary secretary', but he was also tightly hemmed in by a committee of elders. The chairmanship went to Philip Draper, a retired engineer and son of the late Warwick Draper of Sheepleaze, who would soon be telling national newspapers that his first carpentry lessons had taken place in William Morris's house at Hammersmith.[25] Monica Hutchings became a founder member, later introducing her co-author Mavis Caver, who came from a Quaker and socialist background and was then working as a tour organiser in Bournemouth. Ruth Colyer was a footpath vigilante who had initiated the work of the Ramblers Association in Dorset and was well known for re-opening obstructed public rights of way with a slasher or, failing that, a pair of heavy duty wire-cutters.[26]

Rolf Gardiner went into the Vice Presidency, along with Lilian Bond, with whom he corresponded in praise of Philip Draper (as Bond wrote, 'I have known him since he was a boy at Worbarrow and have a great opinion of his soundness, modesty and good sense').[27] The Vice Presidency would soon be joined by Lord Salisbury, the Tory peer who as Viscount Limborne, had been MP for South Dorset for twelve years before Hinchinbrooke took over in 1941. Fenner Brockway, the veteran anti-imperialist and pacifist who was by then a Labour peer, joined after being approached by Mavis Caver, who had known this fiercely anti-Stalinist socialist in the days of the old Independent Labour Party. He would later record his own highly simplified version of the broken pledge that had drawn him to the cause, writing that Tyneham had been 'patriotically surrendered to the Forces in preparation for D-Day and in acknowledgement Winston Churchill promised that it would be returned at the end of hostilities, a letter going to each tenant with this assurance'.[28]

SEVENTEEN

NEW LIFE FOR THE VALLEY OF LOST CAUSES

> We must all pull together over this matter and show that there are some civilians with red blood in their veins ... there are still iron men going to sea in wooden ships. The spirit is not dead.
>
> Tyneham Action Group wellwisher.[1]

THE TYNEHAM ACTION GROUP's renewal of the long dormant campaign was spurred on by the continuing 'rape' of Tyneham House. One of the first hard truths to dawn on the Actionists was that their promise, made at the inaugural meeting, to visit Tyneham in a cavalcade of protest the following August Bank Holiday, seems to have provided the Ministry of Defence with a date by which their demolition of Tyneham House and a number of other prominent buildings should be completed.

Sheepleaze was levelled after some handcut stone tiles from its roof had been carted off to an undisclosed destination, and so too was Mrs Wheeler's unmourned modern bungalow nearby. On 9 April 1968, *The Times* reported that The Ministry of Defence was in the process of completing the dismemberment of Tyneham House. Telephoned in Osnabrück, where he was serving with the British Army on the Rhine, Brigadier Mark Bond declared, 'This is the end of a long, sad and rather disgraceful story. I feel pretty sour.' As for the aristocrats who had salvaged pieces of Tyneham House for incorporation into their seats nearby, Lord Southborough of Bingham's Melcombe, who had taken a fourteenth or fifteenth-century stone doorway and a porch dated 1583 over to his house, remarked 'It makes you want to weep to see an old house in this state. It has cost me four figures to remove, transport and absorb these pieces into my house, but I regard it as a patriotic act.' At Athelhampton Hall, *The Times* found Robert Cooke, Tory MP for Bristol West, wondering what to do with a number of stone facing blocks: it was far from clear how this fourteenth and early fifteenth-century material could be incorporated into his rather more recent mansion. Brigadier Mark Bond may have sighed heavily, but he declared himself 'very grateful to these public-spirited people who have taken some of the pieces. At least something of Tyneham will be preserved.'

Formed the following month, the Action Group was to cast an altogether less generous light on these events. The destruction of Tyneham House was 'a sickening and terrible situation' brought about by the 'deplorably irresponsible policy of Ministry officials'.[2] Writing in the second issue of his *Dorset Magazine*, Rodney Legg reiterated that 'retentive memories are an embarrassment to the military; and perhaps the house became a link with the past which was too strong for their comfort'.[3] Far from participating in a selfless act of patriotic salvage, those lordly removers of valuable 'features' were plunderers who had gone along with what Philip Draper described as the 'deliberate destruction of a scheduled ancient Manor House'.[4]

The emergence of this sharply critical perspective was embarrassing for the County. Lord Southborough communicated his concern to Rolf Gardiner late in 1968; and Gardiner passed his letter to Lilian Bond who was quick to concede that Southborough had surely 'acted in what I believe was good faith'.[5] Lilian Bond was not aware of having slighted any attempts at conciliation. She had indeed been invited for tea at Bingham's Melcombe by a 'mutual acquaintance' then living in the house, who offered to show her the fragments of Tyneham since incorporated there. Lilian had replied — 'I hope gently and kindly' — that she would 'rather not see what could only bring back the ache of old scars'.

Others in the Action Group took a less forgiving line. On 24 August 1968, it was minuted that stone was still being taken from Tyneham House at the rate of two loads a day, and that it was being transported to Athelhampton Hall where it was to be used for the 'rebuilding of domestic quarters'. Mark Bond appears to have been encouraged when he met Monica Hutchings in 1968: 'I showed him the piece of stone which Cooke will NEVER have & he said he'd use it for a cornerstone of his new home in the valley — one day!' Even in the late Eighties, former Tyneham actionists were observing sarcastically that at least some of the material that had been taken to Athelhampton Hall was on view to the public — at that time a considerable quantity of faced stone was still heaped up in chipped and moss-covered piles at the edge of the car park at that nearby mansion.

The dust of demolition was still hanging in the air on 30 August 1968, when the Press announced that the Tyneham Action Group would be going into action for the first time that bank holiday weekend.[6] Supporters were invited to join the Tyneham Action Group on a 'pilgrimage'. The moderate chairman, Philip Draper, was already reassuring journalists that his Tyneham liberationists were not student anarchists: 'People are sick of banners and protestors: we are not doing it this way.'

The event had been widely publicised in the national as well as local media, and it was reported that 'hideous traffic jams built up on the narrow road through the bracken', as hundreds of people wandered about between the barbed wire. Gathered at a trestle table in the car park, the Group turned a brisk trade. There was a 'nostalgic display' of photographs of Tyneham before and after the military occupation, and quotations from perfidious government statements were also on display. A number of theatrical inserts had been fitted into the valley: noteably a six-foot cross painted red and mounted at a former entrance to Tyneham House to 'mark the spot of a broken promise'. Throughout the day the Tyneham Action Group held a 'running dialogue' with the public, including 'a military-looking gentleman in a blazer' who barked 'You've got to have gunnery ranges somewhere. Now haven't you?'[7]

Monica Hutchings had written an article in the *Western Gazette* urging people to visit the area over the bank holiday, and she returned to sum up. Some six thousand people had visited the Tyneham valley over that weekend, and a 'very large number of the visitors appeared to be old and to have personal connections with Tyneham'.[8] Among the pilgrims had been the man responsible for making Tyneham House weatherproof in the early days of the range. He had sealed up the chimneys, boarded up doors and windows and his verdict was that the house 'would have stood for another five hundred years'. Another former resident, who had brought his son over to see where he had lived as a boy, spoke admiringly of Lilian Bond's book: 'She's right about this place. As a sailor I have travelled the world and there is nowhere like Worbarrow Bay, Gold Down and the Tout.' Many moving scenes were enacted along the track from Tyneham to Worbarrow Bay — one frail old native was eased down on a motor scooter; while another, who had 'walked scarcely anywhere for years, being crippled with rheumatism', insisted on hobbling down herself to see the ruins of the house where she had worked as a maid.[9]

Other connections were being made behind the scenes — and none more important than those devoted to winning over the soldier who would, were it not for the pressing requirements of his own employer, have been the squire of Tyneham. The Group had been in communication with Brigadier

Mark Bond. Initially, this former ADC to Montgomery of Alamein had kept his distance, explaining that, painful as it was for him to see the valley 'deserted and ruined', he knew as a professional soldier that there was 'a military justification for the continued occupation of Purbeck' and could not therefore support the campaign.[10] As for Legg's idea that Tyneham should be handed over to the National Trust, Bond remarked that, on the contrary, it was 'to those evicted, or to their heirs and successors that Tyneham must eventually return if the "pledge" is ever to be properly honoured'. He also repudiated the insulting suggestion that the Army take-over had kept the area 'unmarred by development' and prevented encroachment by caravans, bungalows and 'blocks' of Forestry Commission fir:

> In fact, Purbeck's unrivalled and unspoilt coast is due to the gentleman's agreement entered into by the Welds of Lulworth, Bonds of Tyneham and Creech Grange, Mansells of Smedmore, Scotts of Encombe and Bankes of Kingston Lacey.
>
> These families agreed at considerable financial sacrifice to preserve their heritage — and England's heritage — in all its unspoilt beauty. In these days when 'landlord' is almost a dirty word, their action might well be remembered and their example followed.

Brigadier Bond was considerably less reserved by the time he visited the valley during the August 'pilgrimage', telling the *Western Gazette* that the present state of Tyneham House 'makes one sick at heart', and saying, when asked whether he would like the house and valley back, 'Yes, very much so . . . I would have to scrape up some money somewhere to buy it back.'[11] He still felt unable to join the Tyneham Action Group, but he suggested that 'if there is any justice in this world, Tyneham would be handed back'. He agreed that it was not easy for a man in his position to speak out against the Army, 'I shall probably get called up before Denis Healey for saying this, but if they are going to muck around with Tyneham they must expect comments.'

By October 1968, Brigadier Bond and the new Tyneham liberationists had come to terms. The Action Group now accepted the precedent of Crichel Down, and had aligned itself with the non-socialist approach to preservation that Bond had described in terms of the 'gentleman's agreement'. The Group adopted a statement of 'aims and objects' in which Legg's original cry of 'Surrender Purbeck' had been cut down to cover the

Tyneham Valley alone, and the goal of National Trust ownership had been dropped too. The declared objective was, first, 'to have restored to its rightful owners, the land in the Tyneham area, which was requisitioned by the War Department in 1943'; and secondly, 'to regain, with the already expressed approval of these owners, such public access as is compatible with conservation, its usage and natural features'.

In a statement drawn up with his new collaborators, Bond described how he had initially suspected that 'the protest contained in the *Dorset Magazine* was no more than an ephemeral publicity stunt for a new publication'. He now understood that he had 'badly underestimated' the Group, which he recognised as 'a practical, sensible organisation composed of sincere, reasonable people with practical, reasonable aims'. As a serving officer he could not take part in any controversy involving the War Department, but he was happy to 'agree unequivocably' with the Action Group's aims. Brigadier Bond's described position would only become more awkward as his career developed through the years of this campaign. In 1968, he was appointed from the British Army on the Rhine to the Imperial Defence College in London. From there he went to Hong Kong for a brief spell as Chief of Staff, returning to London in 1970 and by now as a Major-General, to become Director of Planning at the Ministry of Defence. His prospects for further promotion were hardly enhanced by the dispute over Tyneham, and it was only after retiring early from the Army in the early Seventies that he felt able to join the Tyneham Action Group as Vice-Chairman. Informally, however, Brigadier Bond was on board by 16 November 1968, when the Group first spelt out its plans at a public meeting in Wareham.

It fell to Rolf Gardiner to launch this windblown ship of vision across the waters of pragmatic self interest and public disbelief. Dorset's veteran rural reviver, who as long ago as 1933 had observed that 'the word "State" emits a foreign tang',[12] commenced by identifying 'the lesson of Tyneham', which should, so he suggested, be written up and affixed to every notice board on the range: 'Put not your trust in bits of paper nor in any official department.'[13] Ministers, Members of Parliament and Civil Servants were the agents of 'remote control; a form of government against which we are nowadays more and more rebelling'.

Quoting from Lilian Bond's 'beautiful, eloquent and often witty' book, Gardiner contrasted the many centuries it had taken to make Tyneham a place of beauty and peace with the 'very short time' in which our discarnate modern age had turned it into 'a shell-shocked wilderness'. Nowadays it was 'widely supposed that inheritance of any kind is wrong or selfish', but Gardiner condemned this 'decadent theory', asking 'Are we becoming an unhistorical people, a collection of footloose nomads who belong nowhere?' Such was the trend against which the Tyneham liberationists should work, cleaving to the unfashionable knowledge that 'It is only by belonging to a place that we are really in harmony with our surroundings, with nature, with all God's creation.' Gardiner pronounced that the 'Subconscious of the Tyneham valley had been rudely dislocated and injured', insisting that 'the devils which prowl around it must be exorcised'.

Gardiner's revitalised valley would certainly have had its archaic features once the rusting metal of the encroaching state had been cleared from its soil. The harvest festivals would have been more vibrant affairs than Bill Douglas was able to bring off in his film *Comrades*, and Post Office Row would have become a lane of childhood vision as described in one of Gardiner's favourite passages from Thomas Traherne, for whom 'the green trees seen at the end of the streets seemed the end of the world, whose beauty ravished him with delight'.[14] Baltington might have become a farmhouse like the one in which the poor rural poet John Clare described growing up, where the annual rent could be raised by selling the harvest from a single apple tree in the garden. Transistor radios would surely have been impounded at the frontier, but Gardiner, who was no timorous preservationist, would not have excluded all modern development. As he told the Wareham meeting, the valley would have to be redesigned around such mixed priorities of contemporary life as farming, wildlife conservation, public access and recreation. He called for a generous provision of 'tree cover', beneficial not just from the practical perspectives of timber production or water catchment, but also, as he had argued elsewhere, as a spirited habitat needed by people for such ingenuous purposes as quiet reflection and love-making.[15]

Gardiner knew the dangers of private ownership sufficiently to stress that 'Tyneham should not be turned into a sort of Butlin's Camp.' Yet he remained convinced that 'no public body', including the National Trust, could achieve a properly organic restoration, because public bodies are impersonal and 'vulnerable to arbitrary changes and decisions'. Fortunately, Tyneham had a willing heir — a man who, in Gardiner's monarchist terms, might even become the benevolent 'Duke' of the recovered valley. Costs would be 'exceedingly high', but it was to be hoped that the nation would provide 'substantial financial help' to the General who was prepared to reclothe a small stretch of broken England in the colours of its banished archetype.

Anyone in that audience who knew Gardiner would have recognised that his plan for Tyneham was to carry out the same revitalisation he had earlier pioneered at Springhead. The Forbidden Valley was to be another pilot-project for the restoration of England Herself – a nation in which all the pledges of history, and of Creation too, had been betrayed for the sake of Profit, Expediency and the convenience of the metallic State. Tyneham was to be the place where the tide was finally turned. Here, as at Springhead thirty-five years previously, Gardiner spoke 'of rebuilding that dwindling natural capital, of creating fresh life from the herb to the hymn'. The redemption of Tyneham would, as he said, require 'immense efforts, far more than most of us envisage'. But with teamwork and the expert assistance of Sylvia Crowe, the landscape architect Gardiner would soon introduce to Mark Bond, it could surely be achieved. Gardiner signed off with the hopeful promise that 'one day there will be Thanksgiving Services in Tyneham Church for what may be a pioneer act of reclamation done for the nation and its good name'.

Bad News from Prague

While Gardiner pressed on with his plans for the organic redemption of Tyneham, a host of ambient liberationists were picking up their pens to fill the newspapers, national as well as local, with fervent letters written in the candlelight of the exiled English soul.

One of the most moving appeared in April 1969, after the *Observer* had printed a feature article that took the usual journalistic liberties with the condition of Tyneham and its valley, lamenting that the rectory had been 'set on fire and gutted by camping hippies'; and that the telephone kiosk, which was actually never shot at, stood 'up to its waist in weeds, pitted with bullet-holes'.[16] This prompted a reply from Mrs Phoebe M. Rees, whose father had been rector of Tyneham up until 1928: 'My bedroom had double windows to protect it from the terrific gales that sometimes blew in from the sea, yet in the sheltered garden I ate the fruits of a loquat tree, native of the Mediterranean, and picked daffodils that flowered in January.' Now blind, she remembered the church with its commemorative east window by Martin Travers, the design for which had been given place of honour in the Exhibition of English Art then being held in London. There, still radiant in her mind's eye, was the blue-robed Virgin Mary, with the butterflies and the little scenes of local husbandry below: 'How symbolic that window has now become — and what a comment on our civilisation! The little bay, which Sir Frederick Treves called "the most beautiful bay in England" has been given over to the obscenities of modern warfare.'

The Tyneham Action Group found its supporters in the House of Commons too. The incensed Tory MP Angus Maude had the rising breeze of Crichel Down tickling his ears as he penned a blistering letter to the *Daily Telegraph*, condemning the hapless military spokesman who was reported to have announced that the Lulworth ranges would be opened that August as a 'concession' to the people in the area: 'Punch-drunk as we are now becoming with official arrogance we should recognise this specimen as being out on his own.'[17] Individual freedom was being squeezed from all sides, and this was just one more example of creeping encroachment: 'We must not acquiesce in the monstrous assumption that the Executive and its servants have a prescriptive and permanent right of ownership in anything that takes their fancy, and that private rights are a "concession" graciously bestowed by our masters.' People should 'protest strongly against each official outrage'. His point was amplified by Lady Sylvia Sayer, who had her own battles with the Ministry of Defence as leader of the Dartmoor Preservation Association. She declared herself reluctant to believe that the British people had become so apathetic that they would allow 'the Ministry's powerful senior officials' to ride roughshod over 'the ordinary processes of democratic justice. Are there not more MPs who, like Mr Maude . . . are prepared to stand up for our rights?'[18]

There would in fact be many others, and of all parties too, since the Tyneham Action Group was pleased to enlist supporters of every political hue.[19] One of them was the ebullient David Mellor, a young son of Dorset who had a bright future ahead of him as Tory Cabinet Minister and — once the lowering cloud of an adulterous mishap had turned, as the darkest clouds over the Dorset coast so often do, to reveal a broad silver lining — as a prodigiously successful commentator and talk show host. Mellor made his debut over Tyneham, bouncing on to the letters page of the *Western Gazette* to defend the Tyneham Action Group against the criticisms of retired Vice-Admiral Sir Robert Ross Turner, who had suggested it was time to 'stop sniping at the armed forces' and, moreover, that without the

Tank Corps, the liberationists 'would probably have lost the freedom to act as they are doing'.

Members of the TAG committee promptly unmasked the compliant Vice-Admiral as the very man who had been chairman of the 'Hands Off Purbeck' committee in the Forties, a campaign which had been 'much more extreme' than the Tyneham Action Group.[20] But David Mellor preferred to engage him on higher ground, declaiming that 'the essence of our democracy is that nothing is above criticism, and when a Government department breaks a solemn promise, and wilfully disregards individual rights it surely deserves harsh words'.[21] 'Who will guard the guardians?' he asked. Mellor fired other missiles at the apologists who argued that the Army must stay in Tyneham because the shells could never be cleared, or who declared themselves grateful to the Army for 'preserving' the valley in a 'wild and natural state'. It was, he ventured, 'an odd nature lover' who could derive pleasure from seeing 'an ancient manor, and the remains of a charming village decaying in a tangle of common vegetation and barbed wire'; and it was an 'even odder nature lover' who could 'shut from his view the violently coloured signs, posts, barbed wire, burnt-out tanks and other military paraphernalia which complete this idyllic rural scene'.[22] Mellor would surely have agreed with another correspondent who wanted to know what kind of people the British had become if they needed 'a military occupation, albeit by the British Army, to protect our glorious countryside from landsharks?'

The Actionists put up a confident show against their critics, picking holes in their arguments with spikey Osmiroid pens and raking the Royal Armoured Corps' tanks with rapid fire from their clattering manual typewriters. Yet, even with Major-General Mark Bond giving tactical advice from the sidelines, they could hardly match the Soviet machines that, just as they were consolidating their campaign, had 'rolled' into Czechoslovakia to oppose them from Prague.

It was after the Wareham meeting that Mrs Rachel Lloyd condemned the Tyneham Action Group for having 'poured venom' on the Army at a time when the Cold War seemed to be heating up dangerously. Citing the Soviet suppression, that August, of the Prague Spring, she pointed out stiffly that 'With seven army divisions on the borders of Czechoslovakia and West Germany; the balance of power in Europe upset and NATO's grim warning', this was surely a time 'to keep silent' about Tyneham and the Lulworth ranges.[23] Retired Squadron Leader Bernard Brooks thought similarly. He wrote from Bournemouth to assert that 'many people, like myself, would view the aims and activities of the Tyneham Action Group with more consideration and enthusiasm if its spokesmen substituted rural realism for their present anti-Army propaganda'. 'Messrs Gardiner and Legg' had apparently already forgotten 'the countless dead of two world wars'.

Miss Joan Begbie, last seen walking down to Arish Mell Gap with her dogs in the Thirties, was also concerned on this point. Writing from her home in Worth Matravers, she explained that, even though she was herself a member of the Tyneham Action Group, she shared Mrs Lloyd's disgust at 'the gibes made against the Army by a small minority of those on the platform'. Miss Begbie was pleased Monica Hutchings had got up to rebut the idea that the Army was the Action Group's target, and to point out instead that it was 'foresworn Whitehall, not the Army, that is to blame for the loss of our lovely valley'.

Senior members of the Tyneham Action Group did what they could to limit the damage caused by this unanticipated development. Chairman Draper wrote to the paper regretting the 'extremist views' that may have been expressed at the Wareham meeting, reassuring readers that the Tyneham Action Group had never intended to close the ranges at Lulworth or on the Heath or — even less — to drive the Royal Armoured Corps from Dorset. Monica Hutchings also held her position. The Czech crisis was just 'a very red herring', and Tyneham House could probably have been saved had the Tyneham Action Group started speaking out a few months earlier. The Russians might believe that 'brain-washing succeeds by forcing people to busy their minds with refuting lies and giving them no time to arrive at the truth', but so too did Whitehall.

But none of these arguments would stick now that Soviet tanks were on the move, and it wasn't long before some Actionists started trimming their sails to the new wind of moderation. As a member of the Royal Dorset Yacht Club, Lieutenant-Commander K. N. Hoare had been rather slow to adjust. In December 1969, he told the *Sunday Times* that he was prepared to organise a flotilla of yachts to sail through the Lulworth sea-exclusion zone in protest against the illegal manner in which the Army patrol boat was excluding sailors from the area.[24] He also threatened to unleash his friend Harold Penrose, chief test pilot at Westlands, who would fly up and down the range with a squadron of private planes. Two months later, however, the Soviet threat had finally sunk in, or been quietly impressed upon him, and Hoare, who now recognised that 'it was the duty of citizens to support the Armed Forces of the Crown', suggested that the Tyneham Action Group should give up its idea of removing the military and concentrate instead on improving public access at weekends and in the summer block-leave period.[25]

From Virtual Reality to Flying Saucers

The Tyneham Action Group's morale is unlikely to have been damaged by rumours of Army infiltration, or by the 'reliable source' who informed Ruth Colyer that there was a police file, and 'considerable interest in those connected with the Tyneham business. And phone-tapping'. Newsletters remained spirited, and gallivanting lampoons of official attitudes were circulated to cheer the membership.

Yet with Philip Draper in the Chair, this campaign would not be taking the insurrectionary road. Draper and his committee bent over backwards to emphasise that they were not 'long-haired idealists', but rather, in the words of their letter to the Duke of Edinburgh, a group of 'public-spirited and patriotic' people. They did their best to fetter errant committee members — especially Rodney Legg, who seemed to think he could say just what he wanted on the pages of his own *Dorset Magazine* — by passing a capital-lettered decree that 'NO COMMITTEE MEMBER OF T.A.G. PUBLISHES ANY ARTICLE, OR EXPRESSES PUBLICLY AN OPINION WITHOUT FIRST GETTING APPROVAL FROM THE COMMITTEE.' But, with Russian tanks on the move, it was no longer enough to reiterate, as Draper invariably did, that the Group's modest and entirely reasonable ambitions were confined to the Tyneham valley itself. If even that limited area was to be restored according to Gardiner's lights, the Tyneham Action Group would have to come up with a practical scheme that would allow the tanks to continue blasting away on the other side of the hill without need of an overshoot area.

Some members of the Tyneham Action Group preferred to concentrate their objections on peripheral matters, like the tank officer's autumnal habit of gathering with his fellows to wander through the supposedly shell-strewn Tyneham valley on an unofficial pheasant shoot.[26] But as a 'certified engineer' in that futuristic age of moon-landings, Chairman Draper led the Tyneham Action Group into its own variation on Harold Wilson's 'white-hot technological revolution'. Having studied the Solatron Simfire system, which used infra-red beams and sensors to simulate live fire and was then being tested on the Lulworth ranges,[27] he lined up his technical qualifications after his name and declared himself satisfied that computer-based simulators could replace much if not all live firing on the Lulworth ranges.[28] £4 million of ammunition costs would be saved at a stroke, trainee tank gunners would no longer have to confine their fire within an unrealistically narrow arc, and the Tyneham valley could be freed.

This piece of wishful thinking, which the Group tried to rest on the combined authority of 'technical advisers' and 'advertising in the Press and TV', proved impossible to sustain in public discussion. Rodney Legg remembers being mangled by a tank officer when he took this line at a public meeting; and Margaret Kraft, the Press officer, was reduced to claiming, quite unconvincingly, that full details of the simulator could not be given for security reasons. Her weak reassurance that 'we do not speak from Cloud Cuckoo Land'[29] did not convince the mocking opponent who replied that, with top secret information like this at its fingertips, the Tyneham Action Group should obviously be signed up by the Ministry of Defence immediately.

Hiking and renovated squirearchy on one side of the chalk ridge; computers and laser beams on the other — such was the hybrid future vision that the Tyneham Action Group took to London on 22 May 1969, when the day for its long-awaited deputation to the Ministry of Defence finally came up. This procession was arranged by Mr Evelyn King, the supportive MP for South Dorset. The Marquess of Salisbury went, together with Rolf Gardiner, Mark Bond, Philip Draper, Monica Hutchings and Mavis Caver, but not the fiery young secretary, Rodney Legg. They were received by the Parliamentary Under-Secretary of State for Defence for the Army, James Boyden, MP, who introduced himself, encouragingly, as a Dorset man who had camped in the Tyneham valley as a boy scout before the war. After naming absent supporters, who by this time included Baron Lewis Silkin, who had reluctantly broken Churchill's pledge as Labour's Minister of Town and Country Planning in 1948, the liberationists 'stressed the geographical limits' of their case. Unfortunately, however, the Under-Secretary replied that it was quite out of the question that the Tyneham Valley could be separated from the Ranges. As for the latest Direct Fire Weapons Effect Simulator, this had developed faults and the laser beam was thought to be hazardous in its own right.[30]

Philip Draper's vision was sober by comparison with some of the stuff to be found on the Tyneham Action Group fringe. It was hard enough to keep the lid on Rodney Legg and his militant friends among the ramblers and emerging eco-activists of that time, but Draper also had reason to wonder about his Press officer, Mrs Margaret Kraft. Her special powers had been revealed, at least to Kraft's own satisfaction, on 14 May 1969, when Brigadier David Allott, the Commandant of the Royal Armoured Corps at Bovington, was killed in a flying accident. Being of an esoteric turn of mind — one veteran remembers her comparing her own occult potencies with those of the 'Great Beast' Aleister Crowley — Kraft claimed his death as the outcome of a curse she had placed on the late Brigadier.

Kraft led the way through August 1969, which was probably the Group's best ever month for publicity. She began by launching a successful assault against the tankman's unofficial perks. On 31 July, the *Daily Telegraph* reported her complaint that Mupes Bay, on the seaward side of Bindon Hill, was being turned into a 'private playground for officers and their families', who enjoyed water-skiing there. Some civilian employees of the Gunnery School had been ordered off the beach with their families by a regimental sergeant major 'in full uniform' — including an irate West Lulworth man who remarked, 'I said to him we fought wars for this. This is supposed to be a democracy.' Draper seems to have intervened in time to abort the 'bathe-in' that Kraft had threatened in response,[31] but the publicity was enough to get the Ministry of Defence to forbid this preferential treatment, reputedly on the direct order of Denis Healey.[32]

When the Group's second August bank holiday cavalcade descended on the forbidden valley Kraft led the way in a converted jeep, her shouts of 'Freedom' and 'Geronimo' filling the air while a soldier complained of the extreme rudeness with which waiting members of the public had treated him before the gate was opened: 'Some almost went as far as to call me a fascist.'[33] Meanwhile, a Granada television crew from *World in Action* was setting up down by Worbarrow Bay. The Tyneham Action Group had managed to persuade the elderly Lord Salisbury to break his resolution never to appear on television; and in a recorded address, he looked back over the twelve pre-war years when he had known Tyneham so well as its Tory MP and put in a word for the 'harmless and good' people of Tyneham: 'Nothing could have been more charming, more peaceful, and more remote than it was at that time — a little folded valley between the downs and the sea with a grey Elizabethan manor house, and a church, and a village to match inhabited by families many of whose forebears had been there for generations.' The villagers had left their homes 'as a patriotic duty', and it was time to rectify this 'breach of trust', and reinstate them in the valley. Salisbury's widely reported words floated through the programme, an island of timeless patrician reflection in a 'deluge of claim and counterclaim'.[34]

Margaret Kraft rounded off that busy August by perpetrating a successful hoax against the *Daily Telegraph*. Describing herself as Mrs X, she claimed to have seen a glowing flying saucer land in the Tyneham valley while driving home over the ranges with her pilot husband in the early hours of 29 August: 'There was no sound and it settled. It seemed to come to a sudden stop in the air and, in the light from it, we saw tripod-like legs come down out of it. I was paralysed with fright ... We stayed watching it for about half an hour, when it went up into the air and disappeared fast over the sea.'[35] Speaking in her own name, Kraft denied all association with the sighting, remarking that if the 'so far unexplained phenomena at Tyneham' was a hoax, it had most probably been perpetrated by the army to discredit the action group.[36]

Nobbling Edward Heath

Against this eccentric background, it is remarkable that the event the Tyneham Action Group preferred to claim as the major outcome of its campaign ever came about at all. On 28 October 1970, while speaking at the Duke of Edinburgh's 'Countryside in 1970' conference, Prime Minister Edward Heath announced that he had requested Lord Carrington, the Defence Secretary, to conduct a review of the armed services' land holdings with a view to finding areas that could be released, especially in national parks and coastal areas, where, as Heath quipped, firing ranges had 'a deleterious effect on sailing'.[37] The entire 6,300 acre holding at Lulworth was listed along with Dartmoor and Shoeburyness as one of the three most likely sites to be freed.

Heath's initiative was followed by Lord Carrington's formation of the Defence Lands Committee, under the Chairmanship of the Conservative Lord Nugent of Guildford, in January 1971. The Tyneham Action Group claimed to have played a significant part in bringing this review about.[38] They also claimed to have found a direct route to the Prime Minister who 'personally will receive from us all the relevant facts in a fully documented "brief" '.[39] Draper attributed this access to the good offices of a certain unnamed national organisation, but Rolf Gardiner wrote to Lilian Bond with a different idea, describing it as 'lucky that I have what they call "a hot-line" to No. 10 Downing Street; because Mr Heath's chief secretary is Robert Armstrong, a musician-leader of the Springhead Ring'. Philip Draper had just received a letter from Robert Armstrong announcing that Mr Heath had read the latest 'Brief' from the Tyneham Action Group with 'interest and attention' and was to discuss it with Lord Carrington. 'So we seem gradually to be loosening the tragic and malignant grip that has lasted so remorselessly long. How I wish that by next Christmas we could tell you that Tyneham had at last been released.' The elderly Lilian Bond was not to underestimate her own influence either: Gardiner remarked that the Countryside Commission was proposing the designation of 'Heritage Coasts', adding 'I think the choice of the word Heritage was suggested by the subtitle of your lovely book on Tyneham.'

How true are these romantic claims? The publicity generated over Tyneham was certainly a significant influence on the formation of Lord Nugent's Defence Lands Committee, but the hot-line to Heath is of less certain status. Lord Robert Armstrong, who went on to be so famously 'economical with the truth' over the *Spycatcher* affair, is inclined to play down Gardiner's powers in this area. When I showed him a copy of Gardiner's letter, he observed that while he may perhaps have shown the Tyneham Action Group's 'Brief' to Edward Heath at the time, it would have floated across the desk at glancing speed. As for Heath, to this day he remains — or so his private secretary writes — far too busy to comment.

Gardiner took an optimistic view of his influence in No. 10. but the Tyneham Action Group's other Vice Presidents were also busy, waylaying Lord Carrington in the House of Lords. No sooner had he announced the forthcoming review of defence lands than the socialist Lord Fenner Brockway asked him to confirm that Tyneham lay at the very heart of an area that the Countryside Commission had recently designated a 'heritage coast because of its great natural beauty'; and, moreover that certain promises had been given in 1943. 'Yes,' said Lord Carrington, 'I think that is perfectly right.' At this point Tyneham's erstwhile MP, the Conservative Lord Salisbury, stood up to confirm that 'the people were definitely promised when they left their homes during the war that they would be restored to their homes as soon as the war was over, and that promise was not honoured by the government of the day.' He hoped that the 'special position' of Tyneham would be considered and that 'as much as possible will be done to undo the wrong which has been done to these people'. When Brockway indicated the unusual coalition that he and Salisbury had formed over the matter, the Liberal Lord Foot stood up offering to 'fortify the coalition', but by this time other Lords were begging 'No!' and he only managed to put in a word for Dartmoor. It was in just such an atmosphere — in which urgency intersected with boredom, idealism with torpor, and one person's passion was another's dead horse — that Lord Nugent's Defence Lands Committee set to work.

By this time, the Tyneham Action Group had finally found its President. Lilian Bond had been asked to consider the position, but she insisted on her own obscurity. So too had John Betjeman, who was busy as the patron of countless other lost English causes.[40] It was not until May 1970 that Ruth Colyer wrote to Sir Arthur Bryant asking him to become the figurehead of a campaign that was by now nationally known. England's historian was already overcommitted as President of other bodies like the Common Market Safeguards Campaign, but he agreed to become President on a purely 'nominal basis'.[41] His only contribution would be his longstanding column for the *Illustrated London News*, in which he cited Tyneham as one more example of the progressive 'tyranny of machines'.[42] By this time, he was no longer suggesting that the pledge had been written out and stuck up on notices around the village, but he remained emphatic about the 'sacred' promise with which Churchill's wartime coalition government had guaranteed this most precious landscape in all the world and — a deep breath is advisable at this point — condemned 'the gross breach of faith' perpetrated by the 'Socialist government' that, having gone back on 'the pledged word of its predecessor', had compulsorily purchased the houses at 'grossly inadequate valuations dictated by the War Office' and then brought in the 'noisy and destructive' machines. These had been 'designed for the defence not the violation of England' but would lay waste to a landscape gifted with 'such transcendent and ever-changing beauty that no work of art made by man has ever surpassed or equalled it in loveliness — not the greatest Velasquez or Rembrandt or Memling, not even Chartres, the Parthenon, or Salisbury spire'.

EIGHTEEN

LIBERATIONISTS FALL OUT

TYNEHAM'S LAST MP, Lord Hinchinbrooke, or plain Mr Victor Montagu as he had become on renouncing his peerage, drew his career to a symbolic end in June 1972, a few months after he had written to the *Daily Telegraph*, calling on the British people to mount 'another general strike' against the all powerful trade unions.[1] He signed off at a mock funeral for John Bull, organised in protest against the Texan oilmen who were planning to drill an exploratory bore-hole at Nettlecombe in West Dorset. The cortège was joined by Kenneth Allsop, a television presenter and environmentalist writer who lived in the area. Allsop described how six pall-bearers had set out with the coffin from a nearby pub and marched on to the limestone uplands where the yellow crane and metal cabins of the oil company's drilling rig squatted, with inorganic malevolence, on what had once been the local cricket pitch. There were black flags and native wreathes of campion, foxgloves and ragged robin.[2] Cars were draped in funereal crepe and the mourners were appropriately clad too: the men in top hats, black ties and frock coats; the women in 'heavy lace veils'. The coffin was inscribed: 'Welcome Hill, in an Area of Outstanding Natural Beauty, died owing to lack of protection from greed, stupidity, equivocation and naivety.'

At the appropriate moment, 'the earl who renounced his peerages' proceeded to 'speak the last rites' with full 'Churchillian resonance' as a buzzard wheeled overhead. His words were differently reported by various papers, but their gist was adequately captured by the *Bridport News*: 'We have not come here to bury anything, nor to surrender Dorset's historical-pastoral order to the people opposite. We are not here to give them the impression that they are the masters of this range of hills for all time. On the contrary: we have told them they cannot practise their infernal mechanics undisturbed on the body and soul of Thomas Hardy's prose.' The demonstration went off well enough, yet Allsop had to admit that it 'by no means represented unanimous opinion'. As he explained, 'not marching with us were those who had the sniff of money in their nostrils and perhaps enticing visions of Cadillacs and Texan hats, who like the sound of our slogan "Oil Means Spoil" for its secondary meaning'. The landscape had been 'sanctified by Act of Parliament as heritage for future generations', but the 'murder' took place anyway. The problem, as Kenneth Allsop saw it, was simple enough: 'Money talks. Beauty is voiceless.' After saying his piece, Mr Montagu went home to Mapperton Manor. A few days later, he was fined £5 for possessing an old revolver without a licence.[3]

Strange were the coalitions that formed at the margins of British political life in the Nineteen Seventies. Dope-smoking libertarians made common cause with right-wing zealots in the Society for Individual Freedom, of which Commander Marten of Crichel Down fame was Vice President; and anxious former soldiers teamed up with paranoid industrialists to plot against the day when it might be necessary to go to war against 'communist' trade unions, and the terrible humiliations imposed on Great Britain by the International Monetary Fund. These pressures were enough to drive Edward Heath's chief civil servant Sir William Armstrong to paranoid distraction. By January 1974, he was raving about imminent coups and the communist infiltration that may even have reached into the room where he was standing; and he was eventually removed from his position after he was found lying on the floor in 10 Downing Street muttering about the Red Army.[4] Dorset also had its paranoid right-wing fringe at this time. A patriotic front called 'Civil Assistance' was formed at the last ditch by a retired Colonel with good connections in the county — another English Array prepared to rise up against strikers. The neo-fascist 'Racial Preservation Society' would later transmute itself into the 'Wessex Study Group' under the leadership of Donald Pirie;[5] and Major Ian Souter Clarence, a former SAS officer based in Poole, is reported to have run paramilitary training camps for British and European fascists, and eventually also to have become involved in safehousing wanted fascist terrorists from West Germany.[6] The Tyneham Action Group was a gentle thing by comparison — although Ruth Colyer, who was a member of the Liberal Party, had successfully won the Society for Individual Freedom over to its cause by 1970.

There were many different ways of feeling like a displaced person in those crisis-ridden times, and the Group rallied its supporters from diverse folds in the crumpling fabric of national life. Ramblers concerned about public rights of access made common cause with composting monarchists and landowners for whom private property was the foundation stone of Civilisation. Animal welfare activists stood shoulder to shoulder with beefy nationalists who simply couldn't believe the European Common Market was coming along to exile them from their native inheritance. The old rectories of Dorset had long echoed with discontented mutterings about Tyneham's expropriation, but the call was now also heard by a younger generation of eco-activists whose more globally defined concerns were represented by new campaigning organisations like the Conservation Society or Friends of the Earth. Some of Tyneham's admirers stepped up as if they had just arrived in Narnia, having reached that forbidden country by climbing into a wardrobe and then fighting their way through a dense coniferous wood — surely not another monocultural Forestry Commission plantation — as demanded by C. S. Lewis in *The Lion, the Witch and the Wardrobe*. And there were plenty of pixified Tolkien readers for whom the Tyneham valley was like the enchanting Shire of Middle Earth's hobbits and the Army no better than the invading host of Mordor, given over to metal, mechanisation, and a terrible wasting of deciduous trees.[7]

Rodney Legg remembers some of the more unusual letters of support he received as editor of *Dorset: The County Magazine*. Encouraging postcards arrived intermittently from Khaikhosru Shapurji Sorabji, a Zoroastrian pianist and composer of Parsee and Sicilian extraction, who was then living as a recluse in Corfe Castle and could have done without gunfire disturbing the retirement in which he composed his famously 'unplayable' music. He also heard from Yvone Kirkpatrick, a man who might have walked straight out of an early Le Carré novel. A retired public schoolmaster who had distinguished himself flying Sopwith Camels in the Great War, Kirkpatrick turned up at all the public meetings. He seemed to have access to classified information, and sensed conspiracies everywhere. He would send Legg copies of official documents with a teasing message on a covering card: 'I expect you know all about this,' as one surviving example reads, 'I wonder who is at the bottom of it?'

A fundamental challenge for the Tyneham Action Group was to integrate its older members — exotic traditionalists as they may certainly have been — with those from a younger generation that seemed to be marching to a very different tune. The average tankman stood aghast at the sight of long-haired rebellion, but the veterans of Rolf Gardiner's circle were not quite so dismissive. They had their doubts, but they also tried hard to see the younger generation's cause — undisciplined as its expression certainly was — as the very one for which they themselves had been fighting since the Thirties. Their hope was given general expression by John Stewart Collis, who had worked in the Springhead woods during the Second World War, and now wanted to know why Tariq Ali and his revolting students were not directing their protests against the spoilation of England:

> Could not the youth of England protest against *this*? It would be no vague cause for the youth of England to stand up angrily against the destruction of England. They could do more than just protest and march. They could refuse to allow such proceedings to go forward in the name of democracy. They could point out that it is no good having an affluent society if you destroy your country . . . They could oppose such actions with force — yes, with arms. They could throw bombs at the bulldozers. There would be a battle each time they appeared. It would be war. But it would be a worthwhile one. Those who fought it would indeed, if ever the words were absolutely true, be 'fighting for their *country*'.[8]

Sir Arthur Bryant had also stared into his television set — a gadget with which he can never have felt entirely at home — and worried about the apparently destructive face of youthful dissent. He was horrified to see a young woman at a demonstration with a placard saying 'I hate everyone!' He hoped she was joking, but feared that this kind of nihilism, bred by communism, heralded a second Dark Age. A firm believer in the authority of the elder generation, Bryant was in no doubt that 'a university which degenerates into a youthful pressure-group or a cell for mob demonstrations is failing to fulfil the purpose for which it exists and becomes a handicap, not an asset, to society'. But, like Collis, Bryant found one aspect of 'student protest' that deserved consideration — namely its claim that 'modern industrial society and government are ignoring and repressing the creative and libertarian impulses of man'. Having 'so pathetically little knowledge', the students didn't realise that anarchy was invariably the parent of 'even more rigid and far more ruthless and cruel tyrannies than those they fear and resent'. But once he had ordered haircuts all round, Bryant observed that 'their instinct that something is "rotten in the state of Denmark" and needs amending is not at fault. Vietnam, Porton, Aldermaston are the symbols to them of nightmare fears that encompass humanity's pilgrimage towards the light.'[9]

Rolf Gardiner looked on with similar thoughts in mind. He had found no redeeming qualities in the 'Rumba' favoured by urban members of the Women's Land Army at Slape flax mill during the war, but by 1966, he was straining to hear the lingering echo of old polyphonies in another raucous urban racket. As he told readers of the Soil Association's journal, *Mother Earth*: 'Much of the protest manifested by the youth of today, whether it be CND, "Beat", "Pop", Mod or Rocker, springs from a deep-seated bewilderment as to the purpose of existence, and of what used to be felt as Britain's mission in the world.'[10] Speaking out from the pulpit at Cerne Abbas two years later, this early prophet of the post-modern age proclaimed that, misled as their protest may well have been, the young were at least expressing their discontent against the abstracted and 'discarnate' culture of a mechanised and industrialised world that Gardiner himself had been fighting for so long: 'What has happened this year among students in so many parts of the world is, I believe, largely a wild, violent resentment against the de-humanisation and de-naturing of life and society, against being trapped in a relentless organised processing machine.'[11]

Tyneham was to cast its spell far and wide, but it was quite another thing for the Action Group to build a seaworthy ship on that visionary shore where young and old eyed each other in unaccustomed encounter. Survivors from both generations remember wondering just what they had got themselves involved in.

General Mark Bond looks back on the Group as a collection of enthusiasts and oddballs whose 'hearts were in the right place'. Philip Draper was a most genial man, but as chairman he could hardly stick to an agenda, and the meetings were all the more chaotic for the fact that at least one of the more passionate women on the committee seemed to have a drink problem. It was a curious company in which this NATO General chose to fight his last battle: romantic, excitable and not a little bizarre.

Rodney Legg also had his doubts. He remembers finding himself among a formidable muster of middle-aged women who seemed as old as the hills to his young eye. Monica Hutchings, Mavis Caver, Margaret Kraft and Ruth Colyer were at the centre, but the matriarchal circle radiated outwards to include a whole host of forceful upper class ladies. Some of the most active women had complicated personal lives — there were Polish lovers who fled to Spain and husbands who ran off with local girls to the West Indies, or merely came up to thank Legg for providing their wives with such a useful 'alternative to therapy'. Adamant that the campaign would never have taken off without these women, Legg also remembers them with a certain exasperation, recalling that the inner circle held their own meeting to indulge in prurient speculation about his sexuality. 'They all looked like horses,' he says a little vengefully, adding with a shake of his head that he found it 'amazing that there were so many of them'. They could be unbelievably catty too. Margaret Kraft, whose posh manner could be irritating, had a serious falling out with Monica Hutchings, who was suffering from breast cancer throughout the campaign, and dividing her still formidable energies between Tyneham and the Women's Institutes, where she was a much-invited speaker on the case for radical mastectomy. As Legg remembers it, Hutchings had asked Kraft what method she would choose if she was thinking of committing suicide, and Kraft is said to have answered, just a little too briskly, that Hutchings might try getting into the bath with an electric fire.

There was little chance that this motley collection of English Idealists would ever really settle down together. Monica Hutchings did what she could to conciliate, writing to Legg to reassure him that, having met Mark Bond, she could vouch for the fact that he was a very decent and unpriggish man. As for Legg himself, the impression he left with other members was of uncompromising left-wing militancy. Hutchings informed Legg that the matrons of the Dorset CPRE thought he should be got rid of, and there were mutterings to the effect that this troublemaking upstart was 'as pink as smoked salmon' and 'ought to be at the LSE'. As a radical socialist peer, Fenner Brockway would have used different metaphors, but he too considered Legg to be typical of 'the radical new generation' that was not cowed by notices saying 'Trespassers will be Prosecuted'.[12]

Rolf Gardiner remained a controversial figure too. Ruth Colyer had already tangled with him in 1965, when pressing for the legal recognition of public rights of way over Springhead land; and General Mark Bond still wonders about the man with whom, as the Action Group minutes show, he might once have written a book about the future of the Tyneham valley. Gardiner, observes Bond, was an enthusiast who didn't always seem to know the difference between dream and reality. General Bond's father, Ralph, had always viewed Gardiner as a little unhinged, and the county folk who later gave up on his CPRE and formed the Dorset in Danger Committee to head off the threat of new towns were also exasperated by his attitudes. One of them wrote to Legg dismissing Gardiner as 'a *kultur* windbag in the true old German professorial manner' and, 'all high flown gas and gaiters'.

Yet in 1968, Gardiner had ideas for Legg as well as for Brigadier Bond. He set out to adopt this young firebrand with the apparent hope of rekindling the old flame of *Youth*. Legg remembers visiting Springhead, and listening to Gardiner 'going on about Austrian and German youth' and trying to persuade him to move into Gore Farm (at that time semi-derelict), restore it and resume the pre-war programme of work camps: 'pull in the young, and get them to brush up the trees to ensure that they would grow good straight timber'.

It was, says Legg, 'an awesome prospect', but he had reservations from the start. As a sixteen-year-old in 1964, he had written to Gardiner, who was then chairman of the Dorset branch of the Council for the Preservation of Rural England, urging him to take such steps as might be necessary to ensure the removal of the Army from the county. The CPRE seemed pathetically genteel and reluctant to do anything but 'talk about trees being cut down . . . All Gardiner would say was that if the Army did get out the land would have to go back to its former owners, which is rubbish.'[13] He remembers being dismayed again when he heard Gardiner declare that the vast pylons taking electricity down by Eggardon Valley 'added another proportion to the landscape'. As for the mixed woods around Springhead and Gore, these may have been planted as a prelude to resettling the megalithic chalk uplands of Cranborne Chase with new yeomen made from formerly redundant industrial workers, but Legg saw little more than an imposed geometry of conifers, musing that 'anyone who could plant those trees as he did would have to be pretty insensitive to landscape values'. He almost accepted Gardiner's offer but, as he remembers, only decided against joining his revival of Wessex when it emerged that Gardiner expected him not just to rebuild Gore Farm and organise the new work camps, but also to pay rent for the privilege.

The Split

The Tyneham Action Group could have split in any number of ways, but it was Rodney Legg who forced the break, after finding himself trapped on a committee that had apparently turned itself into a society for the restitution of the Bonds. His attendance at committee meetings had fallen off sharply after the Wareham meeting, in which his anti-military remarks had outraged those Dorset patriots concerned about events in Prague. But the decisive provocation did not come until November 1969, when Mr Ivor Richards, the Labour Under-Secretary for Defence for the Army, came to Dorset to launch a 'broadside' against the Tyneham Action Group. Richards scoffed that 'What the Tyneham Action Group represents is the Tyneham Action Group.'[14] He gave an unashamedly pragmatic account of why the Tyneham valley could not be released: British forces were withdrawing from many parts of the world and being centralised in Europe; and, anyway, the Army's relationship with the locals was generally extremely good. He was contemptuous of the simple-minded myth that the Tyneham liberationists had made out of Churchill's pledge: 'It seems to me utterly impossible now, in 1969, to say because a government in 1943 said "x" and because a government in 1948 said "y" a situation which has lain dormant for twenty-one years should be reopened.' Undeterred by a voice from the hall that called out 'It has not lain dormant', he went on to declare it 'utterly impossible to separate the Tyneham valley from the rest of the ranges', and to ridicule the Tyneham Action Group's suggestion that, thanks to the magic of the Solatron Simfire system, adequate training could be conducted without live firing.

This was more than enough for Rodney Legg and Margaret Kraft too. They purloined the group's membership register and issued an 'Emergency Newsletter' calling a special meeting at which members would be asked to elect a new committee and approve a new constitution. Denouncing Draper's simulator argument, the rebels insisted that the Group should be campaigning for the release of the whole area of the range, and that to limit this demand to the Tyneham valley was to settle for the redemption of 'half a pledge'. Legg recommended that the tank ranges should be moved to 'a Celtic fringe on the edge of these islands'.

The attempted takeover was a spectacular failure. Legg was denounced as 'crazy' and 'despicable' from the floor, and the meeting passed an overwhelming vote of confidence in the committee he was trying to depose. Shortly afterwards, Draper's committee issued a statement explaining that, while they had expected 'an outburst from a militant fringe', they hoped that the rebels would now settle down and co-operate. But there was to be no reconciliation, and it wasn't long before the two members involved in the 'attempted hijacking' had resigned from the committee. From this moment, the Tyneham 'resistance movement' would prove as susceptible to angry denunciations and splits as the famously fissiparous Presbyterian Church of Scotland.[15]

Legg was content to coast in other waters for eighteen months or so, but direct engagement could not be avoided once Lord Nugent's Defence Lands Committee started to take submissions on the future of the Lulworth ranges. On 21 May 1971, Legg wrote to the *Western Gazette*, breaking 'the silence over Tyneham matters' that he claimed to have kept since 1969. Identifying himself as 'the founder and instigator of the Tyneham Action Group' he condemned its 'ill-conceived policies', urging members to join the new 'Care for Dorset amenity organisation'.

Fronted by its 'Projects Secretary', who turned out to be none other than Mrs Margaret Kraft, Care for Dorset was an unashamedly elitist body that claimed to represent 'professional' opinion on the Dorset environment. It demanded not just the release of Tyneham but the removal of the whole Royal Armoured Corps establishment at Bovington, imagining a non-firing corps installed at Bovington, or, failing that, 'the nucleus of a New Town'.[16] Kraft can still be seen presenting this vision in a surviving television programme. She strides out over the downs at Kimmeridge, gazing over towards Tyneham as she tosses haughty replics at an invisible interviewer.[17] When told that the Royal Armoured Corps feared it would suffer recruitment problems if it moved from Lulworth to the far-flung Scottish wasteland she had suggested, she drew herself up, and snorted with professional hauteur: 'Well, frankly, you astound me, because if the conditions of our fighting forces are so poor that they can only get their recruits by offering the choicest piece of South Dorset coast . . . well perhaps we should have conscription back again.'

From this point onwards, the Tyneham liberationists would spend at least as much time fighting among themselves as pressing their case against the Ministry of Defence. They harangued one another in endless late night phone calls, and exchanged letters that spluttered with vituperation, self-justification and wounded pride.

A conciliatory member of the Action Group would eventually try to overcome this unseemly squabbling by suggesting that the differences were to do with 'personality rather than principle'. But the split also occurred along doctrinal lines that could have been predicted from the very first meeting. The protestors were not just divided over tactics, hot or cold, or whether the campaign should press for the release of the entire range, as Rodney Legg and his supporters had argued from the start, or confine its demands to the Tyneham valley alone. It was also a choice between organic Creationism, of the sort Gardiner had advocated in opposition to the centralised state, and a more secular Environmentalism that was not afraid of using the State to achieve its ends. The Tyneham Action Group imagined their valley privately restored under the benevolent but watchful eye of a reinstated squire. But Legg and the other rebels opposed this 'return to feudalism' and wanted the entire range released into public protection as a nature reserve. They aimed, as General Mark Bond remembers to this day, to bring about the final 'disappropriation of the Bonds'.

Dorset being what it is, however, this is only to say that each side eventually found its own road to the National Trust. For Legg and his allies at the Commons, Open Spaces and Footpaths Preservation Society, National Trust ownership had always been a straightforward alternative to the kind of private ownership that would soon enough resort to caravans, bungalows and the other lucrative excrescences of the tourist trade.

For those who followed Bond and Gardiner's opposed scenario, the prospect of National Trust ownership at first only promised to complete the metallic state's alienation of this precious landscape. But they changed their tune once they discovered that the Crichel Down rule stipulated that previously compensated owners would have to buy back their former lands at current market valuation. This was more than the Bonds could be expected to manage, and the Tyneham Action Group had carried out a reluctant adjustment to Legg's scheme by the end of 1970, when Gardiner spoke at a public meeting in Bournemouth. Major General Mark Bond still featured as the ancestral reinstator of the valley, but Gardiner admitted that it might be necessary for the National Trust to buy the valley and then return it to Bond on a long lease so that he could run it on an agricultural basis: 'If this can be done within the terms of a designated Heritage Coast we can look forward with confidence to the future. If Tyneham is handed over to a faceless authority, it will be indeed and forever a Lost Heritage.'

So there was a lot for Lord Nugent's Defence Lands Committee to contend with when it visited Dorset over a few days in October 1971 to gather evidence about the Lulworth gunnery school. The Tyneham Action Group put the case for simulators again, and then retreated to the high ground of patriotic principle from which they declaimed that 'Pledge' was 'the axiom that an Englishman's word is his bond' and that to claim 'Administrative Convenience' as the excuse for 'negating Dorset's Heritage' was no better than 'converting the National Galley into a shooting range simply because it happened to be convenient for Whitehall'. Rolf Gardiner would have been there, but for the fact that he was overseas receiving a gold medal in recognition of his work as an 'internationally famous Conservationist'.[18] So it fell to Derek Gregory to remind the committee of Gardiner's previously expressed thoughts on the dangers of 'remote control', and of the State's ever increasing 'encroachment' on the organic heartlands of the nation. But that was to be the end of Gardiner's fight for Tyneham. By the time a record of the Tyneham Action Group's submission to Nugent had been written up it included an expression of deep regret that Gardiner had died unexpectedly on 26 November.

Members of the Tyneham Action Group would later congratulate one another on the success of their presentation. But Rodney Legg, who addressed the committee in a purely personal capacity, had done what he could to undermine their case. Declaring himself 'the sole founder and instigator' of the group, he said the Group had done 'a great disservice' to the cause by limiting its redemptive ambitions to the Tyneham valley and thereby discriminating between the various rightful owners: 'TAG asks that Brigadier Mark Bond should go back to his family ruins at Tyneham House. But it does not argue the equal right of Mrs S. B. White [a former heath-cropping smallholder] to return to her humbler family ruin on the other side of the Purbeck Hills at Whiteway Farm.' The only sensible course was to free the entire Lulworth ranges as 'a single unit'.

Hollow Victory

> Tyneham exists for a different sort of visitor: the type of person who appreciates natural beauty and scenery; the type of person who views cafes, caravans and beach-huts with repulsion. We do not want to urbanise Tyneham.
>
> The 1943 Committee, *Blueprint for Tyneham*

By March 1972, the leaders of the Tyneham Action Group were no longer content with the fact that Legg had resigned from their executive committee. They had resolved by five votes to three that he and his fellow mutineers should be tossed out altogether. Having launched yet another rival organisation — this one named 'The 1943 Committee' and dedicated to an undisguisedly 'militant' course of action — Legg denounced the Tyneham Action Group's attempt to muzzle its founder as 'pathetic', writing to remind the secretary of the days before he was a 'lackey': 'I know you had a former

Nazi in your Vice Presidency,' he jeered, 'but the dictatorial weight of your pathetic demand makes me turn to the envelope for the Russian stamps.'[19]

Having broken with the 'Tyneham Inaction Group', Legg wasted no time gathering in its disaffected members — including Mavis Caver and Lord Fenner Brockway — and recruiting new ones through his *Dorset Magazine*. For a while, the car park in Tyneham proved exceptionally busy on public access days, while the rival campaigns battled for public attention. As Philip Draper reported to the Tyneham Action Group's treasurer in late May 1972: 'We had three very windy days at Tyneham which were made most uncomfortable by the unscrupulous behaviour of the 1943 hotheads . . .' By July, Draper's group had given up its pitch altogether.

The 1943 Committee combined their willingness to provoke trouble with a gift for publicity, which they used to fire insults across the traditionally walled spaces of the rural class structure. Yet even though committed to the public interest rather than the private and refeudalising idyll, they were still not blind to Tyneham's traditional charms. They took over the idea of Churchill's pledge, and they recognised the telephone box too, dubbing it the 'John Betjamanism' of the valley and taking parts of its iron top into 'protective custody' so that one day this 'much-loved vintage gem' could be 'restored to a free Tyneham'.[20] They also published a series of picture postcards, having 'crossed barbed wire' and 'risked death from unexploded shells around the village', to take the pictures that would spread 'pictorial evidence of Tyneham's plight all over the country'.

Having recruited Kenneth Allsop to their cause, the 1943 Committee staged a large 'Conservation Rally' in the Tyneham car park without Army permission. A month later, in September 1972, they mounted a 'sit-in' by the gate when the Ministry of Defence tried to see them off by proposing new bye-laws that would enable the Army to take trespassers into custody without warrant and also to confiscate their vehicles.[21] In June 1973, they attended General Mark Bond's Presidential address to the Dorset Natural History and Archaeological Society. The written plan for this piece of direct action asked members to rendez-vous in a Dorchester pub before joining the county audience to 'heckle and disrupt' Bond as he presented his 'feudal' vision of the Tyneham valley restored.

Legg's publicity-seeking 'freedom fighters' delighted in petty vandalism. They cut the wire around Tyneham churchyard, so that John Gould, their adopted former villager, could get through to plant four rose bushes where his grandparents lay. They scrawled 'Free Purbeck, Free Tyneham' over the

Army signs and daubed Army sentry boxes with unlikely slogans like 'Hand it over to the National Trust', using an unusually viscous, greenish-black paint acquired from the National Coal Board. They uprooted many of the Army's red warning signs, sinking them in old clay pits on the heath. So diligent were the 1943 Committee in this, that Legg was thanked by two young officers for guaranteeing the jobs of the civilians employed to produce replacements. The National Trust, meanwhile, was horrified.

The report of Lord Nugent's Defence Lands Committee, finally published in July 1973, turned out to be a pragmatic document, which spurned dramatic change for piecemeal improvement. It favoured tree-screening and such other scenic ameliorations as might be achieved with the help of landscape architects, and it thought the country might be improved if 'buffer zones' were placed between military installations and civilian populations in order to reduce 'environmental pollution by noise'.[22] But though it only recommended a modest reduction in Defence Lands over all, the Nugent Committee had succumbed to the romance of Tyneham, and come down on the side of those who had likened the Army's use of the Tyneham valley to 'playing football in the National Galley'. After surveying the options, the report recommended that the Lulworth gunnery school be moved to a firing range at Castlemartin in Wales, thus freeing not just the Tyneham valley, but the heath, Arish Mell Gap and Bindon Hill too.

Philip Draper was cautiously jubilant, telling the *Daily Telegraph* that 'a great battle has been won, but the struggle is not yet over'. Legg, who had jumped the gun by announcing victory six months previously, now rushed in to steal another march on the flagging Tyneham Action Group. It had been Draper's idea that, if Nugent recommended removal, his Group should reform itself as the 'Friends of Tyneham' to help General Bond with the agricultural restoration of the valley, but, on the very day of Nugent's publication, the 1943 Committee pre-empted them by launching their own 'Friends of Tyneham' to press for their opposed 'natural wilderness' scenario.

The Tyneham Action Group had never had any time for the argument that the Army had actually 'conserved' the Lulworth ranges as an 'accidental nature reserve'. The suggestion that the Army had actually been practising a benign form of neglect had seemed grotesque to Rolf Gardiner, for whom the bewildered ranges were evocative of nothing so much as the tumbled down agricultural landscape he remembered from the depression of the Twenties and Thirties. Draper now put the same line more vehemently, pronouncing that it was only 'vermin' that had ever thrived on the firing range.[23] Legg quickly replied that if Draper could refer to 'Tyneham's teeming wildlife in association with the word "vermin" ', then he should be taken on 'an educational tramp across the ranges by the Army's Lulworth game-keeper. He knows the roe deer, the badgers, buzzards, peregrine falcons, Dartford warblers and a multitude of common and rare animals and birds that have been sprayed and shot to the verge of extinction in civilian owned Dorset.'[24] Draper's claim, which was certainly mistaken, also drew a sharp response from a member of Poole Friends of the Earth who insisted, with the characteristic vehemence of that young organisation, that the real vermin was man: 'be he farmer, tourist operator or artillery commander'.[25]

The 1943 Committee knew that, over the years since 1943, a worse fate than tanks had overtaken much of the English countryside. By this time, the Lulworth ranges contained the largest surviving stretch of heathland in Dorset. The hedges may have wandered but the fields had never been ploughed or amalgamated; and no pesticides or herbicides had silenced the Tyneham valley's spring. The blasted downland had also fared better than privately owned stretches nearby, which had been ploughed up with government grants — including, as Ruth Colyer noted in a letter to *The Times*, the cliff-top downs of the Weld estate, where Llewelyn Powys used to encounter gipsies on the ancient Roman Road: 'Gone is the fragrant downland turf with its flowers and insect life, and walkers will face a solid crop of barley affording no sign of where the various paths were.'[26]

This state of affairs made nonsense of Draper's remarks about 'vermin', and was irreconcileable with the predominantly moral and aesthetic argument that had previously been used to champion the cause of both Bindon Hill and Tyneham. Indeed, the whole romantic idea of Tyneham, centred on the story of Churchill's betrayed pledge, was to be replaced by an environmentalist conception in which the Lulworth ranges were seen less as a fragment of old England brutally encroached upon by the modern state, than as, in the words of the 1943 Committee's 1972 *Blueprint for Tyneham*, 'a vast nature reserve' that was 'restocking much of civilian-held South-East Dorset with animals and birds'.

The Return of Crichel Down

Nugent's recommendation gave new urgency to the Crichel Down rule, which now loomed up as the main obstacle between the Friends of Tyneham and the realisation of their plans. The problem had been indicated on 12 July, a few days after the publication of the Nugent report, when Lord Fenner Brockway had stood up in the House of Lords to inform his fellow peers that he was 'in love with Tyneham', and to express the sincere hope that, despite the precedent of Crichel Down, the land would be transferred to the National Trust. He was answered by Lord Clifford of Chudleigh, who had attended a recent meeting organised by Brockway and heard 'a protégé of his' (presumably Rodney Legg) who was 'violently anti-agriculture and violently anti-private land owning'. He had bitterly resented these comments — especially since one of the landowners concerned was a relation of his and had recently been knighted for his services to Dorset (i.e. Colonel Sir Joseph Weld). For Lord Clifford, Crichel Down was another name for natural justice, and he hoped 'that on no account will it be permitted that land which belonged to local families for hundreds of years will be stolen to satisfy the political theories of fanatics'.[27]

Perhaps Clifford spoke for the Weld estate, but other landowners affected by Nugent's recommendation were a good deal more apprehensive about buying back their expropriated land at market valuation. A Dorchester estate agent estimated that the land could be worth up to £750 an acre, or as much as £50,000 an acre in the unlikely event of building permission being granted.[28] 'It would bankrupt me completely,' said the horrified septuagenarian Lieutenant-Colonel Ashley Bond of Creech Grange. After catching his breath, he looked over towards Baltington Farm and the eastern stretch of the Tyneham valley that had been his before 1943, and observed that 'Buildings have been allowed to fall down and the heart of the land itself has been let go to hell.' Asked how he would react if the land was offered directly to the National Trust, he replied 'I would have to give it very careful consideration.' His cousin, General Mark Bond, was also quoted as remarking 'I would very much hope I could come to some agreement with the National Trust.' So the Tyneham Action Group held meetings with the National Trust, hoping to win it over to their own vision of the agriculturally reinstated valley.

In the other liberationist camp, Legg and his Friends of Tyneham had first been alerted to the likely effects of the Crichel Down rule some months before in January 1973, when civil servants from the Department of the Environment stated that, should the Ministry of Defence decide to release the Lulworth ranges, the land would be offered back to the former owners 'in accordance with the Crichel Down rules', and that it would therefore not be likely that 'the opportunity would arise for the land to be transferred to the National Trust except by arrangement between the former owners and the Trust'. Informed of this, Legg had replied in 'a state of shock', appalled at the thought that 'the county families seem poised to snatch a victory from the backs of the conservation lobby'.

The sense of emergency was only increased when Fenner Brockway 'had a talk' with Lord Carrington on this subject and was told that 'under the law the site would have to return to the previous owners'.[29] That same month, Legg completed his journey across the political spectrum, expressing his worries in an article written for the communist *Morning Star.* John Gould, who had been the 1943 Committee's most picturesque villager, was photographed once again — presented not as a hobbit this time but as an unjustly transported working-class hero in the tradition of the Tolpuddle Martyrs. Identified as a 61-year-old Wareham roadsweeper, he was quoted as saying 'Tyneham is always in my thoughts. My home will always be there. If I could, I'd go back tomorrow. It's a wicked shame the pledge hasn't been kept.'[30] Unfortunately for Gould, as Legg told his communist readers, the Crichel Down rule only guaranteed the rights of landowners, and certainly not of mere tenants like Gould who 'may never see the honouring of that wartime pledge'.

Surveying the three large landowners who might acquire the firing range under the Crichel Down rule, Legg and his comrades realised that, given the limited restraining powers of the county planners, the removal of the Army might turn out to be a Phyrric victory after all. The trustees of the Weld estate, which had formerly owned Flowers Barrow as well as Bindon Hill and Arish Mell Gap, were certainly not lining up at the National Trust's door, and Legg was not impressed by their commitment to conservation. He had seen the caravans at the Weld estate's park at Durdle Door (in this part of Dorset the phrase 'serried ranks' is applied interchangeably to caravans and Forestry Commission conifers), and he feared that Tyneham and Arish Mell Gap could suffer the same kind of exploitation.

As for Lieutenant-Colonel Ashley Bond of Creech Grange, who had owned much of the heath and the west side of the Tyneham valley, he had sold his ball clay quarrying firm to English China Clays for £1.3 million in 1968, and it would hardly be in the commercial interests of that company — in which Colonel Bond was said to retain a financial interest — to leave the heath unbroken. The Attlee government may have been content with an arrangement whereby the material for the sinks, lavatories and bathtubs of the welfare state could still be quarried from the firing range, but Lord Fenner Brockway was horrified that the heath had been 'desecrated' by the ball clay quarriers.[31] Only a month before Nugent's report was published, he had asked Baroness Young, Under-Secretary of State for the Environment, 'whether she is aware of the almost mystical beauty of this Heath, described wonderfully by Thomas Hardy? May I further ask: if china clay were to be found under Westminster Abbey, would not we all oppose the suggestion that it should be blown up?'[32]

This dreamy stuff was not going to compel those who saw money in the heath. Legg had only to read the Nugent report, to find the Managing Director of English China Clays explaining that there was a 'great need' for ball clay from Dorset, and that his company would like a lease over the mineral rights of any area released. The market was growing, and the company, which had already quarried thirty acres on the range and was ready to expand its operations, felt severely constrained by the Army. Legg deplored the fact that Clement Attlee's claypit had already become 'the biggest hole in Dorset' — 'a quarter of a mile wide and seventy-five foot deep'. As he told a reporter, 'It threatens that there will be total destruction of the area by the end of the century.'[33]

General Mark Bond wasn't planning to dig up his inheritance and turn it into lavatories and washbasins, but Legg and his friends had no difficulty imagining him as an agriculturalist of the most destructive kind. Not content with referring to the thriving wildlife of the Tyneham valley as 'vermin' in his Presidential address to the Dorset Natural History and Archaeological Society, Bond had refused to banish bulldozers from the area and, so these hostile witnesses claimed, announced his intention of building 'modernistic breeze-block and asbestos farm buildings'. His advocacy of cattle and sheep was actually quite reconcileable with their insistence that grazing alone would be tolerable, but Legg and his Friends of Tyneham still converted Bond into an unsparing advocate of intensive agriculture, who would have ploughed every remaining trace of history out of the Tyneham landscape if there was money to made by so doing.

Their suspicions were only strengthened when Lord Fenner Brockway met General Bond on 27 May 1973 to discuss the chances of the National Trust being given the land without payment. He was alarmed to gather that Bond intended to oversee the restoration from his present home at Moigne Combe — as what Legg would later call a 'middleman landlord steward', and an absentee one at that. As Brockway concluded, 'I hadn't any doubt that his main aim was to make profit.' This ungenerous interpretation was enough for Legg, who quoted the words of a neighbouring farmer who, not content with repeating the canard that it was only 'vermin' that thrived in the militarised Tyneham valley, had told a reporter that the agricultural reclamation of the Tyneham valley could only be achieved by 'a man of steely character and steely sinews'. With extractors like that just waiting to move in with their machines and pesticides, the Tyneham valley's historic fields stood to be converted into another featureless grain-prairie. As one Friend of Tyneham said, 'Tyneham could easily become the factory floor for intensive farming methods.'

This was certainly a travesty of General Bond's intentions, but the Friends of Tyneham were justified in wondering what the future held for their 'accidental Eden'. Thanks to the Crichel Down rule, as Allsop wrote for the *Observer*, things did not look good for the 'strange enfiladed Arcadia', so long sealed off behind the wire of Britain's 'domestic Iron Curtain'. Allsop regretted the lack of the 'centralist idealism' that prevented the British state from abandoning the Crichel Down rule. Six weeks before the Nugent report was published in early July 1973, Legg had already come round to the view held by the Nature Conservancy and also Roger Peers, the curator of the Dorset Natural History and Archaeological Society. He informed Kenneth Allsop that 'the situation is a shambles. If there is going to be a share-out among the big landowners, the campaigners who have fought for the rights of the dispossessed and to safeguard this unique wildlife reserve will have been taken for ride. It would be better left in the Army's hands than degraded for day trippers and the factory farmer.'[34] He made the same comment when Nugent's recommendation was officially published: 'Unless the National Trust gets the land it would be a hollow victory, and even worse than Army occupation.'[35] Tanks, once again, were better than the available alternatives.

Allsop killed himself three days after the publication of that article. Perhaps there was no connection. Yet there were many suicides among Tyneham's admirers and liberationists — not just John Gale and Kenneth Allsop, but also Monica Hutchings, who swam into the sea off the Mull of Kintyre in 1977, and her fellow animal rights campaigner Mavis Caver, who took her leave on 1 January 1978, and whose ashes were scattered in Tyneham churchyard by former comrades on the 1943 Committee. Discrete as these deaths were, they still shape the memory of the Tyneham campaign for a survivor like Rodney Legg. Suicide hangs over the whole story as the shadowy attendant of passionate idealism. It testifies not just to the oddity of the Tyneham cause — which some veterans now admit — but to the fleeting quality of individual endeavour when pitted against the permanence of government and state: stout-hearted people come and go, but metal endures.

NINETEEN

THEY CAME IN THROUGH THE BATHROOM WINDOW: REFOUNDING BRITISH ARCHITECTURE IN THE TYNEHAM GAP

> If you look to your left, ladies and gentlemen, the view is not very inspiring. Ah, but if you look to your right . . .
>
> courier in The Beatles' Magical Mystery Tour, 1967

EARLY IN 1974, shortly after the Nugent Committee had recommended the release of the Lulworth ranges, a small party set off from the Architectural Association in London's Bedford Square. There were two vehicles, one of them a Land-rover, and a patchily remembered collection of final year diploma students. Fred Scott, the tutor who initiated this expedition, has not forgotten pugnacious, street-talking Lola from London via Los Angeles. In an unexpected fit of piety she had once plastered the walls of that famously avant-garde institute with posters of the child guru Mahara Ji, and when he teased her about this, she took her revenge by breaking into his lectures — rambling period slide-shows with, as Scott now volunteers with retrospective severity, 'no content whatsoever' — to condemn him for talking 'absolute crap'. There was a mad Pole too, a beret-wearing fellow named Adam who probably went off to become a gardener; and a leaping hound that has proved more memorable than its owner — a 'hippy' who has since evaporated into the mists of time.

The distance from London was greater in those pre-motorway days, but the Land-rover travelled at terrible speed through a country beset by larger problems than traffic congestion. As Scott remembers, the whole social order seemed on the point of collapse. The three-day week was still at hand: imposed by a sinking Edward Heath in December 1973 in an attempt to conserve coal supplies during the miners' strike; and the gloom was hardly lifted when the junior energy minister urged the British people to save energy by cleaning their teeth in the dark.[1]

We may reasonably imagine an intermittent stream of cannabis smoke escaping from the back, and the sound of music too — Miles Davis, perhaps, or the never less than fading airs of the Incredible String Band.

There may have been a few books on board, selected from Fred Scott's gloriously jumbled reading list: William Cobbett's *Cottage Economy*, Kropotkin's *Fields, Factories, and Workshops*, Lilian Bond's *Tyneham: A Lost Heritage*. The Nugent report would have seemed unbearably bureaucratic, but somebody may well have chosen Richard Mabey's *Food for Free*, John Michell's *The View Over Atlantis* or Alfred Watkin's book on leylines. As Fred Scott once wrote, the most marked differences between the Architectural Association and other schools of architecture at that time were 'its size, its minimal administration, and its reliance on myths'.

The hoteliers of Swanage are broadminded in a strategic kind of way: able to smile at almost anyone as they count the money into their tills. But the man who opened his door to the members of this architectural excursion was expecting something very different. Not content with cleaning up his guests and cladding them in tweeds, he had solemnly married them off to each other and then assigned them to rooms equipped only with double beds. Dismayed by the tatterdemalions now drifting in, he tried to revise the sleeping plan with the help of a wild-eyed Fred Scott, breaking off in bewildered frustration to ask if there was another teacher in the party. At that moment 'Professor' Warren Chalk strode up to the bar along his own already chosen road to ruin and demanded 'a large Scotch and a large Scotch', both plainly intended for his own immediate consumption.

Warren Chalk might have reassured that hotelier a little by pointing out that the Architectural Association had included a number of eminent defenders of Dorset in its membership, including Sir Clough Williams Ellis and even Thomas Hardy, who had, regrettably, been struck off in 1872 for not paying his subscription. Chalk might even have been able to cast new light on this problem of rooms, beds and the associated questions of use and propriety. He was after all, a founding member of Archegram, the avant-garde group that had spent the Sixties working to detach architecture from 'the decaying Bauhaus image which is an insult to functionalism'. Archegram never directly addressed the problem of the double bed, but its members had carried out a thorough-going demolition job on the idea of the single-purpose room.

There were limits, however, even in Swanage, the capital of Paul Nash's 'seaside surrealism', and Chalk's conception of architecture would have seemed no less disconcerting than his personal demeanour. It is a singular kind of architect who gets up to call, as Archegram had done, for a moratorium on buildings. And Chalk had gone further, arguing what while art, architecture and design may have no 'relevant role in society' there could at least be no doubt that 'leaping about stimulates hide-bound mentalities'.[2] Not content with condemning conventional architecture as a 'fantasy world brought about through a desire to locate, absorb and integrate into an overall obsession a set interpretation of the everyday world around us', he had done his best to replace it with a theory of 'ghosts'. It was, he thought, becoming 'increasingly apparent that due to historical circumstances the most tangible ghosts of the past — those grim, humourless, static, literary or visual images — will succumb to the onslaught of the invisible media, the psychedelic vision, the insight accompanying a joke; the phantoms of the future'.

With housing reduced to the level of 'a consumer product', Chalk had long since declared it time to find new inspiration in unusual places. Science-fiction provided him with 'prophetic information regarding geodesic nets, pneumatic tubes and plastic domes and bubbles'; and he had been quick to hail Pop music as another rich source. Its success, so he wrote in the early Sixties, was largely due to audience participation: the musicians were close to their audience in dress and habits; and the dances — Chalk singled out 'the Frug' and 'the Jerk' for special commendation — were 'self-expressive and free-forming'. Later he had sung the praises of Woodstock nation ('a field turned into a three day city, half a million young people; the only hardware, mindblowing amplification. Beautiful'), and proclaimed, with a nod towards the Whole Earth Catalogue, that 'Our very survival depends on an ecological utopia.'

Chalk may have harboured a romantic aspiration for harmony with nature, but he also admired the high-tech architecture of the space-rocket launchers he and other members of Archegram had admired on a visit to NASA headquarters in the United States. While tower blocks went up all over the country, these anti-architects preferred to sing the praises of Mappin Terrace, built for the bears at London Zoo, and to dream about 'Gasket homes', underwater cities and 'Plug-in Capsule Homes' that might redeem the idea of 'mass-produced expendable component dwellings'. They favoured pods, mounds, clusters and even mole-hills ('a natural environment "heap," with perhaps biological and psychological overtones as well'). They modelled new combinations of ecology and technology as 'part of a strategy for the hinterlands of the new Foulness Airport': Crater City was to be a deep circular hole in the ground, with hundreds of floors sunk down into its perimeter to produce an inward-looking structure shaped like the rim of a wheel; Hedgerow Housing consisted of submerged strip villages, each one a 'relaxed and ramshackle' combination of architect designed houses, sleeping bags and tents sunk into vast trenches along the edge of fields so as to become 'imperceptible from a country lane'. And now, here was Chalk in Purbeck, accompanying a field trip that had come down with the purpose of refounding the fallen discipline of architecture in a much fabled and hypothetical hollow that lay somewhere between vision and pragmatic reality; between the military State and its civilian redemption; between a broken past and a crackpot future that would never quite arrive to redeem it.

Electric Aborigines in Tyneham Valley

The Architectural Association's project was entitled 'Utopian Village'. In part, as Fred Scott recalls, it was prompted by the *Blueprint for Survival*, an influential call to action, published as a special issue of Edward Goldsmith's *Ecologist* magazine in 1972. But its location was the Tyneham valley: nationally famous thanks to the bickering action groups, and full of unregimented future potentiality now that the Defence Lands Committee had recommended its release. So, in January 1974, final year students in the Diploma School had begun work on a two-term project designed to establish 'possible uses of the Wareham and Bovington Army Ranges'. The project opened with a series of lectures presented by course tutors and a collection of visitors: Rodney Legg was given pride of place as 'organiser' of the 'Save Tyneham' campaign, and Roger Peers of the Dorset County Museum also came up to talk about the archaeology. A man from the Department of the Environment lectured about 'philosophies of the countryside' and the architect Cedric Price was booked to expound the virtues of 'non-planning'.[3]

The Architectural Association was not much given to mourning the traditional England lost at Tyneham. The introductory course dossier, which testifies to a greater level of organisation than Scott remembers, may have been ornamented by the trespassing postcards issued by the 1943 Committee, but Scott encouraged his students to approach the Tyneham valley not through the exhausted myth of Churchill's pledge, but by way of Breughel's *Fall of Icarus*. He reproduced that marvellous painting, in which a man tills the earth while the mythological disaster occurs unnoticed high up in the distant sky, captioning it with a quotation from Alan Watts's New Age classic, *Nature, Man and Woman*: 'Sometimes, it catches us right below the heart with an ache of nostalgia and delight compounded when it seems that this is, after all, the world of sane, enduring reality from which we are somehow in exile.'

Scott's 'Modest Manifesto' focussed on the 'current massive schism' between the rural 'visions' pervading British culture and actual 'rural practices'. This was attributed partly to the 'new farming technologies', but much more fundamentally to the eighteenth-century enclosure acts and to the 'Arcadian' landscaping practices 'made possible by the countryside being cleared of its people'. Like pre-war critics of the picturesque, Scott reckoned that

> Current popular myths of nature, although overlaid and degraded by a heavy Victorian romanticism, still stem from this period. Their potency can be seen in the popularity of debased Arcadian themes in advertising . . . The vision of Laura Ashley bedecked girls in a picturesque high summer setting could hardly be more remote than the realities of 'rationalised' food production, factory farming, the poverty of rural workers, and their decreasing numbers, and the flow of capital into the land as our industrial future becomes less certain.

The situation was still deteriorating. The rural population continued to decrease, and there would surely be a further concentration of land ownership among interests concerned only with profit. Meanwhile, 'the mass of people would be increasingly squeezed between two environments apparently unsuited for living in'. Survival in 'the central urban areas' would become increasingly untenable, while the countryside would be preserved in the name of 'a myopic picture post-card consciousness', which refused to countenance the idea of population increase, neglected the dwindling indigenous population and assumed that the most appropriate use for these areas was 'as settings for second homes'. The students were invited to explore the 'counter proposition' that, in the Tyneham valley at least, it might be possible to demonstrate that 'a form of rural resurgency is possible, that the countryside should be reoccupied, that it can become a support and a setting for everyday life'. It was time for 'putting figures back into the landscape'.

The students were to explore the 'privilege' that architectural activity can 'bestow upon a habitat'. They were to consider the differences between the country and the city and, 'perhaps in the spirit of Marxist ideas, to

21 Tyncham House 'taken over by trees', *Illustrated*, 13 September 1952

22 The Taylor sisters revisiting Tyneham, August 1952, *Illustrated*, 13 September 1952

23 Major-General Mark Bond, walking in the Tyneham valley, 1968

24 Rodney Legg in the ruins of Tyneham House, 1972

25 Philip Draper with red cross placed near Tyneham House to mark the broken promise, May 1968

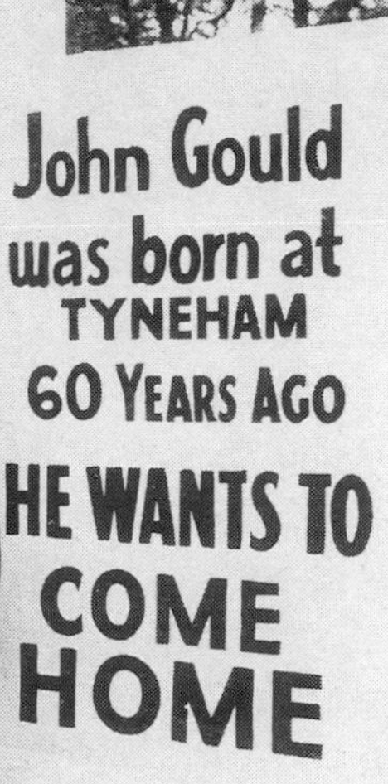

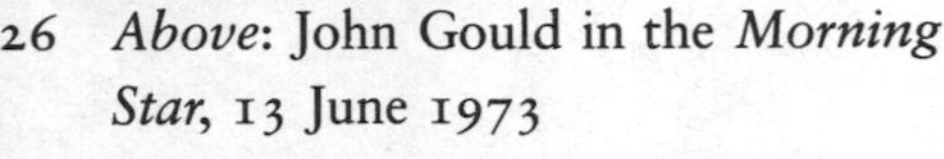

26 *Above*: John Gould in the *Morning Star*, 13 June 1973

27 *Top right*: Monica Hutchings, 1968

28 *Right*: Helen Taylor, 1989

29 *Below*: Peter Wilson and Jeanne Sillett, 'Dorset Monuments', 1975

FORTIFIED HEADQUARTERS OF THE SPECIAL BRANCH OF POPULAR HARASSMENT
CEMETERY OF HIERARCHICAL SOCIAL ORDER
CHAMBER OF JUDGEMENT (SANCTUARY OF MORALS)
ARCH OF PROFESSIONALISM
TEMPLE OF CONSUMERISM
MUSEUM OF CONVENIENTLY CLASSIFIED CULTURE

30 In the 'Sacred Wood', South Egliston, 1993

overcome the contradiction between them'. It was hypothesised not just that the Army was out, but that the Bonds were gone too — taking the whole deeply sedimented nature of feudalism with them. The entire range area had been nationalised and the intention was that it should be repopulated at a density of 860 people per square mile, to accommodate about twelve thousand people. Students were asked to find an alternative to the existing 'new town formula', contriving a low density settlement that could be sustained without a large urban area nearby. The Tyneham valley was to be like the biosphere (a special 'Biosphere' edition of *Scientific American* was on the reading list), and every aspect should be considered: forms of government and management, systems of education, healthcare and transport, agriculture and the distribution of a population that should surely not just be settled according to the cottage utopia of 'one man per acre'. Hovercrafts and cable cars might be introduced, since roads presumed 'some form of centralisation', and there would presumably also be plenty of walking if students were really to bring off the transformation envisioned by Warren Chalk: 'A no-man's land becomes a nomads' land.'

Recent AA graduate Will Alsop suggested that students might consider themselves to have been commissioned by the government to build a new town capable of protecting its population during a Third World War. Most civil defence was all about defending the ruling elite and its government and protecting it against revolution. Orthodox planning models had failed dismally, but one based on Civil Defence might just, so Alsop hoped, 'produce an alternative that is preferable to the results of careful studies of the needs of the people'.

Warren Chalk contributed a page of spaced-out epigrams. For him Dorset was 'SEA, SHINGLE, SAND, CLIFF FACE, LAND CONTOURS, GRASS, HEATH AND THE MEANING OF TREES'. As they traipsed into the soon to be liberated Tyneham valley students should open themselves to 'VISUAL CLUES', which might present themselves 'AS IN A DREAM', approaching their long forbidden destination in the awareness that 'THERE IS A WHOLE AREA OF LOST DISCOVERIES AND FORGOTTEN LIFESTYLES, THE ENTIRE NATURAL WORLD ATTEMPTING TO REGAIN RECOGNITION.' They should recognise that 'THERE IS NO LEGITIMATE PLAN, ONLY A PERSONAL SPECIAL EARTH/HOME UNDERSTANDING THAT DOES NOT EXCLUDE EXCELLENCE AND WIT.' Beyond this there was the usual list of options: 'INDIGENOUS COTTAGES, REINFORCED COTTAGES, THE AUTONOMY OF GROUNDED SPACE CAPSULES, UNDERGROUND LIVING, SEA FARMING, PEOPLE'S PARK, DUDE RANCH,

DISNEY WORLD, STONE/WOOD HENGE, A FOLLY IN A FOREST, A LINEAR SETTLEMENT, A HIGHLY SERVICED LAND PIER, THE ARK ROYAL, A RESERVOIR, A TECHNOLOGICAL MATRIX . . .'

Scott also turned to David Greene, the erstwhile poet of Archegram who had long since declared it obvious that 'the idea of rooms for specific purposes is not viable any more'. The Living Pod was altogether more promising — a plug-in urban structure that might bring an element of nomadism into the settled idea of home, the principle of 'breakaway and regroup' would replace strict hierarchy in the organisation of cities. There would be 'hybrid assemblies' and 'villages' that were both 'instant' and 'invisible', composed entirely of momentary interconnections. A resident of West Lulworth, Green had already used the southern parts of Dorset to explore his idea of a 'moment village' made up not of crumbling and officially vandalised old buildings of the sort that would draw so much melancholic attention at Tyneham, but of the 'instant' relationships 'created by any communal act'. Indeed, in an earlier project described in the 'Gardener's Notebook' he wrote for Archegram, he had adopted the area of land lying between the B3351 and Poole Harbour — which included the now demilitarised village of Arne — taking it 'beyond structure' to produce a 'Cybernetic Forest' and, within that, a 'Bottery', defined as an experiment with 'the temporary placing of bits of hardware in the natural scene'. The 'Bot' may have been 'a machine transient in the landscape', but it was altogether more sophisticated than the Army's trundling tanks. Greene's idea was to go beyond 'the Cowboy international nomad-hero' who carried his environment with him as saddle, bedroll, matches and horse. As a 'robot-serviced landscape' the Bottery enabled the environment to be 'called up wherever you are'. As 'Cybernetic Forest' and home to 'the Electric Aborigine', it offered a way of 'doing your own thing without disturbing the events of the existing scene'.

It would be convenient to imagine Warren Chalk gazing out over Worbarrow Bay and muttering, 'We seem to have found the art of suspended time. What we must look for now is the linkage of the simultaneous and not the vista of the successive.' But in fact the first visit to the Tyneham area was not very revealing at all. Fred Scott remembers stumbling about in a dense sea-mist of the sort that Herbert Weld Blundell once hoped would keep the Army from entrenching their hold on his Lulworth acres. He then goes on to describe the project as 'a failure on a heroic scale'.

The student drawings preserved in the Architectural Association's slide library give a fair impression of what he means. They also reveal how little the Architectural Association's students were touched by the posthumous cult of Tyneham, which measured out the valley with diverse fables of encroachment in which metal was set off against turf. A host of 'foliage shelters', covered lanes and hedge bridges or arches were offered by students who seem to have imagined architecture as a kind of topiary, and Tyneham as a rampant wilderness of greenery waiting to be cut into shape. There were glass houses and geodesic-looking structures, primitive huts that seem to be lost in the jungle of a reverted garden centre, and 'reinforced streams' that might have been borrowed from the junk yard in Richard Brautigan's *Trout Fishing in America*, which sells stacked up lengths of trout-stream by the yard. One drawing shows a warehouse door, almost obscured from view by heaped tins of alligator steak, and designed to look like 'a somewhat stylised Pudental cleft' with the words 'Venite, Videte' cut into the stone above this opening — meaning 'Come! See!', as a helpful note explains, and derived from 'Caesar's famous quote'. Another scheme sought to repopulate the range with a 'Zodiac Community', consisting of twelve circular 'Astro-Units', each one based on an astrological sign and equipped with twelve houses. As the legend explained, the circular form denoted 'the wholeness of harmonious unity, the centring of psyche with cosmos, the resolution of opposites, beyond time and space, the source of all creativity and power, the cycles of earth and universe'. The Astro-Units were to be placed according to 'planetary symbolism': so the one called Leo, for example, would be on the hilltop nearest the rising sun, and landscaped with sunflowers, daffodils, marigolds and walnut.

Melanie Richardson got further into the charismatic valley than that particular Fool on a Hill. She had come down on Fred Scott's initial trip and later returned for another visit: she remembers trespassing in the valley to photograph the village and feeling grateful when the Army, which came along to evict her, obligingly drove her back up the hill. Her drawings, which are branded with a little tank that has an emblematic post-Prague '68 flower protruding from its barrel, show large artificial lakes on the site of Heath Range, and more extensive woodlands than would have occurred even to the Forestry Commission. Her layout for a renewed Tyneham village seems conventional enough with its reinstated duck pond, village green and the burned-out rectory restored as a town hall. Yet her Terraced House Elevation shows Tyneham's Post Office Row, 'merging with the country'. The enfolding turf creeps up until the house becomes a swollen and earthy mound with stone chimneys protruding above grassy windows and a symbolic sheep grazing on the roof. She designed this 'Mole House', in which Archegram seems to merge with Middle Earth, partly, as she now recalls, to demonstrate that a town or village 'needn't necessarily be extended in the absolute vernacular', and partly because she had looked at the mossy holes and finger-like roots of old trees in the Tyneham valley and imagined living, vole-like, among them. As she remarks, breaking off with the self-deprecating laugh to which everyone is entitled when looking back at their own student work, 'we were all into flower power then'.

Richardson had read Tolkien only a few years before she joined that first expedition to Dorset. She was probably also influenced by lectures presented the previous year by Keith Critchlow, since appointed director of studies at Prince Charles's Institute of Architecture, but at that time more concerned with the New Age iconography of leylines, land zodiacs, Avalon and the mythical signatures of ancient Britain. But though she remembers imagining the folds of the Tyneham valley as tumuli with ancient and mythical kings buried beneath their turf, her drawings are not merely the doodlings of another pixified hippy. She had grown up in Kingston, Jamaica, and walking through the verdant 'dream-world' of Tyneham, she felt she had walked into the pastoral image of England that had been so vividly projected into her Jamaican schoolroom. She remembers the primroses, the folded turf beside the road down to Tyneham village, and the rabbits — each one a flopsified tribute to Beatrix Potter. The place was intensely present and yet 'utterly unreal' — a concentrated 'land of English fictions'.

The Story of a Promised Future

The most memorable work to emerge from the Dorset Programme came a little later. Jeanne Sillett and Peter Wilson weren't students on Fred Scott's unit, but there was a lot of 'milling about' in those days, and they borrowed the Dorset location for their own purposes. As Sillett recalls, the country was at that time still reeling from the tower-block fiasco, and the Architectural Association was very anti-building. The challenge that she and Wilson set themselves was to overcome the prevailing idea that all architecture was 'wicked'. They dedicated their Dorset Project to the belief that 'Reality depends upon perception. Thus if we begin with Duchamp's observation that "There is no solution because there is no problem" perhaps one might be justified in attempting to establish one's own relationship with reality by avoiding the given cultural language, and instead probing the cracks between defined areas of experience.'[4]

Their 'houses' were playful and novelistic inventions that would never make it into the Barratt's Premier Collection. The 'Birdman's House' or the 'House for a Kite Flier' began not with bricks and mortar but with 'feelings that cannot be rationalised. Perhaps the desire to fly, or the experience of being glued to the surface of the earth by the force of gravity . . .' When they entered a competition for 'A House for a Superstar', it was with 'A House for any Fred Astaire'. Designed to accommodate 'an image more than a person', this ideal home was full of sky and included a grass amphitheatre, a restaurant, a cinema screen and a bandstand. The public moved through the house to enjoy these amenities; and there were other features too: a private catwalk leading to a library, a stone armchair with a view out over the sea, a billiard room, a place to sunbathe and from which to fly kites.

Sillett and Wilson made their first trip to Dorset with Nigel Coates and Jenny Lowe: driving down in a Deux Chevaux and staying in a freezing bed and breakfast establishment in Worth Matravers — well-known to Nigel Coates, whose father had been stationed at the radar station there during the war. Coates remembers their initiative as being in opposition to Archegram, which belonged to the generation before. They were intent on rediscovering 'the central experience, even the essence' of architecture. Having already visited Avebury to consider how marking the landscape inferred certain ceremonial dimensions, they chose to continue their quest in Purbeck because it was 'the nearest piece of ancient landscape to London'. They struck out along great dry stone walls said to have been built by French prisoners during the Napoleonic wars, and then down to Dancing Ledge, an old cliff-top sea quarry since colonised by outward bounders. It was on this terrain, which Coates describes as an 'ancient landscape with a cultural archaeology that was almost invisible and yet massive at the same time', that they set out to rediscover 'the symbolic dimensions of architecture'.

These young architectural excursionists — and they were, as they stress, very young at the time — came with a 'useful box' of equipment, including a pot of lawn whitener and some reels of shimmering coloured tape, with which they proceeded to mark the landscape. Peter Wilson still has a sequence of photographs showing the reinauguration of architecture they carried out here. In the first, a hexagonal brick-faced box materialises in a stonewalled field somewhere up above Dancing Ledge.[5] A cross is then pegged out, marking what Wilson describes as 'the architects' first move: division, measurement, orientation'. Each architect then constructs a 'domestic tableau', using coloured tape and assorted objects chosen from the useful box. As Wilson observes, Jeanne Sillett's 'green and white suite' survives to this day with 'a certain dignity': its perimeter, outlined in white chalk, encloses a small hummock with an alarm clock on top of it, and a larger rectangle of synthetic astroturf laid over the downland grass nearby. Wilson used a lot of red markers on thin yellow stalks and a blue-cushioned chair to create a beach-like 'placement for view'. Jenny Lowe produced an 'elementary earthworks', a somewhat shamanistic meditation upon the architect's initial gesture of breaking into the soil: a square pit of exposed earth, a line of limestone rocks extending through a mound of excavated soil, and the whole thing strung together along an intermittent white line. Nigel Coates made the most of an upright vacuum cleaner, a cardboard housewife and an upturned milk-crate.

The members of this experimental band went their separate directions after this ceremonial collaboration. In the early Eighties Nigel Coates would draw 'a House for Derek Jarman', built into the quarry engine house at Dancing Ledge (the bedroom is a cave and the house is fitted with 'tourist traps', which sling curious imposters over the cliff edge).[6] But Sillett and Wilson went on to adopt the Lulworth tank ranges as the site for their own allegorical story of ruin and abandonment.

Their 'intervention' took the form of a series of paintings accompanied by a brief written narrative. They show a strange collection of buildings imposed upon the firing range. There are sombre fortified walls on the ground and stone lions recumbent against the sky. An immense electric hair-dryer crowns a hill. There are vast glass cubes, broken temples, and a monumental avenue, which leads up to a vast, fractured triumphal arch made up of different styles. Sillett remembers how she and Wilson would pass drawings back and forth, 'escalating ideas' and deriving passages of text in a manner that resembled the Surrealist practice of automatic writing: 'We were going to live in the future now . . . ' Wilson looks back on it as a 'mythological' endeavour and, with a self-deprecating laugh, a 'post-Sixties meditation on the state of the twentieth century'.

At that time he was much interested in the 'questioning of urban values' that had been carried out by so-called 'visionary architects' of revolutionary

France: Boullée, Ledoux and Lequeue. These architects of the 1790s drew buildings of colossal scale, and sheer geometrical simplicity, as they set out to immortalise the Revolution and celebrate the new order. Their search for what Wilson calls 'an architecture that speaks' — a member of an art jury at the height of the Revolution declared that 'Grand monuments should make great impressions . . . the walls should speak; maxims should turn our buildings into moral textbooks'[7] — led them to experiment with monumental forms, and to combine an austere classical language with masonic symbolism. Some of these dreams were realised by the revolutionary planners, but many only ever existed as visionary drawings showing symbolic mountains, vast triumphal arches and houses conceived as cylinders with rivers running through them.

Sillett and Wilson also set out to 'demystify' and dramatise the limits of accepted cultural attitudes by 'monumentalising' them. The accompanying narrative told the 'story of a promised future' that had been partly realised and then abandoned to remain only as fragments. It opened with a monumental phase called 'Celebration' in which the prevailing powers, sensing 'a lack of confidence, both moral and financial, in industrial capitalism', decide to establish a model settlement that would celebrate 'contemporary establishment ideology' and generate 'a new attitude of enthusiasm and investment'.[8] The Lulworth ranges are adopted as the site of this exemplary endeavour, and the Army retreats to 'a secluded area' so that work may begin in secret. The ground is cleared of explosives, and the 'heroic monumentalism' of the initial triumphal arch is repeated in other expositions. News of the project leaks out, attracting a consortium of capitalists and entrepreneurs who sense 'incredible profit' and start building a 'pata-supermarket' which expresses their 'goals and values in monumental terms'. People start visiting — prospective inhabitants together with industrialists, investors, speculators, priests and the Press — but suddenly the scheme backfires. Indeed, it turns out that 'in expressing totally through the monuments their real aspirations, the capitalist beneficiaries undermine the mystification which has guaranteed their existence for so long'. So the site is abandoned 'almost in an instant' and the rational proposal never completed.

As 'the great disillusionment' sets in, the whole site takes on new meaning: incomplete, speculative and fabulous. The various decaying monuments become the 'sacred reminders of the folly of the old days', but they also initiate a whole set of subsequent myths and parallels. People filter back gradually, but 'the landscape above the horizon remains forever the manifestation of a rejected culture and the territory of the myth'. The new inhabitants live in the ruins of the old order, interpreting the monuments in a way that 'preserves a critical perception of the past'. The various monuments are described by Sillett and Wilson.

The Cemetery of Hierarchical Social Order
The graveyard is completely uniform, being laid out with identical headstones, each bearing the inscription 'Herein Lies Working Class Repression Liberated in Death'. In the middle is a grass-covered earthwork through which the Staircase of Bourgeois Aspirations ascends around the Mausoleum of Universal Middleclassness. At the four axial points on the ziggurat, the view is framed by a stone arch. The view is of the Sarcophagus of Entrepreneurs and Retired Decadents (an Elitist Club in the Empire Style) towards which the staircase progresses. However the top of the staircase is ruined, preventing admission to the Elitist Club.

The Triumphal Arch of Professionalism
Built on what was previously one of the main access routes according to the Rational Proposal, but now isolated since the Proposal was not carried out. The Arch is structurally unsound since an irreparable crack exists in the keystone.

The Museum of Conveniently Classified Culture
Situated at the north end of the monumental avenue from the Sanctuary of Applied Morals, it is a sunken paved square approached by a flight of stairs. A fully computerised Culture Classifier in the centre of the square gives access to the art objects which are filed according to the establishment classification. Ultimately, the visitor's response could become fully conditioned, making it unnecessary to indulge in a personal subjective experience. Beyond the Museum Square, a Transmission Tower for Legalised Brainwashing, resembling the Statue of Liberty, stands half-hidden in the wood.

The Sanctuary of Applied Morals
The Sanctuary is dominated by the Chamber of Judgement. It is in a heroic modern style but seems strangely commonplace. Below the Chamber of Judgement, on a ledge cut into the side of the hill, is a ruined Chapel of Christian Virtues. The ancient Chapel was moved to the site to add historical respectability. Towards the bottom of the slope below the Chapel an Amphitheatre is cut into the hillside. The

steps of the Amphitheatre are lined with sculptural hedges painstakingly trimmed into the shape of confessionals.

The Temple of Consumerism
Blocking and ruining the monumental avenue from the Museum of Conveniently Classified Culture to the Sanctuary of Applied Morals, its placement at the centre of the site expresses the obsessional profiteering of its builders. On top of a conical flat-topped hill, its delicate ring of classical temple columns in 'plastic marble' houses an exotic holographic display of consumer products. These desirable but ironically intangible objects have, since Disillusionment, been reduced to one pathetic holographic electric carving knife, faithfully preserved by the Temple's only occupant, a hermit caretaker, existing in his private, loyal, pre-Disillusionment mentality. The central Rotunda of Profit and Gain encloses a glass cube which contains a pyramid of gold ingots, and is surrounded by waterlilies.

The Fortified Headquarters of the Special Branch of Popular Harassment
Built by the Army to house their activities and equipment, and later taken over by various unnamed investigation and law enforcement agencies. The isolation is reinforced since the adjoining land had not been cleared of unexploded mines, and only the occupants could safely trace out known routes using the patterns of the coloured lichens as a guide. The Fortress seemed to be surrounded by star-shaped bastillions, but perhaps this was an illusion created by the red heather peculiar to that place. Casual observers occasionally referred to a red glow emanating from the structure, and two identical observation and signalling towers on the coast have never been satisfactorily explained. One theory that the Fortress and the Chamber of Judgement lie on a perfect conceptual arc also aligning the two observation towers is still being hotly debated, but if true might prove that there was some sort of mystified relationship between the Moral Bureaucracy and the Law Enforcement Agencies.

Sillett remembers this Dorset project as being 'satirical from necessity rather than wilful desire': it was a 'rite of passage' which she and Wilson undertook in the hope of reaching 'the point where you could be an architect comfortably, and without feeling that you were merely an instrument of the status quo'. So they moved through the allegory they had projected on to the Royal Armoured Corps' firing range, and went on to break soil elsewhere: Sillett as architect to community organisations in places like

Brixton and Hackney, and Peter Wilson as an internationally regarded architect now based in Germany. Their 'Story of a Promised Future' is a commentary on the trials of an architecture trapped in the broken achievements of its own modern history; but it can hardly be recovered twenty years later without reverberating through the flattened canyons of post-modern thought, which finds itself after history, after the reforming state, after the plan.

The memory of the Architectural Association's project still lingers at the back of some Dorset minds. Roger Peers, who was then curator of the Dorset County Museum, remembers leaving his Tyneham-panelled office and going up to the Architectural Association to deliver his lecture to Fred Scott's final year diploma students. He found the group 'very laid back, arrogant and interesting'. The Architectural Association impressed him as an 'exciting' and energetic place — 'sort of disorganised and marvellously scruffy' in comparison with the smooth professionalism of the Royal Institute of British Architects over in Great Portland Street. He recommended that the students might consider including a centre for the interpretation of Tyneham and its landscape. Peers sensed that the practicalities of archaeology and conservation were not taken at all seriously and, indeed, that the vulnerability of the range area was hardly on the agenda. Jeanne Sillett confirms: 'We didn't really have any interest in that site at all — except to tell a more general story.' She and Wilson felt no compunction about bulldozing the entire heath to clear explosives, levelling hills and tumuli and then covering the whole site with concentric green rings that radiate out from the Temple of Consumerism — as if Flowers Barrow had suddenly expanded to engulf the entire range. It was enough for Sillett that this spiral signified a 'different principle of organisation'. Roger Peers remembers hearing of one student's plan to cut a canal through the heath and resolving that, though this was doubtless no more than flippant fantasy, he would 'lay down the law very firmly indeed'. So he came up with another strongly-worded cautionary notice, announcing that the archaeology of the range was both 'extremely valuable and very delicate', and not to be disturbed at any cost.

As Rodney Legg recalls, people were talking about canals because the Soviet Union was at that time announcing heroic engineering schemes that would divert vast rivers in order to prevent desertification, 'and we thought why shouldn't we move a little southern English river like the Frome?' But 'Utopia was the word up at the AA', and none of this was ever going to happen. That, he says, was a 'nutty spasm — planning the rebirth of Tyneham'. And then, sitting back in a plush floral sofa in the sedate Wincanton hotel where we had this conversation, he raised his glass, stared into the fire and concluded, a little wistfully, of Fred Scott and his diploma students, 'We gave a rural English experience to a whole load of shaggy-haired Maoists.'

TWENTY

THANK GOD FOR THE SILENT MAJORITY!

A PILLAR OF West Lulworth's political establishment, the late Mrs Daphne Franklin served as a tireless defender of local interests on both parish and county councils. She picked me up at Wool Station, and her elucidations of the local landscape accelerated as we approached West Lulworth. At Burngate T junction, where the B3070 branches off for East Lulworth, she explained how the Franklin Viewpoint came to be built in the mid-Seventies. The road was becoming unsafe as people drew up suddenly to study the tank then displayed near the junction, so it was decided to remove this exhibit and adjust the road a little. While the work was underway the Colonel in charge of the gunnery school let Mrs Franklin know that he could do with a proper car park and viewing-point just down the road towards East Lulworth, where drivers were also inclined to stop suddenly to watch the tanks practising against Bindon Hill. Mrs Franklin had replied, briskly enough, that she could do with a new driveway herself, but this was no way to use ratepayers' money. As it happened, however, her late husband had been able to help: a national building contractor and local parishioner of good will, he donated the required gravel as a gift.

From the stockaded heights of Lulworth Camp the road runs down Camp Hill and into the village of West Lulworth. A motorist could easily drive down it without noticing the footpath that was Mrs Daphne Franklin's next achievement. No ordinary roadside pavement, this hardwon facility winds along behind the hedge, enabling pedestrians to journey safely between the camp and the village. Mrs Franklin was especially proud of this path, having argued for it and won it from the council. She was also happy that it had been camouflaged so successfully: fitted into the leafy verge as an unobtrusive and perfectly organic-looking addition to the local scene.

In order to persuade the county council of the importance of this proposed amenity, Mrs Franklin had prepared an inventory of the hazards faced by pedestrians trying to negotiate their way through the traffic on Camp Hill already. Ninety-four military wives walked to the village to shop and use the post office. These women were responsible for taking seventy-six children of pre-school age up and down the car-torn hill in pushchairs and prams. There were seventy children under eleven who had to come down the hill to attend school, and forty-two older ones whose use of the road was frequent if less regular. Whether their destination was the pub or the church, the three thousand soldiers who stayed at the camp during the year also had to take their chances on that busy road — along with visiting hikers, Boy Scouts, and campers from Lulworth Castle Park. By this time the interdependency of village and camp was a far more diversified thing than could ever be represented by bald employment statistics of the sort that had been thrown in Herbert Weld Blundell's face, as he had tried to win back Bindon Hill in the early 1920s. The military iron had entered into West Lulworth's soul and Mrs Franklin's metalled footpath was its hardwon symbol.

Mrs Franklin did not dwell heavily on the social side of things when she listed the ties that bound West Lulworth to the gunnery school. She didn't attempt to quantify the courting couples who met halfway up Camp Hill, and neither did she include the villagers found rolling down the same road late at night and considerably the worse for wear. According to Major Mike Collins, a gunnery instructor who was appointed second-in-command there from 1970, Lulworth Camp was known as an unusually 'reactionary' place in the days when the Tyneham liberationists were making the running — clinging to its old ways in a democratic age of cuts and increased austerity all round. The gunnery school was unusual in having a Sergeants' Mess as well as an Officers' Mess, so it wasn't just at the top of the class structure that the invitations sent out into the nearby villages helped to define who was really who in the local community.

The flamboyant parties run by the officers' mess are well remembered in West Lulworth to this day. People recall an amazing costume party when every officer's room was done out as a different ethnic restaurant — French, Indian, Italian, Chinese ... Others remember the officers' mess being painted maroon for a vast ball, and staying that way for months afterwards. A former officer once sailed into the cove in his private yacht to regale his erstwhile colleagues with champagne and oysters from noon until long past midnight. Lulworth was a genial place for a young officer and gentleman before the principle of pay parity with civilian jobs put an end to so many advantages of the military lifestyle. There was, as Collins remarks, 'more room for characters in those days'.

The true master of Lulworth's spectacular evening ceremonies was Major

Michael Parker — then a young gunnery instructor with the Queen's Own Hussars who is reputed even to have automated his bachelor room in the mess, rigging it out with gadgets so that he could do everything from his bed. Kenneth Allsop may have likened the wire surrounding the Tyneham Range to a 'domestic Iron Curtain',[1] but Parker — who would go on to become the undisputed king of the nation's large-scale pyrotechnical display organisers — had a different idea of Moscow in mind. It all started, as he explains of his interest in spectacle, with a review he wrote and produced at Sandhurst. Then, shortly after he had joined the Queen's Own Hussars, there was a big regimental party at Headquarters in Detmold, West Germany. In those extravagant days, regiments would devote a great deal of money and effort to parties. 'You had to be better at everything,' Parker explains, 'gunnery, equipment and parties too.' He remembers doing something with the Taj Mahal, but he really got into his stride when he thought of burning Moscow. He had the band belting out the 1812 Overture, with booming cannons lined up along the edge of the garden. At the bottom of the garden, he had erected a model of the great Russian city, which burst into flames at the climactic moment.

'I can't count the number of times I've burned Moscow since then,' says Parker. The activity seems to have kept him warm through the most glacial stretches of the Cold War. By the mid-sixties he was stationed in Berlin. He had only just been made a lieutenant and was still only twenty-two or thereabouts, but the Brigadier had heard something of his dramatic achievements and asked him to take over an enormous tattoo at the Olympic stadium with a cast of a thousand and ninety thousand visitors.

This time Moscow was huge, six or seven stories high, and the conflagration was intensified by blazing diplomatic argument. Berlin was a four-power city then, and the Soviet Union objected to their capital being burned. Parker mollified the Russians by pointing out that the events of 1812 actually marked a Russian victory over the French, but this displeased the French; and there were further objections from the German authorities in Berlin who did not want to be associated with burning any city. In the end it was agreed that Parker could go ahead, but only if Moscow burned in less than thirty seconds and looked more like a firework than a realistic event. So Parker stationed fire-engines behind his cardboard city, and when the massed band was right into the climax of the 1812 overture, they pumped kerosene into the fire so that it went up in one huge explosion.

Parker has since gone on to greater things, devising spectacles for such patrons as the Queen, Prince Charles and King Hussein of Jordan. For one of his recent state receptions, he even gained permission to affix powerful fireworks to the walls of Buckingham Palace — and that despite the fact that the Queen 'doesn't like bangs'. In Dorset, however, his skills were well-known by the late Sixties, when he came to work as a gunnery instructor at Lulworth Camp. One year, he built Pompeii next to the officers' mess. There were lots of little houses full of petrol, and a looming model of Vesuvius, behind which he stationed military prisoners ('in those days, we used prisoners for everything') whose job was to pump kerosene up into a tray of sand. This fiery riposte to the picturesque cult of the English Bay of Naples came unstuck when Vesuvius went off by mistake in the final rehearsal. On another occasion Parker took the Bayeux Tapestry, enlarging it with a projector, so that he could paint it on the walls of the mess. He remembers opting for complete accuracy but the Bayeux Tapestry is quite small, and there was considerable mirth about the vast size of the copied horses' genitalia.

His greatest Lulworth moment came after the Torrey Canyon super-tanker disaster in March 1967. Attempts had been made to burn the oil slick threatening Cornish beaches by bombing it with napalm, but when these failed the commandant at Lulworth found himself responsible for a lot of unused napalm: the stuff was unstable, and simply had to be used up. Parker realised it was time to burn Moscow once again. So that summer they took two thousand gallons of napalm and a thousand infantry flares, and etched the date 1812 on the blasted flank of Bindon Hill in numbers five or six hundred feet high. The band was installed on the terrace of the officers' mess, and Moscow lay ready to burn on the lawn nearby. It was, remembers Parker, 'very spectacular actually and the whole hill burned, it was lovely'. There is no record of what the Nature Conservancy thought about that.

Loyalist Uprising

Down in the village, Mrs Franklin pulled up at Mrs Jessie Firmstone's house in the row of coastguard cottages that also housed the crab-fishing Millers. Mrs Firmstone was chairman of the West Lulworth Women's Institute at the time of the battle over Tyneham; and she also served as clerk to the West Lulworth Parish Council. The two lady chairmen of West

Lulworth hailed from very different valleys of the English class structure, but they formed a powerful united front in the neighbourhood. Mrs Franklin was a Tory who preferred not to define her activities in party terms; and her voice, both high-pitched and stentorian, was a formidable instrument of social control with which she had been obliged to impose civility on many howling mobs in her time. Its upper register could grate and pierce, and, when she wanted to be especially emphatic, she used it to pursue words, rather as a rogue dog might force sheep towards a tiny gap in a hedge, and then clip the end off them just as they thought they had squeezed through unscathed. Mrs Firmstone had come to Dorset during the war from a mining-village in the northeast, working on the Weld estate to begin with, and later marrying a gunnery instructor. She has retained the accent of her birthplace, and still honours the socialist politics too. She remembers once being visited by Lord Hinchinbrooke, who wanted to meet this West Lulworth socialist, and to know how she held on to views formed in the northern hardship of the Thirties.

The local unanimity of West Lulworth's two chairmen included a highly critical judgement of at least one of Margaret Thatcher's policies. Both were worried by the sale of council housing. They had watched as even the old people's flats for which the parish had struggled so hard, were bought by relatives of those housed in them, and turned into holiday lets. This only went to show the folly of applying a policy that may suit a 'great run-down estate in the middle of a city' to a little village where council housing was one of the few means of ensuring that local people could hold their ground. Watchful for inappropriate commercial development in West Lulworth, they were also concerned that the local planning process was being unduly influenced by middle-class incomers, who had no sooner bought into the village than they became overzealous defenders of the local environment and started doing everything they could to block the Weld estate's plans for this undeniably improvable resort. Firmstone and Franklin were loyalists thrice over: vigilant defenders of the traditionally mixed village and its poorer population; of the Weld estate, of which Mrs Firmstone remarked, 'I'm not anti-anybody who improves the lot of everybody'; and of the Army.

Mrs Franklin stressed that the West Lulworth Parish Council had taken a long and active part in the argument over the tank firing ranges: 'we have a unique relationship with the Army in this parish', and 'it's been lovely to have this relationship'. Conferring with Mrs Firmstone, she ventured that 'we've never asked them to do something for us that they haven't done. In the heavy snows of 1963, well, they dug us out didn't they? And we got the mains sewer here before anybody.' As for the campaigners who tried to get the gunnery school removed at the time of Lord Nugent's Defence Lands Committee, Mrs Franklin described them as 'erudite outsiders', emphasising that few if any were of 'indigenous stock'. She had no time for 'these pressure groups who really think we are yokels and not intelligent enough to fight our own battles'.

Things hadn't always been this straightforward. Jessie Firmstone remembered the shock she experienced one day in December 1959. She was accustomed then to walking on the ranges after the day's firing had stopped. But when she walked out towards Mupes Bay on this occasion, she came upon 'a newly erected notice on a post'. Walking over to investigate, she found herself reading that the Minister of Transport proposed permanently to stop up the footpaths on the range area.

Dismayed, Mrs Firmstone had 'turned tails jolly quick', going straight to the post office to ask if anybody knew what the notice was about. She had been right behind the West Lulworth Parish Council when, on 23 January 1960, she wrote to the Minister of Transport to 'protest most strongly' against the proposed restrictions: it was really too much to propose that the loyal people of this 'minor seaside resort' should now be 'deprived of their ancient rights to fifty per cent of the coastline within their Parish'. She remembered attending the public inquiry held by the War Works Commission in Dorchester on 11 January 1961. As chairman of the West Lulworth Women's Institute, she had told her members, 'I want you all in that court on Monday morning'; and she made no concessions for those who tried to excuse themselves with the plea that Monday was their washing-day: 'I said "Oh Yes, and when your grandchildren grow up and they can't get over there are you going to tell them you did your washing that morning"? I had a whole row of them sitting there. Little old ladies.'

And she made them work too, as the transcript of that inquiry confirms. On expressing her wish to be able to walk along the top of Bindon Hill when there was no firing, Mrs Firmstone was told by Colonel Watson of the gunnery school: 'It's all very well for you, Mrs Firmstone, to use the road, but can you imagine children who might go along there, they see mother go that way . . . and there is a lovely thing to pick up and it blows their hand off.' Mrs Firmstone had an answer to that. 'Without being personal, why is it that Army personnel and their wives and children are allowed to do that? Are their children better behaved than ours?' Colonel Watson replied, 'No they are not allowed to do that', but Mrs Firmstone pressed back with 'Oh, they do', and by this time she was supported by a chorus from the Women's Institute who echoed, 'they do'. Mrs Firmstone had seen them drive up on to Bindon Hill and go for a walk; and she had also seen Army parties unlocking the gate and driving down to the sea at Worbarrow Bay, overtaking the civilians who, on the few days when access was granted, were obliged to park at Tyneham and walk. Taken aback, Colonel Watson could only say 'I am astonished to hear that.' But Mrs Firmstone closed in still further: 'You may be astonished, but this happens every day.' And, once again, there were 'Cries from the public of "Every Day" '.

Organisations like the National Parks Commission and the Commons, Open Spaces and Footpaths Preservation Society defended those rights of way in the name of public access, but the women of West Lulworth had a different aim. They wanted to know why the public could not be reclassified so that the indigenous population were granted access that might not be offered to summer visitors. Mrs Firmstone pleaded on behalf of all West Lulworth's frustrated natives, 'Couldn't we have passes? If you are satisfied we are intelligent enough, couldn't we have passes?' 'Yes, couldn't we?' begged the chorus . . .

The good ladies of West Lulworth had come to terms with the military by May 1968, when Rodney Legg pushed in to renew the campaign. After discussing the newly formed Tyneham Action Group, the parish council had passed a resolution deploring 'the action being taken by the instigators of this campaign' and 'dissociated itself entirely' from their arguments. The Wareham and Purbeck Rural District Council was also quickly brought out behind the West Lulworth Parish Council's resolution. On 18 May 1968, the *Daily Telegraph* had quoted the Clerk to the Council, Mr Durant-Lewis, as being in support of Rodney Legg's initiative, but he had submitted to contrary pressure by the time he prepared papers for a council meeting held on 6 June 1968. In an appendix to the agenda he regretted that while he had indeed described it as 'a dirty trick not to return the land as promised', the *Daily Telegraph* had taken his words right out of context when it printed them as a statement of support for the Tyneham liberationists. He had since declined an invitation to the Action Group's inaugural meeting in Dorchester, and it had been he who derided this new attempt to gain release of the land as 'flogging a dead horse'.

Firmstone and Franklin fought the protestors in other arenas too. As chairman of the West Lulworth Women's Institute, Mrs Firmstone had attended the Annual Council of the Dorset Federation of Women's Institutes, in October 1969, to speak against a resolution demanding that Tyneham should be freed. The resolution was passed, but not before Mrs Firmstone had told the meeting that, although the West Lulworth Institute was indeed 'full of sympathy and compassion for the people of Tyneham and Worbarrow, who had to leave their homes over twenty-five years ago', time had since moved on. Every living person 'must look forward to the day when armies no longer exist and when all these problems will have solved themselves, but if we accept the fact that our men have to be trained efficiently, then we must also face the situation that exists in this area'. She described the range as a 'wild life sanctuary and nature reserve' that would be 'destroyed by the masses' who would surely descend on the area if it were surrendered. The pattern of life had changed so much since 1943, 'mainly due to the motorcar', and it was to be hoped that the land would only be freed when 'we will have learned a great deal more about the conservation and preservation of the countryside'. Tanks, once again, were better than trippers: 'Our village of West Lulworth is an example of what can happen to a beauty spot through sheer pressure of numbers.'[2]

Mrs Franklin hadn't immediately found time to engage with the Tyneham liberationists: as a properly elected local politician, she had been far too busy 'to get involved with a lot of pressure groups'. Yet as their campaign advanced, she realised it was going to be necessary not just to defend the Royal Armoured Corps, but also to buck up some of its senior officers. When members of the Tyneham Action Group made the mistake of asking Mrs Franklin to sign their petition, they received a suitably mincing reply: 'I was very forthright in my opinions, and said we were perfectly able to fight this battle as local people, and we didn't need outsiders' signatures or intervention, thank you.' She remembered chairing meetings at which she had to face down Monica Hutchings, who was 'very anti-me' by that stage. The mere thought of facing 'that lady from Church Knowle' had been enough to reduce one senior tank officer to a quivering jelly but 'I said just sit by me, close by me, and you will be fine, and we shall see it through.' Some of these officers found their own ways of dealing with the liberationists. Brigadier Roy Redgrave remembered that it was always best to engage them singly, picking them off one at a time, rather in the manner of a sniper. Chairman Franklin preferred to rely on forceful application of proper procedure: 'I can remember clearly saying at the beginning of the meeting, only people who were on the electoral roll — this is how I had them — would be invited to speak and to vote.'

West Lulworth's two Chairmen had already put up a good fight by the time Lord Nugent's Defence Lands Committee visited Dorset. Addressing these visitors as a representative for the parishes of Wool, Bovington and West Lulworth, Mrs Franklin had enumerated the many benefits the Army brought to the local community, adding that since mechanisation had destroyed most of the agricultural jobs that had existed in the area before 1916, it was doubly 'providential' that the Army had turned up to provide alternative regular employment for an indigenous population that would otherwise have been forced into emigration. As for conservation, she too believed that 'the wildlife of the lands held would be in far greater danger from the masses of people who would descend on it in ever growing numbers . . . The Army have created a wildlife sanctuary and nature reserve.'

Traders' Takeover

It would be too much to say that Mrs Franklin still smarted with wounded pride when I met her, but she was sensitive about the way the campaign had gone after July 1973, when the Defence Lands Committee had recommended the removal of the gunnery school. When she announced that it was time to set the record straight, I thought she was still assailing the memory of those Tyneham liberationists who had condemned the Army's supporters as venal hirelings. But she was actually arguing with the memory of the West Lulworth men who had formed their own committee in support of the gunnery school, claiming that the parish council run by Mrs Franklin and Mrs Firmstone had not done enough to defend the local economy. There was, she remarked a little haughtily, nothing to stop these traders banding together to form yet another pressure group, but as West Lulworth's elected representative, Mrs Franklin was in no doubt that local politics could be conducted perfectly adequately through the proper democratic channels.

Nugent's recommendation came as a profound shock to West Lulworth. The late Peter Rudd was among the initiators of this traders' array, a hotelier, shop-owner and developer who saw at once that local business would suffer if the gunnery school was moved. When I talked to him in May 1988, he recalled how the campaign had been triggered after a meeting in the officers' mess up at Lulworth Camp. He and another hotel proprietor, Mr John Wright, had been told by Colonel George Forty, who later became curator of the Tank Museum at Bovington, that if the Army was forced to leave, it would be because of 'local default and lack of interest'. By 17 September the *Daily Telegraph* was reporting that the villagers blamed 'their own complacent belief in the Army's continuing presence for their failure to present a fuller case to Lord Nugent'. It also announced the formation of a 'Keep the Army in Lulworth' committee, which warned that the Lulworths, both East and West, would be turned into 'ghost villages' like Tyneham itself. As chairman of this loyalist outbreak, John Wright pointed out that 'this is not an army of occupation. The soldiers have been here since before the First World War, they are our friends, they marry our local girls and they help us to live fuller lives . . . this place would be dead without the Army.'

A survey of local opinion was organised, with Colonel Sir Joseph Weld allowing the questionnaire to be distributed in East Lulworth as well as West. The results, overwhelmingly pro-tank, were announced at a meeting in West Lulworth village hall on the evening of 3 August 1973. A hundred and fifty authentic locals are reported to have risen from their 'somnolent security' to demonstrate that they wanted Lulworth Camp to stay, and to convince the Tory MP for South Dorset, Mr Evelyn King, who had organised the Tyneham Action Group's delegation to London in 1968, that it was now time to change horses. As chairman, John Wright proclaimed: 'We are the silent majority whose views are rarely heard.' Sir Winston Churchill's 1943 pledge should certainly have been honoured after the War, but circumstances had changed since then and 'the dream of public ownership, perhaps through the National Trust, would prove a nightmare'. It was classic stuff for the period: the self-styled silent majority rising up against unrepresentative 'pressure groups' perceived to have taken over far too much of British public life.

Some speakers pointed out how heavily dependant the village was on the Army, but others preferred to set traps for the Tyneham liberationists. Mr George Clark claimed that, before the ranges could be returned to civilian use, it would be necessary for the Army to 'move in with bulldozers and dig down five feet: "What will happen to Tyneham's beautiful natural flora and fauna then?" ' Peter Rudd 'raised the spectre of the Army camp becoming a holiday camp'. The county planners might deny that this could ever happen, but Rudd, a canny operator who had fought his own battles with the planning authorities, knew better than to trust the bureaucrats: 'I see it ending up as a Butlin's or a Pontin's if the Army goes. We don't want a holiday camp, and I don't see why we should be forced to have one.' I well remember the triumphant look in Mr Rudd's eye as he described how adroitly the Keep the Army in Lulworth Committee had exploited this threatening prospect of Bindon Hill converted into a lewd vulgarian's paradise. As we gazed out over the swimming-pool in his garden on the lower slopes of the private road known as Millionaire's Row, and down towards the private 'Heritage Centre' he was then building beside the Weld estate's car park, he remembered the journalists asking him if he didn't regret all the Army's ugly wire fences. He had answered that they were 'better than commercial exploitation'. In retrospect, this adroit commercial exploiter had no doubts that it was the Keep the Army at Lulworth committee that had been the truly 'conservationist one' — so long, that is, as 'conservation' is understood to mean 'what it does now that it is no longer a loony notion'.

So the Keep the Army in Lulworth campaign swung into battle. Mr Evelyn King MP declared himself convinced at their initial meeting. Changing sides more quickly than Lord Hinchinbrooke before him, he promised to ensure that local opinion was 'put strongly across' to Lord Carrington. Plans were laid to take a deputation to 10 Downing Street and the House of Commons. Rodney Legg might daub 'Surrender Purbeck' over the Army's signs, but the Keep the Army in Lulworth campaign now replied with legally posted signs and window stickers of their own: 'LOCALS SAY "LEGG OFF".' 'OUR WORK — OUR HOMES.' 'ARMY TO STAY.'

The formation of this committee stimulated a different kind of letter writer too, lending confidence to opinions that had looked low and self-interested when the high-minded idealism of the Tyneham liberationists dominated the correspondence pages. Civilian employees wrote from Bovington Camp to protest against the plans of 'Lords, MPs and rich landowners', declaring it obvious that 'big business' was behind the liberationists' campaign.[3] Refusing to be cowed by the accusations of self-interest, Army employees owned up in the manner of the man who explained that, having previously worked for twenty-six years in low-paid Dorset industries, he was not inclined to apologise for taking the side of the Ministry of Defence, which had enabled him to improve his standard of living so considerably.[4] As Terry Knight of the Keep the Army in Lulworth Committee remarked, 'Surely there is no hypocrisy in recognising and accepting a fair reward for services rendered.'[5]

A former villager wrote in to debunk the idyllic picture of Tyneham put about by 'that group of busybodies calling themselves the Tyneham Action Group', who evidently knew 'very little about the real Tyneham':

> Tyneham as I knew it, consists of a pond, a village tap, a church, school, post office and general shop, a vicarage and about eleven houses, one used as a laundry. A Mrs Pitman kept the post office and shop and the governess was a crippled lady, a Mrs Fry, and her assistant was a Louie Milsom, who later emigrated to Canada.
>
> The parson was a big bully of a man who went around in plus-fours and carried a dog whip, with which he corrected his sons, and anyone else who was fool enough to let him. I know because he tried it on myself, and I knocked him out with a broom and my father horse-whipped him.[6]

One anonymous tank supporter sent Mavis Caver, chairman of the 1943 Committee, a threatening letter made up of words cut from newspapers: 'Your life is in the balance. You can't beat the Army, We must do anything and everything to win.'[7] But the Keep the Army campaign declared its abhorrence for this 'cowardly and stupid form of protest', insisting that reason alone would win the day. Their cause was even sanctioned by ancient history: 'Let the iron men who train on the sites of iron age forts long defend their country and by their continuing presence save Dorset from commercial spoliation and destruction quite beyond repair.'[8]

The Bishop of Salisbury wrote to *The Times* to dispel any illusion that 'Mrs Caver and her 1943 Committee in any way represent local opinion';[9] and, by the end of August 1973, Mr Evelyn King MP had gained the assurance of Prime Minister Edward Heath that careful consideration would be given to his constituents' views before the government made its decision on Nugent's recommendation. Their deputation went to London on 7 November, carrying a two-thousand signature petition to Whitehall, where they were met by King and taken into a three hour discussion with Mr Peter Blaker, Minister for Defence.[10] They presented their petition at 10 Downing Street, leaving copies with the leaders of the two opposition parties — Harold Wilson and Jeremy Thorpe. Peter Rudd remembered the television cameras that met the deputation at Waterloo station and accompanied them to Buckingham Palace, where they delivered a pleading letter to the Queen. He still admired the nimble way in which John Wright had answered the jaded interviewer who wanted to know what right a small community had to press its case on the Crown. Wright had replied 'When a man loses his locality, who else is he to go to but his Queen?' Wright had come home in good spirits, saying 'almost the whole of Dorset is in favour of the Army staying and I would think the people of Dorset count . . . '[11]

The West Lulworth Parish Council was not happy with the upstart Keep the Army in Lulworth Committee. In November 1973, Mrs Franklin had prepared an inventory of all the properly elected representatives in the area, sending it to John Wright with a terse note: 'I trust that you will find this list helpful as I feel it would only be right and proper to inform these people if you intend making representations on their behalf in London.' Yet the parish council also battled on for the gunnery school, writing to Lord Carrington at the Ministry of Defence to emphasise that 'Conservation of wildlife in the range area has been greatly helped by the presence of the Army. On the occasions when the public are allowed access, one realises that here is an area where time has stood still, and thus, a uniquely beautiful part of England has remained intact, protected from the pollution and man-made development, such as we experience in our own village.'[12] Lord Carrington is said to have remarked that 'he'd never before heard of a civilian population campaigning to have the Army stay in their area' — a line that the activists of West Lulworth frequently quoted as the sign of their own unusual loyalty.

The South Dorset Labour Party felt similarly. Mr Alan Chedzoy, the prospective candidate, wasted no time writing to the Prime Minister for confirmation that the larger encampment at Bovington was not also threatened. After enumerating the jobs and services that would be lost if the camp closed, he offered his own variation on the ghost-town scenario: 'Thirty years ago the Army entered Tyneham and a community was destroyed. I believe that if the Army is now to leave Lulworth without some compensating factors, then this will be a second blow to the population of the Dorset coast.'

The Keep the Army campaign could soon claim the support not just of numerous local councils and the National Farmers Union, but also of the trade unions. By September, the members of the Transport and General Workers Union employed by the Army at Bovington and Lulworth had come out almost unanimously against the idea of removing the ranges; and Poole and Wareham district committee of the National Union of Agricultural and Allied Workers had also supported a proposal that the ranges should be retained.[13] The committee recalled the disasters that had been caused by lack of military training in the last war and insisted that proper facilities had to exist somewhere. Members felt that there would be little gain to agriculture, food production or job opportunities if the land was handed back to private owners. Given the Crichel Down rule, such former tenants as might have survived would have no legal right to return to their fields and cottages: under these circumstances, 'any sentiment about old people being allowed to return was misplaced'. By early December, when Evelyn King spoke out against Nugent's recommendation in the House of Commons, he could declare it hard to imagine greater unanimity of opinion within his constituency than existed on this matter.[14]

Going Down with the Tolpuddle Martyrs

As chairman of the Tyneham Action Group, Philip Draper had attended the Keep the Army in Lulworth Committee's meeting in West Lulworth village hall, but he was 'shouted down uncompromisingly' when he got up to float the conciliatory suggestion that a different Army unit — that didn't need a firing range — might be moved into Lulworth Camp, thereby safeguarding local employment. Indeed, 'the reaction to his statements was so strong that near uproar ensued, and it was some minutes before the chairman restored order'.[15]

Draper would later try to 'correct some misunderstandings' expressed at the meeting.[16] It was 'most understandable' that the people of Lulworth should be afraid of losing their jobs and fringe benefits, but instead of putting a balanced view to these 'frankly biased' locals, the Keep the Army Committee preferred to 'dish out wild and colourful statements' such as 'that a Butlin's-type camp is the only alternative ... which is nearly as absurd as the suggestion that unexploded shells can only be cleared from the Tyneham Valley by bulldozing it to a depth of five feet and thus "making it a second Sahara with mounds of clay instead of sand" '. He hoped that Mr Evelyn King's reference to 'silly pressure groups' referred not to the Tyneham Action Group which had always pursued its cause in a 'responsible and diplomatic' manner and without 'adopting colourful or militant actions', but to the 'irresponsible antics of the so-called "Friends of Tyneham" '.

The biggest gaffe was made by Mrs Margaret Kraft. She launched a haughty and insulting attack against the 'concoction of muddled thinking' displayed by the people of East and West Lulworth. Deriding the claim that without the Army, these settlements would become 'ghost villages' she remarked that 'no one with a flicker of intelligence' could believe that this was a real prospect. As for 'holiday camps', the other fear raised by this 'moribund population', here again the answer was 'stuff and nonsense'. Mrs Kraft admitted that she was not 'native born', but she had attended a village school in Dorset and served as a district councillor. Recent researches into 'the conduct of one of our early rural councils' had provided her with an explanation for the attitude of the people of Lulworth: 'It is a picture of almost incredible insularity and adoration, no less, of the status quo.' Dorset's country folk consisted of a 'dumb bulk' that needed pushing into a twentieth century that was already three quarters spent: 'This county must be the original home of the "Damn you Jack, I'm all right" faction.'[17] This insouciant stuff played right into the hands of the Keep the Army Committee, which concluded that Mrs Kraft should ask herself, 'If that's what she really thinks of Dorset and its people, why stay?'[18]

The Friends of Tyneham also dismissed 'the selfish and hysterical outbursts' of the Lulworth Camp followers. Condemning the Keep the Army in Lulworth Committee for parading 'the old "bogey-man" of irreparable damage being done to Tyneham in the clearance of unexploded shells', the Hon. Membership Secretary, Marjorie Hillman, pointed out that 'vast areas on the continent, notably in Eastern Europe', showed no signs of devastation 'despite the clearance of great amounts of lethal ironmongery with less sophisticated equipment than is currently available'.[19] Legg also lampooned the arguments against their bid for National Trust ownership: as he wrote to one interested journalist: 'In 1968 it was "You can never fight the government and win." In 1969, it had become "Without the Army, Czechoslovakia would be here." In 1970 the landscape came into vogue: "What a pity, it's so lovely here." In 1971 the Army found some friends: "You people are no better than the IRA." '

They kept up the 'direct action' too. On 29 August 1973, they cut through the wire to 'reopen' Tyneham's battered post office and, in the ten minutes before police and the army ejected them, two members sold a special set of commemoration postcards to visitors, stamping them with an improvised postmark reading 'posted at Tyneham post office' before dropping them into a homemade pillar box.[20] That Christmas fourteen members of the Friends of Tyneham sneaked over the fence to mark the thirtieth anniversary of the dispossession by holding a carol service in Tyneham Church, with the help of an obliging Salvation Army minister. Afterwards they laid a wreath at the church door as 'a reminder to those in authority of a broken pledge'.[21]

The Friends of Tyneham were at County Hall in Dorchester for the October meeting at which the County Council decided to follow the recommendation of its own planning committee and, in the light of the Crichel Down rule, to reverse its decision and come out in favour of the retention of the ranges. Rodney Legg took some stick from a retired Colonel for having called for a local referendum rather than 'listening to the prejudiced views of parish councillors', but by this time he and his fellows were wavering.[22] They had formed a 'small picket' to confront councillors entering the meeting, but most of their slogans were aimed at the Tyneham Action Group rather than the Army: 'Save Tyneham from Bondage', 'Farming will wreck Tyneham's ecology' and 'No to Private Estates — Yes to National Trust ownership'.[23]

The Tyneham Action Group was on its last legs by the Annual General Meeting of April 1974. Draper accused Evelyn King MP and Dorset County Council of being 'turncoats', but he also had to report a decline in membership from five hundred to four hundred.[24] The Group had long since concluded that the National Trust should have control of the land, but General Mark Bond's 'very sincere efforts' to achieve a truce with the Friends of Tyneham had been rebuffed. Other members wanted to dilute the campaign's goals even more. Commander N. Hoare was worried that 'a large body of opinion in Dorset is strongly against any move to get the Army out of the ranges. Partly this is because of employment, but also people who are conservationists claim that the Army has preserved something there that is unique. I often wonder whether you take into account these powerful arguments of conservationists, and I am frightened of the spread of "caravanitis" along the coast.'[25]

On 22 August 1974, the Friends of Tyneham sent a deputation to London. Led by Brockway and the Tory MP Neil Macfarlane, they put their case to Lord Brayley, Labour-Under Secretary of State for the Army, who seemed well disposed to their cause and reassured the deputation that 'the Government would not forget its moral obligations'.[26] But it wasn't to be. The Friends of Tyneham went back to Dorset, and were dismayed seven days later when the government released a White Paper announcing its rejection of Nugent's recommendation that the gunnery school be removed from Dorset to Wales. There was great upset, ranging from the 'sheer disgust' of the Ramblers' Association to the quieter disappointment of the Countryside Commission and the Council for the Protection of Rural England.[27] But the response in Lulworth was jubilant. Contacted in one of his hotels where he was firing champagne corks at the ceiling, Peter Rudd reported that: 'Everyone who comes into the hotel is in a celebration mood over the decision.'

Philip Draper declared himself hugely disappointed, adding pathetically, 'We don't know what we are going to do now. We will have to have a committee meeting to decide.'[28] But Rodney Legg was incandescent, remarking that the White Paper must already have been printed by the time that Lord Brayley was promising John Gould that Churchill's pledge would be taken into account. Rejecting the decision of 'a minority government made just prior to a general election', the Friends of Tyneham unloaded everything they had on Lord Brayley, preparing an article for Martin Walker of the *Guardian*, which told the true story of their meeting with this Labour buffoon. As chairperson of the Friends of Tyneham, Mavis Caver had suggested that it was especially appropriate to ask a Socialist Minister to honour the pledge, 'since Dorset had given the labour movement the Tolpuddle Martyrs'. They had been surprised when the vague Lord Brayley had asked in reply: 'Who, the Tolpuddle Marchers? Who were they?'[29]

Labour's Defence Secretary, Mr Roy Mason, made the usual sheepish noises in support of the government's reluctant decision. It had been impossible to please everybody, but the minister believed 'that our final judgement was right when all the factors are weighed in the balance'. The outcome would 'generally be welcomed in Wales, and also by the majority of those who live near the range in Dorset'.[30] Mr Mason came up with the usual concessions too, adding that 'it is our intention to take steps to improve access for the public, and I very much hope that these plans and our willingness to co-operate in conservation policies will increase public enjoyment of the area'.

The Tyneham liberationists went out in customary style — beating one another to death in a final convulsive implosion. In September 1974, General Mark Bond and Philip Draper told fellow committee members that the time had surely come for the Tyneham Action Group to fold. The decision was made, but chaos broke out when it was presented to the membership at a special General Meeting. Draper urged members to accept that their voyage had come to an end: 'We must be realists and face facts as they are.' But Ruth Colyer mustered a dissident faction on the committee, arguing that 'it would be most inadvisable for us to give up now. We must be ready to lobby MPs.' A 'high-speed demonstration' was mounted by the Friends of Tyneham, with Rodney Legg and Mavis Caver bursting into the meeting to denounce those who wanted to desist campaigning as 'traitors to the Tyneham cause' and to tell Draper he was doing 'the most treacherous and despicable thing you can do'.

The Tyneham Action Group was finished, its visionary ship well and truly broken on the reefs of history, but the squabbling stretched well into the summer of 1975, when General Mark Bond wrote to thank former executive members for their efforts. He observed that it only remained to the old TAG executive committee to pay its outstanding bills and then transfer any remaining funds to the Watch Committee that had been set up to work with the Army on amenity and access issues. But the mutinous committee members disputed the legitimacy of the Watch Committee, and the funds were abandoned to the bank where they may even still languish to this day. General Bond quoted Schiller as he walked out on his last campaign: 'Against stupidity the Gods themselves battle in vain.'

The Friends of Tyneham fought on for longer, but their cause was dying too. Their last effective gesture had been made on Thursday, 19 December 1974, the anniversary of the original evacuation, when they took their lost cause to Downing Street. Led by Lord Fenner Brockway, the deputation included Philip Watkins, Treasurer of the Liberal Party, and Brian Jackman, Environment Correspondent with the *Sunday Times*. The part of symbolic villager was played, once again, by John Gould, former resident of Tyneham and now a roadsweeper with the Dorset Water Board. He had been the first to send a postcard from Tyneham's briefly reopened post office in August 1973, and now he came to Downing Street bearing a wreath made of ivy picked from the ruins of the gardener's cottage in which he had been born in 1912, and inscribed 'We remind those in authority of a broken pledge.'[31] Gould presented this to Harold Wilson, along with a letter in which the story of Churchill's pledge found its most sentimental expression:

Dear Prime Minister

I was born on 24 October 1912 in the Gardener's Cottage at Tyneham on the Dorset coast. I lived and worked in the village until 1940 when I joined the Army.

Then in 1944, when I was fighting with the Devonshire Regiment in India, I had a letter from my mother saying they had been evicted from their home on 19 December 1943, which is 31 years ago today.

Our home was taken over by Major C. H. Miller of Southern command who gave written and verbal promises that we could return 'at the end of the emergency'. This pledge was made at Cabinet level by Winston Churchill. The eviction notice stated: 'The Government appreciate that this is no small sacrifice which you are asked to make, but they are sure you will give this further help towards winning the war with a good heart.'

In 1948 the Government accepted that we had a right to return home but said that priority had to be given to national defence needs. Then in 1961, Mr Silkin legally closed 92 miles of public paths in and around Tyneham. We no longer even had any right to see our old homes again.

You can imagine my tremendous pleasure and excitement when Lord Nugent's report in 1973 said these tank ranges should be returned to the people of Dorset. I had always wanted to return, and at last it seemed this was going to happen.

Tyneham to me is the most beautiful place in the world and I want to give the rest of my life and energy to its restoration . . .

As a life-long member of the Labour Party, I appeal to you to look again at Tyneham's plight before there is a Parliamentary debate on this matter.

If you reject this plea, I must make a second request, that when my time comes I will be interred in Tyneham Churchyard. It is there — and in memory of many old friends, my Grandparents and Uncle Tom, who were allowed to live out their lives at Tyneham — that I would like this wreath to go. Most of all, I want to go home.

If there was to be no homecoming in the Tyneham valley, it was partly because the tanks had long since won their place by the firesides of Lulworth. While talking with Mrs Rena Gould in the sitting-room of her stone cottage in East Lulworth, I looked up and noticed what she called 'the brass' on her mantelpiece — diverse ornaments carved from shellcases at the time of the Great War, and polished, faithfully, to the highest shine. At the other end of the village, I glanced at the walls as Jack Scutt and Harry

Westmacott remembered Llewelyn Powys striding about on the downs and explained that 'think' had meant 'that' rather than 'this' in the lost dialect of their youth. There was an oil painting of Corfe Castle on the wall, but their proudest picture is a colour photograph showing a tank firing at night, a dark silhouette with a great jet of flame spurting from its barrel and tearing off in the direction of Bindon Hill. This Lulworth nocturne had been presented to Harry Westmacott when he retired from years of service as a cook in the Sergeants' mess at the Lulworth gunnery school.

Over in the Weld Arms, a young officer nearing the end of his time with the Royal Armoured Corps, was tempting a new girlfriend with glimpses of his career prospects as a civilian: he had considered the law and even the Catholic priesthood as possible vocations, but he was now much more interested in politics. He promised that the Conservative Party had a very good proxy system which means that a chap didn't have to be in London all the time. As Joan Berkeley wrote in 1971, the boom of the guns from the Army ranges may still shock the visitor, but 'it disturbs the inhabitants not at all'.[32]

PART SIX

After the Great Disillusionment

No more dreams, but failure at last, and death; happier so in the Hollow Land.

William Morris

TWENTY-ONE

EXILE'S RECKONING

'I'M A STATELESS person, definitely . . . a displaced person.' When I first met him in March 1986, John Gould was still adamant that his home was in Tyneham, freely admitting that some people 'jibbed' him for this apparently unwordly claim: 'I say, you don't want to laugh mate, 'cause it's true. I didn't want to leave Tyneham; I wanted to stop there, because it was a nice place. It's what you get used to — if you've been born there, I mean. They say you'll get quiet, but I say I don't mind quiet, I like it quiet to a certain extent.'

At that time Gould was a resident of Tyneham Close, the little council estate built at Lewis Silkin's order on the fir-clad heath at Sandwell. The man who had been turned into Tyneham's most famous evacuee lived in a small brick bungalow, identified as 'Tyneham' by a handpainted sign prominently displayed over the door. In April 1973, he had stood in the ruins of Tyneham as 'Roadsweeper John Gould' and told a reporter, 'I was born in the village and my heart has always been there.' And even though he had nothing against the modern amenities of Tyneham Close, here he was thirteen years later describing Tyneham as a paradise and 'the most beautiful valley in the whole world'. Its fate still seemed 'unbelievable': 'when you go over there, when you enter that valley — it seems another world . . . perfect. But there you are.' When he went over to visit Tyneham, he could see two places at once — Tyneham as it had been, and Tyneham as it is now. As he talked, he moved freely between these two superimposed impressions, turning wilderness into cottage garden, and explaining where one could find houses that had disappeared long ago. His regret filled the Tyneham valley, even brimming over Rings Hill to reach the half of Flowers Barrow lost to the sea centuries before the tanks came along.

Gould was born in Tyneham, where his father worked as gardener to the Bonds, but he left after the Rector wouldn't agree to increase his pittance of a wage, joining the Devonshire Regiment in 1933. The war took him to India, but he was invalided home in 1943, and embarked on a lifetime of light manual work: on farms and in the railway goodsyard, as gardener for the Brigadier at Bovington Camp, and, latterly, cleaning pumps and roadsweeping for the water board. When asked about Lilian Bond's book, he observed, with the cautious expression of one who knew that he was about to cut hard against the grain of the Tyneham myth, that she had never given more than one view of the story: 'Her book, you see, was from a different society.' And he didn't just mean it was from an earlier age: 'It was in a different class, you understand . . . The thing is, she never talked about the people like myself, or the children, and how they had to . . . ' He trailed off, explaining that there was this thing called 'class distinction', which was surely 'the worst thing going'. Standing back from the idyll, Gould volunteered that it had been 'a hard life, there's no doubt about it'. His father, being head gardener, was earning about thirty shillings a week, but the farm workers at that time 'were only getting ten'. The old fishermen at Worbarrow Bay had a measure of independence, but everyone else, including the tenant farmers, lived under the thumb of the Bonds. Gould's map of Tyneham was not defined like Lilian Bond's in terms of birds, fauna, folklore and ancient field names. Instead, it was dominated by the rural class structure that had shaped every detail of life, and squeezed vast canyons of social distance into that tiny English valley.

Tyneham Great House stood at the centre of Gould's remembered world too, but for him it had been a point of centrifugal repulsion. Having visited it when the Bonds were away and his father was looking after the place, he could remember the vast corridors, the lino in the passages, and marvelling at the huge quantities of food that had been bought in from the big stores. In the normal run of things, however, 'you'd never go near a place like that'. His father would sometimes take his reluctant son up to the garden, and 'it was a job to get me to go . . . 'Yeah, because . . . you know . . . it was like a . . . you know, Big Brother. You'd never go in there like that.'

In Gould's Tyneham, the wise child was cautious — reluctant to cross a field or linger on the wrong verge for fear of the rector's or master's eye. His remembered village was like one of the vigilant settlements in T. F. Powys's novels, where the powerless have nowhere to hide from the powerful. The villagers went to church because 'Big Brother' expected them to be there: 'If you never went to church, and you worked for the Bonds, oh dear, dear, dear.' There were other rules of everyday life: 'Never put washing up on a Sunday', and if you go out wooding, 'look round twice' before you pick anything up.

John Gould lived in awe of William Bond. He remembers the squire surveying his valley through field glasses: 'Going down into Tyneham, you'd often see him with his binoculars, you see, and he was six feet tall, terrific height he was, and he'd be up there looking around, and we'd think he was looking for us . . . looking to see that we didn't do nothing wrong and then tell our fathers, you see — because most of them worked there.' On this point, Gould had found Lilian Bond's book enlightening: 'I found out then he was a bird-watcher, and he used to be watching the birds!'

Of course, Gould added, that's only the way he saw it as a child, and the Bonds were probably very kind . . . 'No, it was a different life completely. I mean Mrs Bond didn't have to look to find the money for a pair of socks or a pair of shoes for the children. It was no problem at all, money wasn't, with them, you see. And, of course, they'd definitely vote Tory' — which meant that the village did too, including Gould's own father and mother: 'You see, in those days . . . '

Gould had been the figurehead of the 1943 Committee's campaign for the release of the ranges, their symbolic villager. Looking back, he claimed to have known all along that the liberationists would never win, but he fought because his conscience would not have been clear otherwise: 'I mean I was a rebel in the sayings of the other people around, but I was only just doing that because I loved my Grandad and that, as a child . . . you know, I mean it's natural . . . You're very callous if you don't.' There was a more general principle at stake too, as Gould knew from his own war experience: 'I mean, you fight for democracy, and all our chaps got lost in the war fighting for democracy, and you think sometimes, for what . . . you know, when you come back and find your own home taken away.' The fault lay not with the Army, but with the government that had enforced the evacuation: 'They was so crafty, they said, "Well, we'll offer them a pledge to come back" . . . I mean they just couldn't care less.'

Gould well remembered the split that had divided Tyneham's liberators. He still suspected that the Tyneham Action Group would have 'cheapened' the place with holiday camps, caravans and the rest — 'hunting and all that'. And he was full of boundless admiration for the people on the 1943 Committee. People might run down Rodney Legg, but for Gould he had done a marvellous job: 'Yeah, he's a good chap.' He remembered Lord Fenner Brockway, too: ' "Call me Fenner," he used to say, "call me Fenner, John!" . . . he was out of this world, he was . . . and to speak to him, you'd never have thought he was a Lord.' Brockway was 'a different chap' compared with others of his class too — most of whom wouldn't, Gould felt certain, have hesitated to kick the 'peasants' out of a place like Tyneham.

Gould spoke of Kenneth Allsop with similar admiration — 'Oh he was fantastic he was, he was really for Tyneham.' He remembered the August Bank Holiday actions in the Tyneham car park. The Conservation rally had drawn a 'huge crowd . . . And they were for us again when we reopened the post office in the village and the police came and wanted to chuck us out. We were very close to being in the Black Maria — the Black Maria was there . . . very, very close.' The situation had been tense but then 'the people' spoke out saying, 'You know, you want to leave them alone — that was civilians, come from up North you know . . . like miners or something like that . . . big chaps.' They had come down for the beach at Worbarrow Bay, but they had paused to hear the speeches, and were ready to take action of their own. And neither had the police reckoned with Mavis Caver, who faced them down as they tried to remove the homemade pillar box she had mounted on a post, telling them to leave it alone, and that it was her property.

'That was quite something,' mused Gould, explaining that the Tyneham Action Group would never have done anything like that: 'They was disgusted with that. But I mean you've got to really fight, you can't just sit back and wait, you've got to do something . . . You must have action — see they was Tyneham Action Group but 'twas Tyneham Silent Group . . . ' He didn't doubt that Sir Arthur Bryant was a patriotic fellow, but he insisted on a deeper truth: that 'Conservatives never alter . . . you understand what I mean . . . they're always the same. They're monied people.' So their patriotism is not the same as that of the working man or woman — 'you've got that thought haven't you?' Retrospectively, Gould seemed to have the Bonds rolled up together with the evicting government and the cautious elders of the Tyneham Silent Group. They were all part of the moneyed class faction that controlled everything: 'the bosses and the barons like, you know'. He was in no doubt that Mark Bond 'wanted to make it all up with caravans and what have you, for his own ends'.

To begin with Gould had found it 'queer' to hear the sound of his own voice on a tape recorder, but he soon got used to it, becoming quite adept at performing the turns that the television people expected of him as a representative example of Tyneham Man. Whether it was on *World in Action*, or a children's programme like *Magpie* or *Blue Peter*, the typical Gould appearance opened with an establishing shot in which he was seen sweeping the roads in Wareham. He would then ride his bike over the Wareham bridge, peddling valiantly towards his lost home, while the TV crew filmed him from a car in front. After that was in the can they would drive him to Tyneham, lend a slight tilt to his flat cloth cap and give him a bunch of wild flowers to hold: 'Then they would say, well, there's a tree trunk, sit there and tell us about your life, like . . . ' The formula was simple enough — 'Pick a bunch of flowers, sit down and talk about Tyneham' — and Gould quickly got used to reciting the same things over and over again. Like the newspaper photographers, the television people treated Gould as a villager betrayed by modern history: a hobbit-like creature who had popped out of the primrosey bole of an oak tree only to find England's most enchanted valley invaded by the terrible machines of State. Gould played the allotted parts well. He was the expropriated roadsweeper; an invalided war veteran whose hopes had been betrayed; a latter-day Tolpuddle Martyr; a Native who had been barred from making the Return that natural justice, to say nothing of Thomas Hardy, demanded.

'Oh I kept all the pieces about Tyneham that I could get . . . ' Looking back through his album of press cuttings, Gould repeats that the problem lay with the government not the Army, and the civilian employees who used to get 'pin money' from poaching deer, or beating on the Army's pheasant or rabbit shoots. 'Oh, there was a lot of that going on . . . that was our opposition, you see . . . came from people like that.' He remembered going over to darts matches at West Lulworth and being greeted by the loyalists. 'Here's a rebel coming,' they would say, joking but not really: 'They'd make a lot of money, you see.'

The final defeat of the campaign had been another bitter betrayal. The reception of the Friends of Tyneham's deputation to Lord Brayley had truly shocked him. That Labour Minister had stood there with his civil servants, smiling away and saying 'It's all right, you don't want to worry, everything's being taken care of, you know, we'll see you get a fair hearing and all this and that.' Heartened by this reception, the deputation had returned to Tyneham late that afternoon, lifting the gate off its hinges and driving down to place a wreath on the church door. Gould ruined his new suit evading the Army patrol that came down to evict them, but the real disappointment came, so Gould thought, having contracted what was actually an interval of a week into one night, with the very next morning's papers, which announced that Nugent's proposal had been rejected, thus confirming Gould's worst suspicions about the true nature of British government: 'When you got in there, you knew that the government wasn't the boss. The civil servants were the bosses, definitely. Him with a file with a crown on.' Having studied Harold Wilson, Brayley and Roy Mason, the reneging Minister of Defence, Gould had no doubt that these politicians were just helpless 'pawns' or 'underdogs' to the faceless civil servants. 'Democracy? No, I don't think that was democracy . . . Since then I've had no confidence at all in any government.' Casting himself in the role of Tyneham's last Labour supporter, he had resigned his membership of the party in disgust.

Gould had been disappointed by the sudden collapse of the campaign too. Once the government decision had been taken, people like Fenner Brockway and Rodney Legg seemed to vanish: 'They just went.' He missed Margaret Kraft too, who used to pick him up on Sundays and take him over to the valley whatever the weather: 'I've often said to her, I says you was born in Tyneham the way that you carry on.' He had extended the same honorary belonging on Mavis Caver, who replied that, by this stage, she had indeed been born there. But all that seemed to disappear, and Gould found himself back in the adequately plumbed obscurity of Tyneham Close.

He remained proud of the 1943 Committee — 'We were all together then' — but he had since found a replacement for that lost solidarity in the Royal British Legion. His fellow Legionnaires had no difficulty grasping why Gould had fought for Tyneham. 'You've got to fight. You've got to fight a hundred percent.' This had been the lesson of Tyneham, and Gould went on to apply it to the welfare state and the health service, and to the British Legion too. It was in the same determined spirit that he now set out to raise sponsors for the Legion's benevolent fund: 'You've got to be a hundred per cent or it's no good at all.' He hoped that, when his time came, his ashes would be taken to Tyneham churchyard and scattered over his grandparents' grave.

Miss Helen Taylor, or 'Beatie', was almost the last villager to leave the Tyneham valley; and until very recently, she was still living in Sunnymount, the bungalow in Corfe Castle that had been requisitioned in 1945 for her, her elder sister Bessie, and her father, William Taylor, woodman on the Tyneham estate. A singular-looking garden chair stood by the front door, made by a local carpenter from the timbers of an old brandy barrel said

— although she didn't necessarily believe it — to have been deposited in the cellar of Tyneham House by smugglers as unofficial payment for the use of a cave in the woods.

By 1986, when I first met her, Helen Taylor had told the story of Tyneham and its evacuation so many times that every detail had its habitual place. Like John Gould, she admitted to having suffered childish misconceptions. There was no Big Brother in her valley, but as a child she had been too literal in her understanding of the biblical legend carved above the village tap — believing that the water, always in short supply, had been put there to tempt them, and that if they did drink it they would 'thirst for ever', rather than receiving everlasting life. As for Lilian Bond's portrait of Tyneham as an organic and mutually dependent Christian community, Taylor had none of Gould's misgivings: 'It's exactly right, what she says,' remarks Taylor of the lady who had referred to her and her sister as 'you children' right up to her own dying day.

Helen Taylor remembered the quality of Tyneham House ('Panelled and all that. Yes it's a shame'), and was pleased to confirm that everyone had indeed been in the habit of going to church. She told of the boot club she used to run — partly financed by Mrs Bond's jumble sales — for the farm worker's children, who were especially likely to get their feet soaked coming across the fields to school; and also of the dances at which they used to introduce the village 'clodhoppers' — the farm labourers — to the polka. She remembered visiting elderly villagers who had been transferred to the Wareham workhouse for their last years — 'they call it Christmas Close now,' she said with nineteenth-century dread still echoing in her voice. Yet she had no doubt as to the satisfaction that had pervaded the valley. 'Oh yes . . . there was no . . . not like today, when they're counting all their minutes, aren't they, and time and all the rest of it. They'd work till they'd finished the job and was happy about it, happy in their jobs. Yes, you didn't hear any grousing about it.'

When I asked if there had ever been trade unions in the valley, she waved the thought aside, saying 'None of that stuff,' speeding on to explain that 'We were all more or less Conservatives and that sort of thing . . . had to be because of the Bonds.' She remembered Lord Salisbury visiting at election times during the years when he was MP for South Dorset. He would come to speak in the school, where a little concert would also be held to draw people in. The Tory candidate was always a friend of the Bonds, but the Liberal was less welcome. There would be no reception got up for him, and, since the schoolroom wasn't made available, he was obliged to make do with an outside stand instead. As for the Labour Party, Helen Taylor was not at all convinced that it had even existed. The Bonds were Conservatives, and although agitators might have tried stirring up militant thoughts among the farm workers elsewhere, 'Well, we didn't have 'em in Tyneham!'

Taylor cherished the story of the villagers' patriotic sacrifice and had done what she could to ensure that it was only the correct version that received national propagation. She counted up the journalists who had come to interview her over the years. Like Gould, she had done her bit for the television cameras, walking into the church or saluting the flag by the schoolhouse just as the children had done as they filed past it each day. Yet even though she could wring considerable pathos from the story, she also seemed remarkably detached from it. She dwelt on the cruelties of the evacuation, and on the superior way of life that had been lost in 1943, but she was emphatic that she herself had certainly never wanted to go back after the final decision in 1948. This was not just a matter of pragmatic resignation either. It was her form of idealism, her stand for the truth of Tyneham as she had known it.

Taylor was a stickler for accuracy. She had recently noticed certain omissions on the list of former villagers displayed in the church alongside the encased bible, presented by officers of the Royal Armoured Corps. She had been on to the Army but, suspecting, rightly enough, that they would be loathe to remake the display, she was thinking of naming the missing persons on her own roll of honour and then squeezing it under the glass. She was particularly eager to commemorate Mrs Wheeler, who had made an important contribution to life in the valley even though she was not indigenous, and, far more embarrassing for the posthumous cult of Tyneham, had lived in an ugly modern bungalow of exactly the kind that the Army were now praised for having kept out.

Taylor had also defended the memory of Tyneham against those who used the idea of Churchill's pledge to turn Tyneham's story into an evocative myth of England's post-war ruin. I once showed her a representative cutting from the *Daily Mail*, which, besides putting the usual bullet holes in the telephone box, claimed that: 'Old Mrs Pearce's garden, a village spectacle in pre-war summer days, is an overgrown jungle like all the others, though the wallflowers and Canterbury bells still struggle through.' 'What nonsense,' said Taylor, 'There never was a Mrs Pearce in Tyneham village.'

She was in no doubt that the liberationists had been the worst and most meretricious falsifiers: the Tyneham Action Group and the 1943 Committee alike. 'We called them the Suffragettes,' she remembered to the amusement of her chuckling sister — a reference back to pre-war days 'when they used to be kicking up a disturbance, didn't they, those suffragettes.' Counting her way through the regiment of militant women — Colyer, Caver, Hutchings, Kraft — Taylor asserted that they had all come from Blandford and other distant places: they had probably never even been to Tyneham, and they certainly hadn't lived there. As for Rodney Legg, well he wasn't even born when Tyneham was evacuated, which, in her eyes, wholly disqualified him from any legitimate involvement.

As a defender of parochial truth, Helen Taylor had gone into action against the Suffragettes and their male allies: 'Yes, I saw them at the car park, yes — lecturing — all these people round the cars, you know, and all the dreadful things, you see, that the Army was doing and all this and that; and, oh, a lot of lies about the people that had gone. So I listened for a bit, and there were so many untruths that I just stepped in and said, "I'd like to say a few words . . . " ' Having declared on her own experienced authority that, far from having been 'booted out' by the Army, the villagers had actually accepted their fate in a spirit of patriotic sacrifice, she was gratified to find some people falling in behind her as she marched off: 'I walked through the gate and went on down the road. Several of the women ran after, not the Action Group but the visitors that had been listening, ran after me and said, "Well, that was clever of you, speaking up . . . Do you know, we hardly believed it, what they were saying." I said "It's a lot of lies you're listening to." So they came for a walk with me down the road.'

Miss Taylor had been vigilant too when Rodney Legg or any other Tyneham liberationist wrote to the Press, 'If it doesn't suit, well I write back and tell them.' She starts reading out hand-written letters that she had sent to the local papers condemning the protestors for their fictionalised accounts of her home: 'Oh why doesn't someone see their folly and put it in print for the public to read, has been my wishful thinking, as I am a poor correspondent.' In one letter she accused Philip Draper of having started the campaign, explaining that she had phoned to tick him off for presuming to speak on behalf of the former villagers. 'We were all worried because we felt it seemed so ungrateful to the Army and Whitehall, who have done so much to resettle us all in good houses, and seen to our welfare, and the village and the churchyard is kept tidy, the beach at

Worbarrow free of litter.' Moreover, 'none of the speakers that have been on television knew Tyneham before this, except Mr Draper and his house on the cliff was only a holiday home, and let most of the summers . . .'

As for *The Fight for Tyneham*, the booklet written by Monica Hutchings and published for the Tyneham Action Group by Rodney Legg's Dorset Publishing Company, she was pleased to find her letter rejecting it as a tissue of lies. After scoffing at the claim that all the villagers had left the valley on the same 'chill, damp, raw December day', she moved on to the next sentence, which read: 'They gave up the homes they had known from birth; squire and gardener, postmistress and schoolteacher, parson and pupil, cowman and shepherd, and fisherman.' Taylor had been pleased to dismantle this particular lyric word by word: 'No schoolteacher, as the little school had been closed ten years. Pupils? — No children there of school age. Shepherd — no sheep had been kept for two years. Fishermen — all too old, nineties and eighties, to row about.' The rector was already in the Army, and had left two years previously: 'If this is their cast iron case, as they put it, then it is time it was broken down, like they are doing to the fences.'

So it was with Helen Taylor: one fiercely localised fact piled up on another, and then thrust in the way of an encroaching tide of poetry and make-belief. As far as she was concerned the Tyneham liberationists were interfering busybodies, who had no right to claim that the former villagers wanted to go back. 'Well, as I said, I could count them all on one arm, one hand, the people that were left, and I said, well none of them would go back, they were too old to start up again. They were all comfortably settled . . . And even if they had wanted to return, it could never have been the same.' The situation had changed. The Bonds would not have been able to keep on the staff, and most of the farm workers had been replaced by tractors before the war. As for John Gould, the Taylor sisters were hardly fair in their disparagements. They sang the praises of his father Tom Gould — a true Tyneham loyalist — in order then to cast aspersions on the son's educational attainments; and they suggested, quite unjustly, that he only joined the campaign to draw attention to himself or because he was paid to by the protestors — or in the slighting words they attributed to the council rent collector, 'well he'll do anything for a pint — they gave him a pint!' As far as Helen Taylor was concerned, John Gould had been barking up the wrong tree: 'We often said he couldn't keep his own garden tidy, he couldn't put that place right over there! Couldn't put Tyneham right!'

Like Margaret Bond, who had long since become a friend, Taylor saw the Army as the defender of Tyneham; the guardian of its landscape and memory and in that sense the custodian of parochial experience. Rather tanks than the development that would surely have followed now that the Creech Bonds had sold out to English China Clays. But it wasn't just the 'least worst' line of argument that made the Taylor sisters so loyal to the Army. Helen Taylor had always taken a more positive view in her letters to the Press, and she was happy to explain why. As she and her sister knew from personal experience, soldiers were often sent abroad for training: 'We knew what it was for other people, for their men to have to go abroad to be trained, whereas if they could be trained in England, it was far better for the men, as well as their parents or whatever it is. So we took it in that light.' With the saddest tremor in her voice, Helen Taylor started to talk about her three brothers, who had joined the Dorset Yeomanry in the Great War and marched off to be killed, one after the other. The news had broken her mother, who had died in her early fifties in 1917: as Helen Taylor observed, the shock 'hastened her life'. For the Taylor sisters, Tyneham was a war memorial, and the Royal Armoured Corps stood there as its guard of honour.

In the Eighties Helen Taylor had been pleased to use her deeply scored memories to guide the conservationist reinstatement then underway, even though she had her doubts about the ecological blueprint. She had once told the head warden that the roof of the schoolhouse would cave in if he didn't clear the prodigious ferns growing from its stone tiles, and was surprised when he answered that, while the schoolmistresses of old may have been careful to nip that wayward growth in the bud, the conservationists now thought 'it shouldn't be moved, it should be allowed to ramble and all that sort of thing. And I said no, not in our time.' She also had her own conception of the village pond, which she remembered as a barely working thing where the cows used to drink on their way to be milked at the farm. 'I outlined it for them, to show them where the pond was, and they cleared it out and they had the old pond back again, but then these conservation people go over there and stick a lot of reeds in to attract the dragonflies and that sort of thing . . . filling it up with a lot of rubbish.'

Helen Taylor attended the service in the restored Tyneham church on Remembrance Day 1987; and she had been back the previous June, when she took her sister Bessie's ashes over to be buried in the churchyard. She was much obliged when the Army volunteered to stop firing so that the ceremony would not have to be carried out on a weekend, when it was likely to be interrupted by visitors. Once the interment was completed, she had asked the undertaker to take her down to the overgrown remains of her old house, which she found being cleared at last. She stepped into the roofless ruin with the range warden, who told her to return in August, when she could bring a picnic and have tea in the parlour again.

Back in her sitting-room in Sunnymount, Helen Taylor has found another newspaper cutting, quoting her praise of the Army's renovation of the village: 'I hope it will continue to be under Army administration as long as possible,' she reads, looking up to add 'That's me!'

TWENTY-TWO

THE MILITARY ORCHID

> The Mess, when I arrived there, seemed deserted . . . There were polished tables and chairs in the hall, and the whole place looked oddly unmilitary. On one of the tables stood a bowl full of tall, pinkish flowers. I went to look at them: I looked again; at last I took one out of the bowl. Yes, there could be no doubt: the plant I held in my hand was the Military Orchid.
>
> Jocelyn Brooke (1948)

WHO COULD EVER forget Keith and Candice-Marie Pratt? Leaving their Purbeck campsite to visit Lulworth Cove, these paragons of ecological correctness set off down the winding lane in their convertible Morris Minor. They paused to wonder which of the many cows gathered in a gateway might have produced the unpasteurised milk they had bought the previous day, and then, like so many nature lovers before them, they drew up in overdramatised surprise before the military notice announcing that the road over Povington Hill and down the Whiteway to East and West Lulworth was closed for firing.

So the Pratts — the aptly named heroes of Mike Leigh's television film *Nuts in May* — reluctantly turned north for a long detour around the perimeter fence before approaching Lulworth across the heath on the B3070. Somewhere in the vicinity of the Franklin Viewpoint, Candice-Marie started to wonder: 'If we didn't have an Army — just think about it . . . ' If Britain were the first country to scrap the Army, 'everyone else might gradually follow suit and then we'd have no wars at all, and no trouble and no killing and maiming of people'. Her organic husband Keith counters this emotional stuff with a dose of bearded realism: 'There are some very unscrupulous people about, you know . . . '

Here was 'conservationism' of the kind that Peter Rudd and the Keep the Army in Lulworth Committee had fought off so successfully a couple of years previously: guitar-strumming and woolly-hatted faddism, whose cranky advocates adhered to the country code with a fierce intolerance of the swarming masses who thought that communing with nature could be done with a transistor radio. Leigh's researches extend to a dimly remembered meeting with Rodney Legg, but his parody remained beside the significant point. It placed conservationism where it had been through most of the century — on the outside of the military wire looking in aghast. Yet even in January 1976 when *Nuts in May* was first broadcast, the Pratts were a small thing compared with what the Ministry of Defence were beginning to get up to on the range itself.

The conservationist card had previously been played to good effect by the atomic energy establishment on Winfrith Heath. No sooner was the effluent pipe under construction in 1959, than the trench diggers unearthed a Romano-British farmstead, thereby ensuring there had been much talk about 'Atoms and Archaeology' and 'pipelines leading to potsherds' by the time they got to the remains of the village cleared in the late eighteenth century to make way for Lulworth Park. But the greening of the Lulworth ranges, which followed implementation of the Nugent report, was to be more thoroughgoing than anything achieved by the 'atomic gardeners' of Winfrith.[1] To begin with, as Rodney Legg remembers, the Ministry of Defence may have hoped to get away with 'throwing footpaths at the problem', but it was ecology rather than just improved public access that was to be the Army's ultimate weapon.

The Ministry of Defence's Slide Show

Were it not for one flagrantly wayward detail, Colonel J. H. Baker's headquarters in Chessington, Surrey, would seem entirely unremarkable. The visitor travels along a suburban stretch of the Leatherhead Road and then passes through high metal gates into a typical government compound featuring checkpoints and low-lying concrete buildings, with car parks and the usual profusion of signs scattered about between them.

Colonel Baker's offices stand next to HM Treasury Computer Centre. Trees march alongside the path to his door in evenly spaced columns, and though the lawn to the left may be a little scorched, it is neat and tidy as can be. On the right-hand side, however, the lawn has given way to a herbaceous riot that defies all the rules of bureaucratic order. This is Colonel Baker's 'conservation patch', a tiny 'grassland management scheme'. Thanks to his intervention, it is mown only twice a year, and its flora and fauna are studied in close detail. More than fifty Bee Orchids appeared in 1991; the Pyramidal Orchids produced twelve flower spikes, and the cowslips were profuse. Blue butterflies have come to flutter over this anomalous patch. Lady's Bedstraw has been recorded, and a single Common Spotted-Orchid was recently discovered by a Senior Civil Servant 'not normally noted for his deep knowledge of natural history'. Barrows and megalithic earthworks will no doubt be found there before long.

Not content with establishing a stretch of reverted chalk downland on his official doorstep, Colonel Baker has also converted his office to the outdoor life. Doors and windows are flung wide open. A prehistoric stone implement, of the sort collected by Llewelyn Powys, stands in as a paperweight, and the native flora and fauna of England undulate in the breeze, suspended on pictorial wall-charts behind the desk. Colonel Baker is an enthusiastic, slightly frantic fellow who tends to jump up and down as he talks, rushing about in pursuit of papers or copies of the Ministry of Defence's annual conservation magazine *Sanctuary* — free copies of which are sometimes available in the Tyneham schoolhouse — and firing flinty, chap-like remarks at the 'revolting' students attached to his Conservation Office.

Attempting to pin him down in mid-flight, I ask exactly what kind of Colonel he is and how he came to be the Ministry of Defence's Conservation Officer. Long since retired from the Irish Guards, he explains that he also runs the family estate in Sussex, so 'one's always had a great interest in all things natural history'. As for the job, he owes it to Lord Nugent's Defence Lands Committee, which notified the Ministry of Defence that the old system of blasting on regardless could no longer be sustained. A Conservation Officer should be appointed to co-ordinate activities across the different services and act as a link between the military and concerned civilian bodies.

Colonel Baker has pursued his goals of 'active management' and 'positive conservation' by building a network of M.o.D. Conservation Groups, each of which is charged with surveying its particular site from the point of view of the various conservationist disciplines, and then advising the military authorities on future management. There are now over two hundred such groups in Britain. Chaired by the Commanding Officer of the M.o.D. site in question, they bring together people from the military side — the Service Authority, the Defence Lands Agency, grounds maintenance staff, the M.o.D. Conservation Office, etc. — with people from the Nature

Conservancy Council, and the various specialists, who can themselves be as curious as any branch of wildlife. As Colonel Baker puts it, the botanists tend to be women — 'Miss Marple-like' creatures who stalk about with eyeglasses and are 'absolutely divine'. Birds are relatively straightforward, but the British are less keen on insects and a good general entomologist is especially hard to find: 'You can have someone who knows everything about butterflies but nothing at all about bugs!'

Soon enough, this energetic human fig leaf has whisked me down the hall and launched into the slide presentation he has given up and down the country, the precise opposite of the anti-military one that Monica Hutchings used to show on behalf of the Tyneham Action Group. Colonel Baker looks me straight in the eye and launches his introductory salvo. 'People are accustomed to thinking of Army ranges as blasted heaths, but we are now running what is in effect the largest and most important nature reserve in Britain.' The Forestry Commission may have most land, but the Ministry of Defence has more Sites of Special Scientific Interest. The Defence holding includes some three thousand sites around Great Britain, with peerless examples of all the major kinds of habitat: moorland, wetland, dry heathland and chalk downland. At 93,000 acres, Salisbury Plain is 'the largest stretch of unimproved downland in the country'. The gunnery range at Castlemartin in Pembrokeshire is 'a marvellous place', complete with choughs that are no longer even to be found in Cornwall. The chemical research establishment at Porton Down may specialise in poisons and their antidotes, but this deadly place is also 'mind-blowing' for its flowers and surely 'the premier butterfly site in England'. The coastal sites are 'marvellous stepping-stones for migrant birds'. Britain's defence lands are blessed with 'frightfully rare' flowers, even if, and here Colonel Baker allows himself an unprompted moment of regret, the Military Orchid has so far not been found.

Colonel Baker declares his theme to be 'the interaction of wildlife and the military artefact', and, as the slides clatter by, it becomes clear that he relishes this as a story of paradoxical co-existence. Such is the M.o.D.'s version of the pastoral tradition and, as its leading exponent, Colonel Baker likes nothing better than a picture of an ammunition case that has been turned into a breeding box for owls, or of a moorhen pecking at the fins of a mortar bomb stuck in the mud of a pool. He concedes that some of these images are poetic constructs, specially assembled for the camera: the smooth snake coiled over a discarded clip of ammunition, or the short-tailed field vole peering out of a shell-case. But he guarantees that there really are places where wagtails nest in the rusted engines of abandoned vehicles, and where barn owls sit sleepily on the barrels of much blasted Soviet target tanks. And where this fortunate coincidence of metal and wildlife doesn't occur spontaneously, why not give nature a helping hand? Click. That scaffolding was put up to provide a nesting-site for herons. Click. The Royal Engineers are wonderfully co-operative. 'Look! They've graded this pond so that the natterjack toads — charming little chaps — can get in and out.'

It would be a singularly resistant cynic who wasn't a little impressed by this stage of Colonel Baker's slide show, but the man is only just getting into his stride. Throwing another stretch of brooding wilderness up against the wall, he proclaims that, were it not for the M.o.D., even more of the nation's heathland would have been built over or turned into golf courses: 'The yuppies don't want to keep it clear, so it is jolly lucky that we've got lots of it.' But while conceding that conservation may have started as an accidental 'spin-off' from training, Colonel Baker is not content to rest with this passive idea of benign neglect. The 'interface' between military training and conservation can be managed in a way that provides benefits on both sides. Fallen trees, if left to lie, provide good cover for riflemen as well as for beetles and fungi. Soldiers train for surveillance duties in Northern Ireland by guarding the nests of red kites in Mid-Wales and ospreys in the Scottish Highlands.

Not content with such happy coincidences, there are places where the M.o.D. is positively working towards the reinstatement of the traditional British landscape. As Baker explains, 'The one thing we don't want is an eroded dustbowl in which to train, and that's what you get if you overuse armour.' The best training ground is actually normal countryside. The M.o.D. has taken to planting hedgerows of the traditional type, having discovered that they serve as good 'lines of approach' for infantry soldiers. The reinstatement of native woodland is also promised: monocultural blocks of conifer may have suited the Forestry Commission, but they are not much good for training, so 'we are planting eighty per cent broadleaf now, with some conifer for air cover'. The military have been playing the conservation card in a half-embarrassed, opportunistic kind of way since the early Twenties, when apologists ventured to suggest that Lulworth's tanks might be less worse than charabancs, but Colonel Baker is pursuing a more thoroughgoing strategy. There is nothing sheepish about his version of the English pastorale.

The Crater As Habitat

The Lulworth firing range is one of Colonel Baker's favourite M.o.D. sites. 'It's got everything,' he says: heath, coastal cliff, sheltered valleys, woodland and rolling chalk downland. And he would be delighted to arrange a visit. So it was thanks to him that, a few days later in the summer of 1991, I was finally invited for lunch at the Officers' Mess, a large brick building with a vaguely Edwardian ambience and a couple of good-natured regimental dogs scampering about. The terrace commands a marvellous view of Arish Mell Gap, once the exclusive property of Lulworth Castle. This prospect is much appreciated up at the Officers' Mess, and no one feels much inclined to apologise for the variations that seventy-five years of military occupation have added to the scene since Bindon Hill was taken over during the Great War. The landscape may be gouged and covered in numbered arc-markers, but it is not as if this is the first time the area has been remade in the name of defence. Colonel Alexander Lindsay, the Commandant at the time of my visit, pointed to the signs of prehistoric earthworking which have led archaeologists to identify Bindon Hill as an early Neolithic beachhead. Anyone wanting further proof of the tank man's devotion to the landscape only has to walk along the ridge of Bindon Hill and consider the small cairn where the ashes of deceased tank veterans are scattered to the winds. The request is not that unusual, and the range officers are happy to fulfil the wishes of these veterans who reach the end of their days with no better loved place in mind than the hill into which they fired as trainees.

The Heritage Coast Path was established in the early Eighties, and most of the range area has since been declared a Site of Special Scientific Interest. Tyneham itself has been reinstated as a 'heritage attraction' — the buildings levelled in the name of safety and then capped with cement, paths established and the whole site themed up with signs and exhibitions. Lieutenant-Colonel Mike Butler, who was responsible for the non-service side of the range, described the requests from companies wanting to make films on the range (the Tyneham area has been in particular demand ever since it developed a reputation in the late Sixties as 'the valley without pylons').

Bill Douglas had been allowed to make *Comrades*, but the Lulworth Ranges were not routinely available as a film-set. Explaining that some requests have to be refused, he pleaded for understanding: 'We are, after all, a firing range.'

Then there was the Conservation Committee. A young major let slip that its meetings could be 'mind-bogglingly boring', but Colonel Butler insisted that he and his fellow officers were all in favour of protecting the environment: 'I feel deeply, in myself, that what we are doing here is good. There is no alternative, until such a time as we can do without tanks. Then it should become a National Park.' The committee really was taken seriously — even though it can be an uphill struggle getting the different 'ologists' to see eye to eye. As Colonel Lindsay observed, our job is to be 'mildly encouraging' and 'try to stop them murdering each other'. There had been disagreement over the Sika deer. To the deer man these creatures may be everything, but they can be a plague to local farmers, and other members of the committee regretted them as non-native immigrants. The deer man was concerned about the cows trampling down his deer patches, but if the cattle were fenced out the grassland would revert to scrub, and that would worry other members of the committee. The flower people might like to clear the gorse and encroaching scrub, but the bird man — who turned out to be the photographer over at Bovington Camp, and adamant that he was not one of those 'twitchers' who are only interested in sighting exotic specimens — values dense thickets for the nightingales that now congregate in the Tyneham valley, and also for the small passerines of his ringing programmes. And then there was Colonel Prendergast, the dragonfly chap, who is 'very keen on explosions'. It's all 'quite weird' said the Commandant with a brisk laugh, adding that since Prendergast is a retired sapper he knows what he's talking about.

After lunch Major Mick Burgess, the range officer, took me down to the control centre to show me how the range worked. He distinguished two types of red flag which are posted all around the perimeter fence: the fifty-five boundary flags that fly permanently, and the lesser number of access flags that only fly when firing is taking place. The area within is broken up into three distinct ranges. The Bindon Range, also known as the 'School-master' Range is for static firing, while the other two are both battle run ranges. The Heath Range takes heavy tanks; whereas the Tyneham Range is dedicated to lighter compact-vehicle reconnaissance. One of his range control staff stands at the computer console, demonstrating the far from aristocratic perspectives that govern the landscape for him. Each type of ammunition comes with a 'template' of its own, drawn up in advance by the Ordnance Board in London. This is all about estimating possible ricochet distances, and when the template is laid over the map, it defines the area within which firing may safely occur. The measures on the computer screen are correlated with the numbered arc-markers planted on the hill-sides, and the Range Safety Officer uses these to guide the gunners, confining them to an arc that may extend from say, 1 on the left over to 9 on the right.

For the sea danger area, the main problem is expressed in terms of 'plots' — dots on the radar screen with little arrows indicating their projected movement. These are the boats that may be approaching or already sailing within the overshoot area. The technology is so impressive that it has been known to register shoaling mackerel, but thanks to generations of protest, the Army's powers of exclusion remain less perfect. The Inner Sea Danger Area is governed by special bylaws which don't quite remove the right of passage. In the Outer Sea Area it is all down to the negotiating skills of the men on the Royal Armoured Corps's three patrol boats, who can only request and advise yachtsmen to choose another course. Burgess observes that neither of the two danger zones had proved entirely safe against the freeborn 'yuppie' of the Thatcher era, who was bloody well going to sail his shiny yacht through, and to Hell with the twenty tanks that may have to stand idle at the taxpayers' expense as he did so.

Mick Burgess then took me out in his Land-rover. We approached Bindon Hill across gouged and littered ground that is prized as one of the few areas of unimproved downland left in Dorset. Burgess pointed out some old Soviet target tanks, T 54s and T 34s, and remarked that some of the blasted sections of armour plate scattered about the place came from the original Ark Royal. Bindon Hill had been under fire for seventy-five years and no attempt has ever been made to clear the land behind the target track. Indeed, Burgess described a unique ecology of shell-disclosure. The rain combines with the continual churning of gunfire to bring things to the surface: recently, a lot of American shells from the Second World War had been turning up. We passed Arish Mell Gap, now a 'scrap area' loaded up with old skips full of rusty and twisted metal waiting for the contractor to come and take it away. Undeterred by this or the prominent nuclear waste pipe, Major Burgess indicated an old bunker he had recently battened up as a refuge for bats: 'I mean the place is alive,' he said, gazing out after a retreating bird — 'Is that a buzzard or a hobby?'

We drove past the ruined farm where the controversial Trappist monastery of St Susan had stood, and then headed off on to the southern edges of heath range at the foot of Whiteways Hill. The old track leads past the obliterated site of Whiteway Farm. Beyond that, we encountered an elaborate, winding construction over which official silence ruled: this was the recently installed multi-million pound target track known as the Lulworth Multi-Path Rail System. Designed to run targets close to each other and at unpredictable speeds, it uses a software package derived from the London Docklands Light Railway, and I had gathered the reason for the silence on a previous visit to the Weld Arms: after even more tinkering than was required by its famously delinquent inner city cousin, the damn thing still wasn't working: besides costing vast amounts of money, it had rendered the heath range barely usable for years.

Mick Burgess pointed to damage left over from the 'ignorant' pre-ecological days when tanks roamed freely over the heath and prominent tumuli were likely to be adopted as targets or challenging obstacles to be driven over at speed. He also slowed to indicate an unexceptional-looking shallow pool, the product of a recent collaboration between himself and the Conservation Committee. He had a load of plastic explosives to dispose of, and Colonel Prendergast, the retired sapper who is said to be 'ecstatic' about explosions, wanted more pools in which dragonflies could breed. So they detonated the landscape, and here was the result, a teeming ecosystem already looking as if it had been there for a hundred years.

We later headed east down Povington Lane, where a few bewildered fruit trees and daffodils in the spring are the last memorials of a settlement that was also extinguished in 1943 but never found its posthumous cult or liberationists. Near the end of this road, we gazed into the dazzling white void that has only become more vast since Rodney Legg denounced it as 'the biggest hole in Dorset'. Here was Clement Attlee's claypit, still busy even though it is no longer producing sanitation-ware for an expanding welfare state. As we stood rubbing our eyes at its brightness, Burgess said it was strange to think of the millions of urinals that had come out of that lunar chasm. We drove on past a perfectly reinstated field where, only a few weeks before, BP had been drilling for oil, drawing up at a farm left over from the days of traditional husbandry, this one called West Creech, and still equipped with an ancient wooden granary barn mounted on stone stilts to keep the rats from the seed corn. I thought of H. J. Massingham as we wandered around this more or less intact fragment of Old England. Mick Burgess described his job as 'a dream come true — I get up in the morning and I'm dying to go to work'.

Laughing with the Tankman

Seen from a distance, the Army's conversion to conservation suggests the final triumph of the metallic state over the old organic nation of romantic protest. It also raises questions about the ecological cause, and the lengths to which its activists are prepared to go in their eagerness to place a limit on environmental transgression — preferring tanks to the limitless principles of private property and the individual's right to choose. The wider affinity between green activism and military power is already being explored by environmentalists who have imagined a new role for modern military technology in the battle against global environmental threats like the depletion of the ozone layer.[2]

Yet there is also a rising sense of incredulity: a sudden disbelieving laugh, familiar to everyone who has ever tried to advance this unlikely claim that tanks are good for the natural environment, and shellfire a force for conservation. Many snort with contempt on first hearing this argument — saying, just as the Tyneham Action Group used to do in the late Sixties, that the Army surely can't expect to get away with an absurd claim like that. And the promoters of this new military logic also smile at the irony, remembering their own surprise when they were first introduced to this unexpected weapon of self-defence.

Yet the laugh is short-lived, and the joke really only appreciable on the upper heights of the descending path that has brought us from the high country of romantic protest, where everything is touched with visionary simplicity, down to the lower plain where 'management' determines the shape of things. Up there is Peace, Cosmic Insight, and Organic Understanding: English idealism wrapped in green megalithic rings and vigorously defended against the evils of Encroachment, Defilement, and Metallic Interruption. Below is the unillusioned world of pragmatic compromise, where the 'least worst' is as much as anyone dare demand. Laughter measures the distance between those two realms, yet it also dwindles in the descent, becoming an irritant when people start insisting that this, for better or worse, is actually where we live now and there is a job of work to be done.

This new definition of the firing range marks a break between the predominantly cultural and anti-statist valuation of English rural life that motivated the preservationist cause in the Thirties, and the scientific idea of conservation that emerged in the Forties and found its basis in the state with agencies like the Nature Conservancy. It is fitting that Norman Moore, who pioneered the Nature Conservancy's work on the Dorset heathland, should have got to know the Dorset heath while serving as a gunnery instructor on Salisbury Plain.[3] Aware of the place from pre-war holidays, he organised an artillery exercise on the heaths around Purbeck, and remembers driving around the range area on his motorbike. He met Rolf Gardiner and attended a few events at Springhead while serving as the Nature Conservancy's Regional Officer for South-West England in the Fifties. But as a scientific ecologist he was not to be detained by dreamy stuff about the soil — the 'muck and mystery', as it was called at the time. His main concern was to demonstrate how dramatically the Dorset heaths had been diminished and fragmented by modern development, and then to press for its practical conservation. From this point of view there is nothing funny about the fact that the land some might still consider to be 'lost' within the Lulworth ranges includes the largest unbroken remnant of Thomas Hardy's Egdon Heath.

This is not to say that everyone is entirely happy with the present compromise. Some members of the Conservation Committee fear that the recently awakened commitment to conservation remains cosmetic, and could easily be wiped out by any development that led to increased pressure on the ranges. The Ministry of Defence's green fig leaf slipped badly in the first months of 1994, when serious damage was reported on defence lands all over Britain as tank and artillery regiments returned from overseas, and Colonel Baker, the M.o.D's Conservation Officer, quickly discovered the limitations of his own modest rank. The Lulworth ranges have not yet been badly affected, but the settlement remains frail.

Some longstanding observers of the Tyneham Valley are pleased to cite the Army's 'robust' management of the range as proof that nature is not the fading flower that some conservationists seem to imagine, but they too admit there have been problems: some participants in the Army's shoots can't tell rooks from ravens, and there was a range-warden or keeper who left out rabbit carcasses injected with strychnine in the name of 'vermin-control'. Public access is also a cause for concern. Some would like to see it further increased; others suspect that the allowances made after the Nugent recommendation was turned down are already proving too much for the wildlife. Major Burgess, the Range Officer, hears a third objection from visitors to the Franklin Viewpoint. He has been reproached by people who are disappointed to be told that the firing is in abeyance so that the range can be opened for walkers. They protest that they've come down with their families from as far away as Manchester or Scotland. They've been to the Tank Museum over at Bovington, and now they've come to the coast hoping to settle into a picnic and watch as the tanks line up at firing points Alpha, Bravo, Charlie, and Delta and start blasting away at Bindon Hill. So Burgess laughs too, rubbing the faded tattoo on his arm, and saying there's no pleasing some people ...

Over at the gunnery school the talk about conservation finds a different significance. The officers' mess is full of testimony to a glorious past: the fireplaces have great rough fenders made from the unditching beams of old Great War tanks, and famous pioneers from the heroic first days gaze out from portraits. But the cavalry regiments have been reduced and amalgamated many times over since the Second World War and the cuts are not letting up. Colonel Lindsay, the Commandant who was himself on the brink of retirement when I met him, remarked that tanks have taken the brunt of the recent reductions in Britain's armed forces. Under present plans the number in service would go down by fifty-two per cent and though every single tank commander in the Gulf War had been through Lulworth, no one expects this to make any difference. They felt let down by John Keegan, who had been using the *Daily Telegraph* to advocate further reduction in the armed forces; and, casting an eye on events in the former Soviet bloc, they doubted the wisdom of the review process 'Options for Change'. So conservation, which has proved a remarkably elastic term over the years, is now stretched out to provide cover for the Army itself. With its picture of a crater being detonated for dragonflies, the exhibition in Tyneham School spelt out the danger: making the double-edged observation that the current ecological balance of the range would be threatened by drastic changes in defence policy. But it is Colonel Baker who has the perfect slide to illustrate this anxiety. It shows a commando hiding in undergrowth next to a coiled adder, and the carefully primed question is released with perfect timing: 'Which is the endangered species?'

Concerned to keep the fading myth of Tyneham in perspective, I drove to Slape Flax Mill, near Netherbury in West Dorset, curious to see what remained of the place where Rolf Gardiner had tried to resuscitate the Wessex flax industry. The river Brit still meandered through the fields in which Gardiner revived ancient techniques like dew-retting, before the mass-productionists at the Home Flax Directorate ended his experiments. The mill where Gardiner tried to prove that the 'romantic' and 'business' outlooks could co-exist, was still there, a Georgian building of stone with brick extensions, along with the large concrete outhouses into which the operation had expanded before the post-war Labour government closed it down. Slape has not been fortunate since. For a time it was a stinking maggot factory, but the drive is now littered with old skips, the ground of organic revival is black and hardened with oil, and the site heaped high with old cars. Overtaken by what Gardiner deplored as 'petrol England', Slape has become a wrecker's yard. A modern rural industry stands in the place of defeated organic revival: the metal has won.

Tyneham has fared better than this. For a brief moment in the Eighties, its no longer so forbidden valley seemed to gain new enchantment as an exceptional coastal resort where uncommercial austerity still governed the beach, and where the state never did get rolled back — except for those range wardens whose jobs, created by the Labour government that rejected Nugent's recommendation, disappeared in the cuts imposed under Margaret Thatcher. Curiously, however, the recent conversion of the village into a signposted monument and teachers' aid, has greatly diminished its aura. As its thoroughfares were named again, and the houses won back from the undergrowth and levelled to an officially recognised safe height, Tyneham became thinner in its significance. English Nature was worried when the range wardens scrubbed the lichens off the old gravestones, but that wasn't all these overzealous restorers scraped from the encrusted ruins. Their labours had the accidental effect of clearing the village of the sedimented post-war cult that had settled over it: even the church seemed emptier as the pews were brought back in, the memorial window to Grace Draper was put back into place, and the commemorative bibles were installed.

Tyneham has lost much of its post-war charisma. The measures taken to convert it into a tourist attraction have demythologised the place — chasing its spectral and nostalgic elements over the hill, and back into the wider national culture from which they had originally been imported. One version of Churchill's pledge landed between the covers of Kenneth Baker's anthology of *English History in Verse*. Another took refuge in the speeches of Prince Charles, with his revivalist fable of the 'second chance' — in which the sacrifices of the war, so grievously betrayed by the peace, could be redeemed if only ordinary people stuck to tradition and rose up against the progressive experts. Perhaps the dynamited dragonfly pool even found its civil equivalent in the organic reed bed sewage system that Charles has installed at Highgrove. The spirit also lives on in the works of Lady P. D. James, the Conservative detective novelist and moralist who has remembered the pre-war village of lost English constancies in articles written for the *Salisbury Review*, and who once said of Tyneham: 'Every time I've been there I've felt a strong need to write about that village.'[4]

It is far from clear where, or whether, the honourable Christian virtues of Tyneham will re-emerge, for it is only the weakest of temporary accommodation that they have found in John Major's misfired 'back to basics' campaign, or his attempt to conciliate the 'Eurosceptics' in his party by promising that 'Britain will survive unamendable in all essentials.' As for *This England*, the 'heritage' quarterly in which such stuff really belongs, it may, in the early Seventies, have rejected Rodney Legg's suggested article about Tyneham as 'too depressing', but it got round to reprinting Arthur Bryant's 1949 *Illustrated London News* article about Tyneham in 1982. By the early Nineties, editor Roy Faiers had handed Bryant's occasional 'Forever England' column over to Stuart Millson, an erstwhile British National Party member, who was soon writing mushy elegies defending 'England' against the 'unnatural multi-cultural society' that will surely soon overwhelm us all. This is the man who, in 1992, launched a 'Revolutionary Conservative Caucus' dedicated to turning the nation into a human conifer plantation by restoring 'the monocultural hegemony of the majority'. Such are the weak echoes of a dying cult: Tyneham as homeless cliché and dim travesty of Tory values; Tyneham as sick white trash. As Dennis Potter once remarked of the easily hijacked language of patriosm, 'The trouble with words is you never know whose mouths they've been in.'[5]

There is quite a lot to be said for the village in its present reduced state, and Rodney Legg seems content with it too. He is now the Chairman of the Open Spaces Society (formerly the Commons, Open Spaces and Footpaths Preservation Society) and, in that capacity, also a critical member of the National Trust's executive committee, who has not tired of tilting at the patrician culture of that organisation. In the autumn of 1993 I went trespassing with him. We walked along the limestone ridge from Kimmeridge and left the clearly marked path near the remains of the old RAF radar station called Brandy Bay, to climb down towards South Egliston, the house that stood at the centre of Mary Butts's Hollow Land. This forgotten building has fallen into ruin since the Army took it over, but it was still possible to find the three French windows and the flagged terrace on which Butts's doomed young things put on their gramophone to play jazz at the woodpeckers. The garden is completely bewildered, so there is no way of knowing whether the yucca that flowers significantly on the lawn of the house at the close of Butts's *Armed With Madness* had its original here, or over at Tyneham Great House, where old photographs show just such an exotic plant blooming on the lawn. The Sacred Wood is still shaped like the clasped fan of Butts's evocation, but inside it is overgrown, dank and repellant. Rodney Legg took the lead, snipping away as he went, his heavy duty wire-cutters traded for secateurs, pointing out a rare spread of yellow irises and discoursing knowledgeably about ilex trees. We unearthed a forgotten tar-walled stone house at the lower end of this bristling thicket, but there was no lost world in that disenchanted grove.

A few months later, we met again in the Tyneham car park. It was 19 December 1993 – the fiftieth anniversary of the eviction. Only a handful of people showed up: a few habitual Tyneham enthusiasts and a farmer from the Isle of Wight, who still remembered the *Daily Telegraph* article of May 1968. Kiwi, the New Zealander range warden, was there too. He explained that the Colonel had been over earlier that morning to pay his respects. Reminiscing about the campaign with Legg, he agreed that it was probably the Soviet invasion of Prague that finished it off, and then wondered why the last former villager who sometimes still made the sad pilgrimage – a solitary fellow whose father had been a coachman for the Bonds – hadn't come along. Legg hung his final wreath up in church, dedicating it to the memory of the villagers who had been evicted and recalling the broken pledge. But the Press hadn't shown up. The story was ended.

As we left the church, I asked about Bill Douglas's relocated sycamore tree, the one that had been moved to serve as the Martyrs' tree in *Comrades*. Douglas had hoped that this tribute to a contrary rural tradition would survive, but Kiwi shook his head. It had looked fine for a few years, but its roots must have been damaged for one spring it died. That stack of rotting logs was all that remained of it. Rodney Legg, who now serves on the committee that advises the Army over its maintenance of Tyneham village, was pleased to find the exhibition in the schoolhouse being changed. Military ecology may, as Legg says, be better than no ecology at all, but it was still a relief to find the picture of the ecological explosion had been removed, along with all the other propagandist statements about the Army's benevolent custody. The new exhibition opted for kitsch evocation of an uncontroversial kind, thereby completing the evacuation of Tyneham as a mythological site. The schoolhouse is now filled with imported desks. Authenticated names are written by each coathook in the hall and there is a blackboard on which some imaginary schoolmistress has written a sentimental allegory about thrift — surely the only old Tyneham virtue that still flowers pink along the wild edges of Gad Cliff.

NOTES

CHAPTER 1

[1] Philip Brannon, *Sea Coast Retirement at West Lulworth, East Lulworth and Kimmeridge, Dorsetshire, being a guide and companion to the enjoyment of the exquisite scenery and eminent sanitary advantages of these sequestered sites*, London, 1864, p.15.

[2] Father Paul's account of the monastery at Arish Mell was published in the *Gentleman's Magazine*, April 1813, and is quoted in John Hutchins, *The History of Dorset*, Third Edition, Vol. I, 1861, p.389.

[3] John Hutchins, *The History and Antiquities of the County of Dorset*, First Edition, London, 1774, Vol. II, p.163.

[4] For Thomas Hardy's poem 'At Lulworth Cove a Century Back' see James Gibson (ed.), *The Complete Poems of Thomas Hardy*, London, 1976 p.602. Lulworth Cove features in *The Dynasts*, and the 'tradition' asserting that Napoleon, 'the Corsican ogre', landed on the coast hereabouts, to prospect his intended invasion, is used in the story 'A Tradition of Eighteen Hundred and Four', in Thomas Hardy, *Wessex Tales*, London, 1986, pp.21–6.

[5] Malcolm Andrews, *The Search for the Picturesque: Landscape Aesthetics and Tourism in Britain, 1760–1800*, London, 1989, p.45.

[6] Brannon, p.15.

[7] Polufloisboio Thalasses, Esq., *The Excursionist's Guide to Lulworth*, Weymouth, 1886 (?). The passage is similar to that attributed to W. G. Maton's *Observations on the Western Counties*, Vol. I. p.46. in John Britton and E. W. Brayley, *A Topographical and Historical Description of the County of Dorset*, London, 1805, pp.362–3.

[8] Cecil M. Hepworth, *Came the Dawn: Memories of a Film Pioneer*, London, 1951, pp. 107 & 116.

[9] Ian Cox, *The South Bank Exhibition: A Guide to the Story it Tells*, HMSO, 1951.

[10] John Hutchins, *History of Dorset*, First Edition, Vol. II, p.163.

[11] F. J. Harvey Darton, *The Marches of Wessex: A Chronicle of England*, London, 1922, p.31.

CHAPTER 2

[1] Joan Berkeley, *Lulworth and the Welds*, Gillingham, 1971, p.xi.

[2] *Ibid.*, p.105.

[3] *Ibid.*, pp.182–3.

[4] See John Hutchins, *A History of Dorset*, Third Edition, Vol. I, p.389.

[5] The anonymously published *A Tale of Lulworth* (Bath, 1888) was written by Revd William Henry Chamberlain, who enjoys the thought of those silent Trappists living with an open grave in the cemetery to remind them of their mortal condition, and scourging one another with the flagellum that was later cherished as a souvenir of the monastery. He savours the lurid denunciations that followed when a disaffected Irish monk named James Power repudiated the monastery as a den of unnatural practices. He also enjoys the gender-bending romance of the young lady of Lulworth who befriended Power, and is said to have dressed up as man in order to visit the monastery to which females were 'on no account admitted'. The same rule is said to have been broken earlier in the monastery's life when George III and Queen Charlotte visited, and the Abbot was obliged to concede when the Queen insisted that neither she nor the King 'could abandon their right to enter any lands or mansions in their dominion at whatever time they might desire to do so'. This story was still running in the 1930s, when the diaries of that girl, who was actually Julia Woodforde, were published. See D. H. Woodforde (ed.), *Woodforde Papers and Diaries*, London, 1932.

[6] *On the Building of a Monastery in Dorsetshire*, Oxford, 1795.

[7] *The Canonization of Thomas ..... Esq. who has lately erected at East L .... H Dorset a Monastery and there established a body of monks*, London, 1801.

[8] Notice dated 14 August 1803, Dorset Record Office, D/WLC: R17.

[9] This fact was recorded along with other noteworthy items of local memory by a late Victorian vicar in the Tyneham register of births, marriages and deaths, 1694–1808, Dorset County Record Office.

[10] John Hutchins, *A History of Dorset*, Third Edition, Vol. I, p.378.

[11] Berkeley, p.175.

[12] Quoted from, The Parish Church of St Andrew, East Lulworth, an appeal document dated 1967, which I take to have been written by Revd John Stone, the incumbent of that time.

[13] Brannon, p.10.

[14] P. J. Fowler, 'A Note on Archaeological Finds from the AEA Effluent Pipe-line, Winfrith Heath to Arish Mell, 1959, *Proceedings of the Dorset Natural History and Archaeological Society*, Vol. 84, 1962, pp.125–31.

[15] M. Cressey, 'East Lulworth Park Earthworks: a Survey and Interpretation', HND Practical Archaeology Dissertation, Bournemouth University, 1987.

[16] Sylvaticus [John Fitzgerald Pennie], *The Tale of Modern Genius: Or, The Miseries of Parnassus*, London: 1827, Vol. I, p.6.

[17] Sylvaticus, Vol. III, p.51. As one of Pennie's critical champions asked, in what can only be called a begging review, 'Will it alleviate the pangs of a husband and a father surveying his helpless family, that years hence, when the oblivion of the grave has enveloped him, he shall be counted among the company of the great?' See 'The Spirit of the West', a Memoir of J. F. Pennie, that was printed in *West of England* (Undated Copy in the Dorset County Museum). Pennie loved the Lulworth landscape and its ancient relics with a passion that was to prove altogether too 'poetic' for the Victorian antiquarians of the Dorset Natural History and Archaeological Society. Indeed, when these gentlemen included a note of Pennie's life in their enlarged edition of Hutchins's *A History of Dorset*, it was to disapprove of the 'histrionic career' of this upstart who ran too close to 'professional mendicacy' for their liking and was inclined to value himself 'on a higher estimate than he can find others willing to accept'. See John Hutchins, *A History of Dorset*, Third Edition, Vol. I, 1861, p.381.

[18] Pennie was both a Tory and a mason, and his vision of Lulworth is in the tradition described by Nigel Everett in *The Tory View of Landscape*, Newhaven and London, 1994.

[19] Quoted from W. H. Parry Okeden, 'The Agricultural Riots in Dorset 1830', *Proceedings of the Dorset Natural History and Archaeological Society*, Vol. LII, 1930, pp.75–95.

[20] Barbara Kerr, *Bound to the Soil: A Social History of Dorset 1750–1918*, Wakefield, 1975 (First Edition 1968).

[21] J. L. Hammond & Barbara Hammond, *The Village Labourer 1760–1832: A Study in the Government of England before the Reform Bill*, London, 1920, p.284.

[22] John Soane, 'The Modern Period: 1761–1914', in Laurence Keen and Ann Carreck (eds), *Historic Landscape of Weld*, Lulworth: The Weld Estate, 1986, p. 52. For Frampton's conduct as 'the Draco of the fields' see also Kerr, p.102.

CHAPTER 3

[1] William H. Bond signed a consent form for the placing of 'a concrete telephone kiosk in garden of my premises known as the Tyneham Post Office' on 29 September, 1929. (Information provided by the BT Archives and Historical Information Centre, London). For Bond's rage and claimed stroke, I am indebted to Julie Astin's unpublished account of discussions with the Warrs. Rodney Legg reports a discussion with Mr Wilson Coombes, who installed the controversial

phone box and received a 'tirade of abuse' from the rector who resented the innovation. See Rodney Legg, *Lulworth and Tyneham Revisited*, Wincanton, 1985, p. 88.

[2] Alain Robbe-Grillet, *Snapshots and Towards a New Novel*, London, 1965, pp.78–9.

[3] John Junor, *Listening for a Midnight Tram*, London, 1990, p.280.

[4] Albert Fry & Simon Appleyard, 'Tyneham: Dorset's Hidden Sanctuary', *This England*, Winter 1980, p.35.

[5] *This England*, Autumn, 1969.

[6] *This England*, Spring, 1973.

[7] *This England*, Autumn, 1975.

[8] *This England*, Winter, 1976.

[9] *This England*, Winter, 1977/8.

[10] See Molly Dineen's television film 'Home from the Hill'.

[11] *Sunday Telegraph*, 20 December, 1987.

[12] Edward Pearce, 'Mother of all festivals', *Guardian*, 25 August, 1993, p.18.

[13] Edward Pearce, 'Lager leaves a bad taste', *Guardian*, 13 October, 1993, p.22.

[14] John Gray, 'Looting the Leviathan', *Guardian*, 2 February, 1994.

[15] Dennis Potter, 'The Long Goodbye', *Guardian*, 6 April, 1994.

[16] These remarks are quoted from Bill Douglas's friend Peter Jewell. Telephone conversation, 1/12/93. For an account of *Comrades*, see Duncan Petrie, 'The Lanternist Revisited' in E. Dick, A. Noble, D. Petrie (eds), *Bill Douglas: A Lanternist's Account*, London, 1993, pp.173–96.

[17] Quoted at the front of Bill Douglas, *Comrades*, London & Boston, 1987. The film *Comrades* was produced by Simon Relph of Skreba Productions, and distributed by Curzon Films.

[18] Douglas, *Comrades*, p.73.

[19] *Ibid.*, p.62.

[20] Conversation with Michael Pickwoad, designer of the *Comrades* set, February 1994.

[21] *Bournemouth Evening Echo*, 8 January, 1986.

[22] Conversation with Miss Margaret Bond, 29 March 1986.

[23] 'A private chronology of Denis Bond of Lutton in the Isle of Purbeck, made A.D. 1636 & 1640. With notes by Thomas Bond of Tyneham, and entries continued by Lilian Bond from 1919', (manuscript in the County Museum, Dorchester), p.74.

CHAPTER 4

1 Brevet-Colonel J. F. C. Fuller, DSO, *Tanks in the Great War 1914–18*, London, 1920, p.74.

2 Joan Begbie, *Walking in Dorset*, London, 1936, p.1. *Walking in the New Forest* was issued by the same publisher in 1934. According to her publishers, Joan Begbie had inherited her literary skills from her father, the poet Harold Begbie.

3 Major General Sir Ernest D. Swinton, KBE, CB, DSO, RE (Retired), *Eyewitness: Being Personal Reminiscences of Certain Phases of the Great War, Including the Genesis of the Tank*, London, 1932, p.174.

4 Sir Albert G. Stern, KBE, CMG, *Tanks 1914–1918: The Logbook of a Pioneer*, London, 1919, p.46.

5 Swinton, *Eyewitness*, p.190.

6 Major Bertram Clough Williams-Ellis, MC & A. Williams-Ellis, *The Tank Corps*, London, 1919, p.18.

7 G. E. Lanning, 'From Rifle Range to Garrison: An Essay on Bovington Camp 1899–1925' (Southampton University, 1973), mimeographed paper in the Tank Museum library, Bovington.

8 Miss Bohl's poem 'Tanks. A True Story 1917' is printed in Alan Brown, *A Backward Glimpse of Wool*, Wool, 1990, pp.99–101.

9 Quoted from *The War History of the Sixth Tank Battalion*, privately printed, August 1919, p.4. The Sixth Battalion moved to Wool from the Elveden Explosives Area on 27 October 1916.

10 Quoted from Brown, *A Backward Glimpse of Wool*, p.98.

11 Fuller, *Tanks in the Great War*, p.163.

12 Capt D. G. Browne, *The Tank in Action*, Edinburgh & London, 1920.

13 See Rodney Legg, *Lulworth and Tyneham Revisited*, Wincanton, 1985, p.86.

14 Quoted in Care for Dorset, Memorandum to the Defence Lands Committee concerning lands held by the Ministry of Defence in South Dorset, June 1971.

15 Lieutenant C. Patrick Thompson, *Cocktails*, London, 1919, p.246.

16 B. H. Liddell Hart, *The Tanks: The History of the Royal Tank Regiment and its Predecessors*, London, 1959, Vol. I, p.201.

17 Hart, *The Tanks*, Vol. I, p.205.

18 Browne, *The Tank in Action*, p.505.

19 See 'Acquisition of Lands Acts — 1916 & 1920; Closing of Roads and Rights of Way', a War Office memorandum dated 4 May 1922 and signed D.G.L., Public Record Office, WO/32/2662.

20 Letter from Grant Stevenson & Co, *The Times*, 31 May 1917.

21 Such assertions came from Sir Thomas Hood and Mr John Jones. A full transcript

of this debate, which occurred in the Commons on 26 July 1922, is contained in PRO WO/32/2662.

[22] This correspondence is held in 'Quarter Sessions: Miscellaneous 15 (P)', Dorset County Record Office, Dorchester.

[23] For land acquisitions at Bovington Camp, which were completed in March 1924, see Lanning, p.31. A copy of this article is held in the Tank Museum Library at Bovington Camp.

CHAPTER 5

[1] *The Times*, 3 August 1923. *The Times's* first report on the Lulworth argument appeared the previous day.

[2] 'A Tank Offensive', *Manchester Guardian*, 4 August 1923.

[3] 'Threatened Dorset Beauty Spot', *The Times*, 4 August 1923.

[4] 'Further Opposition to War Office Scheme', *The Times*, 30 August 1923.

[5] Dorset Natural History and Antiquarian Field Club, *Proceedings*, Vol. XLV, From May 1923 to May 1924, p.xlvii. This resolution was reported in *The Times* on 23 August, 1923. This organisation would later change its name to the Dorset Natural History and Archaeological Society.

[6] *Observer*, 5 August 1994.

[7] Cecil Roberts, *Alfred Fripp*, London, 1932, pp.161 & 11.

[8] Major Yerburgh's letter was printed in the *Observer*, 12 August 1923.

[9] *Observer*, 19 August 1923.

[10] This information is gathered from the Weld estate account books held in the Dorset County Record Office, Dorchester.

[11] Herbert Weld Blundell, 'The Last Act', *Morning Post*, 5 September 1900, p.11.

[12] Herbert Weld Blundell, 'White Flag Tactics', *Morning Post*, 18 July 1900, p.7.

[13] Herbert Weld Blundell, 'A Visit to Cyrene in 1895', *The Annual of the British School in Athens*, No. 2, Session 1895–6, pp.113–40.

[14] Herbert Weld Blundell, 'A Journey through Abyssinia to the Nile', *The Geographical Journal*, February 1900, pp.99–100.

[15] Herbert Weld Blundell, ibid. p.111.

[16] There was protest when a film screened before an invited audience at London's Pavilion Theatre in November 1921 showed Captain Bede Bentley presenting Lord Kitchener with a drawing of the original idea for the tank. Bentley was undeterred, however, and in 1925 he made an unsuccessful claim for £300,000 compensation from the government under a Petition of Right. See Rear-Admiral Sir Murray Sueter, CBMP, *The Evolution of the Tank: A Record of Royal Naval Air Service Caterpillar Experiments*, London & Melbourne, 1941, p.177.

[17] Clifford Hallé, *To Menelek in a Motor-Car*, London, 1913, p.178.

[18] The manuscript, written by an Abyssinian called Alaqâ Wald Maryam, was obtained by Weld Blundell in Addis Ababa and translated as 'History of King Theodor', *Journal of the African Society*, Vol. VI, No. XXI, October 1906, pp.12–42.

[19] For the story of King Theodore and the 'bomba' see also Henry Blanc, *A Narrative of Captivity in Abyssinia*, London, 1868 and Theophilius Waldmeier, *Autobiography*, London, 1886.

CHAPTER 6

[1] 'Gunnery School at Lulworth: The War Office View', *Bournemouth Daily Echo*, 15 August 1923.

[2] *Bournemouth Daily Echo*, 17 August 1923.

[3] *Spectator*, 11 August 1923.

[4] This suggestion was made by Mr Harvey of Wandsworth Common, whose letter was published by *The Times* on 4 September 1923.

[5] This claim was made by S. G. Owen, Student and Tutor of Christ Church, Oxford, in *The Times*, 21 August 1923.

[6] *Nation and Athenaeum*, 15 September 1923.

[7] *Bournemouth Daily Echo*, 26 July 1924.

[8] Koffman's letter appeared in the *Daily Herald*, 7 August 1923, p.8.

[9] Rovator, 'Lulworth Cove by the Open Road', *Daily Herald*, 13 September 1923, p.8.

[10] Alec Dixon, *Tinned Soldier: A Personal Record, 1919–1926*, London, 1941, p.40.

[11] *Tank Corps Journal*, Vol. I, No. 53, September 1923, p.124. See also *Tank Corps Journal*, Vol. 5, No. 57, January 1924, p.236.

[12] *Tank Corps Journal*, Vol. 5, January 1924, No. 57, p.229.

[13] *Tank Corps Journal*, Vol. 5, No. 60, April 1924, p.365.

[14] *Bournemouth Daily Echo*, 31 August 1923.

[15] Letter from 'Wilsaetas', *The Daily Graphic*, 9 August 1923.

[16] *Tank Corps Journal*, September 1923.

[17] *The Times*, 7 September, 1923.

[18] *The Times*, 13 August 1923.

[19] Letter from Rayner Goddard KC, *The Times*, 21 August 1923.

[20] See Fenton Bresler, *Lord Goddard*, London, 1977 and John Parris, *Scapegoat*, London, 1991.

[21] *Bournemouth Daily Echo*, 4 September 1923.

[22] Colonel Sir Joseph Weld remembered this 'plage' idea, adding that he threw it out when he inherited the estate in 1935.

[23] Revd John Lawrence, letter to *The Times*, 7 September 1923.

[24] Reported in *Westminster Gazette*, 31 July 1924.

[25] See 'Railway and Canal Commission', *The Times*, 23 July 1924, p.5.

[26] Ibid., p.5.

[27] *Bournemouth Daily Echo*, 26 July 1924, p.5.

[28] Reported in *The Times*, 5 August 1924.

[29] Goddard's letter is quoted in 'Lulworth Cove: War Office Move for Compulsory Purchase', *The Times*, 8 September 1924.

[30] *The Times*, 8 September 1924.

[31] Rayner Goddard, letter to *The Times*, 11 September 1924, p.13.

[32] Herbert Weld Blundell, letter to *The Times*, 17 September 1924.

[33] *The Times*, 21 September 1924.

CHAPTER 7

[1] F. J . Harvey Darton, *English Fabric: A Study of Village Life*, London, 1936, p.5.

[2] For an early account of Hardy Country, see Wilkinson Sherren, *The Wessex of Romance*, London, 1908.

[3] J. Heneage Jesse records that the prince attended a prize fight in which one combatant killed the other. As for his friend, Lord Brudenell, such was the debauchery of the prince's circle that he came to be known as 'Cockie' instead of Your Honour. See Jesse, *Memoirs of the Life and Reign of King George III*, London, 1867, Vol. III, pp.30–1.

[4] The change was dramatic, as is recorded in a representative guidebook of the time: 'It is indeed astonishing that a place which a few years since consisted of very little else than a knot of fishermen's huts, should in so short a space have undergone such an amazing change, as now to be the first watering place in the kingdom.' Quoted from *A New Weymouth Guide*, Dorchester, n.d., p.16.

[5] Charlotte Barrett (ed.), *Diary and Letters of Madame D'Arblay*, London, 1891, Vol. III, pp.188 & 199.

[6] Anon., *A Trip to Weymouth*, London, 1790.

[7] *A Trip to Weymouth*, Vol. II, pp.61–2.

[8] D'Arblay, Vol. III, p.196.

[9] Ibid., p.191.

[10] See, for example, *The Weymouth Guide*, Weymouth, 1790.

[11] *Companion to the Museum of the late Sir Ashton Lever*, London, 1790, p.84.

[12] *A Trip to Weymouth*, Vol. I, p.106.

[13] On 26 September 1856, the Weld estate issued a notice informing 'Persons about to Visit Lulworth Castle' that 'in consequence of the mischief done by certain persons who have been brought thither by the Steamers from Weymouth, during the past Summer, and their otherwise misconduct, the Owner of the Castle is under the necessity of ordering an admittance fee of ONE SHILLING each'. It was further announced that 'if this does not remedy the evil complained of and ensure a more orderly class of Visitors, the Castle will not in future be shewn but by an Order from the Owner'. A copy of this notice is held in the Weld estate papers at the Dorset County Record Office, Dorchester, D/WLC: E94.

[14] Alfred Downing Fripp (1822–95) was a member of the Society of Painters in Watercolour and, for a time, secretary of the Olds Society. He spent most of the 1850s painting in Italy, and some examples of his later Dorset work are in the collections of the Victoria & Albert Museum and the Museum of Childhood at Bethnal Green.

[15] B. H. Liddell Hart, *The Tanks: The History of the Royal Tank Regiment and its Predecessors*, London, 1959, Vol. I, p.226.

[16] *The Times*, 30 October 1925.

[17] *Western Gazette*, 30 October 1925.

[18] *Bournemouth Daily Echo*, 21 July 1923, p.5.

[19] Eric Benfield, *Southern English*, London, 1942, p.29.

[20] *Ibid.*, p.109.

CHAPTER 8

[1] S. W. Colyer, *Unspoiled Dorset: A Book of Photographs*, London & Melbourne, 1940, Plate 14.

[2] Edric Holmes, *Wanderings in Wessex*, London, n. d. (1906?), p.114.

[3] Donald Maxwell, *Unknown Dorset*, London, 1927, p.80.

[4] This account is assembled with reference to the collection of 'Eggs', the earliest of which concerns the camp of Summer 1927, held in the library of Eton College. This account draws on the following: SCH/SCO/5/1A, SCH/SCO/5/1B, SCH/SCO/5/2, SCH/SCO/5/3. Quotations are reproduced by permission of the Provost and Fellows of Eton College.

[5] George A. Birmingham, *Bindon Parva*, London, 1925.

[6] Mary Butts, *The Crystal Cabinet*, Manchester, 1988, p.261.

[7] Mary Butts, *Armed With Madness*, New York, 1928, p.61. See also William Morris, *The Hollow Land*, London, 1903, pp.154–208.

[8] *Ibid.*, p.91.

[9] Mary Butts, 'In the South', *Speed the Plough*, London, 1923, p.193.

[10] *Armed with Madness*, p.143.
[11] Butts, 'In the South', p.193.
[12] *Armed With Madness*, p.133.
[13] Mary Butts, *Death of Felicity Taverner*, London, 1932, p.6.
[14] *Armed With Madness*, pp.205–6.
[15] *Ibid.*, p.3.
[16] *Ibid.*, p.186.
[17] *Armed With Madness*, p.81.
[18] John Cowper Powys, *The Meaning of Culture*, London, 1930, p.176.
[19] *Armed With Madness*, p.15.
[20] Mary Butts, untitled note on Christopher Wood, dated June 1931, Tate Gallery Archive (Christopher Wood collection).
[21] *Armed With Madness*, p.62.
[22] Mary Butts, 'Corfe' in Louis Zukofsky, *An 'Objectivist's' Anthology*, Le Beausset, 1932, pp.36–9.
[23] *Death of Felicity Taverner*, p.84.
[24] *Ibid.*, p.27.
[25] Mary Butts published both these pamphlets in 1932. *Traps For Unbelievers* was issued by Harmsworth, while *Warning to Hikers* was printed as the sixth 'Here & Now' Pamphlet, by Wishart.
[26] *Death of Felicity Taverner*, p.115.
[27] In a previous account of Mary Butts's writing, I suggested that Mary Butts's character Kralin was based on her estranged husband John Rodker (see 'Coming Back to the Shores of Albion' in my *On Living in an Old Country*, London, 1985). However, I have since seen a letter Butts wrote to Hugh Ross Williamson on 2 November 1932. Here she admits the autobiographical basis of *Death of Felicity Taverner*, but stresses that she does not want it said that Kralin is Rodker: 'He gave me one or two ideas, I admit'; but the figure of Kralin 'really grew from some evil Jews' she had known in Paris. This correspondence is now in the University of Texas Library, but I am grateful to Bertram Rota, the antiquarian book dealer, for allowing me to read it in London.
[28] For H. G. Wells comments of 1916, see Sir Albert G. Stern, KBE, CMG, *Tanks 1914–1918: The Logbook of a Pioneer*, London, 1919, p.100–3. For a reference to the tank as a 'cubist steel slug' see Major General Sir Ernest D. Swinton, KBE, CB, DSO, RE (Retired), *Eyewitness: Being Personal Reminiscences of Certain Phases of the Great War, Including the Genesis of the Tank*, London, 1932, p.5.
[29] Maxwell, p.80.
[30] *Ibid.*, pp.88–9.

CHAPTER 9

[1] 'Uses for Tanks in Peace Time', *Tank Corps Journal*, Vol. I, No. 9, February 1920, p.264.

[2] The phrase 'Esprit de Tank' was used by Brigadier F. R. Mathew Lannowe, in the *Tank Corps Journal*, Vol. 1, April 1919, p.5.

[3] *Tank Corps Journal*, Vol. I, No. 10, February 1920, p.272.

[4] 'Warfare on the South Downs', *Sunday Times*, 23 September 1923.

[5] 'Gunnery School at Lulworth', *Bournemouth Daily Echo*, 15 August 1923.

[6] 'Castle v. Camp at Lulworth', *Bournemouth Daily Echo*, 17 August 1923.

[7] *Tank Corps Journal*, Vol. I, No. 7, November 1919, p.200.

[8] Quoted from Major The Hon R. T. R. R. Butler, DSO, MC, and dated March 1926, these words appear in a manuscript article written for the Royal Armoured Corps Journal by Colonel P. H. Hordern, former director and curator of the Bovington Tank Museum, dated 1973 and available in the Tank Museum library. On the development of this museum see also Hordern's, 'The Royal Armoured Corps Tank Museum' in *Armor* (Washington DC), Vol. LXXIX, No. 1, pp.5–10.

[9] A. Saunders, about whom nothing else is known, commended 'Old Ironside's' conversion into a 'patriot tank' in a poem called 'Wolverhampton's Tank' in the *Wolverhampton Chronicle*, 6 February 1918. The poem was written to glorify the tank brought to Wolverhampton as part of a 'tank bank' campaign run by the War Savings Committee to persuade ordinary people (or 'small investors'), to buy War Bonds and Certificates.

[10] *Western Gazette*, 30 October 1925.

[11] 'The King and the Tanks: Visit to Training Centre', *The Times*, 25 April 1928.

[12] Produced by W. H. Bishop with E. Foxen Cooper as adviser, the uncompleted official film of this visit is held in the Imperial War Museum's Film Archive as 'Visit of the King of Afghanistan to England', IWM 809. Details of the visit are given in the Imperial War Museum Film Catalogue, pp.1198–2000.

[13] 'We'll all go A Tanking Today' opens as follows:

> 'It's a fine tanking day and as balmy as May
> And the crews to the Tank-park have gone;
> I saw each man go down in his overalls brown,
> And his eyes with intelligence shone.'

See *Tank Corps Journal*, Vol. II, No. 11, March 1920, p.317. The Futurist ode, which appears alongside Swinburnian and Classical variants, is in *Tank Corps Journal*, Vol. II, No. 13, May 1920, p.7.

[14] Herbert Weld, 'The Blue Nile and Irrigation', *Journal of the African Society*, Vol. XXVII, No. CVI, January 1928.

[15] For a discussion of this 'curse', see Christopher Frayling, *The Face of Tutankhamun*, London, 1992. I was informed of the part this popular myth played in East Lulworth's pre-war interpretation of Herbert Weld's troubles by Jack Scutt and Harry Westmacott. To the best of my knowledge, Herbert Weld had no connection at all with Howard Carter's excavation. It is just conceivable that he visited the site some time after it was commenced in 1922, and more than likely that his determination to organise and fund the excavation of the Babylonian city of ancient Kish was increased by Carter's remarkable discoveries. Perhaps it was a Babylonian Curse of Gilgamesh that Herbert's Dorset villagers were thinking of.

[16] Herbert Weld, letter to *The Times*, 30 July 1930.

[17] Quoted from an explanatory note printed as part of a letter from P. Morley Horder, in *Country Life*, 1 March 1930, p.329.

[18] Interview with Colonel Sir Joseph Weld at Lulworth Manor, 7 March 1989.

[19] The sale was planned to take place at Dorchester Town Hall on 21 September 1929. A copy of the catalogue, *The Weld Estate, Dorset: Wool, Winfrith Newburgh & Chaldon Herring*, is held in the Dorset Record Office, D/WLC: E 151.

[20] 'Mansion in Ruins', *The Times*, 30 August 1929.

[21] *Western Gazette*, 6 September 1929.

[22] *Bournemouth Daily Echo*, 29 August 1929.

[23] The holiday makers are mentioned in the *Western Gazette*, 6 September 1929.

[24] 'Noted English Castle Burnt Out', the *Daily Chronicle*, 30 August 1929.

[25] *Bournemouth Daily Echo*, 29 August 1929.

[26] *Western Gazette*, 6 September 1929.

[27] *The Times*, 30 August 1929.

[28] *Daily Herald*, 30 August 1933.

[29] 'Lulworth Castle Destroyed by Fire', *Dorset County Chronicle*, September 5, 1929.

[30] Letter from an employee called Sargeant to Mrs Weld, Dorset County Record Office, D/WLC/E 107.

[31] 'Lulworth Castle Destroyed', the *Daily Mail*, 30 August 1929.

[32] 'Tragic End of Famous Castle; stronghold of the faith in penal days', the *Universe*, 6 September 1929.

[33] The *Illustrated London News*, 7 September 1929.

[34] The *Graphic*, 7 September 1929.

[35] *The Times*, 3 September 1929.

[36] Letter from Joseph E. Weld to Miss Joan Weld, 30 June 1930, Dorset Record Office, D/WLC/E107.

37 Major Rudolph C. Mayne, letter to *Country Life*, 15 March 1930, p.397.

38 See the Weld estate account book for 1 April 1930–31 March 1931, in the Dorset County Record Office, D10/AE 188. The costs of establishing and running the car park in that first year are given as £204. 14s. 11, while the income was £743. 18s.

39 *The Spirit of Dorset; Pageant at Lulworth Castle* (Book of Words and Programme), Dorchester, July 1939. A copy of this programme is in the County Library, Dorchester.

CHAPTER 10

1 Rudyard Kipling, 'Cold Iron' (1910) in Peter Keating (ed.), *Rudyard Kipling: Selected Poems*, London, 1993, pp.130–1.

2 Rolf Gardiner, 'On Harbottle, Geometry and Tradition', *Youth*, Summer, 1924.

3 S. Langton, *Excavations at Kish: The Herbert Weld (for the University of Oxford) and Field Museum of Natural History (Chicago) Expedition to Mesopotamia*, Paris, 1924, p.11.

4 Malcolm Elwin, *The Life of Llewelyn Powys*, London, 1946, p.217.

5 Jonathan Gathorne-Hardy, *The Interior Castle: A Life of Gerald Brenan*, London, 1992, p.257.

6 Kenneth Hopkins (ed.), *Gamel Wolsey: Letters to Llewelyn Powys*, North Walsham, 1983.

7 For an account of this circle see Judith Stinton, *Chaldon Herring: The Powys Circle in a Dorset Village*, Woodbridge, 1988.

8 H. J. Massingham, *Remembrance: An Autobiography*, London, 1942, p.137.

9 H. J. Massingham, *Genius of England*, London, 1937, p.15.

10 H. J. Massingham, *English Downland*, London, 1936, p.75.

11 H. J. Massingham, *In Praise of England*, London, 1924, pp.148–9.

12 W. H. Hudson, *Nature in Downland*, (1923) quoted from Futura edition, 1981, p.31.

13 F. J. Harvey Darton, *The Marches of Wessex: A Chronicle of England*, London, 1922, p.29.

14 Massingham, *Remembrance*, p.86.

15 H. J. Massingham, 'October Trees and Flowers', *Untrodden Ways*, London, 1923, p.144.

16 *English Downland*, p.53.

17 B. Clough Williams-Ellis (ed.), *Britain and the Beast*, London, 1937. Forster's contribution was entitled 'Havoc', and included the observation that 'The fighting services are bound to become serious enemies of what is left of England. Wherever

they see a tract of wild, unspoiled country they naturally want it for camps, artillery practice, bomb-dropping, poison-gas tests . . .'

18 If this is the visit mentioned by Llewelyn Powys in a letter to Gamel Woolsey, it actually took place in 1936. Powys describes being visited by Massingham and his wife in a letter dated 7 April 1936, remarking that Massingham thought 'very highly of our flints'. See M. Elwin (ed.), *So Wild a Thing: Llewelyn Powys' Letters to G. Woolsey*, Dulverton, 1973, pp.71–2.

19 *Downland Man*, London, 1926, p.151.

20 *Remembrance*, pp.20–1.

21 H. J. Massingham, *People and Things: An Attempt to Connect Art and Humanity*, London, 1919, p.193.

22 *Remembrance*, p.93.

23 *Genius of England*, p.23.

24 *Ibid.*, p.5.

25 *English Downland*, p.4.

26 *Ibid.*, pp.4–5.

27 *Genius of England*, p.24.

28 *Downland Man*, p.151.

29 *English Downland*, p.4.

30 See 'What is Degeneration', in H. J. Massingham, *The Heritage of Man*, London, 1929, pp.149–72.

31 *Downland Man*, pp.267 & 311.

32 *Ibid.*, p.347.

33 *Ibid.*, p.272.

34 *Ibid.*, p.241.

35 H. J. Massingham, 'Maiden Castle: A Theory of Peace in Ancient Britain', *In Praise of England*, p.181.

36 *Downland Man*, p.127.

37 *In Praise of England*, p.175.

38 *Downland Man*, pp.377–8.

39 H. J. Massingham, *Fee, Fi, Fo, Fum: The Giants of England*, London, 1921, pp.167–8.

40 H. J. Massingham, *The Golden Age: The Story of Human Nature*, London, 1927, p.54–5.

41 *Ibid.*, p.87.

42 *Remembrance*, p.33.

43 F. J. Harvey Darton, *The Marches of Wessex*, p.7.

44 *Downland Man*, p.377.

45 *In Praise of England*, p.199.

46 *Ibid.*, pp.147–203.

47 *People and Things*, p.24.

48 Massingham's account of *New Age* and his involvement in it is to be found in his autobiography, *Remembrance*, pp.31–3.

49 *People and Things*, p.24.

50 *Ibid.*, p.208.

51 *Remembrance*, p.32.

52 *People and Things*, p.86.

53 *Downland Man*, p.90.

54 *Ibid.*, pp.83–4.

55 *The Golden Age*, p.65.

56 *People and Things*, pp.90–1.

57 In his tribute to W. H. Hudson, Massingham counts 'the sense of birds' alongside the sense of colour and the sense of smell (*Untrodden Ways*, London, 1923, p.24).

58 *People and Things*, p.191.

59 For Massingham's suggestion that modernist experimentation may have been enough to drive an (already schizophrenic) English artist mad, see his memoir of Thomas Hennell in Hennell's *The Countryman at Work*, London, 1947, p.11.

60 This sense of the 'metallic' enemy is at its most desolate in *People and Things*, a book Massingham wrote during the Great War.

61 *The Golden Age*, p.78.

62 *Remembrance*, p.32.

63 H. J. Massingham, 'From Nature to Man', *The Heritage of Man*, London, 1929, p.31.

64 *Downland Man*, pp.159–60.

65 *In Praise of England*, p.50.

66 *Downland Man*, p.329.

67 *In Praise of England*, p.147.

68 H. J. Massingham, 'Egdon Heath', in *A Countryman's Journal*, London, 1939, pp.119–20.

69 *Downland Man*, p.377.

70 H. J. Massingham, *Field Fellowship*, London, 1942, p.18.

71 H. J. Massingham, *Country Relics*, Cambridge, 1939.

72 *Country Relics*, p.161.

73 *Genius of England*, p.25.

74 Llewelyn Powys, 'Poxwell Stone-Circle', *Dorset Essays*, London, 1935, p.85.

75 Llewelyn Powys, *The Glory of Life and Now that the Gods are Dead*, London, 1949, p.58.

76 Llewelyn Powys, *Skin for Skin*, London, 1926, p.4.

[77] Letter to Emily Brue Hoyt, in L. Wilkinson (ed.), *The Letters of Llewelyn Powys*, London, 1943, pp.164–5.

[78] *Glory of Life*, p.25.

[79] Llewelyn Powys, *The Pathetic Fallacy: A Study of Christianity*, London, 1930, pp.128.

[80] *Letters*, p.165.

[81] Diary entry for 22 November 1931 in Alyse Gregory, *The Cry of a Gull; Journals 1923–48*, Dulverton, 1973, p.61.

[82] *Skin for Skin*, p.110.

[83] Llewelyn Powys, 'Gypsies' in *Dorset Essays*, London, 1935, pp.36–7.

[84] *Glory of Life*, p.60.

[85] This is the assessment of Frances Partridge, who remembers being given a worked flint by Powys — rather in the manner that hippies used to hand out 'significant' stones.

[86] *Glory of Life*, p.27.

[87] Alyse Gregory, diary entry dated August 1931, *The Cry of A Gull*, p.59.

[88] H. J. Massingham, *Remembrance*, p.100.

[89] Elwin, *The Life of Llewelyn Powys*, p.243.

[90] *Ibid.*, p.210.

[91] On T. S. Eliot, see Elwin, p.214; on cocktails, see *Letters*, p.126.

[92] *Letters*, p.141.

[93] *Ibid.*, p.227.

[94] The parallel between Dorset and East-African natives is explored in Llewelyn Powys, *Ebony and Ivory*, New York, 1923.

[95] He once remarked to a correspondent that 'Wherever I go I like to speak out my mind in broad country English.' *Letters*, p.165.

[96] *Letters*, p.213.

[97] *Dorset Essays*, p.200.

[98] Llewelyn Powys, 'Thomas Shoel' in *Somerset Essays*, London, 1934, p.143.

[99] Llewelyn Powys, '1834 The Seventeenth of March 1934' in Herbert Tracey (ed.), *Dorchester Labourers Centenary 1934: Souvenir of the Trades Union Congress, Weymouth, 1934*, London, 1934, pp.91–4. Collected in *Dorset Essays*.

[100] *Letters*, p.192.

[101] *Glory of Life*, p.13.

[102] Elwin, p.177.

[103] Llewelyn Powys, *A Baker's Dozen*, London, 1941, p.51.

[104] *Letters*, p.258.

[105] Llewelyn Powys, 'Dorchester Characters' in *Dorset Essays*, p.136.

[106] Letter to Littleton Powys, 23 May 1936, in *Letters*, pp.209–10.

[107] Letter to Theodore Powys, June 1918, Elwin, p.133.

108 *Somerset Essays*, p.269.

109 *Dorset Essays*, p.268.

110 Llewelyn Powys, *Earth Memories*, London, 1934, pp.155–6.

111 Llewelyn Powys, 'Dionysus', in *Rats in the Sacristy*, London, 1937, pp.8–11.

112 Llewelyn Powys, letter to John Cowper Powys dated late August 1933 in *Letters*, pp.175–6.

113 *Letters*, pp.176–7.

CHAPTER 11

1 S. Langdon, *Excavations at Kish*, Paris, 1924.

2 For this particular rat see Vanda Cook (whom I take to be Valentine Ackland), 'Picture of a Dorset Village', *Country Standard*, Vol. IV, No. 1, March 1939, p.10.

3 Claire Harman, *Sylvia Townsend Warner: A Biography*, London, 1991, p.139.

4 Valentine Ackland, 'Country Dealings II', *Left Review*, No. 8, May 1935, p.311.

5 Valentine Ackland, *Country Conditions*, London, 1936, pp.30–1.

6 Valentine Ackland, letter to Alyse Gregory quoted in Gregory's *The Cry of a Gull; Journals 1923–1948*, Dulverton, 1973, pp.135–6.

7 Llewelyn Powys, letter to Valentine Ackland, 1935, in *Letters*, p.201.

8 Powys's description of his own contrary 'country cottage' — 'I hate the dainty cottage of modern nicety' — was printed in the *Countryman* in the Thirties, and collected in J. W. Robertson Scott (ed.), *The Countryman Book*, London, 1948, pp.127–9. His pride in the ugliness of his house is remembered in Gerald Brenan, *Personal Record 1920–1972*, Cambridge, 1979, p.221.

9 For an account of this settlement, see Judith Stinton, *Chaldon Herring: The Powys Circle in a Dorset Village*, Woodbridge, 1988. See also Claire Harman, *Sylvia Townsend Warner: A Biography*, and, for a stronger account of the political involvement of this pair, Wendy Mulford, *This Narrow Place: Sylvia Townsend Warner and Valentine Ackland: Life, Letters and Politics, 1930–1951*, London, 1988.

10 Harman, *Sylvia Townsend Warner*, p.47.

11 T. F. Powys, *Mark Only*, London, 1924, p.20.

12 T. F. Powys, *The Left Leg*, London, 1923, pp.30–1.

13 *Ibid.*, p.17.

14 T. F. Powys, *The Key of the Field*, London, 1930, p.12.

15 T. F. Powys, *Mockery Gap*, p.4, London, 1925.

16 Gamel Woolsey, *Middle Earth*, London, 1931.

17 T. F. Powys, *Mr Weston's Good Wine*, New York, 1928, p.282.

18 Solomon J. Solomon, *Strategic Camouflage*, London, 1920, p.1.

19 It was not just Powys who was inclined to trigger his narratives in this way. David Garnett wrote a novel called *The Sailor's Return* (London, 1925), which tells the story of an African princess, who becomes the consort of a sailor, and is then brought back to a thinly disguised East Chaldon — where her unexpected arrival prompts a drama of bigotry and prejudice. Philippa Powys's *The Blackthorn Winter* works on the same principle, bringing some travelling gipsies into its neighbourhood, and then pursuing the drama that follows.

20 *Mockery Gap*, p.83.

21 Sylvia Townsend Warner, 'The Way By Which I Have Come', the *Countryman*, July 1939, pp.472–86.

22 These articles were collected in Anon. [J. W. Robertson Scott], *England's Green and Pleasant Land*, London, 1925.

23 J. W. Robertson Scott, *The Dying Peasant and the Future of his Sons*, London, 1926, p.3. Scott talks about 'the week-ending classes' in 'The Power in the Air' in *England's Green and Pleasant Land*, p.124.

24 Sylvia Townsend Warner, *The Espalier*, London, 1925, p.13.

25 Valentine Ackland, 'Winter', *Left Review*, March 1936, p.250.

26 Quoted from *Left News* in Mulford, *This Narrow Place*, p.82.

27 Sylvia Townsend Warner, 'In this Midwinter', *Left Review*, January 1935, p.101.

28 Sylvia Townsend Warner, 'An English Fable', *Left Review*, August 1937, p.406.

29 Valentine Ackland's 'Country Dealings' pieces appeared in *Left Review*, No. 6, March 1935; No. 8, May 1935; No. 12, September 1935.

30 *Country Conditions*, p.17.

31 As Ackland writes, ' "Sport" is not the least of the pests by which farms are ravaged. A vast area of fine land is left uncultivated, and much cultivated land is spoiled because of the country gentleman's passion for game. Damage done by pheasants, hares and rabbits (this last and worst of pests being virtually protected by the custom of keeping breeding grounds for game which, despite the desultory efforts of the keeper, inevitably become rabbit sanctuaries), amounts to hundreds of thousands of pounds yearly; while foxes and deer are likewise preserved solely for the sport of idlers.' *Country Conditions*, pp.65–6.

32 As Amabel Williams-Ellis pointed out, 'Russia's love of tractors and of concrete mixers comes in for so much surprised and slightly shocked criticism from certain quarters.' Her critical explanation of this phenomenon was printed as 'Reverence for Machinery' in *Left Review*, Vol. 1, No. 5, February 1935, pp.188–90.

33 Harman, *Sylvia Townsend Warner*, p.148.

34 Mulford, *This Narrow Place*, p.65.

35 *Ibid.*, p.67.

36 Harman, *Sylvia Townsend Warner*, p.144. Ackland and Warner also signed a 'Protest against the Jubilee' in *Left Review*, No. 8, May 1935.

37 Valentine Ackland, letter to Julius Lipton of the Communist Party, quoted in Mulford, *This Narrow Place*, pp.61–2.

38 STW letter to Julius and Queenie Lipton, quoted in Mulford, *This Narrow Place*, p.63.

39 Perhaps the band was along the lines of the one mentioned by 'Vanda Cook' in her 'Picture of a Dorset Village': 'Musicians in this village have united with those of the next to form a band that plays voluntarily at the village festivities, and an excellent combination of fiddles, concertinas, piano accordions, banjos and drums it is.' See *Country Standard*, Vol. IV, No. 1, March 1939.

40 Ackland, letter to Julius Lipton quoted in Mulford, *This Narrow Place*, p.63.

41 First published as *The Country Worker* from Diss in Norfolk in 1935, this publication was moved to Cambridge and relaunched as the monthly *Country Standard* in March 1936. Researchers interested in consulting this exceedingly rare publication will find an almost complete run in the Marx Memorial Library, Clerkenwell.

42 See 'Save the Sussex Downs', *Country Standard*, Vol. III, No. 2, April 1938.

43 *Country Worker*, Vol. 1, No. 1, January 1935.

44 Harry Self, 'Agriculture has a future', *Country Standard*, Vol. 1, No. 1, March 1936, p.4.

45 See the column by 'M.C.' in *Country Standard*, Vol. 1, No. 7, September 1937.

46 Sylvia Townsend Warner, 'Unofficial Drought', *Country Standard*, Vol. 1, No. 6, August 1936.

47 Sylvia Townsend Warner, 'Underpayment of Agricultural Workers; Black Figures from Blue Books', *Country Standard*, Vol. I, No. 2, April 1936, p.5. The previous year Warner had published an interesting dialogue about the inspections that government officials carried out to ensure that agricultural labourers were not being underpaid. See her 'Without comment', the *Countryman*, April 1935, pp.75–85.

48 Valentine Ackland, 'Diddle-Diddle', *Country Standard*, Vol. 1, No. 1, March 1936, p.8.

49 Vanda Cook, 'Picture of a Dorset Village', *Country Standard*, Vol. IV, No. 1, March 1939, p.10.

50 Vanda Cook, 'Shortage of Feeding Stuffs . . .', *Country Standard*, Vol. V, No. 1, April 1940, p.4.

51 Jane Smith, 'Life in Our Village', *Country Standard*, Vol. IV, No. 9, November 1939, p.5.

52 Mulford, *This Narrow Place*, p.158.

53 Ibid., p.142.

54 Maurice Cornforth, *Country Standard*, Vol. III, No. 3, May 1938.

[55] Letter to Nancy Cunard and Morris Cuthbert, 9 June 1944, in *Letters of Sylvia Townsend Warner*, p.85.

[56] *Country Conditions*, p.12.

CHAPTER 12

[1] Quoted by Gardiner in 'Ten Years of Gore Farm, 1927–37', *North Sea and Baltic*, Midwinter 1937, p.71.

[2] Ibid., p.64.

[3] Rolf Gardiner, 'AGENDA: The Vision and the Task', *North Sea and Baltic*, Midwinter 1940–1, p.169.

[4] Rolf Gardiner, 'Notes on the Centres: Springhead', *North Sea and Baltic*, Harvest 1936, p.25.

[5] Rolf Gardiner, 'On the functions of a rural university', Pamphlet issued for 'the dedication of a Wessex Centre at Springhead', *North Sea and Baltic*, 1933.

[6] Gardiner, '*AGENDA*', p.174.

[7] Rolf Gardiner, 'Rural Reconstruction', in H. J. Massingham (ed.), *England and the Farmer*, London, 1941, p.92. Gardiner published the same article under the more revealing title of 'Estates as Centres of Rural Reconstruction', in *North Sea and Baltic*, Midwinter, 1940–1, pp.155–64.

[8] Gardiner, 'Ten Years of Gore Farm; 1927–1937', p.68.

[9] Simon Pugh, *Garden-Nature-Language*, Manchester, 1988.

[10] Rolf Gardiner, 'AGENDA', p.175. Gardiner republished a revised version of this text in his book *England Herself; Ventures in Rural Restoration*, London, 1943, p.81.

[11] Fritz Schumacher had admired Gardiner since the early days of the Intermediate Technology Development Trust, and became a founder trustee when Mrs Marabel Gardiner got the Trust going. The patrons have included former members of the Springhead Ring like Lord Robert Armstrong of Ilminster and the composer John Gardner, along with Green eminences like Jonathon Porritt, the landscape architect Dame Sylvia Crowe, and Yehudi Menuhin.

[12] This sneer is repeated by Georgina Boyes in *The Imaginary Village: Culture, Ideology and the English Folk Revival*, Manchester, 1994, p.158. Gardiner is easily 'unmasked' by anyone who is content to gather up his most reprehensible statements. I have tried to come up with a more fairly nuanced account of his project. For another attempt at a balanced assessment see Malcolm Chase, 'Rolf Gardiner: An Inter-war, Cross-cultural Case Study', in B. Hake & S. Marriott (eds), *Adult Education Between Cultures*, Leeds, 1994, pp.225–41.

[13] John Stewart Collis, *Bound Upon a Course: An Autobiography*, London, 1971, p.161.

[14] Telephone conversation with Sir George Trevelyan, 5 May 1992.

[15] Rolf Gardiner, *Springhead Harvest Camp 1934: A Report to the Chairman of the York Trust and to the Ministry of Labour (South-Western Division)*, Fontmell Magna, 1934.

[16] Michael Pitt Rivers is cautious about overestimating this side of the Springhead Camps. As he recalled there were a few talks — rural writers like A. G. Street came along — but people were too young for genuine political and cultural discussion to take place.

[17] Llewelyn Powys, *Damnable Opinions*, London, 1935, p.57.

[18] Thomas Hennell's apocalyptic drawing of this scene stands at the front of *Country Relics*, H. J. Massingham's book about his collection of redundant rural tools and implements. Hennell's own written tribute to that discarded world is to be found in his book, *Change in the Farm*, Cambridge, 1943.

[19] Ackland, *Country Conditions*, p.69. The article appeared in the *Dorset County Chronicle* on 14 February 1935, and not 1934, as Ackland mistakenly claims.

[20] *Dorset County Chronicle*, 21 February 1935.

[21] *Dorset County Chronicle*, 28 February 1935.

[22] *Dorset County Chronicle*, as quoted by Valentine Ackland, *Country Conditions*, p.69.

[23] *Dorset County Chronicle*, 21 November 1935.

[24] *Dorset County Chronicle*, 24 October 1935.

[25] Ackland, *Country Conditions*, p.68.

[26] *Dorset County Chronicle*, 20 June 1935.

[27] *Dorset County Chronicle*, 21 November 1935.

[28] *Dorset County Chronicle*, 23 May 1935.

[29] Wessex Agricultural Defence Association, *The Tithe Dispute and Justice for British Agriculture*, published from Blandford by W.A.D.A., 1936, p.13.

[30] *Dorset County Chronicle*, 14 November 1935.

[31] *Dorset County Chronicle*, 25 July 1935.

[32] G. H. Lane-Fox Pitt Rivers, *Conscience and Fanaticism: An Essay on Moral Values*, London, 1919, pp.99–100 & 103.

[33] G. H. Lane-Fox Pitt Rivers, *The Clash of Cultures and the Contact of Races*, London, 1927.

[34] George Pitt Rivers, *The World Significance of the Russian Revolution*, Oxford, 1920.

[35] This claim is quoted from Pitt-Rivers's, *Who's Who* entry in Richard Griffiths, *Fellow Travellers of the Right: British Enthusiasts for Nazi Germany 1933–39*,

Oxford, 1983, p.322.

[36] George Pitt Rivers, *Weeds in the Garden of Marriage*, London, 1931, pp.8–9.

[37] George Pitt Rivers, *The Peace that Passeth All Misunderstanding*, Oxford, 1938.

[38] The Wessex Music Festival is reported in the *Dorset Daily Echo*, 3 & 9 October 1945.

[39] William Sanderson, *A Treatise on Freemasonry and the English Mistery*, London, 1930, pp.117, 78, 60.

[40] Viscount Lymington, 'Jazz in Basel', *Git le Coeur*, Paris, 1928. Lymington sowed his 'wild oats' in company with a friend called 'Bimbo', who turns out to have been Stephen Tennant, later known as the famous bed-ridden eccentric of Wilsford, in Wiltshire. See Earl of Portsmouth, *A Knot of Roots: An Autobiography*, London, 1965.

[41] Viscount Lymington, *Horn, Hoof and Corn, the Future of British Agriculture*, London, 1932, p.13.

[42] *Quarterly Gazette of the English Array*, No. 1, September 1937.

[43] The English Array was keen to fly the flag of St George, worrying that with the rise of the composite British type, the 'English stock' was getting 'deficient in that healthy and legitimate egotism which is necessary to self-preservation'. *New Pioneer*, Vol. I, No. 2, January 1939.

[44] *New Pioneer*, Vol. I, No. 1, December 1938, p.6.

[45] *Quarterly Gazette of the English Array*, No. 6, January 1939.

[46] Lymington was appalled by the effects of the Milk Marketing Board on small producers — claiming that it removed the risk of surpluses from big distributors, but did nothing to help the small producer of less than 500 gallons who got no subsidy at all. *New Pioneer*, Vol. I, No. 1, December 1938, p.11.

[47] *New Pioneer*, Vol. I, No. 10, September 1939.

[48] *New Pioneer*, Vol. I, No. 8, July 1939.

[49] G. K. Chesterton, 'The Ballad of the White Horse' (1911), in S. Metcalf (ed.), *Poems for All Purposes: The Selected Poems of G. K. Chesterton*, London, 1994, p.156.

[50] 'Obituary for a Craftsman', *New Pioneer*, February 1939, p.74.

[51] Richard de Grey's poem 'The Old Servants', *New Pioneer*, Vol. II, No. 14, January 1940.

[52] Hugh Seaton, 'Trees in Agriculture', *New Pioneer*, September 1939, p.239.

[53] Letter in *New Pioneer*, Vol. I, No. 1, December 1938, p.16.

[54] *Quarterly Gazette of the English Array*, No. 2, December 1937, p.4.

[55] Between 1929 and 1933, Ralph Coward farmed Gore as Rolf Gardiner's Warden and Guestmaster. He left, as Gardiner records, after disagreements over the

acquisition of Springhead.

56 'The English Array; King Alfred Muster, Newsletter No. 1', January 1940. This document, handwritten by Ralph Coward, includes a short report of the situation of eleven corresponding members of the muster — artisans, farmers, Lord Arundell and Rolf Gardiner. Other letters from Coward to Gardiner, reveal that Springhead supplied him with the wholemeal flour he could not acquire more locally, and also that Coward sold Gardiner portable poultry pens for £2 a piece.

57 Boyes, *The Imagined Village*, p.157.

58 In his retrospective assessment of the English Array, Lymington concedes that 'we acquired the odd crank and near fascist', but insists that 'these were mostly weeded out'. See *A Knot of Roots*, p.129.

59 *New Pioneer*, Vol. I, No. 1, December 1938, p.2.

60 Earl of Portsmouth, *Alternative to Death: The Relationship Between Soil,Family and Community*, London, 1943, p.162–3.

61 *Ibid*., p.21.

62 *New Pioneer*, Vol. I, No. 5, April, 1939.

63 *New Pioneer*, Vol. I, No. 7, June 1939.

64 *New Pioneer*, Vol. I, No. 8, July 1939.

65 See 'The "Country Standard" Policy for A.R.P. Evacuation', *Country Standard*, Vol. IV, No. 2, April 1939. For Valentine Ackland's article about evacuation — which concludes that A.R.P. should stand for Attend to Rural Problems as well as Air Raid Precautions — see 'Evacuation in Wartime: A New Problem for Country People', *Country Standard*, Vol. III, No. 12, February 1939. A later article on the same subject remarks 'In these days of conscription let us not forget the country mansions of the rich. The unhappiest evacuees are those who have been given some isolated attic in a wealthy home so that the rich can claim to be doing their bit. Many have had to be removed to poorer, kindlier houses. But we do not believe this to be the answer. Let the country mansions be taken over lock, stock, and barrel, to be used as hostels, properly run and organised. *Country Standard*, Vol. IV, No. 8, October 1939, p.2.

66 *New Pioneer*, Vol. I, No. 6, May 1939 & Vol. I, No. 11, October 1939.

67 Lymington, Letter to the Hon. Richard de Grey, 27 September 1938.

68 *New Pioneer*, Vol. I, No. 13, December 1939.

69 See Lady Evelyn Barbara Balfour, *The Living Soil: Evidence of the Importance to Human Health of Soil Vitality, With Special Reference to Post-War Planning*, London, 1943.

CHAPTER 13

[1] Rolf Gardiner, 'Hitler's Reich and the Real Germany (1929–1939)', *Wessex Letters From Springhead*, No. 4/5, Autumn 1948. Gardiner's extensive papers have for several years now been held at Cambridge University library. Due to building problems, however, they remain inaccessible to researchers. I have therefore relied on published material, correspondence that remained in the possession of Gardiner's daughter and literary executrix Mrs Rosalind Richards, some estate papers in the possession of John Eliot Gardiner, and the typescript of Gardiner's only partially published book about his co-operation with the German youth movement, *Wisdom and Action: A Chronicle of Youth*.

[2] Rolf Gardiner, 'Reflections on Music and Statecraft', *North Sea and Baltic*, early 1934, pp.3–7.

[3] Viscount Lymington, letter to Rolf Gardiner 2 January 1939. Lymington's correspondence with Gardiner gives no support to Anna Bramwell's conjecture that Gardiner 'dominated' the *New Pioneer*, or indeed, that anything by Gardiner was printed in it other than the pieces bearing his name. See Bramwell, *Ecology in the Twentieth Century: A History*, New Haven & London, 1989, p.118.

[4] Rolf Gardiner, 'Notes on the Centres: Springhead', *North Sea and Baltic*, Harvest 1936, p.29.

[5] As Gardiner wrote to Lymington, 'I know that the English Mistery and particularly Sanderson, dislike the idea of Work Camps ... I think that is a defect in their thought; that they fail to re-interpret old functions in terms of present day forms.' He goes on to suggest that young men between the ages of 18–24 deeply need the experience of warm, romantic companionship connected with adventurous purpose, suggesting that while people in their thirties could lead such events, the young would never be won over by 'people too old to share their mood or to give their inchoate longing a purpose in which they can believe' (letter dated 16 March 1938).

[6] On 17 March 1938, Gardiner wrote to Lymington recommending that some sort of 'common activity or expedition by the leading men of the Array' be held before the approaching summer camp. He suggested that 'a weekend walk along the Roman Wall, or along the Ridgeway of the Downs or in the Welsh marches' would have 'a surprisingly good effect' and 'give the camp a power which it otherwise would lack'. On 24 March, Lymington sent out a circular letter inviting 'All Marshalls' to participate in 'a short walking tour either on the Roman Wall or some other unspoilt part of England'.

[7] Rolf Gardiner, letter to Viscount Lymington, 16 March 1938.

[8] Quoted from 'Notes on the Centres: Springhead', *North Sea and Baltic*, Harvest 1936, p.29. A couple of years later, Lymington, who had recommended Gardiner

as a possible outside speaker to the National Socialist League — a 'very intelligent' schism from Mosley's British Union of Fascists led by John Beckett and William Joyce — was writing in response to Gardiner's reservations: 'About Joe Pitt Rivers, the position is that he is just hopeless. He has got a brain, but you cannot deal with a man who is like quicksilver, just at the moment when you want steady work and an objective for some purpose. He is also infernally pleased with himself that you cannot reason with him. Joyce and Beckett may not have been respectable, but by God, they worked hard with intense efficiency, and took orders . . .' Joe's only use was 'to deal with the converted when there was no reporter about!' (Letter to Gardiner, 18 August 1938)

9 Rolf Gardiner, 'Harvest Rides in Wessex; Extracts from a Letter-diary', *Wessex Letters from Springhead*, No. 2, Autumn 1942, p.15. I take it that it is Captain Pitt Rivers who is being referred to here. As Gardiner remarks, he had a son who had 'attended harvest camps at Gore and enjoyed digging potatoes with my labourers during holidays which he might have spent in much more luxurious ways'.

10 Georgina Boyes has recently assumed a connection between Gardiner and the freebooting and murderous bands of men known as Freikorps who roamed Germany in the Twenties. (*The Imagined Village*, pp.162 & 191). Observing that Gardiner 'frequently visited the eastern parts of Germany' during the years of Freikorps activity, she goes on to remake him in the image of the Freikorps provided by Klaus Thewelheit in *Male Fantasies, Vol. I: Women, Floods, Bodies, History*, Cambridge, 1987. This produces an impressive masculine demon, but it is historically unjustified, for while Gardiner did indeed visit Germany east and west, his allegiance was with youth movements that viewed the Freikorps as anathema. In 1935/6 Gardiner did have a brief correspondence with Edwin Dwinger, one of Thewelheit's most horrible proto-fascist novelists, who wanted him to contribute to a book of anti-communist propaganda and seems to have been at some pains to persuade Gardiner that the Church of England was being used as an instrument of 'cultural Bolshevism'.

11 I quote these phrases from 'The Generations and Leadership', an article first published in *New English Weekly* on 12 December 1940, and reprinted by Gardiner in a pamphlet entitled *Youth and the Nation*.

12 Rolf Gardiner, *World Without End; British Politics and the Younger Generation*, London, 1932, p.10.

13 Gardiner's judgement of the leaders of the English Folk Dance Society is here quoted from his review of E.F.D.S. News in *Youth*, No. 10, June 1923, p.240. His feud with the English Folk Dance Society intensified in 1923 when he and Arthur Heffer, a young bookseller in Cambridge, set up the Travelling Morrice to pursue their own more dynamic conception of English folk dance, on the basis that traditional dances were 'forms of joy and fulfilment' which Sharp and

his followers at the centralised E.F.D.S. had confined in a straight-jacket of 'traditional' authenticity. He declared that 'Vulgarity it is true will always worm its way into your buds, if you plant them in artificial conditions where vulgarity is rife, all the more so if you spray them with the germ-killer of a spurious traditionalism.' Gardiner was after the masculine 'spirit' of the Morris Dance, or the sword dance he learned from the ironstone miners of Cleveland, and deplored the way in which that soul, once fallen into the centralised and academic hands of the E.F.D.S., had become 'the façade of a deserted temple of life, the pattern made by the ribbing of a withered leaf, a hollowed stalk'. Gardiner sent the E.F.D.S. a proposed charter for renewal — recommending the cancellation of festivals in which country and Morris dances were 'displayed' for propaganda purposes; the discouragement, but not the banning, of women from the Morris, exchanges with other parts of Europe, and the redesignation of the society as the English Festival Society. For his proposals, which were not accepted, see Rolf Gardiner, 'The English Folk Dance: Some Constructive Considerations', *Youth*, Vol. II, No. 9, October 1923, p.52. His criticism of the academic approach to which Sharp and the E.F.D.S. had 'shackled' the folk dance which should really 'be concerned with the religious and psychological evolution of humanity' is to be found in Rolf Gardiner, The *English Folk Dance Tradition*, London, 1923.

In Gardiner's mind, the project of revitalising folk dance was connected to the much wider task of reconnecting life to the 'rhythmic' basis it had lost as it broke with the land. As he explained in an 'excursion into prophecy' included, with due apologies, in a letter dated 22 September 1937, written to Douglas Kennedy, his friend and dancing collaborator who by that time was Director of the English Folk Dance and Song Society: 'The truth is that not only is the whole question of movement as a technique of personal and national regeneration now a matter of first class expert consideration . . . but the implications in our whole economic and national life have got to be sought out honestly. I see things so terribly clearly from my acquired corner as a practical agriculturalist and would-be reconstructor of rural life. The development of the machine and the frightening automatism of purely mechanical necessities can only be counterweighed by an advance to a rhythmic approach and a consideration of fundamental needs.'

14 Rolf Gardiner, quoted from early chapters of *Wisdom and Action: A Chronicle of Youth*. For a history of the early German Youth Movement, see Walter Laqueur, *Young Germany: A History of the German Youth Movement*, London, 1962.

15 Gardiner's 'paganism' is mentioned in Anna Bramwell, *Ecology in the Twentieth Century*, pp.114–15. Unconventional as it certainly was, Gardiner's vision was actually a Christian one.

[16] Rolf Gardiner, 'German Youth Movements', in *Youth*, No. 9, March 1923, pp.202–3.

[17] Karl Wilker, 'We and Yet Not We', *Youth*, No. 12, Spring 1924, p.112.

[18] Rolf Gardiner, 'Vox Juventutis', *Youth*, No. 10, June 1923, p.216–8.

[19] This phrase is quoted from H. E. Barlow, 'The cult of nakedness in Germany', *Youth*, No. 10, June 1923, p.238.

[20] Rolf Gardiner, review of *Vivos Voco: Zeitshrift fur neue Deutschtum* in *Youth*, No. 10, June 1923, p.241.

[21] A. S. Neill, 'Hellerau International School Transferred', in *Youth*, 1923.

[22] Leslie Paul, *Angry Young Man*, London, 1951, p.55.

[23] As editor of *Youth*, Gardiner would be pleased to publish Pierre Loving's 'African Songs' — adaptations of African folk lore, which celebrated the African as a source of grounded Aboriginal wisdom ('Yeh, yeh, la! Yeh, yeh!/God up high, man on the earth-skin' etc.), but the black troops on the Ruhr were not blessed with these primitive qualities. Loving's verses were published in *Youth*, No. 12, Spring 1924, pp.105–7. Gardiner's comment on the French troops is quoted from the typescript of *Wisdom and Action: A Chronicle of Youth*.

[24] Rolf Gardiner, 'To the Reader', *Wessex: Letters from Springhead*, No. 4/5, Autumn 1948, p.167.

[25] Rolf Gardiner, *World Without End*, p.44.

[26] On March 1931 Max Plowman, a pacifist who worked with John Middleton Murray on the *Adelphi*, wrote to inform Gardiner that he could not possibly print his review of a book by Cicely Hamilton because 'it reads to me exactly like a political manifesto on behalf of German penetration in the East'.

[27] Rolf Gardiner advocated 'interlocality' as an alternative to 'Internationalism', describing it as organic place to place exchange and, with Gore and the Boberhaus in mind, suggested that interlocality would promote articles with titles like 'Regional Reconstruction in Wessex and Silesia'. See Rolf Gardiner, *World Without End*, p.44.

[28] Rolf Gardiner, *England Herself*, London, 1943, p.18.

[29] *Ibid.*, p.28.

[30] Rolf Gardiner, 'Marching in Downland', *England Herself*, p.23.

[31] Rolf Gardiner 'Land Service: A Focus for Youth', *New English Weekly*, 19 December 1940.

[32] See M. Balfour & J. Frisby, *Helmuth von Moltke: A Leader against Hitler*, London, 1972.

[33] Ian Kemp, *Tippett: The Composer and His Music*, Oxford, 1987, p.26. See also Malcolm Chase & Mark Whyman, *Heartbreak Hill: A Response to Unemploy-*

ment in East Cleveland in the 1930s, Cleveland, 1991.

34 Gardiner talks about 'landscape regions' in 'Hitler's Reich and the Real Germany', p.179.

35 Rolf Gardiner, 'Ten years of Gore Farm', *North Sea and Baltic*, Midwinter 1937, p.68.

36 Rolf Gardiner discusses Dartington Hall in 'Rural Reconstruction' in H. J. Massingham, *England and the Farmer*, London, 1941, pp.105–7.

37 Letter to Leonard Elmhirst, 1933. Gardiner's letters to Elmhirst are among the private papers held at Dartington Hall.

38 Rolf Gardiner, 'Hitler's Reich and the Real Germany (1929–1939)', p.170–1.

39 Rolf Gardiner, *World Without End*, p.32.

40 Ibid., p.34.

41 Rolf Gardiner, 'The meaning of the German Revolution', *North Sea and Baltic*, Whitsuntide 1933, p.2.

42 Rolf Gardiner, 'D. H. Lawrence in a Black Shirt', letter to the *Observer*, 11 February 1934, p.11.

43 See M. D. Bryant & H. Rosenstock-Huessy (eds), *Eugen Rosenstock-Huessy: Studies in His Life and Thought*, Toronto Studies in Theology, No. 28, 1986. I am informed of the continuation of this legacy by Mark Feedman, founder and executive director of the Rural Development Service Group, based in New Mexico, which traces its own understanding of the importance of cultural matters in rural regeneration to the work of Rosenstock-Huessy.

44 Ludwig Lienhard, who later escaped from Nazi Germany by organising a party who sailed out of the Baltic on a tall ship, also compiled a statement informing National Socialist students attending Springhead camps that they were not there to convert participants to the Nazi cause, and should treat differences with respect.

45 Rolf Gardiner, 'Hitler's Reich and the Real Germany (1929–1939)', p.182.

46 Leslie A. Paul, 'The Decline of the Youth Movement', *The Adelphi*, Vol. 7, No. 5, February 1934, pp.317–27.

47 Rolf Gardiner's letter appeared in *The Adelphi*, Vol. 8, No. 1, April 1934, pp.63–5.

48 For the 'coefficient of ruralicity' see R. G. Stapledon, *The Land Now and Tomorrow*, London, 1935, p.4. Rolf Gardiner greatly admired this book.

49 Rolf Gardiner, copy of letter to Lymington, 17 March 1939. Lymington agreed with this estimate of events in Czechoslovakia, remarking of the Nazis 'what unutterable B.F.'s they are in their diplomacy, playing straight into the hands of Roosevelt and his few friends ...' Undated letter marked only 'Sunday'.

[50] Quoted from Margaret Gardiner's unpublished article 'My Uncle, Balfour Gardiner'.

[51] Rolf Gardiner, 'Hitler's Reich and the Real Germany', p.213.

[52] Quoted from Gardiner's letter to Leslie Paul, drafted 22 March 1951.

[53] John Stewart Collis, *Bound Upon a Course: An Autobiography*, London, 1971, p.178. For the play in Coward's barn see pp.172–3.

[54] Rolf Gardiner, 'Music and the Soil', in *England Herself*, p.135.

[55] H. J. Massingham, *Remembrance: An Autobiography*, London, 1940, p.142. Massingham also appreciated the 'prehistoric signature' in Gardiner's anciently terraced downs, and said of Gardiner's project that 'its pattern of integral harmonies based on upgrowth from a particular place is a means to winning even more than the war, namely the soil of England back to itself'. (p.143).

[56] See Gardiner's 'Mechanization and the Land: Report on a Meeting of A Kinship in Husbandry held at Corpus Christi College, Oxford, 27th February, 1944', in *Wessex: Letters From Springhead*, No. 5, Autumn 1944, pp.25–9. For a fuller account of A Kinship in Husbandry see 'Can Farming save European Civilisation' in Rolf Gardiner, *Water Springing From the Ground*, Fontmell Magna, 1972, pp.196–9.

[57] Rolf Gardiner, 'Cranborne Chase: Memorandum, January 1944'.

[58] Rolf Gardiner, 'Cranborne Chase Co-operative Group, 31 March, 1953'.

[59] Rolf Gardiner, 'Farewell to Slape Flax Mill', *Wessex: Letters From Springhead*, No. 3, Spring 1943, pp.19–23. The full version of Gardiner's account of his attempt to revive the flax industry is given in 'A Rural Industry', *England Herself*, pp.98–124.

[60] Rolf Gardiner, 'Harvest Rides in Wessex', *Wessex: Letters From Springhead*, No. 2, Autumn 1942, pp.29–30.

[61] Rolf Gardiner, *England Herself*, pp.120–21.

[62] 'In this accumulation of metal, soldiers seemed intensely fragile, objects de luxe ... One stared at the craftsmanship of their eyelashes and fingernails, their eyelids like flower-petals.' Quoted in Claire Harman, *Sylvia Townsend Warner: A Biography*, London, 1991, p.200.

[63] Hugh Dormer, a young Catholic who served with the Second Armoured Battalion of the Irish Guards and was killed in France, appreciated the obvious contrast between his Sherman tank and the Yorkshire landscape in which he trained, describing an evening mass being said behind a haystack in an open field at Duncombe Park: 'All around the hedges the tanks were camouflaged, pointing in their silence so perfectly the contrast of peace and war.' But once he was driving through Sussex on the way to embarkation for France he felt no discontinuity with the landscape: 'All that day we drove across typical English country-

side with thatched cottages and honeysuckle in the hedgerows and the cornfields gleaming in the June heat. I gazed at the experiences of my former travels, I stored up those sun-drenched memories that morning against the bleak and terrible future.' *Hugh Dormer's Diaries*, London, 1947.

[64] John Stewart Collis, *While Following the Plough*, London, 1946, pp.228–9.

[65] John Stewart Collis, *Down to Earth*, London, 1947, pp.181–2.

[66] While approving his support for peasant and yeoman, Gardiner admits of Darré that 'At the same time there was about his theory a pseudo-biological materialism mixed up with a rather cloudy nature-worship.' But he also remarks 'By much of this approach I was strongly attracted, and I still believe that a great deal of both the programme and the performance were sound and praiseworthy.' Rolf Gardiner, 'Hitler's Reich and the Real Germany', p.192.

[67] See his 'Hitler's Reich and the Real Germany', pp.174–5.

[68] Gardiner outlines this Royalist vision in 'Rural Reconstruction' in H. J. Massingham (ed.), *England and the Farmer*, London, 1941, pp.91–107.

[69] Gardiner is quoting from an article called 'The Rediscovery of Wood' from *American Forests*. See his 'Forestry and Husbandry' in H. J. Massingham (ed.), *The Natural Order: Essays in The Return to Husbandry*, London, 1945, p.129.

[70] H. J. Massingham, 'England Laid Waste' in *The Heritage of Man*, London, 1929. Ironically, the Breckland is now one of the Forestry Commission's conservation show-pieces.

[71] Quoted in David Cannadine, *G. M. Trevelyan: A Life and History*, London, 1992, p.156.

[72] See 'A Tree Song' in Rudyard Kipling, *Puck of Pook's Hill*, London, 1987, pp.59–60.

[73] Gardiner would have agreed with Wilfrid Hiley, when he wrote that 'The danger of "preservation" is that in killing the disease it will also kill the patient and that the relics of the countryside, duly and reverentially embalmed, will be preserved as a mummy for the admiration of future tourists.' He would also have agreed with Hiley's insistence that 'In contrast to the mummification of the country is the intensification of its vitality, which comes from the vigorous pursuit of rural industries.' W. E. Hiley, *Improvements of Woodlands*, London, 1931.

[74] Rolf Gardiner, 'Replanting Cranborne Chase', in *England Herself*, p.92.

[75] Rolf Gardiner, 'Forestry and Husbandry', in Massingham, *The Natural Order: Essays in the Return to Husbandry*, p.130.

[76] Rolf Gardiner, 'Silviculture', *Mother Earth*, Vol. 14, No. 8, pp.545–7.

[77] Rolf Gardiner, *England Herself*, p.93.

CHAPTER 14

1 J. R. R. Tolkein, *The Return of the King*, London, 1955, p.296.

2 The notes of Ralph Bond's talk are printed in *Proceedings of the Dorset Natural History and Archaeological Society*, Vol. 58, 1 January–31 December 1936, pp.141–3.

3 Arthur Oswald, 'Tyneham, Dorset', *Country Life*, 6 April 1935, pp.348–53.

4 L. M. G. Bond, *William Ralph Garneys Bond 1880–1952*, a privately printed memorial in the County Museum, Dorchester.

5 W. R. G. Bond, 'Notes on Dorset Bats', read to the Dorset Natural History and Archaeological Society on 27 April 1943, *Proceedings*, 64, 1943.

6 W. R. G. Bond, 'The Common or Garden Bird; its reaction to human habitations', read to the Dorset Natural History and Archaeological Society on 17 October 1944, *Proceedings*, 66, 1945, p.137.

7 Pat Evans, 'War time memories, 1942–3', Dorchester County Museum, Tyneham papers.

8 Reported in 'Spoiled Beauty Spot', *The Times*, 24 September 1949.

9 *Dorset County Chronicle*, 2 December 1943. Quoted from Rodney Legg, *Lulworth and Tyneham Revisited*, p.89.

10 Lilian Bond, copy of letter to Canon Grace, 2 May 1957. In the possession of General Mark Bond.

11 Quoted from Margot Bond's notes of 1977 entitled 'Evacuation of Tyneham and Povington, December 1943'. In the possession of General Mark Bond.

12 Quoted from Margaret Bond's letters to her sister — extracts in the possession of General Mark Bond.

13 'The Annual Dinner of the Society', *The Dorset Year Book*, pp.142–8.

14 John Parris, *Scapegoat: The Inside Story of the Trial of Derek Bentley*, London, 1991, p.49.

15 Michael Foot, the *Daily Herald*, 23 May 1961.

16 *Dorset Daily Echo*, 16 September, 1953.

17 Viscount Hinchinbrooke, 'Address to the Student Federation for International Co-operation, Oxford, 9 January, 1943', *Full Speed Ahead!*, p.7.

18 *Ibid.*, p.8.

19 Viscount Hinchinbrooke, 'The Modern Tory Rejects Individualism', reprinted from the *Evening Standard* (8 February 1943), in *Full Speed Ahead!*, pp.20–4.

20 *Daily Worker*, 7 May 1949.

21 As Hinchinbrooke wrote of the Conservative Party, 'I am conscious that some branches of the old oak have died and not yet been lopped off, and that other branches have tried to spread their foliage but have grown up twisted and stunted and out of the reach of the sun.' From 'New Horizons', (originally

published in the *Empire Review*, September 1943), republished in *Full Speed Ahead!*, p.54.

22 Hinchinbrooke, *Full Speed Ahead!*, pp.4–5.

23 *Daily Telegraph*, 19 March 1953.

24 Hinchinbrooke, *Full Speed Ahead!*, p.7.

25 *Ibid.*, p.39.

26 Hinchinbrooke, 'New Horizons', *Full Speed Ahead!*, pp.52–6.

27 Hinchinbrooke, 'The Course of Conservative Politics', *Quarterly Review*, Vol. 284, No. 570, October 1946, pp.523–4.

28 *Dorset Daily Echo*, 5 October 1945.

29 *Dorset Daily Echo*, 17 December 1945.

30 *Western Gazette*, 17 June 1949.

31 *Dorset Daily Echo*, 7 February 1950; *Daily Worker*, 14 September 1950.

32 *Dorset Daily Echo*, 23 November 1953.

33 *Paignton Observer*, 8 December 1949.

34 *Eastern Daily Press*, 6 October 1952.

35 Wareham and Purbeck Rural District Council, Minutes, 1944–6, County Record Office, Dorchester, DC/WAP 6L 179.

36 *Proceedings of the Dorset Natural History and Archaeological Society*, Vol. 66, 1943–4, p.11.

37 F. Holland Swann, letter to *The Times*, 20 July 1945.

38 *Dorset Daily Echo*, 5 October 1945.

39 *Dorset Daily News*, 25 October 1945.

40 *The Times*, 22 November 1946.

41 *The Times*, 26 February 1947.

42 'The Future of the Countryside: Labour's Opportunity', in Cyril Moore (ed.), *Countrygoing; the Fourth Countrygoer Book*, London, 1945, pp.3–7. C. E. M. Joad chaired the editorial board of this publication devoted to increasing, and also refining, the townsman's interest in the countryside.

43 C. E. M. Joad, *The Untutored Townsman's Invasion of the Country*, London 1946, pp.160–1.

44 Douglas Goldring, *Marching with the Times 1931–46*, London, 1947, p.227.

45 H. J. Massingham, *An Englishman's Year*, London, 1948, p.164.

46 John Dower, *National Parks in England and Wales*, HMSO, May 1945 (Command Paper 6628). Sir Arthur Hobhouse, *Report of the National Parks Committee (England and Wales)*, HMSO, July 1947 (Command Paper 7121).

47 A copy of Brigadier N. W. Duncan's talk to the CPRE is held in the library of the Tank Museum at Bovington Camp.

48 Ministry of Town and Country Planning, *East Holme, Purbeck Use of Land for*

the War Department, Public Local Inquiry, Tuesday 16th March and Wednesday 17th March 1948; Report of Sir Cecil Oakes C.B.E., to the Right Hon. Lewis Silkin, M.P., Public Record Office, W64/43.

49 *Dorset Daily Echo*, 17 March 1948.

50 *Ibid.*

51 This official admitted the existence of the pledge in a manner that also deflected the blame away from the centre of government: 'When those wretched chaps were turned out in 1943, they were promised quite wrongly and without authority by people on the spot that they would be allowed to go back.' Quoted from *The Times*, 3 March 1960.

52 'Note of a Meeting Held at the Offices of the Wareham and Purbeck Rural District Council on Friday, 16 July 1948, at 3.30 pm'.

53 *Dorset County Chronicle*, 22 July 1948.

54 The phrase is quoted from John Durant-Lewis, Clerk to the Wareham and Purbeck Rural District Council in the *Dorset Daily Echo*, 20 July 1948.

55 'Spoiled Beauty Spot', *The Times*, 24 September 1949, pp.2 & 10.

56 *The Times*, 20 July 1948.

57 *Southern Times*, 30 October 1952.

58 For this story, and passing mention of Hinchinbrooke's involvement in it, see I. F. Nicolson, *The Mystery of Crichel Down*, Oxford, 1986.

59 Interview with Peter Farquharson, 14 February 1994.

60 R. Douglas Brown, *The Battle of Crichel Down*, London, 1955, p.31.

CHAPTER 15

1 W. T. Wadham, letter in *Western Gazette*, 21 September 1973.

2 John Gale, 'The Deserted Village', the *Observer*, 3 August 1952.

3 In his autobiography, John Gale tells of visiting Tyneham at a time when it had been 'dead seven years'. His account is a muted version of the *Observer* article cited above. See John Gale, *Clean Young Englishman*, London, 1988, pp.117–9.

4 First printed in the *Illustrated London News* on 7 May 1949, 'St George's Day in Purbeck' is collected in Arthur Bryant, *The Lion and the Unicorn*, London, 1969.

5 Arthur Bryant, *The Spirit of Conservatism*, London, 1929, pp.74–5.

6 Bryant, *The Lion and the Unicorn*, p.269.

7 Arthur Bryant, *English Saga*, London, 1940, p.316.

8 *Ibid.*, p.332.

9 *Ibid.*, p.333.

10 Arthur Bryant, *Unfinished Victory*, London, 1940.

11 L. M. G. Bond, *Tyneham: A Lost Heritage*, Dorchester, 1956.

12 This episode was remembered by Miss Margaret Bond in a conversation of 29 March 1986. As she also recalled of that 'silly old parson', 'we did mix in a way, but not up to that extent'.

13 Bond, *Tyneham*, p.17.

14 Lilian Bond's refusal to revisit Tyneham is mentioned by Mark Bond in his introduction to the Dovecote Press's 1984 reprint of *Tyneham: A Lost Heritage*.

15 Dated 1957, the poem is called 'The Winterborne 'twixt Piddle and Stour (with a copy of Mrs Bond's book "Tyneham")', and included in Rolf Gardiner, *Love and Memory, A Garland of Poems*, Springhead, Dorset, 1960.

16 Gardiner's draft of this letter survives among his papers at the University of Cambridge library. Bond's answer is dated 2 April 1957.

17 Quoted from a note from Rolf Gardiner to 'Marcella and Daffodil', written at the time of the County Council vote, in the archives of the Dorset Branch of the Council for the Protection of Rural England, Dorchester.

18 A draft of this letter survives among the papers of the Dorset CPRE.

19 Quoted from *Southern Journal*, 18 January 1957. Perhaps some differences remained, since I understand from her biographer, Claire Harman, that in her diary Warner also regretted the pathetic efforts of her fellow objectors at this inquiry.

20 'Army Seek Permanent Closure of Dorset Roads', *The Times*, 3 July 1960.

21 For these letters see Public Records Office, T180 107/ W.64/43.

22 *The Times*, 5 March 1960.

23 Quoted in 'Clerk's Memorandum Regarding Battle Training Areas — East Lulworth and East Holme Ranges', Wareham and Purbeck Rural District Council, 3 March 1960.

24 *The Times*, 4 March 1960.

CHAPTER 16

1 Monica Hutchings, *The Walnut Tree: An Autobiography of Kindness*, London, 1951, p.257.

2 'New campaign to remove Army from Purbeck Hills', *Daily Telegraph*, 18 May 1968.

3 Gordon Winter, 'The Rape of Tyneham', *Country Life*, 31 March 1966.

4 Ronald Fraser, *1968: A Student Generation in Revolt*, London, 1988, p.254.

5 Michael Frenchman, 'Tyneham', *Town*, Vol. 7, No. 12, December 1966.

[6] See Rodney Legg, 'How the Tyneham campaign was launched', *Dorset: The County Magazine*, No. 27, Autumn 1972.

[7] Michael Pitt Rivers, *Dorset: A Shell Guide*, London, 1965, pp.31 & 92.

[8] Martin Walker, *The National Front*, London, 1977, p.47.

[9] See David Underdown, *Fire from Heaven: Life in an English Town in the Seventeenth Century*, London, 1992.

[10] Rodney Legg, 'Speech notes for Tyneham Action Group Meeting Saturday 18 May 1968 at Dorchester', typescript in Rodney Legg's archive.

[11] This last passage does not occur in Legg's notes for his speech, but was quoted in the *Dorset Evening Echo*, 20 May 1968.

[12] Monica Hutchings, *The Walnut Tree: an Autobiography of Kindness*, London, 1951.

[13] Monica Hutchings, *Romany Cottage, Timberlake*, London, 1946.

[14] Monica Hutchings, The New Face of Britain, Part Two: Imber was a Village', *The Special Smile*, London, 1951, pp.107–15.

[15] Monica Hutchings, 'The New Face of Britain, Part One: What Price Progress?', *The Special Smile*, pp.97–106.

[16] Monica Hutchings, 'They Noticed this Road', *The Special Smile*, pp.138–49.

[17] *Dorset Evening Echo*, 20 May 1968.

[18] Hutchings, *The Walnut Tree*, p.256. See also Monica Hutchings, *A Farmer's Wife looks at Hunting*, National Society for the Abolition of Cruel Sports, 1965.

[19] *Western Gazette*, 4 September 1970.

[20] Monica Hutchings and Mavis Caver, *Man's Dominion: Our Violation of the Animal World*, London, 1970, p.92.

[21] Gardiner's use of this phrase is remembered by Michael Dower of the Countryside Commission. Gardiner's line did not always seem particularly helpful to those who were involved in the practical compromises involved in rural conservation in a small country with a large, predominantly urban population, and for whom the wholesale rejection of 'petrol England' was not an option.

[22] See, for example, Gardiner's 'Speech to the Duke of Edinburgh's Conference "The Countryside in 1970" ', presented on 12 November 1965, and collected in Rolf Gardiner, *Water Springing From the Ground*, Fontmell Magna, 1972, p.264.

[23] Rolf Gardiner, 'Harvest Thanksgiving: Cerne Abbas', *Water Springing from the Ground*, pp.289–94.

[24] *Western Gazette*, 24 May 1968.

[25] *Daily Telegraph Magazine*, 3 November 1972.

[26] See, for example, Alan Rogers, 'Come rambling with Ruth — and her wire cutters', *The Sun*, 29 April 1966.

[27] As Lilian Bond also wrote, having praised Draper, 'I was struck, too, by your

description of present world conditions as "apocalyptic" — truly le mot juste.' Letter to Rolf Gardiner, 2 December 1968, Cambridge University Library.

[28] Fenner Brockway, *Towards Tomorrow*, London, 1977, p.239.

CHAPTER 17

[1] Quoted in *Tyneham Action Group Newsletter*, November 1970.

[2] *Tyneham Action Group Newsletter*, February 1969.

[3] Legg's 'Obituary' to Tyneham House appeared in *Dorset: The County Magazine*, No. 2, Summer 1968, p.11. Alongside a poem in which I. Geraldine Peart gave her thoughts on pictures in the national Press showing the effluent pipes being laid at Arish Mell: 'Concrete mixers grind away / As you dig, dig deep and well / Smashing, stirring, gouging, whirring / Ring the fate of Arish Mell . . . / Sound the knell on a golden bell / for the sake of poor old Arish Mell.'

[4] Philip Draper, letter to the *Manchester Guardian*, 19 August 1968.

[5] Lilian Bond, letter to Rolf Gardiner, 2 December 1968. Rolf Gardiner papers, University of Cambridge Library.

[6] 'They will plead for action to rescue village from oblivion', *Western Gazette*, 30 August 1968.

[7] Philip Howard, 'The army reclaims a beauty spot — for shelling', *The Times*, 3 September 1968.

[8] Tyneham Action Group, Minutes of committee meeting, 21 September 1968. See also Monica Hutchings, 'Pilgrimage gives source of Hope', *Western Gazette*, 20 September 1968.

[9] Tyneham Action Group, *The Fight for Tyneham*, Wincanton 1969, p.32.

[10] 'Brigadier Bond's view', *Dorset: The County Magazine*, Summer 1968, p.26.

[11] 'Pilgrimage to Tyneham bitter experience for one', *Western Gazette*, August 1968.

[12] Rolf Gardiner, 'Reflection on Music and Statecraft', *North Sea and Baltic*, early 1934, p.3.

[13] Rolf Gardiner's 'Notes for Tyneham Action Group Meeting, Wareham 16 November 1968' are among his Tyneham papers, now in Cambridge University Library. A more detailed script, written after the speech had been delivered, is among the T.A.G. papers at the Dorset County Record Office, D. 1037, B2.

[14] Quoted from Gardiner's 1968 sermon 'Harvest Thanksgiving: Cerne Abbas' in *Water Springing from the Ground*, Fontmell Magna, 1972, p.290. Thomas Traherne's *Vision of Childhood* had been a source of considerable inspiration to the Springhead Ring since the Twenties.

15 It was Dr Frank Fraser Darling, who declared that tree-cover was needed 'to give time to think: to do a little experimentation: and for love-making!' Gardiner quoted this approvingly in 'Farming and Forestry in an Overcrowded World' (1966), *Water Springing from the Ground*, pp.266–78.

16 Patrick O'Donovan, 'Wild, lovely, littered with violent death', *Observer*, 25 May 1969.

17 Angus Maude, letter to the *Daily Telegraph*, 7 August 1969.

18 Lady Sylvia Sayer, letter to the *Daily Telegraph*, 22 August 1969.

19 On the battle against fluoridation see 'Drinking water in a toxic state' in the revised edition of my *A Journey Through Ruins*, London 1993, pp.208–43.

20 Draper's comments, contained in a letter published in the *Western Gazette* on 18 September 1970, was also featured in 'Action Groupers' rap for Admiral', *Poole Herald*, 24 September 1970.

21 David Mellor, letter in *Western Gazette*, 18 September 1970.

22 David Mellor, letter in *Western Gazette*, 4 September 1970.

23 *Western Gazette*, 22 November 1968.

24 'Protest fleet ready for the battle of Weymouth Bay', *Sunday Times*, 28 December 1969.

25 'Aims of Tyneham Action Group Criticized', *Western Gazette*, 6 February 1970.

26 *Daily Telegraph*, 17 November 1969.

27 Richard Cox, 'Laser beam "knocks out" tank in trials', *Daily Telegraph*, 22 September 1969.

28 Philip Draper, 'The Assessment of a Chartered Engineer of the More Realistic Means for Training British Army Tank Gunners by Employing Modern Techniques at Acceptable National Expenditure', Tyneham Action Group, July 1972.

29 'Tyneham Valley — Action Group Statement', *Evening Echo*, Bournemouth, 14 July 1969.

30 'Tyneham — call to action', *Poole Herald*, 5 June 1969.

31 'Beach protest falls flat', *Wessex Gazette*, 4 August 1969. Also 'Army keeps bay for officers' allegation', *Poole Herald*, 7 August 1969. Kraft's denial of all this was printed in the *Western Gazette*, 8 August 1969.

32 *Swanage Times*, 28 August 1969.

33 'It's the "freedom" of Tyneham — for a month', *Dorset Evening Echo*, 5 August 1969.

34 'Village gets lordly aid', *Guardian*, 5 August 1969.

35 'Woman claims she saw flying saucer land', *Daily Telegraph*, 30 August 1969.

36 Margaret Kraft, 'Scotching rumours', *Evening Echo*, Bournemouth, 13 September 1969.

37 'Heath to reduce land held by services', *Daily Telegraph*, 29 October 1970.

[38] As Monica Hutchings wrote, 'As a direct result of our delegation to Whitehall and the publicity achieved by Tyneham Action Group, this present Government appointed Lord Nugent to hold his commission into MOD holdings in coastal areas, giving priority to Tyneham because of the importance of its position and because the case was so fully documented and had received such widespread publicity.' See her letter, signed 'Monica Gauntlett', in the *Poole Herald*, 25 May 1972.

[39] Quoted from Philip Draper, *Tyneham Action Group Newsletter*, November 1970.

[40] Reported in Minutes of TAG Executive Committee Meeting, 16 April 1970.

[41] Arthur Bryant's letter, dated 22 May 1970, is in the Tyneham Action Group Archive, Dorset County Record Office, D1037, E7.

[42] Sir Arthur Bryant, 'The tyranny of machines', *Illustrated London News*, 17 April 1971, p.13.

CHAPTER 18

[1] Mr Montagu's letter was printed in the *Daily Telegraph*, 19 April 1972.

[2] *Daily Telegraph*, 26 June 1972. See also Kenneth Allsop, *In the Country*, London, 1972, p.124.

[3] Reported in *Bridport News*, 7 July 1972.

[4] See Philip Whitehead, *The Writing on the Wall: Britain in the Seventies*, London, 1985, p.109.

[5] 'A guide to the extreme right', *Searchlight*, January 1981, p.8.

[6] On Clarence, see *Searchlight*, March & April 1983.

[7] See Meredith Veldman, *Fantasy, the Bomb, and the Greening of Britain: Romantic Protest, 1945–1980*, Cambridge, 1994, pp.76–90.

[8] John Stewart Collis, *Bound Upon a Course: An Autobiography*, London, 1971, p.183.

[9] Arthur Bryant, 'Student Power', *Illustrated London News*, 29 June 1968. Quoted from *The Lion and the Unicorn*, op. cit., pp.274–7.

[10] Rolf Gardiner, 'Our Rural Future' in *Mother Earth*, Vol. 14, No. 4, October 1966.

[11] Rolf Gardiner, 'Harvest Thanksgiving: Cerne Abbas', *Water Springing from the Ground*, p.291.

[12] Fenner Brockway, *Towards Tomorrow*, London 1977, p.239.

[13] Denis Hart, 'Carry your own case', *Daily Telegraph Magazine*, 3 November 1972.

14 ' "Broadside" by Minister meets backlash from Tyneham Group', *Western Gazette*, 7 November 1969.

15 *Dorset Evening Echo*, 24 November, 1969.

16 'Care for Dorset', Memorandum to the Defence Lands Committee, June 1971.

17 The programme was called 'Westward Diary' and broadcast on Westward ITV, Plymouth, 24 August 1971.

18 It was actually a week later, on 21 October that Gardiner was presented with the Peter Joseph Lenné Gold Medal, by Count Bernadotte of Strasbourg. This award was part of the Europe prize for Landscape Husbandry, and awarded to Gardiner in recognition of his 'lifelong endeavours for European Cultural Unity, work in soil and water conservation, afforestation and landscape planning in Dorset and Malawi, and as Chairman of the European Working Party for Landscape Husbandry, founded by him in 1963'. Quoted from Gardiner's own Chronology of his life in *Water Springing From the Ground*, p.320.

19 Letter by Rodney Legg in Ruth Colyer's files.

20 Quoted from Mavis Caver's report in the 1943 Committee's Annual Report for 1972.

21 'Demo outside gun range', *Bournemouth Echo*, 26 September 1972.

22 Report of Lord Nugent's Defence Lands Committee, HMSO, 1973.

23 *Western Gazette*, 12 October 1973.

24 *Western Gazette*, 19 October 1973.

25 *Western Gazette*, 26 October 1973.

26 Ruth Colyer, letter to *The Times*, 31 May 1969.

27 Hansard, House of Lords, 4 December 1973, Col. 434–5.

28 'Army land's ex-owners priced out', *Western Daily Press*, 11 July 1973.

29 Lord Brockway, letter to Rodney Legg, 28 June 1973.

30 Rodney Legg, 'Government danger to Dorset dream', *Morning Star*, 13 June 1973.

31 Lord Brockway referred to this 'desecration' in the House of Lords on 2 July 1974.

32 Hansard, House of Lords, 11 June 1973, Col. 372.

33 'Action pledge over crater', *Western Daily Press*, 11 July 1973.

34 These lines were in the typescript of Allsop's last article — but never made it through the sub-editors at the *Sunday Times* (20 May 1973).

35 *Western Gazette*, 6 July 1973.

CHAPTER 19

[1] Phillip Whitehead, *The Writing on the Wall: Britain in the Seventies*, London, 1985, pp.106–7.

[2] Archegram quoted from Peter Cook (ed.), *Archegram*, London, 1972.

[3] 'The "non-plan" argument was derived from an influential article written by Paul Barker, Reyner Banham, Cedric Price and Peter Hall, and published in *New Society*, 20 March 1969.

[4] Jeanne Sillett and Peter Wilson, 'Yesterday was as bad as any other day for a solution', *Casabella* (Milan), no. 413, May 1976.

[5] Comments taken from a letter by Peter Wilson, 25 August 1992.

[6] Nigel Coates's 'House for Derek Jarman' was designed for submission to the RIBA 'Festival of Architecture'. See drawings in NATO 2, 1984.

[7] Quoted from James A. Leith, *Space and Revolution: Projects for Monuments, Squares and Public Buildings in France 1789–1799*, Montreal & London, 1991, p.4.

[8] Jeanne Sillett and Peter Wilson, 'Storie di un prossimo futuro; Arbitare un Paessaggio: Dorset,' *Casabella* (Milan), no. 413, May 1976, pp.24–7.

CHAPTER 20

[1] Keneth Allsop, 'Tyneham dream fades', *Sunday Times*, 20 May 1973.

[2] 'Return this land to its owners, W. I.'s demand', *Western Gazette*, 31 October 1969.

[3] J. L. Precey, letter to *Western Gazette*, 30 July 1973.

[4] G. M. Gover, letter to *Western Gazette*, 11 May, 1973.

[5] Terry Knight, *Western Gazette*, 31 August 1973.

[6] W. T. Wadham, *Western Gazette*, 21 September 1973.

[7] *Bournemouth Evening Echo*, 16 August 1973.

[8] Philip Hemingway, letter to *Western Gazette*, 27 July 1973.

[9] Letter to *The Times*, 31 August 1973.

[10] Dorset Evening Echo, 8 November 1973.

[11] *Bournemouth Echo*, 8 November 1973.

[12] Letter from West Lulworth Parish Council to Lord Carrington at the Ministry of Defence, 11 September 1973.

[13] *Dorset Evening Echo*, 24 September 1973.

[14] *Western Gazette*, 7 December 1973.

[15] *Poole and Dorset Herald*, 9 August 1973.

[16] Philip Draper, letter to *Western Gazette*, 17 August 1973.

[17] Mrs Margaret Kraft, letter to *Bournemouth Echo*, 19 September 1973.

[18] Terry Knight and G. Clarke of the KAL Committee, letter to *Bournemouth Echo*, 25 September 1973.
[19] Marjorie A. Hillman, letter to *Western Gazette*, 14 December 1973.
[20] *The Times*, 28 August 1973.
[21] *Bournemouth Evening Echo*, 20 December 1973.
[22] Col. (Retd) Christopher Corfreed, letter to *Dorset Echo*, 17 December 1973.
[23] *Bournemouth Echo*, 5 October 1973.
[24] *Bournemouth Echo*, 29 April 1974.
[25] *Western Gazette*, 3 May 1974.
[26] 'Autumn decision on land held by Army', *The Times*, 23 August 1974.
[27] 'Government rejects army land proposal', *Guardian*, 30 August 1974.
[28] 'Villagers to celebrate decision', *Daily Telegraph*, 30 August 1974.
[29] Martin Walker, 'Good Lord', *Guardian*, 27 September 1974.
[30] Reported in *Daily Telegraph*, 30 August 1974.
[31] *The Times*, 20 December 1974.
[32] Joan Berkeley, *Lulworth and the Welds*, Gillingham, 1971, p.xiv.

CHAPTER 22

[1] Kenneth Hudson's programme 'The Atomic Gardeners' was transmitted on the BBC Home Service on 2 August 1961. It emphasised how thoroughly consoled those who had opposed the 'rape of Winfrith' felt once the tree screening had started and rose-bushes has started to burgeon in the flowerbeds around the atomic installation. The text of this discussion, in which former objector Douglas Pass declared himself at peace with the Winfrith establishment, was later published as a pamphlet by the Atomic Energy Establishment.
[2] See Gwyn Prins & Robbie Stamp, *Top Guns and Toxic Whales*, London, 1991.
[3] Norman Moore, *The Bird of Time: The Science and Politics of Nature Conservation*, Cambridge, 1987, pp.36–7.
[4] See P. D. James, 'Murder, Mystery and Mortality', *Salisbury Review*, September 1990 and 'At School Between the Wars', *Salisbury Review*, September 1992. Lady James's remark about Tyneham was made during an interview with the author in October 1994.
[5] Dennis Potter is here quoted from my profile in the *Guardian*, 15 February 1993.

INDEX